Elizabeth Wormeley Latimer

Russia and Turkey in the nineteenth Century

Elizabeth Wormeley Latimer

Russia and Turkey in the nineteenth Century

ISBN/EAN: 9783743316157

Manufactured in Europe, USA, Canada, Australia, Japa

Cover: Foto ©ninafisch / pixelio.de

Manufactured and distributed by brebook publishing software (www.brebook.com)

Elizabeth Wormeley Latimer

Russia and Turkey in the nineteenth Century

Lisbon Public Library
SUGAR HILL BRANCH.

Presented to
The Library
of the
University of Toronto
by

ETHEL GREENING PANTAZZI

CZAR NICHOLAS.

RUSSIA AND TURKEY

IN

THE NINETEENTH CENTURY

BY

ELIZABETH (WORMELEY) LATIMER

AUTHOR OF "FRANCE IN THE NINETEENTH CENTURY," "SALVAGE,"
"MY WIFE AND MY WIFE'S SISTER," "PRINCESS AMÉLIE,"
"FAMILIAR TALKS ON SOME OF SHAKESPEARE'S
COMEDIES," ETC.

CHICAGO
A. C. McCLURG AND COMPANY
1895

COPYRIGHT
BY A. C. MCCLURG AND CO.
A.D. 1893

NOTE

THE kindness with which "France in the Nineteenth Century" has been received by my critics and the public encourages me to put forth this companion volume on "Russia and Turkey." It was composed under the same circumstances as "France," and if it shall be found to have appropriated too freely what belongs to other writers I make for it the same apology.

E. W. L.

HOWARD COUNTY, MARYLAND.
September, 1893.

Digitized by the Internet Archive
in 2007 with funding from
Microsoft Corporation

CONTENTS.

CHAPTER		PAGE
I.	The Emperor Alexander I. and Madame de Krüdener	9
II.	The Grand Duke Constantine and Janetta Grudzińska	26
III.	The Crescent versus Christendom	42
IV.	Turks, Russians, and Greeks	63
V.	The Czar Nicholas	85
VI.	The Crimean War	103
VII.	The Crimean War (*concluded*)	134
VIII.	The Emperor-Liberator and his Reforms	167
IX.	Four Sultans	197
X.	The Turkish War of 1877.—General Skobeleff	232
XI.	The Assassination of Alexander II.	265
XII.	Alexander III.	282
XIII.	Siberia.—Central Asia.—The Baltic Provinces.—The Persecution of the Jews	303
XIV.	Sultan Abdul Hamid	335
XV.	The two Danubian Kingdoms.—Servia and Roumania	357
XVI.	The Balkan Principalities and Provinces	381

LIST OF ILLUSTRATIONS.

Czar Nicholas	*Frontispiece*
Emperor Alexander I.	*To face page* 16
Madame de Krüdener	24
Grand Duke Constantine	40
Lord Raglan	112
Marshal Saint-Arnaud	124
General Todleben	134
Florence Nightingale	148
Emperor Alexander II.	168
Sultan Abdul Aziz	200
Sultan Murad V.	214
Sultan Abdul Hamid II.	230
General Skobeleff	258
Emperor Alexander III.	282
Empress of Russia	300
Midhat Pasha	336
King Milan of Servia	364
Queen Nathalie	368
King Charles of Roumania	374
Queen Elizabeth of Roumania	376
Prince Ferdinand of Roumania	378
Princess Marie	380
Prince Ferdinand of Bulgaria	400

RUSSIA AND TURKEY

IN

THE NINETEENTH CENTURY.

CHAPTER I.

THE EMPEROR ALEXANDER I. AND MADAME DE KRÜDENER.

SOMEBODY has said of Russia that it is the most extraordinary country on the globe, in the four most important particulars of empire: its history, its extent, its population, and its power. It has risen into importance only since the early part of the last century, and ever since it began to rise it has been the cause of continual alarm to Western Europe. All international efforts have been directed toward thwarting its schemes of aggression, and to the repression of its "manifest destiny," yet it has held the balance of power in its hands in almost every crisis of modern European history.

Peter the Great, who flourished at the close of the seventeenth century, and in the dawn of the eighteenth, was not the reformer or restorer of Russia, he was its creator. He found it Asiatic, he left it European, — a work for which Panslavist fanatics at the present day are by no means grateful.

In the days of the Vikings Russia had been more or less connected with the Norsemen. Its chief kingdom, whose seat of empire was at Novgorod, was a settlement of Northmen, whence Harold Hardrada (killed in England, 1066, three weeks before the battle of Hastings) brought home to Norway Elizabeth, its king's daughter, as his bride.

The kingdom of Novgorod was overturned by invading Tartars, and little more was heard in Europe of Muscovy until in the sixteenth century, when Captain Sir Richard Chancelor, seeking the Northeastern Passage, wandered into the White Sea, and was thence conducted to the barbaric court of Ivan the Terrible. That formidable monarch received Chancelor at Moscow, "seated on a very royal throne," having upon his head a diadem of gold; "his robe was all of goldsmith's work," in his hand "he bore a crystal sceptre, garnished and beset with precious stones, and his countenance was no less full of majesty." Upon one side of his throne stood his chief scrivener, and upon the other the great "commander of silence," or court usher, in costly dresses of cloth of gold. Around the chamber were seated his council of one hundred and fifty noblemen, "upon high seats, all clad as richly."

Having presented letters from King Edward VI., which were received most graciously, Chancelor and his officers were invited to dine with the Czar. The English captain seems to have been much impressed by the profusion of gold and silver plate displayed on the occasion, and especially by four mighty flagons nearly two yards high, wrought on the top with elegant devices of towers and dragons' heads.[1] The servants were arrayed in habits of gold, but the guests wore white linen; and the Czar twice changed his crown during the banquet.

Still more magnificent was Ivan's entertainment on Christmas Day, 1559, of another English guest, who came as an ambassador from Queen Elizabeth, and who was much astonished at seeing twelve massive barrels made of silver and hooped with fine gold, each containing twelve gallons of wine. Ivan was a second Nero, full of promise in his youth, but after he reached full age crazed by the responsibilities of absolute power.

[1] United Service Magazine.

In 1568 Elizabeth despatched her favorite diplomatist, Sir Thomas Randolph to the Russian court. His mission was to negotiate a commercial treaty and to soften her refusal of the Czar's offer of marriage, that potentate having been added to the list of her Majesty's cajoled and rejected suitors.

After that Russia sank back into the obscurity of barbarism for one hundred years.

Early in the seventeenth century, the race of sovereigns to which Ivan belonged having become extinct in the male line, the House of Romanoff, which claimed royal descent through females, ascended the throne. The first sovereign of that dynasty, named Michael, was elected "by an assembly of the States," and crowned July 13, 1613, — that is, two years after King James's Bible was first printed, and three years before Shakespeare died.

The next Romanoff was Alexis. The son of Alexis was Peter the Great, who after being harassed by various conspiracies, and sharing for a few years his throne with Ivan, his elder brother, became Emperor and Autocrat of all the Russias. The title assumed by Ivan I. in 1340 had been Grand Prince of the various provinces called Russias, which though governed by their own dukes, and their own laws, paid tribute, and owed fealty to the Grand Prince of Muscovy.

We are all familiar with the history of Peter the Great. We know how he travelled that he might return home and instruct his people; how he learned ship-building in Holland; how he visited England, — where William III. requested Mr. Evelyn to lend his house, and garden of rare herbs, to his semi-civilized guest; how Peter's amusement was to be wheeled through the trim hedges in a wheelbarrow; how he returned to Russia; how he founded a navy, conquered Livonia, reclaimed a swamp in it, and built St. Petersburg; how he humbled Charles of Sweden; how he acquired all the Baltic Provinces; and how, dying in 1725 at the age of fifty-three, he left his throne to

Catherine his peasant wife, having previously named their son Peter as her heir. Peter was not his oldest son. A year before his accession, when he was seventeen, he had married his first wife, a noble Russian lady, Eudoxia Lapuchin, by whom he had had one son named Alexis. Eudoxia he divorced, but she survived him. Alexis was brought up with neither love nor care. Catherine had naturally no affection for her step-son, and was ambitious to make her own son Peter his father's heir. The customs of Russia at that day gave a father absolute power over the life of his child. The Grand Duke Alexis, neglected and unhappy, led probably an irregular life; at any rate he drew down upon himself the displeasure of his father, who ordered him either to reform, or to retire into a monastery. After trying for six months to conform to his father's wishes, Alexis made his escape to Vienna. He was soon, however, forced to return to Russia. There the higher clergy, the chief officers of state, and the leading nobles were convened at Moscow to try him. Alexis acknowledged himself unworthy to wear the crown, but entreated that his life might be spared. His trial was followed by his confinement in a prison and by the nomination of Catherine as her husband's successor.

Alexis was not left in peace in his imprisonment. His father employed every means to extract from him the names of his confidants and advisors. For five months he was subjected to constant interrogations; at last his father pronounced him worthy of death, and the next day he was found murdered. The father suffered pangs of remorse for this act in his later years. When he died he left his throne, as I have said, to Catherine, who had unbounded influence over him.

Peter, their son, had died before his father, and Catherine, who reigned only two years, exercised the prerogative of a Russian sovereign, namely, that of choosing a successor, by leaving her crown to Peter II., son of the unfortunate Alexis. He was a lad of thirteen, and after the death of her own child, she had shown him kindness, and interested herself in his education. Peter lived only two years after ascending the throne; and then followed a strange entanglement of succession. The Russian nobles, passing over the two daughters of Peter the Great (Anna, who had married a duke of Holstein, and Elizabeth) offered their crown to the widowed Duchess of Courland, Anna Ivanovna, daughter of Peter's elder brother. At her death she left it to Ivan IV., son of her niece Anne, who had married Prince Antoine Ulrich of Brunswick. But Elizabeth, daughter of Peter the Great and of Catherine, easily effected a *coup d'état*, imprisoned Ivan and his parents, and reigned till 1762. She made no legitimate marriage, though she was probably married secretly to a young Cossack whom she raised to many dignities, Alexis Razumoffsky. She adopted as her successor Peter, the son of her sister Anna and the Prince of Holstein Gottorp. She caused him to be brought up at the Russian court and married him to the penniless Princess Sophia Augusta of Anhalt-Zerbst. This lady, who on her baptism into the Greek Church took the name of Catherine, was a woman of extraordinary vigor, ambition, and ability. When Peter began to ill-treat her she made short work of so feeble a husband. She forced him to abdicate, and then suffered him, after his abdication, to be poisoned in a few hours. She is known in Russian history as Catherine II., or Catherine the Great. She applied a strong coating of French varnish to Russian barbarism. She was noted for her many lovers, for her wars with Frederick the Great, and also with the Turks in the Crimea; but most of all for her share in the partition of Poland, a country whose great misfortune it has been to have no natural boundaries.

Catherine had had one son by her husband Peter, the Grand Duke Paul. She kept him, as long as she lived, in a state of servile tutelage, even taking from him his children as soon as they were weaned, and bringing them up under her own eye.

Paul's first wife died very young, and he was then married to the Princess Dorothea of Montbelliard, a tiny principality in the east of France, shut in between the Vosges and Jura Mountains. No sweeter princess ever lived than Princess Dorothea, who, on her baptism into the Greek Church, took the name of Marie Feodorovna. Madame d' Oberkirch was her dearest friend, and has left a charming account in her memoirs of the one bright episode in poor Paul's life, his travels with his wife in 1782, through France, Italy, and Holland, as the Comte and Comtesse du Nord. Though they professed to travel incognito their identity was perfectly well understood in the courts they visited. Louis XVI. and poor Marie Antoinette were lavish of attentions to them. The Princess was beautiful, gentle, and well-informed; the Prince was very plain, with a Calmuck face, and but little education; but he had a kind heart, and for years the married pair were happy together. Paul had strong faith in the supernatural, and believed that he had seen a vision forewarning him of his death by violence, but it seems to need no ghostly visitant to predict to a prince of the House of Romanoff so very probable a destiny.

Paul and Marie had many children, of whom four were sons, Alexander, Constantine (so called by his grandmother, who destined him to enter Constantinople as its conqueror) Nicholas, and Michael. Of these Alexander and Nicholas became Czars.

Catherine one night retired to rest after drinking large quantities of black coffee, as was her custom. In the morning her attendants found her lying speechless and dying on her chamber floor.

Paul ascended the throne in 1796, — in the early days of the French Revolution. He had never been allowed during his mother's life to take the smallest part in the affairs of government. He had been permitted, however, to "play at soldiers," and his first idea on becoming possessed of imperial power was to alter the dress, discipline, and equipments of his army. This made him intensely unpopular. He also sent an army, under his brilliant but half crazy general, Suwarroff, to fight the French Republic, an army that did wonders in Northern Italy, and in the mountains of Switzerland. Soon, however, Paul became dazzled by the brilliant career of Napoleon Bonaparte. The result of their alliance was that he undertook to combine the fleets of the Northern Powers against England. This led to Nelson's Battle of Copenhagen, by which he anticipated and disconcerted the intended movement, by the destruction of the Danish fleet, before England had put forth a declaration of war.

Russia was not in sympathy with her Czar's predilection for the French and their great captain. A party of conspirators secured the army, and declared Paul mad. Indeed, he had shown many symptoms of the malady hereditary in his family. Among other things he built a new palace at St. Petersburg at great expense, and insisted on having its decorations red. The accounts of his behavior to his family during the last weeks of his reign vary exceedingly. Some say that he was affectionate to his wife and children to the last; others, that he was on the point of arresting his sons, and incarcerating the empress, when the conspiracy broke out which ended his life. There is no doubt that he harassed and disgusted his army with vexatious regulations about dress and hair-powder, which last, Suwarroff told him bluntly, had nothing to do with gunpowder; and Paul dismissed his victorious general for saying so.

On the night of March 24, 1801, the conspirators, who had drunk deeply, repaired to the palace. One of them led a troop of soldiers stealthily beneath its walls. Skirting that part of the building was an avenue of lindens. In the lindens roosted a multitude of rooks which, disturbed by the stir at midnight, cawed so loudly that it was feared their noise would wake the emperor. A body of soldiers was then led across the moat, the water in which was frozen. The sentinels on duty were surprised and disarmed. A party was detailed to enter the emperor's sleeping-room. They passed up to it by a narrow private staircase leading from the garden. This party consisted of three brothers named Zouboff, two leading Russian generals, and several others. A faithful Cossack, who kept watch before his master's door, defended the entrance till he was covered with wounds, and then he rushed away to bring assistance. The conspirators were in full uniform, with plumed hats on their heads and swords in their hands. The emperor started up as they entered his chamber. "Sire !" they said, "we have come to arrest you." Paul sprang from his bed. They repeated that they had come to arrest him, and that he must abdicate. As Zouboff went to the door to call in others of the party, General Benningsen found a moment in which to whisper to his master, "Sire, your life is in danger; you *must* abdicate !" As he spoke a number of conspirators poured into the room. Paul tried to defend himself. He sprang behind a table, on which at night he kept two loaded pistols; but the conspirators fell upon him, threw him down, and strangled him, tearing a scarf for that purpose from the waist of a sub-officer who was present. Paul struggled bravely; but numbers overpowered him.

Before morning the Grand Duke Alexander was proclaimed emperor, and St. Petersburg was in a frenzy of joy.

But although Alexander I. acquiesced in his own elevation to the throne, he never got over the melancholy caused by the assassination of his father, and he took the earliest opportunity of manifesting his detestation of the murderers.

His first act was to make peace with England, and to join the alliance against France, and General Bonaparte her First Consul; but six years later, at Tilsit, in 1807, he fell under the spell of Napoleon's personal influence, and became devotedly his friend.

After this friendship had lasted some years, Napoleon's overbearing conduct in enforcing what was called "The Continental Blockade," drove Alexander into alliance with his enemies. "The Continental Blockade" prescribed that

EMPEROR ALEXANDER I.

no article of English manufacture, nor any article that had been shipped on board any English ship, or had been previously landed on the shores of England, should enter any port of France or any port of her allies. All such goods were to be burned upon the beach in a public conflagration.

When Alexander I. joined the allies, Napoleon retaliated by the invasion of Russia. He did not strengthen himself by making Poland, which lay behind him, into an independent kingdom, nor by raising, as he was advised to do, a force of fifty thousand Polish Cossacks to keep open his communications with France. He pushed on in the terrible winter of 1812 into the heart of the frozen empire. Many a campaign has been won by " pushing on; " but it has always been by " pushing on " to some place where an army could find supplies. Napoleon's army "pushed on" to desolation and starvation. There had never been known so cold or so early a winter. But this is not the place to dwell upon the horrors of the retreat of the French army from Moscow.

The Emperor Alexander, the hero of the day, led the allied armies in return to Paris. There he endeavored to procure generous conditions of peace for the Emperor Napoleon, his former friend. While Marie Louise was abandoning her husband, Josephine, the repudiated wife, caught her death from a cold contracted while walking round the gardens of Malmaison with the Emperor Alexander, trying to interest him in the fortunes of the man whom she still held dear.

In the Congress of Vienna Alexander hoped to get the consent of Europe to his encroachments upon Turkey, and so to approach the object of all Russian policy, — the acquisition of Constantinople as an outlet to the Mediterranean. The allied powers would not further his ambition in that direction. They compensated him by confirming him in the acquisition of Finland, and permitted him to do what he would in Poland.

Alexander sent his brother Constantine (who was a semi-barbarian) to govern Poland as his viceroy. While there Constantine became passionately attached to Janetta Grudzinska, a Polish lady, and this attachment had great influence on his after history.

When Napoleon came back from Elba in 1815, Alexander could no longer stand his friend with the other allies. The ex-emperor was banished to St. Helena, and Alexander, after projecting what was called the Holy Alliance, returned to his own country. Some account may not be here uninteresting of the singular and enthusiastic woman who exercised an all-powerful influence over him for several years.

Her maiden name was Barbara Julie von Wielinghoff, and her age was fifty, when in 1814 she first met the Emperor Alexander. She, however, had been born a Russian subject, and at eighteen had been married to a kind and just man twenty years older than herself, the Baron von Krüdener. She accompanied her husband on several high diplomatic missions, and she was clever, lively, devoted to pleasure, imaginative, and susceptible. No wonder that in the state of society that prevailed in those days in high places, her conduct during an absence from her husband at some baths in the South of France, was such that she deeply repented of it for the remainder of her days. M. de Krüdener, to whom she was sincerely attached, though in his absence she had accepted the attentions of a lover, forgave his wife, and was very merciful to her. He exacted however a promise that she would give up the fascinations of the world, and lead a domestic life with him in retirement. Fifteen years later she took advantage of a permission he had given her to visit the Baths of Töplitz, to extend her journey into Switzerland. Her husband remonstrated, but she took her own way, and was punished by soon receiving news that M. de Krüdener had died very suddenly of apoplexy. She bitterly reproached herself, but was soon again absorbed in frivolity. She published " Valérie," a novel of some merit, and showed a most wonderful vanity of authorship in connection with it. But in 1804, when forty years of age, tired of a life of folly and self-seeking, she left Paris, and sought refuge with her mother at Riga.

Several events that befel her had great influence over her imagination. One day a shoemaker waited upon her by appointment to take her measure for a pair of shoes. As he measured her foot she did not look at him, but sat shading her face with her hand. He asked her some question, she raised her eyes, and fixing them upon his face thought she had never seen a countenance so happy. It sent a pang to her heart, for she by contrast felt herself so miserable. "My friend, are you happy?" she asked. He answered, "I am the happiest of men." She said nothing, but the tone of his voice and the sincerity of his look haunted her, sleeping and waking.

A few days after this she sent for him again. He was a Moravian Brother (in other words, a German Methodist), and in all sincerity and simplicity he preached Christ unto her. Soon, with all the fervor of a forgiven sinner she loved Him who had first loved her.

En peu d'heures Dieu laboure is a homely French proverb. Madame de Krüdener in a short time experienced a great change within herself, and a new stimulus was given to all her powers. She devoted herself to the study of the Scriptures, and to spreading the knowledge of Christ wherever her influence could reach among rich or poor. Two years later, in 1806, she became the friend of the good Queen Louise of Prussia, and together they ministered to sick and wounded soldiers. At this time Madame de Krüdener, accompanied by her daughter, began to travel through all parts of Germany and Switzerland, a wandering Evangelist, preaching Christ to Protestants and Catholics alike.

Sometimes she rested for a while in Christian households. At Geneva she associated with herself a young man, expelled from the ranks of the divinity students for his persistency in holding prayer-meetings. She was found in the cabins of the poor, and in the *châteaux* of the great. Among those ladies of high rank who came under her influence were the mother of the wife of the Emperor Alexander, her daughters the Queens of Sweden and Bavaria, the Grand Duchess of Hesse, the Duchess of Brunswick, and Queen Hortense of Holland. But everywhere she went the police looked upon her as a suspicious person. They feared she might prove dangerous to Church and State. Sometimes she was hurried from place to place, sometimes she was forbidden to speak at all, sometimes her friends were separated from her, sometimes *gens d'armes* set a watch upon her, sometimes her correspondence was intercepted. The movement was so novel in those times that officials knew not what to think of it. One of those persons whom she greatly strengthened in the faith was Joseph Wolff, the future travelling missionary.

But Madame de Krüdener's exhuberant enthusiasm and unguarded disposition brought her into association with two religious charlatans, a Marie Kummer who "dreamed dreams, and saw visions," and a French priest, her follower. These people greatly damaged Madame de Krüdener's mission by their extravagances and their self-seeking.

She had long wished to know and to exhort the Emperor Alexander. She had mentioned this wish to persons high in the Russian court, and she believed herself especially commissioned to proclaim God's truth to him.

Alexander had in 1812 been under strong religious convictions. In 1813, when his armies met with such marvelous good fortune, his heart had been bent on giving God the glory, but in 1814 he wént to the Congress of Vienna, and there, for a while, he gave himself up to "riotous living."

Here is his own account of himself as he wrote it to a friend. He had quitted Vienna, disgusted with himself, and was passing a few days in salutary solitude at Heilbrun in Bavaria. He says : —

"At length I breathed freely, and the first thing I did was to take up a book that I always carry about with me; but in consequence of the dark cloud which rested upon my mind the reading made no impression upon me. My thoughts were confused and my head oppressed. I let the book fall, and thought what a comfort conversation with some pious friend would be to me. This idea brought *you* to my mind; I remembered what you had told me about Madame de Krüdener, and the desire that I had expressed to you to make her acquaintance. 'I wonder,' I said, 'where she is now, and whether I shall ever meet her.' No sooner had this passed through my mind than I heard a knock at the door. It was Prince Wolkousky, who said, with an air of the greatest annoyance, that he was very sorry to disturb me at so unseasonable an hour, but that he could not get rid of a lady who was determined to see me. He said her name was Madame de Krüdener. You may imagine my amazement. I thought I must be dreaming, and exclaimed: 'Madame de Krüdener! Madame de Krüdener?' This sudden response to my thoughts could not be accidental. I saw her at once, and she addressed such powerful and comforting words to me that it seemed as if she had read my very soul; and they calmed the storm which had been assailing me."

"The bearer of the divine message," says the narrator, "drew aside the veil from the emperor's mind. She told him of his sins, of the frivolity and pride with which he had entered on his mission. 'No, your Majesty, you have not yet cried out like the Psalmist, "God be merciful to me a *sinner!*"' . . . The emperor shed tears, and hid his face in his hands. Madame de Krüdener apologized for her earnestness. 'No! go on,' he said, 'your words are music to my soul.'" Three hours passed in conversation of this nature, and the emperor implored Madame de Krüdener not to forsake him. He felt that no one had ever before so touched his conscience, and unveiled the truth to him. At Heidelberg, his next halting-place, he besought her to hire a little cottage connected with the garden of the house he occupied, and there he spent every other evening. He selected chapters in the Bible for reading, and their conversations were often prolonged till two o'clock in the morning. The news of the battle of Waterloo reached them as they were reading the Psalms. The emperor, Madame de Krüdener, and Empaytaz (the ex-student from Geneva) threw themselves on their knees. After a prayer and a thanksgiving the emperor cried: "Oh, how happy I am!—my Saviour is with me. I am a great sinner, but He will employ me to give peace to the nations! Oh, how happy might all be if they would only understand the ways of Providence and obey the gospel!"

When Alexander went with the Allied Armies to Paris he requested Madame de Krüdener to follow him, and in the evenings he came to her house with his Bible under his arm. He was a man who yielded himself always without reserve to any prevailing personal influence. Before he left Paris he was very desirous of making a public profession of faith, and he formed with his allies what was called the Holy Alliance, by which *he* meant an alliance to promote the reign of the gospel by putting down all anarchic and revolutionary ideas, and the other Powers meant an alliance to oppose every movement in Europe calculated to disturb the state of things imposed upon the nations by the Congress of Vienna.

When Alexander returned to Russia and no longer daily saw Madame de Krüdener, her influence over him waned. She took a lively interest in the unhappy Christians of the Greek Church oppressed by the Mahommedans. Alexander, while under her influence, had lent his countenance to a secret society called the Society of the Hetairists. It had been formed ostensibly to alleviate the sufferings of Christians in the Ottoman Empire, but it had for its ultimate object the deliverance of the Danubian Provinces (Moldavia and Wallachia), Servia, and above all, Greece. The Hetairists never doubted that they had the full sympathy of the Emperor Alexander; and in 1821 an insurrection broke out, under their leadership, simultaneously in Wallachia, Moldavia, and Greece. In Wallachia it was headed by Alexander Ypsilanti, son of one of the former hospodars of that country, and a member of one of the Greek families resident in Constantinople. The elder Ypsilanti had encouraged his Wallachian subjects to revolt against the Porte in 1806, and had in consequence been forced to fly for his life to St. Petersburg. There his sons entered the Russian army. Alexander became a colonel, and aide-de-camp to the emperor.

Alexander Ypsilanti, as leader of the Hetairists, when on the top wave of success found himself utterly disavowed by the Emperor Alexander, who ordered him to return at once to Russia there to receive punishment for a revolutionary attempt.

The fall of Ypsilanti, who was defeated in a battle with the Turks, did not prevent a rising in Greece under Demetrius, his brother. In vain had the Greeks presented their cause before the Congress of Verona; the European Powers would only consider their movement revolutionary; they could not see that it was the old struggle of European against Asiatic, Christian against Infidel, Western progress against stagnant Orientalism.

Alexander saw well enough that to support the Hetairists would be to take the first step upon the march that might lead him to Constantinople; but the more he felt that it was to his own interest to take this step, the more his conscience bound him to be true to his engagements with the Holy Alliance, which made it incumbent upon him to oppose all measures that would unsettle the state of Europe as determined by the Congress of Vienna. The opportunity was therefore missed for settling, while the Powers were upon good terms with one another, that Eastern Question which has been the plague-spot in Europe for more than sixty years. But for the influences which superseded that of Madame de Krüdener, and persuaded Alexander to discountenance his fellow-Christians for conscience' sake, the horrible massacres which swept away nearly one half the Christian population of Greece, might have been averted.

After the emperor had renounced all connection with

the designs of Ypsilanti he intimated to Madame de Krüdener that her residence in St. Petersburg would only be permitted so long as she refrained from any expression of opinion as to the affairs of Greece. She left that city, therefore, and not long afterwards she died. A few days before her death she wrote to her son: "The good that I have done will remain; the harm that I have done, — and how often have I not mistaken the workings of my own imagination and pride for the voice of God! — God in His mercy will wipe away. I have nothing to offer to God or man but my many imperfections; but the blood of Jesus Christ cleanseth from all sin."

She died on Christmas Day, 1823. Her chief friend in her later days was Princess Galitzin, who had been head of the Bible Society in Russia, and whose son was the Prince Demetrius Galitzin, known among us as the Apostle of the Alleghanies. He came out as a Roman Catholic missionary to Baltimore, and found his field of work among the German miners in Pennsylvania and Western Maryland. His face was one of almost heavenly benevolence. He was a man whose piety and self-devotion may have been greater than his intelligence, but he gave up all for Christ's sake, and died among his humble people.

After parting from Madame de Krüdener, the mind of Alexander became tinged with melancholy; he lost his activity, and had he lived a few years longer he would probably have become a victim to religious melancholia. This tendency to religious melancholy seems to have been fostered by the people round him. The empress had long been in ill health, and was ordered to a warm climate. She declared it was unfitting that an empress of Russia should seek health out of her own dominions, and resolved to go to the Crimea. Thither her husband followed her. On the morning that he left St. Petersburg, a solemn mass was chanted for him at four o'clock in the morning in the Monastery of Saint Alexander Newsky. The service used on the occasion was, it is said, the Office for the Dead.

MADAME DE KRÜDENER.

And after this solemn service the Emperor was invited to visit a hermit who slept every night in his coffin. All this made a painful impression on his sensitive mind, and had he known, as we know now, that at that very moment a plan for his assassination was ripening, the effect might have been deeper still. He did not, however, live to be assassinated. He took a malarial fever at Taganrog, notwithstanding which he went on a journey of inspection to Sebastopol, and exposed himself to the malign influences of that climate, which proved so fatal to the French and English troops in 1855–1857. He returned to Taganrog, and his last hours were embittered by details imparted to him of the conspiracy which was to have included his assassination. He died Dec. 1, 1825.

CHAPTER II.

THE GRAND DUKE CONSTANTINE AND JANETTA GRUDZIŃSKA.

AS has been said in the previous chapter, the Grand Dukes Alexander, Constantine, Nicholas, and Michael were the sons of Marie Fedorovna (Princess Dorothy of Montbelliard) and of the ill-fated Emperor Paul. When Alexander died of malarial fever in the Crimea, his last hours were embittered by the discovery of the first Nihilist conspiracy, — a plot to assassinate him, — not because he was unpopular or accused of any tyranny, but because he was an obstacle to that programme of reform which, based upon the principle that "whatever is, is wrong," was to begin by making a clean sweep of existing institutions, and reducing everything to nothing.

On Alexander's accession to the Russian throne he had endeavored to associate his brother Constantine with himself in the affairs of government. Constantine had in his father's lifetime made a campaign with General Suwarroff. At Austerlitz in 1805 he distinguished himself by his rash bravery; and he attended his brother Alexander through the campaigns of 1812–1814. After the war was over he returned to Russia, and was married to a refined and gentle lady, Princess Juliana of Saxe-Coburg, sister of the Duchess of Kent, the Duke of Saxe-Coburg-Gotha, and of King Leopold, aunt both to Prince Albert and Queen Victoria. But the eccentricities, the fits of passion, the brutalities, and the savagery of Constantine so terrified and alienated the poor lady that she refused to live with him, and retired, first to Switzerland, and subsequently to her own family at

Saxe-Coburg. Complaints of all kinds poured in upon Alexander concerning the unbearable brutality of his brother's conduct, and Constantine was dismissed from the Russian court to superintend affairs in the new kingdom of Poland.

This kingdom when first restored to Russia, though shorn of what had been its proportions in the days of its elected kings, had been placed under the care of a provisional government, at the head of which was Prince Adam Czartoryski, a true patriot, who in youth had been Alexander's dearest friend.

"But," says a writer in the "London Quarterly," "the czar of all the Russias is by birth and training an autocrat. Alexander was fast losing, under the imperial purple, the liberal tendencies of his earlier years. An independently national and liberal constitution for Poland was, under such circumstances, fated to become a dead letter. The Poles, who had seen the mirage of liberty stretch out before their eager eyes, were given over to the violent and capricious rule of the emperor's brother Constantine."

Yet in Paris in 1814 Constantine had been thrown into contact with some of the Polish leaders, and had conceived a high esteem for them, showing preference thenceforward for the Poles in his personal and private relations over his own countrymen. At Warsaw he was head and chief; in St. Petersburg his position was secondary and uncomfortable. At the beginning of his career he had exhibited his father Paul's strange fancies concerning military dress and drill. It was currently reported at St. Petersburg that he had said he hated war because it spoiled his soldiers' uniforms. A button loose, or boots ill-blacked, or a beard a fraction too long, was sufficient under his generalship to destroy for life the professional prospects of any officer; and yet he had talent and a quick knowledge of character; was generous and industrious. He was an affectionate son to his mother, a kind husband to his last wife, and a good brother; but his fierce explosions of rage, and his general eccentricity destroyed the effect of his good qualities.

His administration in Poland had little to distinguish it. It was a field on which his rude and savage character had full play, but his private life after his retirement from the Russian court is a far more attractive history. Between Constantine in public and Constantine in private life there were strange contradictions. The two characters seem inconsistent, and their reconciliation might form an interesting psychological problem.

At the period when Constantine appeared in Warsaw as generalissimo of the troops, and governor-general of the kingdom of Poland, there was living in that capital a family of good birth but of impaired reputation. Count Grudzinski, who appears to have been a "just man" and even a pious one, had been the first husband of a lady, who, having with great difficulty procured a divorce from him, had married a certain Marshal Broniec, a mere adventurer in spite of the rank conferred on him by his boon companion the King of Saxony. Madame la Maréchale had had by her first husband three daughters, whose custody she was permitted to retain. The names of these young ladies were Janetta, Josephine, and Antoinette.

These young ladies owed much to their careful training under a lady who, although political events had reduced her to needy circumstances, moved in the best society of Warsaw, where she was greatly esteemed. The fair young girls whom she desired to introduce among her friends, were pitied, approved, and soon became great favorites. The state of affairs in their own household was neither creditable nor comfortable. Count Grudzinski, a devout Catholic, had refused to lend his name to his wife's proceedings for a divorce, and while the young girls were growing up, confusion, intrigue, and great pecuniary distress prevailed. Hence it was felt by every one desirable that the three fair sisters should marry early and leave their home. Josephine, an amiable and beautiful girl, married a distinguished Polish gentleman. The youngest sister Antoinette, married General Chlapowski, who was subsequently a leader in the Polish revolt of 1830, and dictator of Poland for a brief period between the overthrow of the Russian government and its terrible restoration. Janetta was not so beautiful as her two sisters, but it was said of her that "in all things she did she charmed." Her sweetness of disposition was as attractive as her powers of conversation. In 1818 she met the Grand Duke Constantine for the first time, and the acquaintance soon ripened into love. The courtship lasted for more than two years. Constantine was still the husband of the Princess Juliana, and in Russia a divorce can only be obtained by favor of the emperor, who claims to be *ex officio* the head of all orthodox Christians in his dominions. In 1820 Constantine repaired to Saint Petersburg, and made it his earnest request to his brother and his mother that he might be divorced from his Saxe-Coburg wife, and marry (with the imperial permission) the lady whom he loved.

It cost him tears and prayers and sacrifices to attain this end. The divorce was at last given, and the consent granted, but a heavy price had to be paid for them. Previous to the marriage an imperial ukase was published depriving the children of any marriage contracted by any member of the imperial house with any lady not belonging to a reigning family, of all rights of succession to the throne. To this Constantine consented, and also agreed that his Polish wife should not be considered a member of the imperial family. Besides these conditions, which were known to the public, there was a third, kept a profound secret, between Constantine, his brother, and their mother. Constantine signed and placed in the hands of Alexander a paper by which he renounced his right of succession as heir presumptive to the imperial throne. This paper was sealed and deposited by the emperor with the president of his Grand Council, only to be opened in case of his death, when it was to be read immediately.

These conditions having been at last arranged, not without much difficulty (for Constantine, though willing to surrender his own rights, was jealous for those of his wife), the imperial lover went back to Warsaw, made his formal demand to Count Grudzinski for the hand of his daughter, and was married to Janetta. It is not known under what influence the bride, as a Catholic, overcame her religious scruples.

A contemporary memoir-writer thus speaks of the wedding: —

"The Grand Duke Constantine Paulovitch, brother and heir of the emperor, married April 24, 1820, Mademoiselle Janetta Grudzinska. For several years there has been talk of his attachment, and those who knew him well predicted how it would end.... Mademoiselle Grudzinska immediately after her wedding took up her residence in the grand-ducal palace, and since then she and the grand duke are seen everywhere together. It is considered very surprising that the emperor and his mother should have given their consent to this marriage. It is said that the grand duke, when last at St. Petersburg, wept three days at their feet imploring their permission. Janetta has no title as yet, but it is said the emperor intends to give her one. This subject is the theme of conversation in all circles. Many ladies envy Janetta, but I pity her."

The marriage on the whole was not unhappy, though the bride soon found herself assailed by annoyances, many of them caused by the insatiable demands of some greedy members of her family. Janetta seems most sincerely to have loved her husband, but from the first he forbade her interference in public affairs, and warned her never to intercede with him on behalf of her countrymen. If she had hoped to stand the friend of Poland, and to assuage the miseries of her own people, she soon found that no influence on such subjects was allowed her.

The emperor created her Princess of Lowicz, and presented to his brother large estates that bore that name. These were settled on the prospective children of the marriage; but no children came. By degrees the princess adapted herself to her anomalous position. She overlooked much, she forgot much. She could "suffer and be still." But though denied all political influence, her influence was great over the semi-barbarian who was her husband. In her society and under the spell of her affection he became calmer and more refined. He always spoke of her as his home angel. Though forced to be deaf to innumerable demands for honors and money which harassed her continually, her correspondence with her mother and sisters was most loving. Never did a family fête day or a birthday pass forgotten. To her family she wrote only of her happiness, of her husband's attention to her, the kindness she received, or the embarrassments she felt when she found herself treated with more distinction than her rank gave her a claim to; yet on April 3, 1821, almost the anniversary of her marriage, she could write thus to a friend of her girlhood:—

"My surroundings are charming; I find all sorts of pleasant things in my home, all kinds of advantages. But this is only of late. At first it appeared to me all gloomy and sad, and its luxury was unbearable. . . . I have suffered very, very much. It seems to me that I never had so many trials in my life as during this year. But all that is over now, and I am completely happy. . . . After some months of married life people know each other far better, as you know, than they can possibly do before marriage. One has to bear, and forbear, and make mutual concessions. I am doing so, and begin to feel happy. You will understand that this letter is only for you and your mother."

Notwithstanding the conditions on which the emperor and the empress-mother insisted before they would consent to the grand duke's marriage, the relations of the princess with the emperor and the court were always friendly. When Alexander came to Warsaw, soon after his brother's marriage, he gained golden opinions even from the reluctant Poles. The Princess of Lowicz felt the attractions of his character, and always spoke of him with enthusiasm.

For three years and a half after this the princess led a quiet life at Belvidere, — a palace which, although almost a country seat, stood within the limits of Warsaw. Her health was not good ; but time and her husband's tender solicitude for her in her weakness drew them more closely together. Besides this, she had the good opinion of the Czar and the affection of the whole imperial family, — more particularly that of the Grand Duke Michael, and his sisters, the Grand Duchesses Anne and Marie.

A few days before Christmas, 1825, the Emperor Alexander breathed his last. Up to the end he persistently refused to be thought ill, or to omit the duties of his station.

The Grand Duke Nicholas, who was residing in St. Petersburg, immediately on receipt of the news of Alexander's death took the oath of allegiance to Constantine, his elder brother. He then despatched two couriers to Warsaw to inform Constantine that he was now emperor. Strange to say, both couriers died upon the road, and the news was brought to Warsaw by an aide-de-camp of the Grand Duke Nicholas, who was charged to present to the new emperor the respectful homage of his brother.

Before, however, this officer was despatched from St. Petersburg, the army as well as Nicholas had sworn allegiance to Constantine. No sooner had they done so than the president of the Council produced the letter that the Emperor Alexander had confided to his keeping. It conferred the imperial crown on Nicholas, and enclosed a letter from Constantine confirming and sanctioning this arrangement.

In spite of the production of this document, Nicholas persisted in despatching his aide-de-camp to Warsaw to assure his brother of his loyalty and submission.

The effect produced at Belvidere by the arrival of this messenger was very great. Some say that Constantine fainted on hearing of the death of Alexander. It is certain that he at once shut himself up alone in a state of great excitement. Even the princess was not suffered to come near him. At a distance she stood with clasped hands where he might see her from his window. At the end of two hours he came forth self-collected and calm, though all the furniture in his room had, during his transport, been broken in pieces. His first words were to the princess, — an assurance that she might make her mind easy, for he was not going to reign.

He at once despatched his youngest brother, Michael, to Nicholas, confirming his resignation of the throne; and Nicholas, when with energy he had thoroughly crushed the projected insurrection of the Nihilists, made preparations for his coronation. But Constantine was still popular with the party of Old Russia, — the party that loved long beards and the national costumes; and Nicholas was anxious that his subjects should receive some personal assurance that he was to be crowned czar with the full consent of his deposed brother. He therefore urged Constantine to be present at his coronation. Constantine returned no answer; but on the eve of the day appointed he drove into Moscow in a travelling-carriage attended by a single aide-de-camp. Nicholas, grateful and delighted, hastened to welcome him; but his surprise and embarrassment were great when Constantine announced that he only meant to stay one night, and should set out on his return the next day after the conclusion of the ceremony. It had to be explained to him, with fear and trembling, that there had been some delay in the preparations, and that the coronation could not take place for a week. With some grumbling at the delay, Constantine consented to remain till after the ceremony. His native ferocity, aggravated by the excitement of the occasion, kept the new Czar Nicholas all that week in a state of great uneasiness; and it is not quite certain what thoughts were stirring in the heart of the elder brother; but not many hours before the coronation took place Constantine became aware that in the preparations for the ceremonial everything had been arranged so as to do him honor. This seemed to produce in him the effect of a sudden revelation. That afternoon, at a review, he abruptly placed himself at the head of his own regiment, and advancing to where the emperor sat on horseback at the far end of the great court of the Kremlin, he raised his hand in military salute to him as his superior. The emperor seized him by the arm. Constantine bent forward, and kissed the hand of his brother. The emperor flung himself upon his neck, and they embraced in a transport of brotherly affection. Next day the Grand Duke Constantine refused to place himself upon the throne that had been prepared for him at the coronation, but took his place simply as a grand duke of the imperial family by the side of his brother Michael. The following morning, in spite of the earnest remonstrances of the emperor, he started back to Poland.

He returned to his home, to the Polish army he was endeavoring to discipline after the Western fashion, and to the wife who loved the wild nature she had subdued. That he was unpopular made her love him with more wifely devotion; and in truth he must have had some qualities well worthy of her love.

Here are parts of two letters written by him to his wife's mother: —

"My affection for my dear wife increases daily; for she is the source of all my happiness, and my sole aim is to try to make her happy and content. Thank God, her health is improved, and she is ever that sweet and charming Janetta whom you have always known."

And again, —

"Thanks to our excellent Janetta, I enjoy a happiness in my home I had never dreamed of, and I pray God it may continue until death."

But events in Poland were in preparation for a crisis. In 1830–1831 all Europe was enveloped in clouds and darkness, and the treaties of Vienna, then shattered by the shock of revolution, were in another generation to be swept away. Revolutionary fires had been smouldering throughout Europe ever since the Spanish Revolution of 1821. In Poland as in Italy there were secret societies which kept up fermentation beneath the social surface.

"Towards the close of 1830 the exasperated Poles broke out into open insurrection. A great wave of hope swept over the whole nation, which rose to vindicate its right to national existence and liberty with overmastering purpose, and at first with signal success. But alas! Poland had against her her internal feuds, the overwhelming superiority of the Russian army, and the absence of any support from foreign nations."[1]

The wrath of the Czar Nicholas at the success of the revolution of July, 1830, in France, which terminated in the triumph of the *bourgeoisie* and the elevation of Louis Philippe to the throne, went almost beyond the bounds of reason. Not only had it destroyed his hopes, and broken up his plans, but it had attracted the sympathies of all unquiet spirits. He at once mobilized the Russian army, that it might be ready to advance on revolutionary France. And this demonstration of animosity against France caused the latent spirit of disaffection in Poland to blaze out into activity. On the night of Nov. 29, 1830, a party of young men began a movement which at first, for a few hours, seemed to fail of success, but by daylight, owing to a variety of circumstances, had become a temporary victory.

Eighteen of the conspirators made their way to the palace of Belvidere, the residence of the Grand Duke Constantine. They entered it without opposition while all within it lay asleep, and in apparent security. They murdered two of the grand duke's gentlemen in cold blood, and made their way into his chamber. He had been awakened by his valet. He sprang out of bed, flung a cloak over his night-clothes, and rushed down a narrow stairway to his wife's apartments. There he found the greatest confusion. The court ladies had all left their beds,

[1] London Quarterly Review, 1890

and were assembled in the salon. The princess made them fall upon their knees around her husband, and pray aloud for his safety. Unhappily, Constantine had wholly lost his self-possession, and though a soldier brave to rashness in his early career, he now trembled with terror. The eighteen conspirators, after searching his apartments, retired in haste, murdering General Gendre, his chief counsellor on their way. They had not gone a hundred yards from the palace when a party of Polish horsemen galloped up to the rescue. Why the little band of conspirators was not annihilated, it is hard to say; but by this time the insurrection had spread among the populace of Warsaw. Polish soldiers were fraternizing with the instigators of the movement; and of all the grand duke's army there remained faithful to him only four regiments of cavalry.

Had he put himself at once at the head of these four regiments he might have won a victory, but he seemed dazed by the events of the night. He trembled like a leaf, and wandered aimlessly among his troops, a prey to despair, which seemed to have stupefied him. He and his wife retired before the fury of the storm, and sought shelter at Wiezbno. There for some days they lived in the poor hut of a gardener, destitute of comforts of every kind. The princess showed courage and capacity in this emergency, but she could not always restrain her feelings.

The leader chosen by the insurgents was General Chlapowski, and one of his titles to their confidence was that he was known to harbor strong resentment against the grand duke for an insult publicly put upon him in 1818. Yet since that time he had married Antoinette Grudzinska, the Princess of Lowicz's favorite sister, and the princess had favored the match in spite of their mother's opposition.

Chlapowski deemed it his duty as a patriot to endeavor to negotiate with the grand duke before proceeding to extremities. The negotiation came to nothing, and it lost him the confidence of his countrymen. But as the deputation sent by him to confer with the grand duke was leaving the camp where Constantine had succeeded in assembling eight thousand men, it was followed by a large part of the hitherto faithful Polish cavalry. There was nothing left for Constantine but flight, and Chlapowski, to the great indignation of his countrymen, took no pains to pursue him.

Not long after this the Polish Revolution lost all prospect of success, though the struggle was continued a few months longer. The Czar hurried his army, already mobilized, to the scene of insurrection. The general in command was Diebitsch, who had won his laurels in 1826 in the Turkish war. He advanced upon Warsaw, but with him came the cholera. The Poles won a battle, but the soldiers who had fought hand to hand with Russians were stricken down by sickness almost on the field of battle. The fever of men's minds, and the absence of all sanitary precautions, made the plague horrible in Warsaw; nevertheless the war went on. Step by step Diebitsch advanced, but early in January, 1831, the Poles gained an important victory. Diebitsch retreated to his camp, and in his despair and self-abandonment gave himself up to drunkenness. It was thus that a messenger from the czar met him, and presented him his dismission. The next day Diebitsch was seized with cholera and died. The messenger passed on to Minsk to carry dispatches to the Grand Duke Constantine. The day after their interview the grand duke also died of cholera. He was fifty-three years of age.

His widow retired to St. Petersburg. On her way she wrote thus to her mother: —

AUGUST 2, 1831.

DEAR MAMMA, — Your daughter is very, very miserable. She has lost him for whom she lived, and now she is alone, without husband, friend, or protector. O mother! you can never know the grief this parting has caused me.

In the middle of September a few words written in a trembling hand close the records in her journal: —

"I am very ill, and have received the last sacraments."

Yet she lingered a few weeks longer. She was watched over with affectionate solicitude by the imperial family. She had a presentiment that she would die upon the anniversary of the dreadful night when, roused from sleep, she fled with her husband from their home at Belvidere. The Emperor Nicholas, with kind consideration, had the dates changed in the little calendar she always used, in order to mislead her; but in vain. She died on November 29, 1831, exactly one year after the attack on the palace of her husband.

She was buried in the Roman Catholic Chapel built by Alexander I. at Tzarskoé-Sélo near St. Petersburg, and the court wore mourning for her for two weeks.[1]

"Many tears," says a French writer often hostile to emperors and kings, "were shed upon the tomb of this Polish lady, so fair, so tender, and so faithful. Her own conjugal devotion, and the beneficent influences of her love upon the character of her husband were no secrets to any one. The Grand Duke Constantine, though fierce in temper, and generous by impulse, gave up a throne to win her, and having won her, he showed her during the remainder of his life the submission of a child and the devotion of a knight of romance in the days of chivalry."

At one time there had been brief hopes that England, France, Austria, and the new Catholic kingdom of Belgium might intervene in favor of Poland, but the diplomatic desire to keep Europe out of a general war if possible, caused all projects of that kind to fall to the ground.

In nine months there were several different forms of government in Warsaw. After the night of Nov. 29, 1830, when Warsaw was in a ferment of joy and of enthusiasm, Chlapowski[2] was the popular favorite and was made head

---

[1] This account of the Grand Duke Constantine and of Janetta Grudzinska has, by the kind permission of the editors of the "Catholic World," been almost entirely copied from an article I wrote for that periodical in Oct. 1888. My material was then drawn chiefly from the "Revue Britannique" in March of the same year. — E. W. L

[2] Spelled by some writers Chlopicki.

of the government by acclamation. Then came a new provisional government by an Administrative Council, at the head of which was Prince Adam Czartoryski; this Council was arbitrarily set aside by Chlapowski not long after, when he constituted himself dictator. Eventually he retired, like Prince Adam Czartoryski, into the ranks of the army. But the lack of some strong man of authority and experience at the head of the government, and as chief commander of the army, led to terrible disorders in Warsaw at a time when all patriots should have been united for the common good. Warsaw became the scene of the wildest confusion. The plague was raging, yet bands of excited revolutionists rushed through the streets demanding the decapitation of traitors. Still there was energy of a certain kind. A *levée en masse* was called for throughout the country. Priests shouldered the crucifix, boys and old men armed themselves, the peasants left their harvests and rushed to battle with their scythes.

Marshal Paskievitch had been appointed to succeed Marshal Diebitsch, and with fresh masses of troops from the interior of Russia was advancing step by step on Warsaw, to crush the revolution by one stunning blow.

On August 15, the birthday of Napoleon, all Warsaw was celebrating his memory. He had behaved perhaps more ill to the Poles than to any other nation, their want of frontier having withheld him from forming Poland into an independent kingdom. Nevertheless the whole country revered his memory. His friendship might not have been worth much to the Poles, but he had been the only sovereign who had ever showed them active sympathy. News that day was brought in that the Russians were advancing on the doomed city. Under cover of this rumor, a rising was made to depose Chlapowski in favor of a man of no experience named Krukoviecki. He incited his followers to burst the prison doors and massacre the Russian prisoners. He was proclaimed Governor of Warsaw and removed at once Dembinski (the only general of ability left since the retirement of Skrzynecki) from command of the army.

Three weeks later the Russians attacked Warsaw and gained important advantages. Marshal Paskievitch had the Grand Duke Michael with his army. On September 6 Governor Krukoviecki went out to treat with the Russian commanders. The terms proposed were amnesty on the one part, complete submission on the other. Till one o'clock the Russians offered to delay their attack upon the city, in order to enable the Polish Diet to accept or to reject these conditions. One o'clock struck and nothing had been decided. A quarter of an hour later a Russian cannon gave the signal for assault. By nine o'clock Warsaw was in flames, and its inhabitants had capitulated. The Governor made no conditions. He threw himself and his country, he said, "on the paternal heart of the Czar."

But such a submission was rejected by the distracted inhabitants. They seized their Governor, and refused to let him sign the ratification. The disorderly remnant of a Polish government marched out of one gate while the Russians were entering Warsaw by another.

Generals Dembinski and Rybinski rallied what remained of the Polish army, and pushed their way into Prussia, where they, and all the men with them, were put under arrest.

Paskievitch, the victorious general, gave his soldiers license to commit all sorts of horrors. Murder, sack, and pillage followed his entrance into the revolted city. Then he sat down and wrote his celebrated despatch, beginning: "Order reigns in Warsaw."

The sympathy, the fury, the distress, this outcome of the Polish revolution caused in France would be difficult to describe. One of the Parisian papers published a few verses which roused the masses to a high pitch of sorrowful enthusiasm : —

"Brave heart! Brave Warsaw! 'T was for us she died —
Died gun in hand, unbending in her pride;

GRAND DUKE CONSTANTINE.

Died for fair France; died with unhumbled knee,
Died, weeping o'er our Bird of Victory!
Died with our cry of pity yet unheard;
Without one fond adieu, one loving word!
Where shall we hide henceforth dishonored lives?
Quick! snatch the distaff from our braver wives!
Fling down our muskets, furl our flags so gay,
Tear off militia plumes, fling belts away!
By fits and starts French courage comes and goes;
Boast we no more of victory o'er our foes;
Let the red shame mount up— Hark! hear the drum!
You wish to see the Russians? Here they come!"[1]

Yet as we look back upon this sad, sad story, we feel that it was the Poles' own want of cohesion and of great men to guide their councils, and to lead their armies, that led to such a disastrous termination of the Polish revolution. Had Europe intervened far better terms might have been made for the brave unhappy kingdom, but it seemed unlikely that Poland in any event could have secured permanently her separation from Russia. Freedom did not "shriek" this time when Poland fell, but rather mourned over the disorders committed in her name, while Pity shed tears over the victims of the struggle.

[1] Louis Blanc, Dix Ans.

CHAPTER III.

THE CRESCENT VERSUS CHRISTENDOM.

BY way of preface to our story of the Turkish Empire during the nineteenth century, it may be well to glance back at the settlement of the Turks in Europe five centuries before. The Eastern Question indeed can hardly be comprehended without this retrospect.

Looking at a map of Europe made in the last century we are astonished at the extent of the Turkish power. Besides the narrow strip of land we now call Turkey in Europe, the Turkish sultan in 1755 (at the time, let us say, of Braddock's defeat) ruled over Greece, Thessaly, the Islands of the Archipelago, Crete, Cyprus, the Ionian Isles, Bulgaria, Bosnia, Herzegovina, Servia, Moldavia, Wallachia, Bessarabia, the Ukraine, and the Crimea. His frontier on the north touched Poland. His dominions were wedged in between Hungary and Russia, and, leaving out of account his provinces in Asia, he ruled as suzerain over all the southern coast of the Mediterranean Sea.

Since then the sultan has been stripped of all these vast possessions (except the Islands of the Archipelago and Crete) and it may be well to see how he acquired them. Subsequent chapters, relating more particularly to the nineteenth century will tell how one by one they have been shorn away.

All educated persons are vaguely aware that the Turks, like every other fierce and migratory horde, came from the sun-rising, and had their origin at the foot of the Altai Mountains. The earliest mention of them is supposed to be found in Genesis, where Togarmak (assumed by antiquarians to have been their ancestor) is enumerated among the grandsons of Japhet, — a circumstance which gives, it would seem, to their introduction into the European family the very earliest date, and cuts the ground beneath the modern argument that Turks, as Asiatics, have no business to be upon the soil of Europe at all.

In Ezekiel "those of the house of Togarmak" are mentioned as great traders in "horses and mules;" and in the final destruction of Gog out of the land of Magog (Gog being a Russian prince, according to the Septuagint) the house of Togarmak out of the north quarter, with all its bands, is in alliance with Jews, Persians, Ethiopians, and the inhabitants of the North African coast, against the common enemy.

Be all this as it may, we know very little concerning the Turks until about five hundred and fifty years after the Christian era. They were then settled on the frontier of China. They inhabited walled towns, were extensively engaged in commerce, and lived under the protection of just laws. Their leader in the latter days of the Roman Empire sent an embassy to the Emperor Justinian. This Turkish chief is believed to have been the son of Toumen the Blacksmith; for the race was already advanced in manufactures, and in the working of iron. Toumen was the founder of the first great Turkish Empire. Under him his people rose in rebellion against the Avars, a mixed Mongolian race, and his dominions are believed to have extended across the continent of Asia, from the Caspian Sea to the Pacific.

The son of Toumen was a rude barbarian, but a sovereign alive to the importance of a balance of power, and the ties of commercial intercourse. He had instructed his ambassadors to procure him, if possible, the silk trade of Europe, and to form an alliance with the Byzantine emperor against their common enemy, the Persians.

During the prosperous years of the mighty power of Rome the commerce of the West with India, which was carried in fleets down the Red Sea, struck Pliny with astonishment.

After the reign of Justinian the disorders in the empire of the East, caused this great traffic rapidly to decline. War, piracy and devastation, depopulation, and destruction of property soon left the eastern coast of the Red Sea as desolate and unproductive as we find it now; and the well-governed dominions of the Turkish khan opened a surer highway to India and the Spice Islands.

Two centuries later, from causes now unknown to us, the eastern provinces of the Turkish khan became subject to China, while the west fell under the dominion of the Saracens; but even in adversity the Turks soon became masters of the situation. They embraced Mahommedanism, and the Saracen caliph, admiring the bravery and hardiness of the Turkish troops, formed them into his body-guard. By the eleventh century these soldiers, called Mamlouks, had become masters of the Caliphat, and being joined by a tribe of their own blood, — fresh from the cradle of their race, and commanded by the all-conquering Togul Beg, — they proceeded to conquer western Asia, and to accelerate the decline and fall of all that was left of the great eastern division of the Roman Empire.

The habits of the new invaders, who are called the Seljouk Turks in memory of Seljouk the father of Togul Beg, were neither commercial, agricultural, nor manufacturing, like those of the tribe which founded the first Turkish Empire. Wherever they came "the verdure," says a contemporary writer, "fled from the bloody sod." Where they pitched their tents, orchards, and fertile fields disappeared for a day's journey round their encampments; and still, in wandering through Asia Minor, we are told that travellers " come unexpectedly on districts fertile as the plains of Poland or Moldavia, on which wheat never grows, but which the page of history informs us were inhabited by an industrious agricultural population until the towns were destroyed and the people exterminated by the generals of Alp Arslan (the successor of Togul Beg) and Malek Shah."

This mighty Turkish Empire of Alp Arslan was soon

divided into three secondary kingdoms: Roum, near the Black Sea,—which took its name (as Roumania has since done) from Rome,—Syria, and Persia.

About 1270, when Saint Louis flung his noble life away upon the sands of Barbary, when Dante was a little boy in Florence, while Guelphs and Ghibellines were distracting hapless Italy, and while Michael Palæologos, a clever and ambitious soldier, having freed Constantinople from the temporary dominion of the Latins, was establishing himself on the Byzantine throne,—there entered the kingdom of Roum, through the defiles of the mountains of Armenia, about four hundred families, forming a small tribe, led by a gallant chief of Turkish race. He had a son called Othman, whose name has been perpetuated in that of the great Ottoman Empire. Othman's fame for judgment and for justice became very great. One celebrated decision of his in favor of a Greek Christian, and against a nobleman of his own race, extended his renown, and added importance to his government. He never, however, became more than the emir of a province, though, according to a Turkish tradition, a vision, the particulars of which every Turk learns in his childhood, was early vouchsafed to him. In it he beheld his family the masters of Constantinople; "which," says the Oriental who relates this legend, "is placed at the junction of two seas, and of two continents, resembling a noble diamond set between two sapphire stones and two emeralds." Before Othman died, his great son Orkhan, in 1325, had conquered Brusa in Anatolia from the Greeks, and laid the foundation of the Ottoman Empire.

The power of Orkhan differed from that of every other conqueror. It was not based on nationality, for even the four hundred families who had followed his father into Armenia, and thence into the dominions of the Greek Empire, had never become a distinct tribe.

"The Ottoman Empire threatened Europe with conquest; Ottoman armies were well nigh invincible; the Ottoman government was an intelligent despotism, superior to any contemporary government; but during the period of Ottoman greatness there never was such a thing as an Ottoman nation." Five centuries of Ottoman power in Europe rest solely on the sagacity and foresight of Orkhan, son of Othman and the princes of his family. When the life that they infused into that empire of "all nations and languages" was drained out of the body politic by an alteration in the traditions of its government, and the suppression of the Janissaries, that final sickness soon set in of which we ourselves may possibly witness the last convulsive throes.

The troops of Othman had been irregular horsemen. His son Orkhan attempted the formation of a body of infantry. He found his followers, however, so rude and insubordinate that the idea occurred to him of educating his troops under his own eye, of literally forming a nursery of soldiers in his household, of owning an army of well-educated slaves. To this end he imposed a forced tribute of male children on every Christian district that he conquered. This tribute was exacted until 1685, when it was finally abolished. These tribute children all became members of the sultan's household. They lost all ties of race, of faith, of family, — their sole law was their master's will. They were ready to defend him against every enemy. Like faithful animals they looked only to the hand that fed them. They formed the celebrated corps of Janissaries, first planned by Orkhan, fully organized by his son after him, and abolished by massacre, after vain efforts for their reform, in 1826, a date which falls within this history of the nineteenth century.

With this corps Amurath, the successor of Orkhan, subdued nearly the whole of the present Turkey in Europe, leaving the Greek emperor little more than his capital. He then marched against those provinces, Wallachia, Servia, and Bulgaria, whose shores are washed by the Danube, and everywhere he went he demanded contributions of male children. By the laws of the Koran, to the victor belonged the *fifth part* of all the property of the conquered. This was interpreted to include a fifth part of the population. The conqueror compounded for male children, seven or eight years of age. "Let them be called Janissaries," said a dervish, who, with great ceremony, gave them his blessing, — "*Yeni-sheri*, or new soldiers! May their countenances be always bright, their hands victorious, their swords keen!"

Strange to say, this horrible tribute does not at first appear to have been intolerable to the Greek Christians. Whether they accepted the fortune of war and were thankful to have universal servitude compounded by such a sacrifice, or whether, their country being laid desolate, they were willing to see their children secured against the horrors of starvation, we do not know; but, as a modern writer says, "had the Greek Christians and the heads of the Greek Church given these very children as good an educacation as Orkhan gave them as his slaves, all Europe might have been spared the Turkish question."

The boys who were the victims of this tribute, were collected once in five years, by officers deputed for the purpose. Their numbers were also increased by children taken in war, and presented to the sultan by his generals and pashas, so that, besides Greeks, Albanians, Servians, Bulgarians, Bosnians, Moldavians, and Wallachians, the corps frequently included Poles, Bohemians, Russians, Germans, and Italians. These were at first lodged in the Sultan's palace, and the first step was to instruct them in the Mahommedan religion. So carefully was this done that while devotion to the Sultan was their duty, devotion to their Prophet became their sole enthusiasm. During the first stage of their education the disposition and mental capacity of each was carefully studied. They then entered on a course of general instruction interspersed with severe bodily toil. At length they were divided into several classes. Those who had been chiefly trained to bodily endurance became Janissaries; those who were believed capable of higher things were educated to fill posts in the administration of the government, with the prospect of being advanced to the highest offices of state. From 1453 to 1617 out of forty-eight grand viziers, thirty were either renegades or the children of Christian parents, brought up in the Mahommedan religion; four only were of Ottoman or Seljouk families; the other fourteen, who had been born Mussulmans, were not of Turkish race.

The discipline of both classes of boys was extremely severe. Those destined to be Janissaries were inured to every kind of bodily privation. They were employed in military exercises during the day, and at night they slept in a long lighted hall, with an overseer walking up and down to see that no one stirred. The higher class, destined to be men of the pen, were separated from the rest, but were kept no less strictly. At the end of three years of training in the "higher education," they had the choice either to remain and ascend in the civil service of their master, or to enter into one of the first four corps of *spahis*, the immediate body-guard of the Sultan.

A *kulah*, or cap of dingy white felt, of which a strip hung down behind, while the front was adorned by a tuft of heron's-feathers, was the distinguishing mark of a Janissary. A fire-lock, a pistol, a mace, a scimitar, and an axe were his equipments, and he prided himself, not only on the temper of his weapons, but upon their elaborate ornamentation.

Besides the standards and horse-tails planted before the tent door of their commander, each regiment had the caldron in which the soldiers made their soup carried before it on parade or in battle. The loss of its caldron was the greatest misfortune that could befall a regiment; and on the rare occasions when they were taken in battle, all the officers were cashiered, and the regiment publicly disgraced.

After the power of the sultans began to decline, the pride and insubordination of the Janissaries became intolerable. As Lady Mary Wortley Montagu says, writing from Turkey to Mr. Alexander Pope in 1717, during her husband's embassy to Constantinople: "These troops have an absolute authority here, and their conduct carries much more the aspect of rebellion than the appearance of subordination. They are commanded by a Pasha Seraskier (that is, General), though the last expression is hardly just, for, to say truth, the pasha is commanded by the Janissaries."

For several generations the Ottoman sultans, who were educated in much the same manner as their tribute children, were even more remarkable for their sagacity, liberality, and occasional generosity, than for their talents and success.

While Orkhan pursued his conquests in Asia Minor, some of his emirs fitted out ships, and proceeded to plunder the Greek islands and the coasts of the Morea. One of them indeed became a model pirate, the chivalrous protector of a Greek empress and her family, the friend and sworn brother in arms of her husband, the Emperor John Cantacuzene. His propensities for plunder were, however, ineradicable. Notwithstanding his "thousand virtues," his name is linked in history with some fatal advice he gave on his deathbed to the Greek emperor. He exhorted his friend to cultivate an alliance with Orkhan.

The Greek Empire was distracted at that time (about the middle of the fourteenth century) by quarrels between the Palæologi and the Cantacuzeni. Indeed there were then two emperors and three empresses at Constantinople disputing with each other the Byzantine throne, and this at a time when a young prince of one of their houses was driven to exclaim: "Alexander complained that his father would leave him nothing to conquer; my predecessors will soon leave me nothing to lose."

Before, however, any arrangement had been entered into for the accommodation of the five personages who, in 1347, agreed to share the Byzantine throne, the flames of civil discord had been raging for six years throughout the Greek Empire, and the Bulgarians, Servians, and Turks were invited by the several parties to the quarrel to take sides in their disputes. The advice and influence of Cantacuzene's buccaneering friend seems to have turned the scale. Orkhan proffered Cantacuzene his alliance, and Cantacuzene accepted it, even listening to a proposal that he would give Orkhan his daughter Theodora in marriage; on which condition alone Orkhan promised to fulfil toward him the duties of a subject and a son. It was stipulated that Theodora should continue in the exercise of her own religion, and the marriage took place with great magnificence, but with no religious ceremonies, on the shores of the Hellespont. Theodora's life, though led thenceforth in a harem, was one of devotion and charity.

Orkhan, in spite of his marriage with a Christian lady, insisted on receiving permission to expose his Christian captives for sale in the markets of Constantinople. Such scenes, and the unnatural marriage of a princess of the reigning family, assisted further to disorganize what remained of the Greek empire. In 1341 (that is, ten years after the death of Robert Bruce, and five years before the battle of Cressy) John Cantacuzene abdicated. His last advice to his countrymen was "to decline rash contests with the Turks, and to compare their own weakness with the hardihood and valor displayed by that great people." He then retired into one of the monasteries of Mount Athos, and took no further part in public affairs, except to urge a union of the Eastern and Western churches, a union which at that time there was some probability of seeing accomplished, under the auspices of the pope at Avignon.

The Emperor John Palæologos, pupil and successor of John Cantacuzene, was the son of a princess of Savoy who had refused the hand of Charles le Bel of France, and had married the Greek emperor. She brought her son up with a prepossession in favor of the Roman Church, and partly from conviction, partly from the hope of foreign sympathy and foreign aid, he offered to bring back his church and people to the Catholic fold. To this end he made a visit to the West, but was not successful. As he was returning home he was made prisoner by the Venetians, to whom he already owed large sums of money. His second son, Manuel, on hearing this, at once sold or mortgaged all he possessed, embarked for Venice, ransomed his father, and pledged his own freedom as security for what remained unpaid of the previous debt.

But present or absent in his dominions, John Palæologos had neither the vigor nor the capacity needed to protect the Eastern Empire, and during his reign the Turks made rapid conquests.

Soliman, the gallant eldest son of Orkhan, was killed by a fall from his horse while throwing the *jereed*, and Orkhan died of grief for the loss of so valiant a son. He was succeeded by his second son, called Murad by the Turks, and Amurath by Christians. Amurath perfected the discipline of the Janissaries, captured Adrianople (a city only one hundred and twenty miles distant from Constantinople) and made it the capital of his empire. This conquest roused some spirit among the Latin Christians of the East, though it was very quietly submitted to by those of the Greek communion. The Servians, Hungarians, and Wallachians, who were Catholics, in obedience to a mandate from Pope Urban V., combined their forces to drive the Turks back into Asia. They were surprised in their camp, however, and completely defeated.

John Palæologos made no effort to recover Adrianople, the second city of his empire; he even sought the friendship of Amurath, and in point of fact became his vassal. Amurath, however, having undertaken an expedition into Servia, was treacherously slain at the close of a victorious day, by a Servian prince who was lying mortally wounded on the field of battle.

His successor, Bajazet the Thunderbolt, first ordered the execution of all princes of his own race, and then reduced the Servians to obedience. He changed the title of emir to that of sultan. He conquered almost all that was left of the Greek Empire, and all the fertile regions lying round the shores of the Black Sea.

After defeating the Hungarian king in a pitched battle, in which a brilliant band of Western princes and knights fought desperately, but without due discipline, against the infidel, Bajazet threatened to besiege Belgrade. Among his prisoners was the Sieur de Boucicault, who afterward, when Constantinople was first attacked by the Turks, defended it successfully. He governed Genoa, invaded Asia, and died at Agincourt. He held pen as well as sword, and wrote a narrative of his captivity, extolling the generosity and chivalry of the Grand Turk on every page. The gay cavaliers of France and Burgundy proved valuable prizes to the Turkish sultan. Besides a ransom of two hundred thousand ducats paid for the survivors, the king of Cyprus sent, to secure their good treatment in captivity, a golden salt-cellar worth ten thousand ducats; while Charles VI. (who was sane at the time of this calamity) sent a cast of Norwegian hawks, six horse-loads of scarlet cloth and of fine linen, besides arras tapestry representing the battles of Alexander. It had been stipulated when ransom was paid for the French captives, that they should swear never again to bear arms against their conquerors; "but Bajazet," says Boucicault, "absolved us, saying to the heir of Burgundy: 'Thou art young and mayst be ambitious of effacing the disgrace or the misfortune of thy first chivalry. Assemble thy powers, proclaim thy design, and be assured that Bajazet will rejoice to meet thee a second time in battle.'"

In 1399 Bajazet's ambition prompted him to subdue Constantinople, but he abstained on the advice of his grand vizier, who represented that such an enterprise might unite the princes of Europe in another formidable crusade. Soon after he was checked in his career of Western conquest by tidings from the East, which called his attention to Asia.

About thirty years before (that is during the latter years of the Black Prince) a mighty conqueror, Timour the Tartar, better known as Tamerlane, had appeared in Central

Asia. He advanced so far to the northwest as to threaten Moscow, conquered Bagdad and Shiraz, left a record of his passage in Siberia, and subdued those parts of Central Asia which, until lately, when the Russians began their Trans-Caspian Railway, have been rarely visited and little known. Thence Timour passed over into Hindostan by way of the Indus, advancing in the track of Alexander the Great. He soon, however, overpassed his Macedonian predecessor. He reached Delhi, and pushed forward to the sources of the Ganges. He there received news that Sultan Bajazet, indignant at his having espoused the cause of some rebellious chiefs, was preparing to invade the western frontier of his dominions. After some correspondence, more like the vaunts of the Homeric chiefs than diplomatic intercourse in modern times, in which the Turkish sultan is styled the Kaisser of Rome, the angry conquerors prepared to measure their strength in a pitched battle.

Timour was a zealous Mussulman, but he belonged to that unorthodox section of the faith which is still the religion of Persia, and reveres the memories of the martyrs Ali and Houssain. His wars with the Saracens and Turks became wars of religion. His army met that of Sultan Bajazet in 1402 at Angora in Anatolia. The Turkish army had four hundred thousand men, and in its ranks were twenty thousand men-at-arms from the countries of Western Europe, besides forty thousand Janissaries. But in spite of the conduct of the sultan, who, though suffering from gout, and but ill-mounted, displayed, it is said, all the qualities of a soldier and a chief, — in spite of the splendid charges of the Europeans, and the faithful self-devotion of the Janissaries, — victory decided in favor of Timour. Bajazet was captured, and a body of Tartar cavalry pursued his flying army to the shores of the Sea of Marmora.

Gibbon has sifted the old story of the iron cage in which Timour imprisoned Bajazet, and finds it probably true. Why should it not be true? Timour was a conqueror always on the march, who in the case of so illustrious a captive must have felt the necessity of a portable prison. Nearly a hundred years after this date Louis XI. held Cardinal de Balue in similar confinement, and the Countess of Buchan was so punished for having crowned the Bruce in Scotland in 1306.

The hordes of Timour were happily unable to cross the Hellespont, which was defended by the Turks, nor could they cross the Bosphorus, which was defended by the Greek emperor.

Soliman, the son of Bajazet, however, humbled himself to solicit the clemency of the conqueror, and the Greek emperor transferred to Timour's military chest the tribute he had been in the habit of paying to the sultan. Ambassadors from Egypt, Arabia, India, Tartary, Russia, Spain, and even France, visited the court of Timour at Samarcand before he set out on his last expedition to China. He died upon the march in 1403, and his tomb is near the present terminus of the Russian Trans-Caspian Railway. His effigy as the Great Mogul adorns every pack of playing-cards printed in England.[1]

The European dominions of the Turkish sultans now fell into confusion and anarchy. Had the Latins joined the Greeks at this crisis they might have driven back the infidel to Asia. But the dislike that in that age was felt for unorthodox Christians was stronger than that inspired by such Mussulman conquerors as Othman and the descendants of his sons.

During the great anarchy that reigned throughout the East for fifty years Constantinople was twice besieged by the Turks, but the strength of its walls resisted them. Gibbon says of the Ottoman Empire: "The massy trunk was bent to the ground, but no sooner did the hurricane pass away than it rose with fresh vigor, and more lively vegetation." When the Turks attacked Constantinople for

---

[1] Playing-cards were first invented about this period. Timour himself was a great chess-player.

the third time, in 1453, they had been instructed by the Genoese in the use of cannon.

Manuel Palæologos, the dutiful son who took his imperial father out of pawn to the Venetians, reigned at Constantinople during nearly all these fifty years. His efforts, and those of his son John Palæologos II., were directed not toward the renovation of their decaying empire, but toward accommodating the disputes between the Latin and Greek churches, and so procuring the support and countenance of Roman Catholic princes. Both Manuel and his son made pilgrimages of supplication to the popes at Avignon. Manuel even passed over into England, where he induced Henry IV. to take the cross for another crusade.

> "I had a purpose now
> To lead out many to the Holy Land,"

says Shakespeare's Henry IV. when dying in the Jerusalem chamber, and his gallant son, who cherished the same purpose, alludes to Turkish history in his speech after his father's death, when he says, desiring to reassure his four brothers: —

> "This is the English — not the Turkish court;
> Not Amurath an Amurath succeeds,
> But Harry Harry."

John Palæologos II. reached Italy in 1438, just as the papal court was on the eve of returning from Avignon. After delay and disappointment he succeeded in effecting a treaty with the pope, which was to secure him help from Catholic Christendom, and bring the Greek Church into subjection to that of Rome. Several of the Greek bishops were made cardinals, and some of them hastened to do their part in carrying out the treaty, the news of which was far from being welcomed by all Greek Christians. Isidor, the primate of Russia, who had been created a cardinal and legate, was at once deposed by his clergy. The patriarchs of Alexandria, Antioch, and Jerusalem, whose sees were under the protection of the Turks, assembled a synod, denounced the agreement entered into by Palæologos, condemned the creed and councils of the Roman Church, and threatened the Greek emperor with excommunication.

Pope Eugenius, on his part, did what he could to gather together forces for a crusade; but France and England were exhausted by long wars, and, though Frederick of Germany promised his assistance, he entered into the scheme with no enthusiasm. Philip of Burgundy (father of Charles the Bold, brother of the prince so courteously treated by Sultan Bajazet) sent a contingent. Venice and Genoa, for once, united their fleets. Poland and Hungary sent their light horsemen, and what was of more importance they contributed a hero. The Servian Catholics promised to rise against their Turkish masters; an Armenian prince offered to make a diversion in Asia, which would favor the Christians; a few knights of renown from France and Germany led their own followers; and the Greek emperor promised to guard the Bosphorus and to attack the Turks when occasion offered.

During this time the four sons of Bajazet had been engaged in strife for his inheritance. It was at last grasped by Mohammed the youngest and the ablest of the family. His son Amurath II. succeeded him. The Greek emperor Manuel Palæologos, hoping to profit by civil discord among the Turks, broke his word by releasing from prison Mustapha, a rival claimant for the throne, who was, or called himself, the son of Bajazet. Amurath, however, triumphed over this competitor, and though unable to revenge himself upon the emperor of Constantinople at the time, bore him a deep grudge for his treachery.

Ladislas, who was then king, both of Poland and of Hungary, believing himself to be acting in concert with the crusaders of the pope, led an army of his confederated subjects in 1444, as far as Sofia, the capital of Bulgaria. Two battles were fought, in which the Christians were victorious through the skill and valor of John Hunniades, a young chief of Wallachia. After these victories Ladislas went back to Belgrade for the winter, and there received a deputation from Sultan Amurath, soliciting peace. The Turks promised to restore Servia, and to withdraw from the frontier of Hungary. These terms were accepted, and a truce for ten years was concluded. But the pope's legate was greatly disappointed, and hardly was the treaty concluded when news reached Belgrade that the Armenians were in full revolt in Asia, that the Greek emperor had invaded Thrace, that the combined fleets of Venice, Genoa, and Burgundy, had passed the Hellespont, and the allies, ignorant of any agreement between Ladislas and the sultan, demanded the co-operation of the victorious Polish and Hungarian army.

The legate, in an eager speech, absolved the Christians from all sin of perjury should they break their oaths to the infidel. In the very room where the treaty with the sultan had been solemnly sworn to a few days before, war was again declared against the Turks. But the army of Ladislas had been already broken up. The German and French knights had departed before the first treaty was signed, refusing to make terms with unbelievers. The Poles were never willing long to keep the field. A Wallachian chief remarked that the remnant of the army remaining with Ladislas was hardly more numerous than the hunting retinue which attended the sultan.

The confederated army, however, which was composed entirely of Roman Catholics, marched through Bulgaria, burning as it went the cottages of the Greek Christians. At Varna, near the shores of the Black Sea, it met the Turks, commanded by ex-Sultan Amurath, who had abdicated in favor of his son Mohammed II.

Amurath marched with a copy of the violated treaty borne before him as a banner, and it is said that he called upon the God of the Christians before the battle to punish the perfidy of His followers.

Ladislas perished in a brilliant charge, and the cardinal legate also fell. A column was erected by the victorious

Amurath to the memory of Ladislas, commending his valor, and recording his unhappy fate. Hunniades fled to Hungary, where at first he was made regent, and afterwards king. He "spent his life in battle with the Turk," whom he repulsed, a month before his death, from before the walls of Belgrade.

The crusading forces returned to western Europe without having accomplished any deliverance for the Greek emperor. But southern Greece was up in arms against the Turk, and Albania, peopled by a race descended from the Macedonians, was making rapid progress in insurrection under George Castriot, better known as Scanderbeg, — which is Turkish for Prince Alexander. He is the only one of the tribute children converted into Janissaries whom we know to have retained any memory of his Christian faith or friends. For twenty-three years after he abjured the Prophet, and his allegiance to the sultan, he fought the Turks as the avenger of his country and her wrongs. At last, for some reason that we do not know (probably because his resources were exhausted), he sought refuge in Venetian territory. The Janissaries, who soon after his death had the opportunity of plundering his tomb, had his bones set in gold, and wore them as amulets. His son escaped to Naples, where his blood still flows in the veins of some of the noblest families.

Four years after the defeat of the Christians at Varna, the Emperor John Palæologos II. suddenly died, and, after a short interval of disputed succession, was succeeded by Constantine Palæologos, not only the last and best, but the sole hero of his family. Our knowledge of him is drawn largely from the memoirs of his chamberlain, Phranza; but all accounts of him agree.

At the time of Constantine's accession (1448) Mohammed II. was already making preparations to besiege Constantinople on a scale of unparalleled magnitude. Cannon, just begun to be used in war, were cast of a size never again equalled until our own day. One cannon threw a ball weighing six hundred and sixty pounds, and was large enough to give shelter in after years to an absconding tailor. Soldiers were recruited in every Mohammedan country, a powerful navy was put afloat, and immense magazines were formed.

Constantinople meantime was a scene of cowardly despair, discord, and confusion. In the doomed city seemed to shine only one noble soul. In the spring of 1453 Mohammed II. appeared before its gates with two hundred and fifty thousand men. Constantine, after using every exertion, could only raise a force of forty-nine hundred Greeks; these were, however, reinforced by two thousand men-at-arms from western Europe, under the conduct of Gian Gustiniani, a native of Genoa. But the princes of Europe stood aloof. The pope, indignant at the obstinacy with which the Greek Christians refused to admit his supremacy, prophesied the success of the Infidels; the princes of the Morea and of the Islands of the Ægean affected cold neutrality.

Constantinople is situated on a triangular piece of ground, and formed at that day almost a semi-amphitheatre. On its northern side is its noble harbor, the Golden Horn; on the south, the Sea of Marmora. The west landline, or base of the triangle, extended in a slightly curved line from the Sea of Marmora to the harbor. This western wall, which was double, was nearly six miles long. It was old, but was defended by a deep moat. The side of the city toward the sea was protected by a strong current; while the harbor was defended by a mighty chain supported on several large vessels. The first efforts of the Turks were directed against the land side. They not only relied on their enormous cannon, but appear to have employed something like the modern *mitrailleuses*. The cannon and the *mitrailleuses* were supplemented by the catapults and moving towers of antiquity. By the combined use of such arts of annoyance, an immense breach was effected in the outer wall; but Gustiniani and the emperor, by great personal exertions, repaired the damage before daylight, and destroyed the wooden tower relied on by the besiegers.

A few days afterward five merchant vessels laden with supplies broke through the Turkish fleet, which was composed only of innumerable small boats and a few war-galleys. In vain did Sultan Mohammed, sitting on horseback on the shore, endeavor by shouts, gestures, and reproaches to animate his followers; the Christian ships swept on, and safely anchored within the chain of the harbor. But the cannon of the Turks were directed by a Christian engineer, and the ambassador of Hungary, relying on a prophesy that the capture of Constantinople should be the last of the Turkish conquests, was in the Ottoman camp directing the operations of the Infidel. The reduction of the city, however, appeared hopeless, unless an attack could be made both from the harbor and the land. Mohammed (resolved that nothing should be impossible where he was concerned) determined to carry his fleet overland six miles, and launch it in the harbor, between the great boom and the city. Relying on the supineness of the Genoese, who, inhabiting the suburb of Galata, might have obstructed the passage, the sultan in ten days constructed a plank-road made slippery with grease and with vast quantities of millet. Fifty light galleys were landed on this road, placed on rollers, and drawn forward by men and pulleys. Every vessel had its sails set to a favoring breeze, and in the course of one night this Turkish fleet surmounted an elevation, steered over the plain, and was launched into the harbor. In vain the Greeks now tried to burn this fleet; the insufficient garrison was too weak to sustain a double attack, and all hope for Constantinople was over.

Still Constantine refused to yield. The sultan offered him safety, riches, and an honorable retirement. He declined to make any terms which included the surrender of his capital. May 29, the 53d day of the siege, was fixed on as propitious for the final assault. Mohammed promised his men the slaves and the spoil, reserving to himself the buildings of the city. On the night of May 28 the Turkish camp was all ablaze with bonfires.

That night, within the walls of the doomed city, the noblest of the Greeks and the bravest of their allies met in the palace at the summons of Constantine. He made them a last speech. They wept together, and kissed each other. Then each commander went forth calmly to his post, and the emperor entered the cathedral of St. Sophia. There the Lord's Supper was celebrated for the last time, the emperor and his few guards kneeling at midnight to receive the elements with prayers and tears. Then Constantine, taking leave of his own household, and imploring the forgiveness of any he might have wronged, mounted his horse, and went forth before sunrise. For two hours his voice was heard above the roar of the assault, encouraging his soldiers. The sultan's troops from Anatolia and from Roum fell by hundreds, and their bodies made a bridge across the ditch over which the Janissaries at last mounted the breach under the eye of their sovereign and commander. At this moment Gian Gustiniani, — the brave Genoese chief, — was wounded by an arrow in his hand. The extreme pain of the wound overcame his power of endurance. In vain the emperor implored him to disregard his anguish. He passed to the rear. The foreign troops lost heart. Hassan, a giant Janissary, with twelve comrades scaled the breach.

Whatever we may think of the Greek people in this struggle with the Turks, the courage of the self-devoted band of friends and nobles who drew around Constantine should never be forgotten. The last words of the emperor that history has recorded were : " Cannot there be found a Christian to cut off my head?"

The Turkish forces poured into the city; the multitude rushed into the Church of St. Sophia. Ducas, a Frenchman, who was an eye-witness, shall tell the tale : —

" The Turks, having reached the cathedral, cut down the gate with axes, entered with drawn swords, and having cast a glance upon the crowd, proceeded to seize them separately as slaves, without encountering any resistance. Who can describe such ruin and calamity? The Turk, with sacrilegious hand, seizes on every nun of delicate form or beautiful person; one carries off his victim bound; another, more powerful, snatches her away from him. The curling hair, the naked breast, the extended arms offer fresh inducements to the plunderers. The mistress was bound with her servant; the master with his purchased slave; the priest with the porter at the gate. Young men were linked in the same chain with virgins on whom the sun had never shone, — whose faces their own fathers had scarcely beheld; and stripes were inflicted on their tender flesh if they dared to offer any resistance. The space of an hour was sufficient for these robbers, these ministers of Divine vengeance, to bind the whole multitude, — the men with ropes, the women with their own fillets and shawls."

At two o'clock on the same day victorious Mohammed entered the city by the Gate of St. Romanus, through which an ancient prophesy had predicted the free passage of a destroyer. He paused at St. Sophia, and ordered the destruction of all Christian emblems, that it might be converted into a mosque, and then rode on to the great Blachernal Palace. As he entered its courts he was heard repeating to himself some lines of Persian poetry, —

"The spider has spun her web in the palace of the Cæsars,
The owl has sung her watch-song on the towers of Afrasiab."

But Mohammed, though a man of generous impulses and literary tastes, was still a savage. He did not, indeed, at first trample on or oppress his Christian subjects on account of their religion; on the contrary, the heads of the Greek Church were treated with respect; and the churches and chapels of Constantinople were divided between them and the Moslems. He caused the dead body of the emperor to be sought, and gave it honorable burial. But cruelties unspeakable, committed in cold blood two weeks after the capture and the fall of Constantinople, filled Christendom with horror, though no combined movement was attempted against the Turks for several years.

CHAPTER IV.

TURKS, RUSSIANS, AND GREEKS.

SUPINE though civilized Christendom might have been on hearing the fate of the capital of the Greek Empire, and the story of the sufferings of Greek Christians, there was one barbarous people in whose hearts the taking of Constantinople roused deep and permanent emotion. "There remains now," said a contemporary Russian annalist, "but one Orthodox Empire. The prophecies are accomplished which long ago announced that the sons of Ishmael should conquer Byzantium. Perhaps we are destined also to see the fulfilment of that prophecy which promises that the Russians shall triumph over the children of Ishmael, and reign over the seven hills of Constantinople."

After the events we have recorded Mohammed the Great reigned nearly thirty years. He rooted out from the Morea the last princes of the house of Palæologos, and forced one of them to give him his daughter in marriage. He conquered Greece, Servia, the Islands of the Ægean Sea, and the tiny Greek Empire of Trebizond, where the last of the Comneni still reigned. The princes of that house were murdered by the Turks, and their mother, the Empress Irene, after digging for them a grave with her own hands, fell dead by the side of her beloved ones, and the earth was filled in over them. Mohammed rent Nigropont from the Venetians, and other important places from the Genoese. Frequent wars with Persia, however, prevented more vigorous operations against Christian princes. The most memorable enterprise he undertook during his latter years was against the Island of Rhodes. That island had been conquered from the Saracens by the Knights Hospitallers about fifteen years after their expulsion from Palestine, in 1291. Its ports were at that time nests for pirates, but the Knights suppressed the pirates, occupied the island, and built fortifications of enormous strength. Rhodes was fertile, beautiful, and picturesque beyond description. The fleets of the Knights kept in check the Mohammedan corsairs, and the inhabitants of the island became prosperous and happy. Against it, however, in 1480, Mohammed sent a force of seventy thousand men, in one hundred and sixty vessels commanded by four Greek renegades. One of these was an engineer of reputation, another, who commanded the expedition, was a Palæologos. The immense guns of the Turks soon made a breach in the great tower. In spite of the efforts of the Knights it grew wider and wider, till the Grand Master, Pierre d'Aubusson, perceived that nothing more was possible, except to resist an assault. This was not long delayed. The Turkish ships bore down upon the Tower of St. Nicholas, which was close to the water's edge. All day the sixteen thousand followers of the Knights defended the position against five times their number. Thousands of Turks were cut down, but thousands more seemed to replace the slain and wounded. When at last the day closed D'Aubusson sent fire-ships into the fleet of the enemy. Several galleys caught fire, and the Turkish fleet was dispersed.

Again Palæologos attacked the place in a new quarter. Men, women, children, nuns, and Jews (a part of the population much devoted to the Knights) joined in the work of strengthening the defences. Again and again Palæologos attacked, but was every time repulsed, until at last, with a loss of more than half his men, he drew off his fleet, and left the island. The sultan sentenced him to death for the failure of his enterprise, but his punishment was commuted to exile. Mohammed himself died shortly after. He directed that on his tomb should be engraved: "I intended to capture Rhodes, and subjugate Italy." As a first step toward the latter purpose his troops had already attacked and taken Otranto, and the kingdoms of the West were filled with fear.

Mohammed's empire was disputed by his two sons, Bajazet and Zizim. Achmet Pasha, the victorious commander who had just returned from planting the crescent on the towers of Otranto, declared for Bajazet. Zizim sought refuge in Rhodes. He was far from handsome, though a prince of great accomplishments, and of a noble soul. The Grand Master d'Aubusson, who lived twenty-three years after his glorious defence of Rhodes, unhappily stained his memory on this occasion with treachery. He sent Zizim to a Commandery of his Order in France, in a sort of honorable captivity. The Order accepted a bribe from Bajazet to keep him safely. Pope Innocent VIII., however, insisted that the Mohammedan prince should be given up to him, in order that he might lead against the Turks a Christian army, which was being raised in Hungary. Zizim was therefore sent to Rome, and was there treated with distinction, but Innocent, who died soon after, was succeeded by Cardinal Borgia, Alexander VI., of infamous memory, who, being bribed by Bajazet, with three hundred thousand ducats, first imprisoned, and then poisoned the Turkish prince on the eve of his surrender to Charles VIII., who was on his march to Naples.

Bajazet II. reigned twenty-one years. He was poisoned by his son Selim, who reigned eight years, and was succeeded in 1519 by his only son, Solyman the magnificent, the most illustrious sultan of an illustrious house. This prince was proclaimed sultan three days before Charles V. was crowned emperor of Germany.

Bajazet and Selim had not pushed their conquests in Europe; they were chiefly occupied by the affairs of Egypt, Syria, and Palestine; but Solyman began his reign by a successful expedition against Rhodes. He commanded it in person, at the head of two hundred thousand men. He also invaded Hungary, laid Moldavia under tribute, and subdued all the kingdom of the Saracens in Western Asia. He then led another expedition through Hungary into Austria, but was checked in 1529 before the walls of Vienna. Subsequently Hungary made an alliance with him, out of hatred for Austria, and his great corsair Barbarossa spread terror and devastation along the coasts of the Mediterranean Sea. The alliance of Solyman was courted by the Most Christian king Francis I., and even the pope was accused of being favorable to him out of enmity to the Greek Christians. His empire extended from the Danube to the Euphrates, — from the Adriatic to the shores of the Black Sea. In 1565 his general Mustapha with thirty thousand men (among them six thousand Janissaries) attacked the Knights Hospitallers, who after being driven out of Rhodes, had found an asylum in Malta.[1]

Solyman before he died united the sacerdotal character of caliph with that of sultan, and became the Prince of True Believers. As such he was addressed by Queen Elizabeth, who was advised to style herself to him Defender of the Faith against Christian idolaters. His subjects called him the Lawgiver, for he completed the code of laws begun by his great-grandfather, — all of which are based upon precepts in the Koran.

Solyman was less of a voluptuary and better educated than his predecessors. In glory he excelled them all; but he was the last of the great Ottoman sultans. From his time the family of Othman has degenerated, and the power of the Porte has declined. Two causes have contributed to this decay. Many changes were permitted in the organization and discipline of the Janissaries; and the sultan caused his promising young son Mustapha to be murdered almost in his presence, that the son of his favorite (a Russian slave) might succeed him on the throne. Instead of receiving the hardy, liberal education

---

[1] The glorious particulars of that most interesting siege have been stirringly told by Mr. Prescott in his life of Philip II.

hitherto given to princes of his race, this young man was brought up, as all his successors have been since, in the voluptuousness and effeminacy of the seraglio.

From Solyman's death in 1566, to the present day, there have been twenty-two sultans, but none of them, save Sultan Mahmoud, the destroyer of the Janissaries, have shown marked talent or great vigor.

All through the seventeenth century the Turks struggled with Austria, often in the character of the allies and protectors of Hungary; and in 1683 Vienna had all but met the fate of Constantinople. In 1699 the treaty of Carlowitz deprived Turkey of the Ukraine and Podalia, gave the Morea to the Venetians, and the strong post of Azof to the Russians.

Lady Mary Wortley Montagu, who passed over the lands rendered desolate by these cruel wars in 1717, thus speaks of what she witnessed: —

"The desert woods of Servia are the common refuge of thieves, who rob, fifty in a company, and the villages are so poor that only force could extort from them the necessary provisions. Indeed the Janissaries had no mercy on their poverty, killing all the poultry and sheep they could find, without asking to whom they belonged, while the wretched owners dared not put in their claims for fear of being beaten."

In that year (1717) the Sultan Achmet again went to war with Austria. The aged hero Prince Eugene compelled him to give up nearly all Servia and Moldavia, but the latter was recovered by the Turks after it had been governed by Austria for nineteen years. Twenty years later the Turks regained Servia and Wallachia, but they gave up the Crimea to Russia.

Such incessant changes make it impossible in a short history to follow the fortunes of the provinces and principalities which once formed part of European Turkey; and it seems to have been equally difficult for those distracted countries to consolidate since their emancipation.

Hostilities hardly at any time ceased between Turkey

and Russia during the seventeenth and eighteenth centuries, and the memory of this strife is so vivid in the minds of the Russian peasantry, that, it is said, they still call all enemies " mussulmans " in their village *patois*.

After the reign of Solyman, the Ottoman Empire seems to lose itself in a number of large, disorderly, ill-organized provinces, in which Christians in Europe were more numerous than the Mohammedans. But they agreed only in their hatred of the Turks ; they differed widely on points of orthodoxy, in race, laws, interests, language, and aspirations.

All the provinces were fertile, all were almost without roads, all felt themselves oppressed by local tyrants, above all by the tax-collector. All were densely ignorant, but all were accustomed to some sort of local self-government, on the village system. Most of them made bitter complaints of the subserviency of the dignitaries of the Greek Church to the Mussulman authorities at Constantinople ; no man seemed to expect justice from a Turk without bribery, not so much because he was a Christian, as because Greek Christians were a subject race. As some one suggested in 1873, " Take all the evils that afflicted France before the Revolution, add those that distracted England under the Norman kings, aggravate them by the bickerings and jealousies of Jews, Mohammedans, Roman Catholics, Renegades, and Greek Christians, — then leaven this mass with a vague hope of coming deliverance, such as will enable every man among them to set his foot upon the neck of his oppressor, and you may form some idea of the condition of things."

Sultan Mahmoud II. — styled "the shadow of the Almighty upon earth " — was the second son of Sultan Abdul Hamid, who died in 1789 when Mahmoud was only four years old. Abdul Hamid, according to the law of succession in Turkey, was succeeded, not by one of his sons, but by his brother Selim III. On Selim's death, in 1807, Mustapha, the eldest son of Abdul Hamid, was called to the throne. It was his purpose to adhere to Turkish precedent and put his younger brothers to death, in order to forestall conspiracies in their favor, in order also that his own sons might, after his death, replace him on the throne. Mustapha was therefore preparing to get rid of Mahmoud in the obscurity of the seraglio, when a military *émeute* suddenly deposed him, and girded Mahmoud with the sword of Osman, a ceremony equivalent to Western coronation. Needless to say that Mustapha was murdered, and that his infant children were destroyed.

The early years of Mahmoud's reign were occupied by incessant disputes with the all-powerful Janissaries. We have seen how Lady Mary Wortley Montagu spoke of them half a century before, and since her time they had only increased in arrogance and insubordination. Alternately they coerced their sovereign into granting their demands, even to the banishment and execution of his personal attendants and favorites, or they were in open revolt against him. When very much exasperated they were in the habit of setting fire to the outskirts of Constantinople. The streets of that city frequently ran blood. But during the early years of the nineteenth century western Europe had no time to turn its eyes upon the East, being absorbed by the conquests and successes of the mighty emperor of the Western world.

The year that Napoleon invaded Russia, that power concluded a long war with Turkey, by the Treaty of Bucharest; but it is Turkish policy to make promises on paper, and never to fulfil them. There were too policies in the Divan at that period: that of Russia and of England, who on the Turkish question were then united; and that of France, which was ably sustained by Marshal Sebastiani, then the French ambassador. But Mahmoud was restive under foreign dictation. His reign continued to be a succession of treasons and rebellions, suppressed (when not submitted to) by revolting cruelty. The Servians rose against him. Mehemet Ali, a Macedonian soldier of fortune, who had been made governor of Egypt, converted himself almost into an independent sovereign. Roumelia, Widdin, Damascus, Trebizond, St. Jean d' Acre, Aleppo, and other places were scenes of revolt and of frightful massacre. Ali, the bold, crafty, energetic pasha of Jannina (the potentate visited in his fastnesses by Lord Byron) made himself master of Epirus, and the war which thereupon ensued with the Albanians might be called a prologue to the Revolution in Greece. As soon as Sultan Mahmoud was convinced that in his conflict with Ali the sympathy of his Greek subjects went with his opponents, he issued the following order to his generals: " Every Christian capable of bearing arms must die. The boys shall be circumcised and educated in the military discipline of Europe to form a supplementary corps of Janissaries."

The Society of the Hetairæ or the Brotherhood of the friends of Greece had been joined by men of influence, wealth, and education in all countries, and by 1821 it numbered eighty thousand members. Prince Alexander Ypsilanti, the fast friend and aide-de-camp of the Emperor Alexander, made not the smallest doubt that his master, then under the religious influence of Madame de Krüdener, would second any movement in favor of Greek Christians and assist it if necessary with material aid. But the conscience of Alexander was torn by what seemed to him conflicting obligations. To abandon the cause of the Greek Christians was hard, especially as to support it might probably give him that paramount influence which every Russian covets in the city of Constantinople. On the other hand he had sworn solemnly and with great earnestness to be faithful to the Holy Alliance, which, as he understood it at the time he took his oath, was an alliance between Austria, Prussia, France, and Russia to put down every attempt at revolution in any country in Europe, — revolution being synonymous with atheism in Alexander's mind.

At the moment when Ypsilanti was lifting the standard of revolt at Jassy in Moldavia, and was assuring his followers of the countenance and protection of the Russian emperor,

— when all Greek Christians throughout Turkey were preparing to unite in the revolt, — a military insurrection took place in Italy, and Spain was convulsed by a constitutional revolution. Those uprisings were considered so formidable to the peace of Europe that the Holy Alliance called on France to invade Spain, and force the constitutionalists into submission to King Ferdinand, the despicable despot whom the Congress of Vienna had set over them. Could Alexander, thus engaged in putting down one revolutionary movement place himself at the head of another, — even though the Revolution in Greece was the cause of his co-religionists against Mohammedan oppressors?

He decided that his honor called him to stand faithfully by the word which he had pledged to the Holy Alliance. He cast off Madame de Krüdener, he disowned all connection with the Hetairists and Ypsilanti; but from that time forward to the day of his death he suffered from fits of great excitement alternating with periods of religious melancholy. He may be said to have died a victim to his sense of honor conflicting with his interests and his sympathies.

Ypsilanti, disavowed by his former friend and emperor, continued his struggle against the Turks in Wallachia and Moldavia. Those pashaliks were then called the Danubian Provinces; they are now the Kingdom of Roumania. As seen on the map their form is much like that of a baby's sock, Moldavia being the ankle, Wallachia the foot, the sole of which extends along the northern or left bank of the Danube. The country is wedged in between Hungary and Russia. For the latter its inhabitants have no great affection, partly on account of religious differences; for they are chiefly of the Greek Church owing allegiance to the Patriarch of Constantinople, whereas the czar is head of the Church to all orthodox Christians in his dominions.

The refusal of Alexander to countenance his aide-de-camp was a death-blow to the rising in the Danubian Provinces; but the spirit of the Greeks was already stirred. Besides, they did not believe that Russia would really desert them in their extremity.

As soon as the news of Ypsilanti's rising reached Constantinople Sultan Mahmoud and his Divan resolved upon a blow that should strike terror to the hearts of all Greek Christians.

On Easter Sunday, the great Festival in the Greek Church, as the Patriarch Gregorius, then eighty years old, was descending the steps of the altar, he was seized and hanged over the gate of his Archiepiscopal Palace amid the furious cries of a vast crowd of Mussulmans. After the body had hung three hours it was cut down and delivered over to an infuriated band of Jews, who dragged it by the long beard about the streets, and finally flung it into the harbor. Thence Christians, by night, recovered it, and transported it to Odessa, where it was at length solemnly interred.

Everywhere, after the death of the patriarch, priests and leading Greeks shared the same fate, and the Christian churches were openly profaned. "Not a day passed," says Alison, "that numbers of the Greek citizens in Constantinople and Adrianople were not murdered, their property plundered, and their wives and daughters sold as slaves. In ten days several thousand innocent persons were in this manner massacred."

On the 15th of June, 1821, five archbishops, three bishops and a great number of laymen, were hanged in the streets of Constantinople without any trial, and four hundred and fifty Greek mechanics were transported as slaves to the Assyrian frontier. At Salonika (the Thessalonica of Saint Paul) the battlements of the city were hung round with a ghastly dangling fringe of Christian heads, whose blood ran down the wall and reddened the water in the ditch. Nor was all this over in a day, nor in a month, nor in a year. It was going on continually in all parts of the Turkish Empire from 1821 to 1829.

The Greeks of the Peleponnesus and of the Islands of

the Archipelago, fought with desperate courage. The successes of their little fleet were due chiefly to fire-ships, which they managed with great daring and dexterity. But bravely as they fought they had no ideas of the virtues and the duties of citizens. At the height of their war against the Turks their leaders turned their arms against each other. "They are the same rascals that they were in the days of Themistocles," said one diplomatist to another.

Saddest among the stories that stirred all hearts in England and America in those days, was that of the great massacre in the Island of Scio. But the massacre at Scio was no worse than other massacres in Cyprus, Crete, Smyrna, and numbers of other places. To Boston in 1826 was brought Garafelia, a little Greek girl who was drawn with her mother from their hiding-place in an oven, and sold as a slave. She was redeemed by an American philanthropist and brought to America, where the very name of Garafelia became popular.

Twenty-five thousand people, it was said, met death in one day in the massacre of Scio, and thirty thousand women and children were sold as slaves. Besides which, the principal Greek merchants who traded with the island and were living at Constantinople were decapitated by order of the sultan.

Here is a description of the Scio massacre, drawn from an account written not long after it took place, by Miss Sedgwick: —

"For a long time, after the war between Turkey and Greece broke out, Scio took no part in the contest. The Turkish dominion was less felt there than in the rest of Greece. The island lies almost under the shadow of the Asiatic coast. It has a rich soil, and in its happy days it was so highly cultivated, so loaded with fruit and so beautiful with flowers, that it was described as 'an island of gardens.' It had schools and colleges well endowed, and its upper classes, both of men and women, were as well educated and accomplished as other members of European good society. The Sciots had wealth, for they carried on an extensive commerce. They had resident merchants in all the great commercial towns of Europe. They carried on nearly all the trade between Greece and the Turkish cities of Smyrna and Constantinople. They had more to hazard in a war than their fellow-countrymen.

"They were allowed some privileges of local government, and their affairs were managed mildly and prudently by a council of elders. In May, 1821, however, when the standard of the Hetairiæ was raised at Jassy, a small squadron of Ipsariots (patriotic Greeks) appeared off their coast. The Turkish Aga (or colonel), the military governor, immediately resorted to measures that had been taken in other Greek islands; he seized about forty elders and bishops and shut them up in the castle, as hostages for the general good conduct of the people. He brought also to his aid troops from Asia Minor, and did not discountenance their depredations on the wealthier inhabitants. The people were stung to madness by the excesses of these troops, and an attempt was made to rouse them to resistance; but it was hard to light the fire that was to sweep over their own homes and gardens. They were still hesitating when two insurrectionists from Samos, with a small band of followers, landed on their shores. The elders in vain urged the peasantry not to join them. The Aga doubled the number of his hostages. He expected further aid from Asia Minor; the Sciots looked for the help of the Greek fleet.

"Their hope was vain. On April 22, 1822, a Turkish fleet of fifty sail moored in the bay and began to bombard the chief town. The Sciots were deserted by the Samians, who had prompted them to rebellion.

"Scio became the scene of indescribable horrors. The male inhabitants were massacred; their houses were plundered and burned, — not one was left standing, except such as belonged to foreign consuls.

"Three days were passed in sacking the city; then the Turks spread themselves all over the island. The following letter is from the pen of an eyewitness who escaped. He says: 'Oh, God! what a spectacle did Scio present upon this memorable occasion! On whatever side I cast my eyes nothing but pillage, murder, and conflagration appeared. While some were occupied in plundering the villas of the rich merchants, and others in setting fire to the villages, the air was rent with the mingled groans of men, women, and children, who were falling under the swords and daggers of the infidels. The only exception during the massacre was of young women and boys, who were preserved to be afterwards sold as slaves. Many of these young women, whose husbands had been butchered, were running to and fro, frantic, with torn garments, dishevelled hair, pressing their trembling infants to their breasts, and seeking death as a relief from the fate that awaited them.' Ten days were given to slaughter. Gardeners and work-people, who had been seized and carried on board Turkish ships, on the supposition that they would reveal the hiding-place of hidden treasure, were, to the number of five hundred, hung. This was the signal for the execution of the hostages in the citadel. The prisoners were for the most part sold in Smyrna or Constantinople; but on June 19 an order came to the slave-market of Constantinople for the cessation of the sale. The Island of Scio had been granted many years before as an *appanage* to one of the sultanas. From it she derived a fixed revenue, and a title to interfere in all matters relating to police or to internal administration. This patroness, at the time of the massacre, was Asma, sister of the sultan, who received about two hundred thousand piastres a year besides casual presents from her flourishing little province. When she was informed of its destruction, her indignation was excessive. Her anger was chiefly directed against the officers in command, — Valid Pasha, who was in charge of the citadel, and the Capitan Pasha, or chief admiral, to whose conduct she chiefly attributed her misfortune. In vain the Capitan Pasha selected from his captives sixty young and beautiful maidens, whom he presented for the service of her Highness. She rejected the offering with disdain, and continued her remonstrances against the injustice and illegality of reducing free sons and daughters of the soil to slavery, and exposing them for sale in the slave-markets. The sultan, at length, yielded to her importunities. The permission for such brutalities was revoked; and it is pleasant to think that this unlooked-for humanity was due to the exertions of a woman!"

This account of Scio by Miss Sedgwick precedes the history of a young girl named Maritza, who, with her boy-brother and her mother, was dragged from a hiding-place by the soldiers. The mother was a lady of high rank in the island. They passed into the hands of a slave-merchant, who sent them to Alexandria. Here the boy, who had provoked his master by obstinately refusing to renounce his Christian faith, was murdered in cold blood before his mother's eyes. Mother and daughter were then offered at an enormous price to the sister of Ibrahim Pasha. As they waited in the anteroom of that great lady, they were seen and commiserated by two young travelling Englishmen. Finding that the princess would not pay the slave-merchant his price, these gentlemen clubbed together their resources, and bought the women. What became of the mother I do not know; but one of the gentlemen, having become the sole possessor of Maritza, sent her to his mother in England to receive an education. He married her when she was seventeen years old. She was very accomplished, exquisitely beautiful, and made a sensation in London society. Her husband, however, took her back to Alexandria, where she died a year and a half after of the plague.

I cannot tell here the long story of the struggle between the Greeks and Turks, which lasted for eight years, and enlisted the warmest sympathies of Christendom. The narrative is the same thing over and over again. It tells of Turks defeated when sometimes ten, sometimes twenty to one, of bravery, of love of country, of desperate valor, and generally of the success of the Greeks, which led to nothing for want of statesmanship. The Greek partisan leaders seem to have been little amenable to any government or authority. The most brilliant deeds were done by the Greek fleet under Frank Hastings and Lord Cochrane, — English naval officers (who forfeited their commissions to join the insurgents), — and by Kanaris, a Greek islander, whose daring exploits with fire-ships again and again discomfited the Turkish fleets. Marco Bozzaris, who perished in 1823 in an attack on the camp of a Turkish general, owes his immortal fame chiefly to the pen of an American poet. In 1823 Lord Byron gave his fortune and his life to the cause of the Greeks. Rousing himself from the *cui bono* lethargy of his life in Italy, he came forward as a statesman and a soldier in a cause which had his fullest sympathy, and he drew after him the sympathies of the civilized world. He was bitterly disappointed, however, on reaching Missolonghi, to find how divided and incapable of civil government were the Greeks themselves. If he had lived it is quite possible he might have been made king of Greece at the close of the revolution; but worn out by worries and malarial fever, he died a few months after reaching the Morea. Doctor Howe, of Boston, who reached Missolonghi in April, 1824, — the day after Byron's death, — said that the place seemed as if covered by a pall. The loss sustained by Greece in the death of the great English poet was counterbalanced by the new prospects that opened for her on the death of the Emperor Alexander. Nicholas was eager to make himself her protector, and three months after his brother's death, he declared war against Turkey on the ground that the stipulations of the Treaty of Bucharest had never been fulfilled. Mr. Canning, the English prime minister, — moved at once by his own generous feelings, and a sense that Russia must not be left to espouse the cause of Greek Christians alone, lest they should learn to look upon her as their only friend, — persuaded France and Austria to join England and Russia in an agreement to *make* Turkey acknowledge the partial independence of Greece.

Strange to say, Sultan Mahmoud chose this time for the annihilation of his great corps of Janissaries, on whom the power of his empire had for centuries seemed to rest.

As the sultans had grown more effeminate after the middle of the seventeenth century, the Janissaries grew more insolent and more and more powerful. Several sultans were murdered by them, or had been set aside. Indeed, what the Prætorian Guards became in the later Roman Empire, the Janissaries aspired to be under the later sultans.

Sultan Mahmoud, from the opening of his reign, had aimed to be a reforming sultan. Especially he desired to break up the power of the Janissaries by abolishing their old dress, arms, privileges, and customs, and introducing among them the discipline of the armies of Western Europe. His reforms were so unpopular that he was called the Giaour Sultan. His idea was to Europeanize his people, beginning with his army. Mehemet Ali had introduced the dress and drill of Europeans into the Egyptian army, under the superintendence of French officers, and Sultan Mahmoud considered the experiment a success.

The Janissaries, being an immense body of men, were distributed all through the Turkish Empire; for, after twenty years of service, they were allowed to marry, and engage in various trades and occupations. They had been highly exasperated by the very meagre success of the Turkish arms against the Greeks; and Mahmoud expected opposition among them to his new plans. At first he demanded only a small contingent from each regiment to wear the new dress, and to adopt the new drill. They consented, but finding their privileges further encroached upon (for indeed the plan of the sultan and his war minister Hussein Pasha was to drive them into rebellion), they broke out into open revolt in Constantinople June 14, 1826. The sultan was fully prepared for this. He sent for the Green Standard of the Prophet, which all true Mussulmans must follow, and planted it in the courtyard of his palace. The Janissaries were then driven into their own barracks, which were set on fire, and every one who attempted to escape was shot down. Thousands were seized and executed throughout the empire. Those who could, sought safety in exile. The corps was abolished, and Mahmoud was left with no soldiers but ill-disciplined new recruits, awkward and half-hearted. He had destroyed Turkish customs, outraged Turkish feelings, and now by the massacre of the Janissaries had sapped Turkish strength. After this he set at nought in his own person the precepts of the Koran. All day he worked with frenzy, at night he indulged himself in frightful orgies, till, dead drunk, he desisted from his madness and slaves bore him to his bed. It was in those days that a

Frenchman of distinction dined with him, and the sultan having promised to grant him any favor he might ask, the guest had the bad taste to request to see the most beautiful woman in the seraglio. The sultan bowed, and gave an order; the feast went on, when presently a slave entered bearing a silver salver covered with a cloth. He was sent round to the French guest, who, lifting the veil, saw to his horror the bleeding head of a beautiful woman, while the sultan calmly assured him that living no member of his harem could be seen.

Sultan Mahmoud, finding that the Greeks were victorious, that the Russians were invading Bulgaria, and preparing to carry their arms into Armenia, while the massacre and dispersion of the Janissaries had just deprived him of a hundred thousand fighting men, bent all his energies to the formation of a new army. He collected European officers to train his Nizam, the name given to his young recruits, who were beardless boys for the most part; for the sultan and his Divan dreaded disaffection, and preferred to recruit inexperienced youths, who would more readily adopt the Christian dress and discipline.

He also called to his aid Ibrahim Pasha, the brave adopted son of his powerful vassal, Mehemet Ali; and he again issued a decree of total extermination against the Greeks, which the ambassadors of the European Powers could not prevail upon him to recall. He besides ordered all the olive groves and fruit trees in the Morea to be cut down. The atrocities committed in southern Greece by the troops of Ibrahim Pasha so shocked the sensibilities of Christendom that a combined English, French, and Russian fleet, under the command of Admiral Sir Edward Codrington, was sent into Greek waters to check, if possible, the Egyptian cruelties. Finding that this could not be done without attacking the Turkish fleet, Sir Edward Codrington did so, without any preliminary declaration of war between England and Turkey, and fought the brilliant battle of Navarino October 20, 1826. His government was not entirely satisfied with this exploit. It did not disavow him, but he was never again employed, and Western governments have since come to consider that the destruction of the Turkish fleet was a great political mistake.

Mahmoud was furious at this interference with his policy of vengeance, and his sovereignty. In 1827 the Greeks formed a provisional government and placed at its head Capo d'Istrias, the private secretary of the Russian emperor. Ibrahim Pasha, having lost his fleet, had to suffer his troops to be carried back to Egypt in English vessels.

Russia, resolved on enforcing the stipulations of the Treaty of Bucharest by the invasion of Turkey, sent Diebitsch with twenty thousand men into Bulgaria, where he laid siege to the important strongholds of Silistria, Brailow, and Varna, which guarded the high-road to Constantinople; while Paskievitch, with another army, made a brilliant campaign in Armenia.

At the outbreak of the struggle it was supposed it would be pitiably unequal. Turkey had been weakened in every way, and the southern frontier of Russia gleamed with more than two hundred thousand bayonets and sabres. But the world did not know then, as it has known since 1855 and 1877, that Turkish troops behind stone walls are very nearly invincible. The defence of Brailow was magnificent. It lasted twenty-seven days, and cost the Russians between four thousand and five thousand men, among them four generals. The garrison capitulated at last on the most honorable terms.

The successes of the Turks at Shumla were such that operations against that place were reduced to a distant and imperfect blockade. But Varna, which is situated on the shores of the Black Sea, was besieged both by a Russian fleet and a Russian army. In the first attack the Russians lost three hundred men; "and a cartful of infidel heads was sent to Constantinople; for the Turks had not yet learned, as they did later, to content themselves with the salted ears of their enemies as trophies."[1]

[1] Harper's Magazine, vol. lvi.

After a siege of eighty-seven days, in which the Russians lost six thousand men, and fired eight thousand shells, and while eight thousand of the garrison were still under arms, confident of success, and as unshaken in courage as ever, a parley took place. There were secret negotiations between General Diebitsch and Jussef Pasha the Turkish commander, and the parley brought about a surrender.

A large Turkish force, however, was still guarding the highway to Constantinople, and was little more than four hours' march from Varna. The Emperor Nicholas came himself to animate his troops, and to superintend their military operations. In spite of the czar's presence his army met with very little success. The sickly season came on. Thousands of the Russians died, or were in hospital. The Russians in this campaign of 1828 fought two or three minor battles, took Brailow, Varna, and several smaller forts, but they had failed before Silistria and Shumla. They recrossed the Danube at the beginning of winter. "The sword, sickness, and hardships had cost them the lives of forty thousand men. Considering their superiority in numbers, armament, and organization the campaign had proved a failure and a humiliation rather than a triumph."

In May of the following year Diebitsch with a large force resumed operations against Silistria. The siege dragged slowly on, until, two fresh armies of Russians coming up, the Turks were forced to give battle in the open. Even then the fate of war remained for some time undecided; but at last a storm of Russian shot spread panic among the irregular troops (who were the strength of the Turkish army) and dispersed the Nizam, or youthful Turks recruited to supply the place of the Janissaries. The entire army dissolved, and escaped, as it is said, "with the dexterity of a rabble." This battle, called Kalewtscha, decided the campaign, and Diebitsch, leaving the fortress of Silistria still untaken in his rear, prepared to cross the Balkans, and to march on Constantinople. On Aug. 20 he was in possession of Adrianople, one hundred and twenty miles from the Ottoman capital.

Meantime, though the sultan showed no signs of fear, Constantinople was in a tumult. The populace threatened to restore the Janissaries; the foreign ambassadors trembled lest Russia should obliterate Turkey, and destroy the balance of power in Europe. England especially was imperative for peace. With tears of rage and shame Mahmoud signed the Treaty of Adrianople, giving up Greece; paying heavy indemnities, and perhaps saving the Russian army; for Diebitsch, who had begun the campaign with one hundred and forty-two thousand men, had so suffered by war, sickness, and other hardships that he had but twenty-one thousand with him at Adrianople.

But the treaty by no means satisfied the aspirations of the Greek people. The new kingdom of Greece was formed with very restricted boundaries. Above all, the islands of the Archipelago, and Crete, and Cyprus, were given back to their Ottoman rulers. A monarchy was established, and the crown was offered to Prince Leopold, the widowed husband of the English princess Charlotte. After some hesitation he refused it, saying he foresaw that the Greeks would never be satisfied with a boundary so restricted as that which his obligations to the Treaty would compel him to maintain. In this decision he was guided by the advice of his friend Baron Stockmar, but Leopold is believed to have long regretted it.

The crown of Greece was finally accepted for Prince Otho of Bavaria, a minor, a Roman Catholic, a heavy lad without talent or vivacity, and a scion of a house afflicted with insanity. He was entirely out of sympathy with the nation he was called upon to govern, became very unpopular, and of his own free will abdicated in 1863, after enduring sovereignty for thirty-one years.

The liberation of Greece was in some sort payment of the debt of gratitude that Europe and America owe to that diminutive but glorious country, the birthplace of the poetry, the political science, the fine arts, and the philosophy of the civilized world. In the war of independence, Greek heroes, such as Kanaris and Marco Bozzaris, did deeds not unworthy of warriors in the ancient world; but that, alas! was all. Every man seems to have fought for his own hand, and to have been as ready to find an enemy in a Greek as in a Turk, if that Greek or his interests were opposed to him.

The resurrection of Greece forms a brilliant episode in modern history, and if she is sometimes reproached because sixty years of liberty have passed over her without any indications of vitality beyond the changes everywhere brought about by the world-wide advance of science and civilization, we must remember that with her restricted limits, her national poverty, her impoverished soil, it would be unjust to expect she should at once renew the age of Pericles. Of late years, under her present king, George of Denmark, — who, standing in his court with his fair locks, presents a strange contrast to his swarthy, dark-haired courtiers, — she has made great advances in education, in credit, and in material civilization. Nevertheless, her best possessions are still the remains of Homer's language, and the ruins she has inherited from the Greece that was once the glory of the world.

"We must at all risks maintain the integrity of the Ottoman Empire" has been long a maxim of European diplomacy. "I decline to argue with any man," said Mr. Pitt, "who does not see that in the interests of England the Ottoman Empire must be preserved."

It is said that when Alexander and Napoleon were intimate friends, they discussed together the division of Turkey, but Napoleon insisted that France must have Constantinople, Syria, and Egypt, which was not satisfactory to the Emperor Alexander. Napoleon from his earliest years had a craving for the empire of the East, and said at St. Helena that had not Sir Sidney Smith repulsed him at Acre he would have been seated on the Byzantine throne.

In 1830, after the formation of the kingdom of Greece, Turkey, in Europe and Asia (not counting the countries which paid her tribute along the northern coast of Africa), consisted of two hundred and eighty-eight thousand square miles of territory, inhabited by seventeen millions of people. The same amount of territory in western Europe was inhabited by ninety-seven millions. This was a powerful argument for those who wished to see the garden of the earth opened to modern civilization; but over and over again the question rose: Drive the Turks out of Europe, and who shall have Constantinople?

CHAPTER V.

THE CZAR NICHOLAS.

A GREAT difficulty presents itself to those who desire to understand any subject relating to Russia or its imperial family; for while the world looks upon Russia as a seething mass of misery and corruption, and holds her imperial ruler responsible for this state of things, all persons brought into personal contact with this terrible autocrat and his household find them (from Alexander I. down to the present day) persons who command respect, — with noble qualities that from time to time conspicuously shine forth as occasion offers, and with every-day household virtues such as make the whole world kin.

When the struggle of all Europe with Napoleon was over, the Grand Duke Nicholas started on a tour to foreign courts and foreign countries. He visited England during the year of Princess Charlotte's brief married happiness, and Stockmar, writing at that period, said : —

"He is taller than Leopold, without being thin, and straight as a pine. His features are extremely regular, the forehead handsome and open, eyebrows finely arched, nose particularly handsome, mouth well-shaped, and chin finely chiselled. There is an air of great self-reliance about him, but at the same time a manifest absence of pretension."

On his return to Russia he married the princess who had been selected for him by his family, and never were husband and wife more devoted to each other. She was Princess Maria Charlotte of Prussia, daughter of King Frederick William II., and of his charming queen, Louise, whose memory is so dear to her descendants and to all Germany. As the wife of every Russian sovereign *must* adopt the Orthodox faith of which her husband is the head, it seems to be the custom of these ladies, on their baptism, to take the name of Marie Feodorovna,[1] a practice which makes it somewhat hard to distinguish them. Thus the uncle of Alexander II. was the old emperor William of Germany. Alexander II. and the emperor Frederick were first cousins, and the present emperor of Germany, William II., and the emperor of Russia, Alexander III., are second cousins.

We have seen in a former chapter how on the death of Alexander I. the Grand Duke Nicholas, then at St. Petersburg, had his elder brother Constantine proclaimed emperor and caused the oath of allegiance to him to be taken by the Council and the army. But no sooner was this done than a sealed packet was presented to him, containing Constantine's resignation of his right of succession. Messengers had already been despatched to Constantine at Warsaw, who brought back his reiterated refusal to ascend the Russian throne. He even went so far as to return unopened letters addressed to him as his Majesty the emperor of Russia, saying that he was not the person they were intended for.

On Dec. 24, 1825, the Grand Duke Nicholas consented to accept the sceptre, and to date his accession to the throne from the day of the death of his brother Alexander. On the next day the great officers of State and the Holy Synod took the oath of allegiance to him. The next day the army was to do the same thing; but unfortunately the common soldiers had not had it made clear to them that Constantine, to whom they had taken the oath two weeks before, had declined to be their emperor.

There was at that moment a vast conspiracy extending all over Russia to depose the dynasty of the Romanoffs and set up a new dynasty pledged to govern as constitutional sovereigns. Some men of true patriotism were concerned

---

[1] Nicholas not being czarevitch, his bride was baptized Alexandra.

in this conspiracy, but its active members seem to have been of the same stuff as modern nihilists.

When the Romanoffs, in 1613, were chosen rulers of Russia by an assembly of nobles, there was a rival candidate, Prince Troubetskoi. It was the representative of this family who was now placed at the head of the conspiracy; but he was not unscrupulous enough to serve the purpose of his followers, and when the time for action came he kept himself in the background. The uncertainty that attended the order of succession, the hesitation of Nicholas, and the distance of Constantine from the scene of action made the moment seem propitious to the conspirators. Agents went among the soldiers, and proclaimed that Nicholas was about to thrust himself into his brother's place, and that the vengeance of Constantine would fall on all who aided and abetted the usurper. By the morning of December 26, the conspirators had succeeded in drawing over to their side three regiments of household troops in garrison at St. Petersburg. These were marched into the great square of St. Isaac, and stationed behind the equestrian statue of Peter the Great. An immense crowd assembled round them, composed largely of sympathizers anxious to vindicate the supposed rights of the absent Constantine. Men went among them rousing their indignation and enthusiasm, some even representing that they had just come from Warsaw, where they had witnessed the arrest of the Grand Dukes Constantine and Michael.

Meantime Nicholas was busy in the Winter Palace, where the oath was being administered to about thirteen thousand soldiers, the remaining troops in garrison at St. Petersburg. On learning what was passing in the great square, he ordered several regiments to face the rioters; then he rode forth surrounded by his generals and staff, and confronted the insurgents.

"At this moment an officer was seen to gallop from the midst of the disaffected regiments, his right hand thrust into the breast of his uniform. As he approached, the emperor advanced to meet him; and when they had arrived at a sword's length from each other Nicholas enquired, 'What do you bring me?' The officer met the emperor's steady gaze; his hand moved convulsively under his uniform; he turned his horse, and without saying a word rode back to his associates. Said he, 'The czar looked at me with such a terrible glance that I could not kill him.' . . . Nicholas seems to have been anxious to avoid shedding the blood of his subjects. He requested General Miloradovitch, governor-general of St. Petersburg, to address the rebels. He did so, but his voice was drowned in shouts of 'Long live the Emperor Constantine!' . . . At the same moment one of the revolutionary leaders rode up to the old general and discharged his pistol. He fell mortally wounded. He had been called the Murat of Russia, and had escaped the shafts of death in fifty-six battlefields."[1]

Still Nicholas seemed anxious to avoid bloodshed. He ordered his cavalry to charge, but the crowd was immovable. He then ordered up his cannon, and volley after volley crashed into the dense mass of the insurgents. The crowd fled across the frozen waters of the Neva.

At six o'clock on the evening of this memorable day Nicholas re-entered the Winter Palace. He found the empress bathed in tears and trembling with terror. Indeed, she never recovered the shock her nerves had received on this occasion.

The emperor had dared the most imminent danger, had exhibited the utmost intrepidity, and had achieved a decisive victory over a powerful and dangerous conspiracy.

All particulars of the conspiracy were revealed by Troubetskoi, who, when he made his confession, fell at the emperor's feet and asked for life. It was granted, with the scornful remark from Nicholas, "If you have the courage to support a life dishonored thus, I grant it. But it is all I promise."

The next morning the emperor, accompanied by only one aide-de-camp, reviewed his troops. The soldiers who had revolted in favor of Constantine were treated with

[1] S. M. Schumucker's History of Nicholas I of Russia.

great clemency. Not so the revolutionary leaders and instigators of the conspiracy. Among these was Pestal, who, on the eve of execution, wrote the march that bears his name. Yet Nicholas showed kindness to his family, and promoted his brother to be his aide-de-camp.

A very remarkable document is in existence called the Will of Peter the Great. Its authenticity in its present form is doubtful, but the existence of some such document containing advice to his successors is indubitable. Podewils reported to the great Frederick, while prime minister, that the Russian envoy at Berlin had told him of a paper in which future Russian emperors were counselled to maintain friendship with Prussia. A Pole subsequently gave to Frederick William, in 1798, a memorandum concerning the Will of Peter the Great, written after the perusal of the original document, which he had seen in the Russian archives.

In 1812 this "plan" of Peter the Great was published in Paris in a newspaper, by Lasur, a clerk in the French Foreign Office. Some persons think that the memorandum of the Pole was cooked by Lasur to suit the views of the Emperor Napoleon, who was then on the eve of his Russian campaign; others, from internal evidence, maintain its authenticity. Be that as it may, it is said that Nicholas, as grand duke and as czar, received it as a message from his great ancestor; and he certainly adopted its advice, which may be summed up as follows:—

Peter begins by a prophetic declaration that as western Europe has repeatedly in the past found itself obliged to submit to swarming races from the East, so Russia, in the progress of the world's evolution, would eventually possess all Europe, such being her manifest destiny and part of the scheme of Providence. Therefore he advises:—

1. That Russia should be always at war with some people or peoples on her frontier, in order that her armies may be kept in a state of efficiency.
2. That foreigners of distinction, especially military officers

should be encouraged to settle in Russia, and to take service there.

3. That no chance should be lost of taking part in the disputes of other European powers.

4. That Russian agents should intrigue in foreign courts and with the legislatures of other peoples on behalf of Russian interests.

5. That Sweden (then owning Finland) should be despoiled of territory.

6. That Russian princes should seek wives in Germany.

7. That England should be propitiated in view of commercial advantages.

8. That the frontier of Russia should be everywhere extended; north along the Baltic, south to the shores of the Mediterranean.

9. That Russia should never cease to desire the acquisition of Constantinople, and the commerce of India; also that she should aim to establish herself on the Persian Gulf.

10. That everything should be done to cement a firm alliance with Austria, but at the same time that Austria's strength should be sapped by fomenting dissatisfaction among her various peoples.

11. That Austria should be reconciled to the Russian acquisition of Constantinople, or, if that were impossible, should be debarred from interference by being drawn into a European war.

12. That the Greeks should be taken everywhere under the protection of Russia.

13. That when Sweden, Poland, and Turkey should be all made Russian, overtures should be made to France and Austria to share with Russia the dominion of the world. If either declined, Russia should find some pretext for a quarrel, the issue of which could not be doubtful, as she would then be mistress of the East and the best part of Europe.

14. If both France and Austria should reject these overtures Russia should invade Germany, sweep the coasts of the Mediterranean and the Atlantic with her fleets, and simultaneously overrun France and Germany. When these countries should be fully conquered the rest would fall easily and without a struggle.

Such is the policy which, whether shadowed out or not by Peter the Great, has been apparently in the main the policy of his successors; and of late years state secrets have come to light which enable us to see how the Emperor Nicholas had laid to heart his ancestor's advice in the 13th clause of his testamentary document, and how in the last years of Charles X. of France he labored to effect with him an alliance which should further his designs upon Constantinople.

Count Pozzo di Borgo was a Corsican, and we might call him a statesman of fortune. He cherished an hereditary enmity to the Bonapartes, especially to Napoleon, with whom, when Corsica became French in 1797, he had a personal quarrel, and decided to seek advancement in other countries.

After various experiences as a diplomatist in the service of England and Austria, he attached himself in 1811 to the Emperor Alexander, and for many years after the Restoration was the Russian ambassador in Paris at the courts of Louis XVIII. and his successor. He tried to marry the Grand Duchess Anna, sister of the Emperor Alexander, to the Duc de Berry; but the negotiation was not successful, as the lady would not change her religion.

The Emperor Alexander, not long before his death, foresaw that there must be war in the end between Turkey and Russia, arising out of the affairs of Greece; and as such a war need not be considered by the world to be prompted by sympathy with revolution, he suggested to the government of Charles X. that, if France would support him in the acquisition and retention of Constantinople, he would repay the service by any return that could be pointed out to him. Nothing further passed till after the battle of Navarino, three years later, when the French government — treacherous to its allies — proposed to the Emperor Nicholas a scheme of alliance, "involving not only the partition of Turkey, but the reconstruction of the map of Europe, from which Holland and Saxony were to be erased as independent kingdoms."[1]

[1] Edinburgh Review, 1892.

The proposition had not been received at St. Petersburg, however, when news reached Paris that the war of 1828 between Russia and Turkey had been abruptly concluded by the Peace of Adrianople. Had the engagement been carried out, France offered to acquiesce in the acquisition by Russia of a large part of Turkey, while she herself was to obtain Belgium, Luxembourg, and the frontier of the Rhine. Prussia was to be propitiated by the annexation of Saxony and Holland; Austria, by receiving Servia, Bosnia, and Herzegovina; while it was hoped England would give her consent if bribed by the offer of the Dutch colonies. It is not certain that this scheme provided for the possession of Constantinople by the czar. It is thought likely that the intention may have been to form a small weak empire of Greece, with Constantinople as its capital. But such schemes and negotiations were defeated by the follies committed by Charles X., which brought on a revolution.

Until the papers of Count Pozzo di Borgo were recently published, it had always seemed to the world as if the rage of the Emperor Nicholas, on learning the elevation of Louis Philippe, had been excessive and unreasonable. We see now that it ruined his schemes. He massed his troops for an immediate war with France; and thus it happened that the Revolution in Poland in 1830 found him prepared to crush it at once.

In vain Louis Philippe attempted to secure from the Emperor Nicholas recognition as a brother-sovereign. The czar remained haughty and irreconcilable, and it was not until four months after Louis Philippe was seated on the French throne that Pozzo di Borgo, as Russian ambassador at Paris, was permitted to present him his credentials.

The Treaty of Adrianople was followed, four years later, by the Treaty of Unkiar-Skelessi. By the Treaty of Adrianople Turkey was to pay Russia about thirty million dollars indemnity, and give up to her the command of the mouths of the Danube, together with certain territory bordering on the Black Sea. Wallachia and Moldavia were to become autonomous principalities, paying only a small tribute to the sultan, who thenceforward was to possess no fortresses on the northern bank of the Danube; nor was any Moslem to hold property there. Sultan Mahmoud is said to have wept and torn his beard with rage as he signed these hard terms, which he would probably have resisted had he known the condition of Diebitsch's army, reduced by sickness to twenty thousand men.

Subsequently, in 1833 and 1834, when the power of the Porte was threatened by the victories of Ibrahim Pasha, Russia stepped forward as the sultan's friend and protector. Nicholas considered that no one should threaten Constantinople but himself. This alliance between the sultan and the czar was cemented by a new treaty, signed June 26, 1833, containing a secret clause, which converted the Black Sea into a Russian lake, and caused great indignation in western Europe when its existence was discovered. By this secret article of the Treaty of Unkiar-Skelessi the straits of the Bosphorus and the Dardanelles were opened to the fleets of Russia, and closed to those of all other nations. The czar posed before Europe as the generous ally and confidential friend of the sultan, who was expected thenceforward to walk by Russian advice in the administration of his government, and to abandon his confidence in England. It was a conspiracy not unlike that in the history of the two showmen recorded in "Master Humphrey's Clock," where little Nell was exhorted to discover that Codlin was her friend, and not Short.

Before Nicholas in 1828 marched his armies on to Turkish soil he had tested their endurance and their discipline in a war with Persia. In this war General Paskievitch won his laurels, and at the close of it he was enabled to harangue his soldiers thus: " Brave comrades, you have conquered in this campaign two provinces, taken eight standards, fifty guns, two sirdars, twenty khans, six thousand prisoners in arms, ten thousand who had cast them away, and great stores of provisions. Such are your trophies!"

I fancy very few of us have any clear ideas as to the geographical relations of Russia, Turkey, and Persia. Between the Euxine and the Caspian seas is a wide strip of land including several states and provinces, which is commonly known to us by the name of the Caucasus. Upon the inhabitants of this land Russia has been making war during the whole of the present century, thus keeping her armies actively employed on her frontier, according to the views of Peter the Great. The countries included in this strip of territory are Georgia, Circassia, Mingrelia, Daghestan, Russian Armenia, and Shirvan, and Karabaugh. Georgia was acquired by Russia in 1802. Its last hereditary prince died in St. Petersburg not many years ago. Circassia became Russian in 1829. Mingrelia, whose hereditary prince (now a Russian nobleman) was the candidate recently supported by Russia for the throne of Bulgaria, was acquired in 1804; Daghestan in 1813; Shirvan at the same time; Karabaugh, by the Treaty of Adrianople, was made Russian in 1828; and Russian Armenia became Russian the same year. But though Russia nominally holds sway over these provinces she wages perpetual war upon the people who inhabit them.

The mountains of the Caucasus run diagonally through these territories. The range, at its northern end, touches the Black Sea, at its southern the Caspian.

To these regions all Russian regiments are sent if they are untrained, or are suspected of disaffection, and all officers who have committed any military offence, or whose extravagance or ill-regulated habits have been brought by their families to the notice of the emperor. In the Caucasus they undergo, as it were, a sort of penal military probation.

The inhabitants of the Caucasus are by some thought to be descendants of the Crusaders. Their complexion and features are European, their dress and military equipments are more mediæval than Asiatic, and though Russia nominally owns their country, with its mountain pastures and its fruitful valleys, they have fought the fight of brave men, and to this day are only partially subdued.

On the accession of the Emperor Nicholas he appointed General Paskievitch to command his armies in the Caucasus; but for some time the attention of Paskievitch was too much absorbed by a war with Persia, and by the war of 1828 in Asia Minor, to give much attention to the mountaineers.

The war with Turkey being terminated by the Peace of Adrianople, Paskievitch had leisure to turn his attention more completely to the yet unsubdued Caucasian tribes, who refused to pay tribute to his sovereign. But he was called away, as we have seen, in 1831 to conduct the Polish War, and to succeed General Diebitsch, who had died of cholera.

While Paskievitch was absent in Poland, Schamyl appeared as the leader of his people. He had risen from a very humble station, but he claimed to have received a mission from heaven through Mahomet the Prophet, who had assured him he should be invincible in war, and that no wound should ever kill him. "Though it is difficult," said one who knew him,[1] "to see clearly through the thick haze which shrouds political events among the wild mountains and defiles of the Caucasus, we know enough of Schamyl to excite our interest, and even our respect for him. By paths unknown to European ambition, by dauntless courage, an austere simplicity, rare self-denial, great firmness of purpose and promptitude of action, by some intrigues, and by many cruelties, he raised himself to a position of unexampled authority among his countrymen." The title by which he was known among them was the Imam. In alliance with Kasi Mullah, another Circassian leader, Schamyl roused all Daghestan, and met with remarkable success. But after desperate fighting, one leader of the mountaineers was killed, and Schamyl himself was so severely wounded that his recovery strengthened the belief of his people in his mission as an envoy of the Prophet. His forces, which had been dispersed, rallied, not as an army, but in innumerable armed bands, and for eighteen

[1] Chambers' Journal, 1861.

years the war was carried on, Schamyl and his men holding the mountain passes, which commanded large tracts of fertile country. The Russians were shut up for the most part in forts or in military encampments, which barely kept open their communications with St. Petersburg, but they were afraid to go beyond the range of their own guns, except in large bodies.

In 1837 the Emperor Nicholas visited the Caucasus with a view of striking terror into the hearts of Schamyl and his followers; but the mountaineers were not to be intimidated, although the czar put forth a proclamation assuring them that he had powder enough to blow up all their mountains. But the terrible corruption which permeates all branches of the government service in Russia, and which in the Caucasus received heroic treatment forty years later at the hands of General Skobeleff, was made known to the czar during his visit. It excited his indignation, and led to some spasmodic attempts at vigorous reform. But even the Autocrat of all the Russias is no match for the spirit of corruption pervading the bureaucracy in his dominions.

In 1840, and for three succeeding years, Schamyl gained advantages over successive Russian generals. But early in 1845 General Woronzoff arrived at the seat of war with powers more unlimited than had been granted to any Russian subject since the days of the Empress Catherine. He was, in fact, made autocrat over all the country, from the Pruth to the Araxes. He began by attacking Dorgo, the stronghold of Schamyl, and took it without difficulty, as it was weakly defended; but as his army was retreating Schamyl suddenly threw himself upon it with such fury that it was annihilated. Only the general, some of his officers, and four thousand men escaped. It is proof of the magnanimity of the Emperor Nicholas that he shortly after raised Woronzoff to the rank of Prince.

Instead of sending great expeditions against the tribes, Woronzoff advised the emperor to weary them by delay, detaching if possible the smaller states by bribes and promises. But the first one that took advantage of such offers was nearly annihilated by Schamyl, and defection was summarily put an end to.[1]

In 1835 the czar met the king of Prussia on the frontier of their dominions under cover of a grand review, but in reality to discuss what might be done to extinguish the little republic of Cracow, the last remnant of Polish independence. The result of this interview was that at the beginning of the next year a requisition was suddenly sent to the republic from Russia, Prussia, and Austria, requiring the authorities to expel all refugees from those nations within eight days, or else recognition of the independence of the republic by those three Powers would be withdrawn. As the Senate of Cracow begged for delay, Russian and Austrian troops marched into the city. The refugees were shipped off to America, and foreign troops were permanently placed in garrison. Cracow has since been annexed to the Austro-Polish Province of Galicia, thus setting aside one of the arrangements agreed upon by European governments at the Congress of Vienna.

At the close of the month of May, 1844, Queen Victoria and Prince Albert were taken by surprise by an announcement that the emperor of Russia was about to pay them a visit. They had only forty-eight hours in which to prepare for his arrival. The king of Saxony was at that moment staying at Windsor. It was the emperor's fashion to make all his visits thus suddenly. On the night of his arrival in London he went to the residence of his ambassador, and the next day was escorted by Prince Albert to Buckingham

---

[1] It may be here added that after this mountain chief had waged war twenty-five years, from 1834 1859, with the most distinguished generals in the Russian service, and had made the country over which he ruled one of the greatest military schools in the world, he surrendered, to save the lives of the mere handful of devoted followers who still remained true to him. The Russian government assigned him a liberal pension. and a pleasant residence in the town of Kalouga: where. until his death, he held friendly social relations with the Russian authorities.

Palace, where he was presented to Queen Victoria. The day following he went to Windsor. The prince, who had preceded him, met him at the station, and conducted him to the Castle. He was greatly impressed by the palace at Windsor and by what he saw of the English court during his five days' stay there. He said that everything seemed to move without effort, and as if nothing more than ordinary were going on. He had come over to England to see things for himself, instead of trusting to diplomatists; and he had, no doubt, the intention, in his interviews with members of the English Cabinet, of feeling his way upon the Eastern Question. He did not talk politics to the queen, but conversed much with Prince Albert and Lord Aberdeen. To almost every one he said in substance: "I know that I am taken for an actor, but indeed I am not; I am thoroughly straightforward. I say what I mean; and what I promise, I fulfil."

He had, he said, been all his life desirous to stand well with England, and mentioned that when he was a little boy his beautiful mother had once taken him to an eminence, and pointing to the West had told him that there lay the nation beyond seas in whom he should ever seek a friend.

France he openly professed to have no interest in, and her opinion he did not care about. To Sir Robert Peel he said: "I do not covet an inch of Turkish soil for myself, but neither will I allow any one else to have one."

He was exceedingly impressed with Prince Albert, expressing to him earnestly his wish that they might one day be found on the same side, should Europe be engaged in any quarrel. To others he said that he wished he had the prince for a son.

The queen, writing to King Leopold, says of this visit:

"A great compliment it certainly was, and the people here are much flattered by it. The emperor is certainly a very striking looking man, still very handsome. His profile is beautiful and his manners most dignified and graceful, extremely civil,—

indeed alarmingly so; he is full of attentions and *politesses*. But the expression of the eyes is severe, and unlike anything I ever saw before. He gives Albert and myself the impression of a man who is not happy, and on whom the burthen of his immense power and position weighs heavily and painfully. He seldom smiles, and, when he does, the expression is not a happy one. He is very easy to get on with. . . . He amused the king of Saxony and me by saying he was *si embarrassé* when people were presented to him, and that he felt *si gauche en frac* (that is, in plain clothes), which he is certainly quite unaccustomed to wear."

Military uniform had become so habitual to him that without it he said he felt "comme si l'on m'avait oté la peau."

"The two last evenings of his stay," the queen wrote in her journal, "we had large dinners in uniform, the emperor disliked so being *en frac*, and was so embarrassed about it."

"He seemed really and unaffectedly touched," she adds at parting, "at his reception and stay, — the simplicity and quiet of which told upon his love for domestic life, which is very great. At parting he said with much emotion: 'I leave you, madame, with a sad heart, and penetrated by your kindness for me. You may be sure, madame, that you may count on me at any time as your most devoted servant. May God bless you.'"

"And now," adds the queen, in another letter to her uncle Leopold, "I will give you my opinions and feelings on the subject, which I may say are Albert's too. I was extremely against the visit, fearing the *gêne* and trouble, and even at first I did not feel at all to like it; but by living in the same house together quietly and unrestrainedly (and this, Albert says, and with great truth, is the advantage of these visits, that I not only see these great people, but *know* them) I got to know the emperor, and he to know me. There is much about him which I cannot help liking, and I think his character is one that should be understood and looked upon for once as it is. He is stern and severe, with strict principles of duty, which nothing on earth will make him change. Very clever I do not think him, and his mind is not a cultivated one. His education has been neglected. Politics and military concerns are the only things he takes an interest in; the arts and all soft occupations he does not care for; but he is sincere, I am certain, — sincere even in his most despotic acts, — from a sense that it is the only way to govern. He is not, I am sure, aware of the dreadful cases of individual misery that he often causes; for I can see by various instances that he is kept in ignorance of many things which his people carry out in most corrupt ways; while he thinks he is extremely just. He thinks of general measures, but does not look into details; and I am sure much never reaches his ears, and, as you observe, how can it? . . . He asked for nothing whatever. He has merely expressed his great desire to be on the best terms with us, but not to the exclusion of others. He is very much alarmed about the East and about Austria. He is, I should say, too frank, for he talks so openly before people, — which is what he should not do, — and with difficulty restrains himself. His anxiety to be believed is very great; and I must say his personal promises I *am* inclined to believe. Then his feelings are very strong. He feels kindness deeply, and his love for his wife and children, — and indeed for all children, — is very great. He said when our children were in the room: 'Voilà les doux moments de notre vie.' One can see by the way he takes them up and plays with them that he is very fond of children."

The queen in her "Journal" also says: "I don't know why, but I can't help pitying him; and the melancholy visible in his countenance made us sad sometimes." She remarks too: "He never takes a drop of wine, and eats very little. Albert thinks he is a man inclined to give way to passion, which makes him act wrongly often. His admiration for beauty is very great."

In spite of this admiration for beauty noticed by the queen, no man was ever more devotedly attached to his wife. He was stern to his sons, but chivalrous to his daughters. When at one time the Winter Palace was on fire, and the safety of his library was threatened, his secretary rushed to him to know what he should save? "Only my portfolio," said the emperor; "it contains all the letters that the empress wrote to me before our marriage."

Of the empress the Marquis of Londonderry writes when travelling in Russia : —

"The indescribable majesty of deportment and fascinating grace that mark this illustrious personage are very peculiar. Celebrated as are all the females connected with the lamented and beautiful Queen Louise of Prussia, there are none of them more bewitching in manner than the empress of Russia; nor is there existing, according to all reports, a more excellent and perfect being."

The Marquise de Custine speaks of her in equal terms of praise. She bore her husband seven children, — four sons and three daughters. The sons were the czarevitch, afterwards Alexander II., and the Grand Dukes Constantine, Michael, and Nicholas; the daughters, the Grand Duchess Maria, who married the Duke de Leuchtenburg, grandson of Eugène de Beauharnais; the Grand Duchess Olga, — a beautiful woman, who married the prince royal of Wurtemburg; and Alexandra, who died in 1851, having been wife to Prince Frederick of Hesse. The present queen of Greece is the granddaughter of the Emperor Nicholas. Her father was his son, the Grand Duke Constantine.

The health of the empress was very delicate. She never recovered from the shock her nerves received when her husband confronted his mutinous regiments in St. Isaac's Square, immediately after his accession. Her life, too, was a very laborious one, being a continual round of receptions, balls, reviews, and all the other functions demanded by her position. In 1847 she went to Naples for her health, and the emperor accompanied her. It is said that he would suffer no one but himself to carry her from her carriage to her apartment.

From 1844, when the emperor visited England, to 1854, when another war broke out between himself and Turkey, the chief events in Russia that concerned Europe were the extinguishment in 1846 of the last remnant of Polish independence, and the assistance afforded to Austria by the Emperor Nicholas in her struggle with Kossuth and Hungary. In 1848 the Hungarians almost believed themselves successful when the Emperor Nicholas, still carrying out the precepts of Peter the Great, marched an army of more than 100,000 men through Moldavia into the eastern provinces of Hungary. Then Görgey, who had been appointed military dictator in 1859, despaired. With divided councils, with divided aims, with divided generals, — nay, even with a divided population, — for the Slavs in the dependencies of Hungary were in revolt, — it seemed hopeless to fight the forces of two emperors. Nothing could exceed the sufferings of the rural population of Hungary when the Slav inhabitants of its frontier provinces felt themselves strengthened and encouraged by the presence of the Russians; nevertheless, so far as the conduct of the regular forces was concerned, that of the Russians was far less cruel than the behavior of the generals and soldiers of the army of Austria.

Görgey, believing that further resistance would only prolong the sufferings of his country, surrendered his army at Villagos to the Russians, his officers breaking their swords, and his troopers shooting their horses after hugging and kissing them. General Paskievitch, who commanded the Russian troops, made in return promises of amnesty in the name of the Austrian government, which were never fulfilled.

Thus we approach the days of the Crimean War, which broke up the general peace of Europe, which had lasted thirty years.

CHAPTER VI.

THE CRIMEAN WAR.

EVERY war that affects Turkey seems like an annex to the Crusades. Three quarters of a century ago it was the fashion to talk much of the folly and the superstition of the Crusades. Apart from their religious aspect we have learned to see how great were the advantages to civilization and learning in western Europe promoted by those wars, and most sincerely to regret that no subsequent crusade followed up the work begun by Godfrey de Bouillon and his successful crusaders.

It was the dream of Columbus to devote all the wealth he might acquire in the new world to a crusade that should complete the work begun four centuries before his day, and which four hundred years after is still incomplete.[1] The Crusades have left us in the nineteenth century an unsolved problem, — the Eastern Question. Not but what the Turks are a fine people, but, as we say of weeds, they are flowers in the wrong place; though the effete or savage Christian nations likely to succeed them are far from being their superiors either in morality, honor, or trust in a Divine Providence.

As we have seen, Russia, ever since the Turks established themselves in Constantinople has aimed to be considered the patron and protector of Greek Christians. For

---

[1] In 1606 the baptism of Louis XIII. at Fontainebleau was accompanied by strange portents in the sky, interpreted by the astrologers to mean that Louis would receive the crown of Germany, reconquer Europe from the Turks, and overthrow the Ottoman Empire. See Edinburgh Review, June, 1893.

four hundred years every Russian has been born to the hope that he may one day follow the footsteps of a conquering czar through a certain gate into Constantinople,—a gate through which ancient prophecy has said that the Russians shall pass in triumph to re-establish Christian worship in the Cathedral of St. Sophia. It has been walled up by one of the sultans in consequence of this prophecy, and remains walled up to the present day.

But although the Russian emperor claims to be the political protector of Greek Christians, Greek Christians out of Russia are by no means willing to accept him as their ecclesiastical head. Politically, however, there have been times when they were not unwilling to welcome him as their protector against the Turks, leaving the religious differences between patriarch and autocrat in abeyance.

The sultan of Turkey in 1851 was Abdul Medjid, son of Sultan Mahmoud, the destroyer of the Janissaries. He had succeeded his father in 1841, when the Eastern Question, complicated by the affairs of Egypt, was threatening a war in Europe,—a war which was only averted by the pacific policy of Louis Philippe and by Lord Palmerston's skilful diplomacy.

We can sincerely sympathize with the feeling that makes the Holy Places dear to all Christians,—those "places where Christ's holy feet have trod;" that Jerusalem which in a certain sense is "the joy of the whole earth" now, and will, we humbly believe, be more so hereafter.

The holy shrines are two,—the Church of the Nativity in Bethlehem, and the Church of the Holy Sepulchre at Jerusalem. To these shrines yearly come hosts of Greek, Latin, and Armenian pilgrims, and at the holy season of Easter such quarrels and disputes for precedence went on among the pilgrims (each church claiming especial privileges in connection with the holy sites) that often Turkish soldiers had to interfere; and once there was a disgraceful massacre, the pilgrims fighting each other until the pavements of the church ran blood.

In 1851 Louis Napoleon (then prince-president) made an effort to have the privileges of the Latins, that is, the Roman Catholics, enlarged. This stirred the Greek Christians into fury. It was they who had had the ascendency at the holy shrines since 1740. They at once appealed to their great champion the czar of Russia. The French ambassador at Constantinople in 1851 was the Marquis de la Vallette, a man of charming manners and of great benignity, who had for his wife a very beautiful American lady, — a perfect woman of the world, in the higher sense of that much desecrated expression. But nothing in the career of M. de la Vallette would have led any one to suppose that his principles of religion or morality were higher than those of Prince Louis Napoleon. One can hardly imagine that either of them had one particle of religious sentiment connected with the dispute about the Holy Places. The great question was whether Latin monks should keep the key of the great door of the chapel in the grotto at Bethlehem, and whether in the chapel above ground they might hang a silver star with the arms of France emblazoned on it. The Greek Christians were willing that the Latins should have a key to the side door, but not to the principal entrance. Such was the puerile dispute that led to war and sorrow and suffering; and its consequences are with us to this day. The quarrel waxed so hot after the czar was brought into it that a Russian army was held in readiness to enter what were *then* called the Danubian Provinces.

The dissensions of the monks about their keys was an entering-wedge by which the czar hoped to carry out the intentions ascribed to Peter the Great, and to obtain the object of desire to every Russian, namely, controlling influence at Constantinople, if not its complete possession.

Russia without Constantinople has no practicable outlet to the high seas. A fleet sent down the Baltic is liable to be frozen in in winter, or attacked while passing through the Sound, Cattegat, or Skager Rack. A fleet launched at

Archangel in the White Sea could sail only in summer, and only in summer return home. It is no wonder then that every Russian covets Constantinople. When Alexander I. lost the opportunity of acquiring it by helping the revolutionary Greeks, he said, and truly: "I am the only man in Russia who would not risk anything on earth to obtain possession of Constantinople."

The state of mind of the Czar Nicholas between 1840 and the breaking out of the Crimean War is thus described by Mr. Kinglake: "He was always eager to come forward as an ardent and even ferocious defender of the Greek Christians in Turkey, but he dreaded interfering with Turkey when the opportunity was offered him, unless he could get the alliance of England." He had sometimes a curious and undiplomatic frankness in dealing with trained diplomatists. One night, January 9, 1853 (nine years after his visit to Windsor Castle) when Sir Hamilton Seymour, the English ambassador, was at a party in the palace of the Grand Duchess Helena, the emperor came up to him and began talking about the close amity that should exist between England and Russia, adding: "If *we* are agreed I am without anxiety as to the West of Europe, but as to Turkey that country is in a critical state, and may give us a good deal of trouble." The emperor then shook hands with Sir Hamilton, and believed that he had closed the conversation; but Sir Hamilton, with his hand still in the emperor's grasp, said: "Sire, with your gracious permission, I am about to take a liberty. Would your Majesty add a few words which might calm the anxiety in England regarding your Majesty's intentions with respect to Turkey?" After a moment's hesitation, the emperor added: "The affairs of Turkey are in a very disorganized condition. The country itself seems to be falling to pieces. The fall will be a great misfortune, and it is very important that England and Russia should come to a perfectly good understanding on these affairs, and that neither should take any decisive step unless the other is apprised." Then he went on: "Stay! We have on our hands a sick man, — a very sick man. It will be, I tell you frankly, a great misfortune if one of these days he should slip away from us; especially before all necessary arrangements have been made. But, however, this is not the time to speak to you upon this matter."

A few days later the czar sent for Sir Hamilton, and set before him in more detail his views of the Eastern Question.

He protested that he desired no more territory than his empire possessed. The time had gone by, he said, when Russia had anything to fear from Turkey; "but there are," he continued, "in that country several millions of Christians, whose interests I am called upon to watch over, while the right of doing so is secured to me by treaty. I may truly say I make a moderate and sparing use of my right, and I will freely confess it is one that is attended with obligations occasionally very inconvenient, but I cannot recede from the discharge of a very distinct duty. Our religion, as established in this country, came to us from the East, and there are feelings as well as obligations which must not be lost sight of. Now Turkey, in the condition I have described, has by degrees fallen into such a state of decrepitude that, as I told you the other night, eager as we all are for the existence of the man (and I am as desirous as you can be for the continuance of his life, I beg you to believe), he may suddenly die upon our hands. We cannot resuscitate what is dead; if the Turkish Empire falls it will rise no more. I put it to you, then, whether it is not better to be prepared for such a contingency, rather than to incur the chaos, confusion, and uncertainty of a European war?"

The plan the czar proposed was that neither he nor England should take Constantinople; that Servia and Bulgaria should become autonomous States, under the protection of Russia, and that England should have Egypt and Candia.

Russia is always well pleased to have weak States on her frontier. She waits until they get into disputes with one another, then she settles their disputes, taking for her pay a portion of their territory. She does this again and again until the remnant left appears hardly worth saving, and then she absorbs the whole.

The English government declined the bargain, and the matter remained secret for rather more than a year. The czar had opened the subject to Prince Metternich before his conversation with Sir Hamilton, and the old Austrian diplomatist, not wishing to discuss the subject, looked full at him, saying: "The sick man? Are your Majesty's remarks addressed to his doctor, or his heir?"

Meantime the little body of Christians who live in the Black Mountains (Montenegro) and have never been subdued by the Turks were attacked by a Turkish army under the celebrated Hungarian renegade, Omar Pasha. The Emperor Nicholas was anxious to intervene on behalf of the brave and primitive Montenegrins, but Austria forestalled him by representing to the Porte very peremptorily that she would not calmly see the independence of the Montenegrins imperilled.

The sultan greatly surprised both the czar and the emperor of Austria by at once withdrawing Omar Pasha and his army from besieging the mountain stronghold of the Montenegrins, and this prompt submission to the representations of Austria deprived the czar of that pretext for a war with Turkey.

But the Russian army lay all ready on the Turkish frontier, and Nicholas was sincerely desirous of hostilities. He despatched Prince Mentzikoff as his ambassador to Constantinople, a man more celebrated for his witty sayings than for his talent for diplomacy. He was to settle the question of the Holy Places, and to force the sultan into making a secret treaty with Russia, by which Russia should be given legal power over the Greek patriarch at Constantinople and be confirmed as the protector of Greek Christians throughout the sultan's dominions.

The English ambassador at Constantinople had long been

Sir Stratford Canning (nephew of the great George Canning, minister for Foreign Affairs in England in 1822); the Turks used to call him the English sultan, so great was his influence at the Porte. Part — indeed the chief part — of Prince Mentzikoff's mission was to put Sir Stratford Canning aside, and to acquire the same influence for Russia with the Porte that Sir Stratford had exercised for so many years.

Sir Stratford was away from his post at that time on a visit to England. The English government made him Lord Stratford de Redclyffe and at once sent him back, to checkmate, if possible, the Russian diplomatist. His first step was to conciliate the French ambassador, and to get him to join in making concessions about the quarrel concerning the Holy Places, which would take that grievance out of Prince Mentzikoff's hands. Accordingly, it was gravely and formally agreed that the key of the church at Bethlehem, and the silver star, should remain where they were, but should confer no new rights upon the Latins, or Roman Catholics. The door-keeper was to be a Greek monk, as before, but without power to exclude from the Holy Place any Roman Catholic worshipper. The Greeks and the Armenians might say their prayers at an earlier hour than the Latins in the Chapel of the Virgin, — the Greeks first, the Armenians after them, then the Latins, each having an hour for their service; and the roof of the Church of the Holy Sepulchre was to be repaired at the cost of the sultan, who was to listen to the remonstrances of the Greek patriarch if he made any mistakes.

Thus the controversy of the Holy Places was settled, but there remained the question of the secret treaty. On this point Lord Stratford de Redclyffe triumphantly defeated his Russian rival, and Prince Mentzikoff quitted the field in a state of great exasperation. By this time England and France had drawn closely together in alliance, — Napoleon III. seizing this opportunity to show how sincere he was in departing from the policy of his uncle, and in being friends with England.

Many amusing stories are told about Lord Stratford de Redclyffe, — "the great Elchi," as he was called familiarly. He was a man of very great talent, with a brain, as some one said, "like an elephant's trunk, equally capable of taking up the largest or the smallest things." The way in which he managed the Turks was amusing enough. He stood their friend in everything, and with a bitter hatred he hated the emperor of Russia, but he was not going to overlook any of the short-comings of his Turkish friends. Here is an instance ; one of his *attachés* tells the story :

" I was with him one day in his ten-oared caïque upon the Bosphorus when we passed a large garden in which preparations were being made for building. Lord Stratford told me to land and inquire whose it was. On being told that the sultan was about building a new summer palace, he ordered the boatmen to row straight to where the sultan was living. He was announced as desiring an immediate audience. It was just at the opening of the Crimean War, and Abdul Medjid received him with smiles, thinking he had come to bring important news from the Danubian Provinces. But the great Elchi, who had a quick temper, burst out with, ' His Majesty has eight palaces already. Ask him would he spend his money, scarcely sufficient as it is to buy bread for his troops in the field, in building a ninth palace for the emperor of Russia to occupy?— for no assistance can be expected from the allies of Turkey if they see such reckless extravagance going on ! ' "

Prince Mentzikoff's departure from Constantinople, after having taken down the imperial arms over the Russian embassy, was equivalent to a declaration of war between Turkey and Russia. England and France were united, whether for war or diplomacy. The next move had to come from the czar. His chief minister at that period was Count Nesselrode, a man of calm good sense, who had grown gray in diplomacy ; but he was not able to appease his master when he learned that the English and French fleets had united, and together had approached the Dardanelles, casting anchor in Besika Bay, which was as near to Constantinople as diplomacy permitted. The czar threatened to retaliate by letting his army cross the Pruth into the Turkish dependency of Moldavia.

As has been said, the Treaty of Unkiar-Skelessi prohibited any vessel of war of any foreign power from entering the Sea of Marmora, either by the Bosphorus, on which Constantinople is situated, or by the Dardanelles, which connects the Sea of Marmora with the Ægean. The Bosphorus is seventeen miles long and in some places not wider than a second-class American river. Russia had built the mighty fortress and naval station of Sebastopol on the extreme southern point of the Crimea, a territory she had wrenched from Turkey about seventy-five years before. But her great ships lay inactive in the harbor of Sebastopol. They had no exit from the Black Sea. So long as the sultan was at peace no ship of war could pass Constantinople. If Russia invaded Moldavia Turkey would no longer be at peace, and the English and French fleets might pass the Dardanelles and Bosphorus and enter the Black Sea.

Meantime plenipotentiaries of the Austrian, Prussian, English, and French governments were trying to patch up a peace between Turkey and the angry emperor of Russia: but Nicholas, inflamed by religious zeal, was almost beside himself.

The "note" prepared as a basis of reconciliation was acceptable to neither party, and moreover a strong Mohammedan feeling was roused in Constantinople against the Infidel. Placards, urging the sultan to declare war against Russia, were posted in the mosques, and the condition of things was so stormy that fears were entertained for the safety of the Christian population. Under these circumstances, after much hesitation, the English and French ambassadors ordered their respective fleets up to Constantinople. The czar at once retaliated. His fleet sailed out of Sebastopol, and stood over to Sinope, a town upon the Turkish coast of the Black Sea, where a small Turkish fleet was lying. The Russian admiral had six line-of-battle ships, the Turkish admiral had no three-deckers. He had, however, seven frigates, a sloop, and a steamer, and was the first to begin the engagement. Every one of the Turkish ships was destroyed (except the steamer), with nearly all the men on board of them. Only four hundred Turks survived, and those were wounded. This was the opening of the Crimean War, — a war apparently without any heart-stirring object; a war that might have been averted by diplomacy. But a desire for war seems to have possessed that generation. Mr. Kinglake, whose animosity to the emperor of the French is conspicuous throughout his able and interesting volumes, seems to think that the desire of Napoleon III. for the English alliance egged on the war. He says of it: —

"This war was deadly. It brought, so to say, to the grave full a million of workmen and soldiers. It consumed a pitiless share of wealth. It shattered the framework of the European system, and made it hard for any nation henceforth to be safe except by its sheer strength."

At this crisis a deputation of English Quakers waited on the czar at St. Petersburg, to urge upon him peace. Nicholas received them in a manner which they felt to be most flattering, and which made them hope that they were the world's peace-makers; but the moment they departed he turned all his attention to war, while in England nothing could exceed the warlike enthusiasm. As the queen wrote to her uncle, King Leopold, "The war is widely popular."

Twelve thousand men were at once sent to Malta, and Lord Raglan (Lord Fitzroy Somerset, a Waterloo hero) was placed in command. Lord Raglan had been second at the War Office while the Duke of Wellington was commander-in-chief, and was much disappointed when Lord Hardinge, instead of himself, had been appointed the Duke's successor. Fifteen thousand men were to follow the first twelve thousand, and France was to send forty-five thousand. Besides these a splendid fleet was fitted out to carry the war into the Baltic, and placed under the command of the dashing but eccentric Admiral Sir Charles Napier.

LORD RAGLAN.

The Russian ambassador left London on Feb. 7, 1854; on the same day the English ambassador was recalled from St. Petersburg; and on Feb. 21 England put forth her declaration of war.

Meantime the English troops were beginning to embark at Portsmouth, and along the southern coast of England. They were in a state of wild enthusiasm. There had been no war with any civilized nation for a generation. In the last great war they had conquered the French, who had conquered the world; now English and French were to fight side by side, and emulate each other.

The queen, writing to her uncle Leopold, said : —

" The last battalion of the Guards (Scots Fusiliers) embarked to-day. They passed through the courtyard here at 7 A. M. We were on the balcony to see them pass. The morning was fine, the sun shining over the towers of Westminster Abbey, and an immense crowd collected to see the fine men, and cheering them immensely as with difficulty they marched along. They formed in line, presented arms, and then cheered us very heartily, and went off cheering. It was a touching and beautiful sight. Many sorrowing friends were there, and one saw the shake of many a hand. My best wishes and prayers will be with them all."

Again, on March 15, 1854, when going down to Spithead to see the fleet that was assembled there to sail for the Baltic, the queen writes in anticipation of the review : " It will be a solemn moment! Many a heart will be very heavy, and many a prayer, including our own, will be offered for their safety and glory."

So commenced the Crimean War. It lasted a year and a half. " For twelve months," says Kinglake, " it raged. It so tried the strength, so measured the enduring power of the nations engaged in it, that, when the conflict was over their relative stations in Europe were changed, and they had to be classed afresh."

The war was undertaken to enforce, as it were, the police regulations of Europe. The idea on which these police regulations are founded is that there are five Great Powers, England, France, Russia, Austria, and Prussia (now Germany). If any of these Great Powers should wrong a lesser State, and that wrong also tends to the injury of any one of the other four Great Powers, the injured Great Power is expected to take up the cause of the little power, and to fight the big one if necessary.

This was the theory on which the Crimean War took place. Russia was oppressing Turkey by threatening her with war unless she put the protectorate over twelve millions of Greek Christians in her dominions in Europe into the czar's hands. England and France argued that this would so weaken Turkey (already considered by Russia "a very sick man") that before long Russia would get possession of Constantinople, and become very formidable to the other four Great Powers; therefore it would be best to cripple her before she attained additional strength.

The fleet that the queen and the prince consort went down to review at Spithead set sail under the command, as has been said, of Admiral Sir Charles Napier.[1] He was cousin to General Sir Charles Napier, the hero of Indian warfare; also cousin to Sir William Napier, the historian of the campaigns in the Peninsula, and second cousin to Lord Napier of Magdala. He had all the dash, bravery, and natural ability of these distinguished members of his family; but he had been at sea all his life, had had no education from books, was uncouth in his appearance, slightly lame from a wound received early in life, and was noted among his brother officers for being a sloven. His opinions in politics were those of an advanced reformer, and his animadversions were dreaded by every ministry as soon as he obtained a seat in Parliament. His professional

---

[1] When Sir Charles was elected Member of Parliament for Marylebone, he applied to my father for one of my school histories of England; saying he had never read an English history, and thought he ought to know something on the subject as he was called to be a legislator. — E. W. L.

reputation rested largely on the magnificent services he had rendered to Maria da Gloria, the Queen of Portugal, in 1828. For offering his sword to a foreign power without permission from his government he was dropped from the English navy list, but was afterwards restored to the navy. In 1840 he distinguished himself in the Levant, where he took St. Jean d'Acre from the Egyptians under Ibrahim Pasha.

The French fleet that was to have supported that of England in the expedition to the Baltic was not ready; indeed it did not get ready till hostilities were nearly over; and the naval part of the war against Russia was a failure, to the deep disappointment of England, and the mortification of Sir Charles Napier. The fleet under his orders was a magnificent one, consisting almost entirely of screw-ships, carrying two thousand guns, and fourteen thousand men. With this armament he sailed for the Baltic, carrying with him the hopes and confidence of the English people. The queen and prince, in the little yacht " Fairy," went in and out among his monster ships at Spithead, and, after the whole fleet had sailed past, the queen stood waving her handkerchief, the " Fairy " remaining motionless as if those on board of her wished to linger over the scene.[1]

This splendid fleet entered the Baltic, and there did absolutely nothing. It tried to take Cronstadt, which was too well defended. It sustained few losses, it suffered no defeat; it was simply a naval illustration of the old saying,

> "The King of France with twenty thousand men
> Marched up the hill, and then — marched down again."

We need speak of it no more.

To tell the history of the Danubian Provinces in this place would interrupt our story. It is enough to say that Moldavia and Wallachia, lying north of the Danube, had long been ruled by the Turks when by the Treaty of Adrianople in 1829 they were put partly under Russian

[1] Life of the Prince Consort.

protection, and were governed by their own princes, called "waiwodes," who paid tribute and owed fealty to the sultan their suzerain. The high-road from Russia into Turkey proper lies through these provinces.

Some months before the declaration of war between Russia, England, and Turkey, the Emperor Nicholas had assembled a large army on the banks of the Pruth. He did this on learning that the Turkish government, by advice of Lord Stratford de Redclyffe, had refused to sign the agreement which had been almost concluded, by which the sultan was to confirm the protectorate claimed by Russia over the Greek Christians in his dominions. At once the army on the Pruth was marched into Wallachia.

It seems desirable to have a clear idea of the provinces of Turkey at that period. North of the Danube lay Wallachia. South of the Danube lay Bulgaria and Servia. Running through Bulgaria were the Balkan Mountains (Mount Hæmus in the days of the old Greeks) which separated Bulgaria proper from Southern Bulgaria (otherwise called Eastern Roumelia); and Roumelia was the very heart and body of European Turkey. In Northern Bulgaria were the great fortress of Silistria, the fortified city of Plevna, the entrenched camp of Shumla, and the port of Varna. Russia cannot approach Constantinople by land without crossing Bulgaria and taking one or more of these places. This is why the Russian government at the present day is anxious that Bulgaria shall have no prince who is not devoted to Russian interests and subservient to the will of the czar.

The Turkish general-in-chief in 1853 was Omar Pasha, a Hungarian renegade. He had committed some small fault during his early youth, and had fled from home to escape punishment. He had crossed the Danube and made himself a Turk. He was a cold, stern man, but a great general. The sub-officers in the Turkish army are in general cowardly, trifling, and corrupt, but the common soldiers are brave and self-devoted, — admirable material for an army if only their officers could be made trustworthy.

In the month of March 1854, Lord Raglan was chosen to command the English forces, and Marshal de Saint-Arnaud to command those of the French. Saint-Arnaud had been the man who so skilfully and successfully conducted the prince-president's *coup d'état* of December 1, 1851, — about two years and a half before the breaking out of the Crimean War. He had in consequence been raised to the dignity of a marshal of France, and was intrusted, though the youngest marshal in the French service, with the command of his imperial master's army in this war.

Mr. Kinglake, in his history of the struggle in the Crimea, says of him: —

"He impersonated with singular exactness the idea which our forefathers had in their minds when they spoke of what they called 'a Frenchman.' He was bold, gay, restless, and vain; but beneath the mere glitter of the surface there was a great capacity for administrative business, and a more than common readiness to take away human life."

He began his career as Jacques Leroy. He ended it as the Marshal Achille de Saint-Arnaud, having had divers aliases during the interval. In 1816 he entered the French army as a sub-lieutenant in the Royal Guard, but his course of life was so dissolute and so disreputable that he was soon dismissed, and was obliged to keep out of France for several years. Part of this time he spent in England, and learned to speak English fluently, as well as several other languages. He lived apparently by all kinds of shifts, and his course of life was not improved. At one time, under the name of Florival, he was an actor in one of the second-rate theatres in the suburbs of Paris. When the Revolution of 1830 broke out he was thirty-three. He changed his name, again entered the army as a sub-lieutenant, and gained favor with his superiors, ingratiating himself in their regard by various little services. General Bugeaud made him his aide-de-camp,[1] and it is to Saint-Arnaud's credit that when arranging the details of the *coup d'état* with Prince Louis Napoleon, he took care to have Marshal Bugeaud sent from Paris to Lyons, so that he escaped the imprisonment and the indignities heaped on the other "African generals." But while aide-de-camp to Bugeaud and a personal favorite with that general, "again," says Kinglake, "the cloud passed over him." That is, he was again dropped from the service "for conduct unbecoming an officer and a gentleman."

No longer eligible to re-enter the regular army, he got a sub-lieutenant's commission in what was called "the Foreign Legion," and went with it to Algeria. "Every man," he says, "in that corps boasted of his *vie orageuse;*" that is, Saint-Arnaud found them all scamps and dare-devils like himself. He had however re-entered military life with a determination to die or to be something remarkable. At the memorable siege of Constantine in 1837 the fortunes of the day were mainly due to his rash courage. When all seemed lost after a great explosion, which blew hundreds of Frenchmen into the air, Saint-Arnaud rallied the foreign devils of his corps — many of them English, Irish, Germans, and Scandinavians — by an English hurrah. The men caught up the shout, and, cheering, followed their leader.

His health was wretched. Half the time he suffered bodily agony, but nothing quenched his spirit. If there was a deed of daring to be done, in or out of his profession, he was the man to do it, and it was often accompanied by acrobatic feats which he must have learned when Signor Florival.

In 1845 he perpetrated a horrible massacre of five hundred Arabs in a cave. I do not mean that massacre which made General Pélissier world-famous, — when he smothered a crowd of Arabs, men, women, and children, at Dahra;

---

[1] Saint-Arnaud was with him at Blaye, and was one of the witnesses to the declaration of the Duchesse de Berry concerning her second marriage.

but this other massacre Saint-Arnaud for a long time kept secret. He so contrived it that the very soldiers who walled up the openings to the cave did not know that there were five hundred living wretches inside it. Saint-Arnaud could himself take the whole credit of the deed, saying with Coriolanus, "Alone I did it — I ! "

After Louis Napoleon became president, he at once meditated how he should make himself emperor, and Fleury, his personal friend (the only one of the inner circle that surrounded him who was really true to him), was sent into Algeria to select a military man fit to conduct the plan of a *coup d'état.* He found Saint-Arnaud, then a colonel and brevet-general. He was secret, daring, reckless, able in administration, unscrupulous, untroubled by political principles, agreeable and intelligent as a companion, and with no character to compromise. Fleury brought him home, and presented him to the prince-president, who as a first step in the accomplishment of his purpose made him minister of war.

We know the result. And this was the man who was to be associated with Lord Raglan as his colleague, and intrusted with the most splendid command conferred upon any French general since the great wars of Napoleon.

Lord Raglan was third son of the Duke of Beaufort, a line of dukes legitimately descended from a morganatic marriage made by a son of Edward III. He was already known in history as Lord Fitzroy Somerset, aide-de-camp, secretary, and nephew by marriage to the Duke of Wellington. He was for forty years so attached to the duke's person that he seemed like the very shadow of that great man. He had lost an arm at Waterloo while carrying orders for Wellington past La Haye Sainte. His name and his honor were unsullied. His life had been woven like a thread into his country's history. Wellington had been probably more closely intimate with him than with any other man living. He was a man of simple habits, hating show, fuss, or parade. Indeed he did not like public demonstrations of enthusiasm even for his soldiers. He would have wished to start off with them to the East, and there serve his queen and do his duty. He was sixty-six years old, but fresh, active, and upright, — a strange contrast in all things to the inexperienced French commander-in-chief with whom he was linked, and whom it was his almost painful endeavor to treat on all occasions with distinguished consideration.

On April 11, 1854, Lord Raglan and the queen's cousin, the Duke of Cambridge, commander of a division of the English army, attended a review of thirty thousand French troops in the Champ de Mars, where, almost for the first time in the history of France, French troops cheered for England. The emperor had known Lord Fitzroy Somerset in London. Indeed it was Lord Fitzroy who had introduced him to the Duke of Wellington at Apsley House during his exile.

On April 13 Lord Raglan had a long and confidential private interview with the emperor, and then was taken into an outer room where he found King Jerome, the Duke of Cambridge, Marshal Vaillant (then minister of war), Lord de Ros, and Marshal de Saint-Arnaud.

What a strange conjunction! — the brother of the great Napoleon, his nephew and successor, the grandson of George III., the nephew and disciple of Wellington, Lord de Ros, bearer of the oldest title in England, Vaillant the oldest marshal in France, and — Marshal de Saint-Arnaud, a man twice dismissed from the French service, and who had not even a legal right to his name.

After this interview Lord Raglan and the Duke of Cambridge hurried forward to join their troops, who were encamped at Gallipoli upon the shore of the Dardanelles, opposite the old camping-ground of the Greeks during the siege of Troy.

Gallipoli was a dull, sad little town; decay and dirt were everywhere, but the place changed suddenly as soon as the fleet of transports arrived. "Trumpet-calls, shouting, and bustle succeeded the death-like repose of the broken-down little city. A camp was soon pitched. Things shook into their places," says an eye-witness. "Drill began, and marching out," to bring the soldiers into a proper state of training. The march past on parade was soon as good as at Aldershot. Had Nicholas been there he might have said, as his son did afterward to the German crown prince, while witnessing a review at Windsor: "They are the finest soldiers in the world. You and I may thank our stars there are so few of them."

While the armies lay at Gallipoli waiting the arrival of military stores, especially the means of land transportation, which would enable them to push forward, Lord Raglan's patience and courtesy were not a little tried by Marshal de Saint-Arnaud's changes of mind. "In the dead of night or in the early dawn he would send word to his colleague that he proposed to make changes that would affect the whole plan of campaign, or alter the whole structure of the armies. With bland politeness Lord Raglan would convince him, or checkmate him, when Saint-Arnaud, with irrepressible buoyancy and good-humor, would submit, and all would be smooth again."

When the army of the czar had posted itself in Wallachia, on the northern or left bank of the Danube, Omar Pasha had massed his troops in Bulgaria on the opposite bank. The czar was not willing that his Russians should cross into Turkey Proper while negotiations were pending, and Wallachia was (at least nominally) Russian ground; but inasmuch as it still owed to the sultan tribute and allegiance, Omar was continually sending troops across the Danube and harassing the enemy by small surprises. At last the Russian army crossed the river and laid siege to the great fortress of Silistria. This was precisely what Omar Pasha wanted. He desired they should waste their time and strength upon stone walls which he knew would hold out against them.

The siege of Silistria was going on under the old Russian general Paskievitch, so successful in Persia, in Poland, and in the Caucasus nearly thirty years before; but Omar Pasha did not make any energetic attempt to relieve the garrison, feeling assured that when protected by fortifications Turkish troops were well-nigh invincible. The allied generals, however, had misgivings on the subject. Lord Raglan had no great faith in Turks, and if the Danubian fortress were to fall while the French and English armies lingered at Gallipoli, he felt that they and their commanders would be disgraced. They could not go anywhere by land for want of the means of transportation, but there was an English fleet and a French fleet at hand, and in these they embarked, sailed through the Bosphorus, passed Constantinople, entered the Black Sea, and landed at Varna, on the shores of Bulgaria. There they were near enough to Silistria to hear the roar of the great guns at night with the ear to the ground, and near enough to Omar Pasha's headquarters to reach them in a long day's ride.

Silistria was immensely strong as a fortress, but it had a very small garrison for so large a place. It had also an indifferent Turkish commander; but two young English officers from India, named Nasmyth and Butler, had thrown themselves into the place, animated the Turks, who soon adored them, bullied the Turkish commander into something like courage, and successfully resisted every effort of Paskievitch and his large army to take the town. Poor Butler was mortally wounded during the siege. He and Nasmyth were joined in the course of it by five other English officers. One night at Varna the usual cannonade from Silistria was listened for by the French and English troops recently landed. It was very heavy. The next night the allies heard none. Had the place then fallen? On the contrary the siege was raised, and Paskievitch had retreated across the Danube. Thither a party of Turkish troops, led by Englishmen, followed him, and obtained signal advantages at a post on the Danube called Giurgievo.

This roused the czar to fury. "I can understand Olenitza," he cried (Olenitza was a battle won by Omar Pasha);

"I can even understand that Omar should have been able to hold out against me on the lines of Kalafat; I can understand Silistria, — the strongest may fail in a siege, and Paskievitch and his second in command were both wounded; but — but — but — that Turks, led on by a general of Sepoys and six or seven English boys, — that *they* should dare to cross the Danube in the face of my troops, that, daring to attempt it, they should do it, and hold fast their ground, that my troops should give way before them, and that this, this should be the last act of a campaign which is ending with the abandonment of the principalities and the retreat of my whole army! — Heaven lays upon me more than I can bear!"

The Russian army having retreated, the English, French, and Turkish allied armies found no enemy in their front, and had to determine on a new point of attack in southern Russia.

Meanwhile the allied generals, Lord Raglan and Marshal Saint-Arnaud with their staffs, started out one hot summer morning to ride over to the Turkish camp at Shumla, and consult with Omar Pasha.

"Lord Raglan," says a civilian who was with the army at this stage of the war,[1] "having served on the Duke of Wellington's staff in the Peninsula and at Waterloo, when feelings were rife in the British army not over conducive to harmony with the French, thought he could not do too much to show that no such antipathies prevailed now. Marshal Saint-Arnaud, whatever other merits he may have possessed, was certainly rather wanting in the chivalrous feeling which ought to have prevented his taking an unfair advantage of his colleague's cordial courtesy. Later on this peculiar feature of their intercourse was of serious importance, as it could not fail to affect their joint operations, to the prejudice of the British army, but in this instance no great harm was done by it, and a little amusement at the good and gallant Lord Raglan's expense for

[1] Laurence Oliphant, in Blackwood's Magazine.

letting himself be jockeyed, was the only result. Shumla is fifty miles from Varna, and in order to ride the distance more comfortably in one day, Lord Raglan proposed to Marshal Saint-Arnaud that they should not pay their visit in uniform, as Omar Pasha would doubtless receive them equally well if they appeared in easy-fitting plain clothes. The French marshal made no objection, and he and his staff started in wide-awake hats, and shooting jackets with gold-laced uniform trousers under them. Lord Raglan and his suite were similarly attired, but with plain overalls. When the cavalcade was approaching Shumla, orderlies brought tin boxes to the marshal and his staff, who halted for a few minutes, and proceeded to unpack cocked hats and feathers, laced jackets, swords, stars, crosses, and medals, all of which they donned with the greatest complacency, while the English general and his staff, helpless in their sober mufti, looked on with astonishment. At the gate of the town the Turkish guard turned out and presented arms to the French officers. It turned in when the English officers rode up to the gate. Omar Pasha had the good taste to receive the two commanders-in-chief exactly alike, and to tell Lord Raglan he was very glad to see him in plain clothes, which he begged to be allowed to treat as an intimation that he considered him a friend. The English general, with his noble simplicity of character, merely replied that it was a long day's ride, and that he had felt sure Omar Pasha would not object to his coming in the most comfortable dress. On this occasion the Grand Cross of the Legion of Honor was formally promised by the marshal to Omar Pasha, while Lord Raglan in his turn announced that the Grand Cross of the Bath would be conferred on him. The sultan had already been invested with the Garter, and much surprise and curiosity were evinced by the Turks, who declared they had never heard of a Bath being used for anything but cleanliness, nor of a stocking being kept up by a gold-embroidered garter as a mark of distinction. 'Mashallah!' they exclaimed, 'the English are the fathers of funny freaks!'"

MARSHAL SAINT-ARNAUD.

In spite of the beauty of the country around Varna, and the excellent sport, the armies became very desirous to move elsewhere. Ague, cholera, and dysentery broke out, and the troops gladly heard the trumpet-call that summoned them to fold their tents and march away.

And yet the war might have been ended by diplomacy, after the cause of war was removed by the retreat of the Russian army from the principalities, but the Emperor Napoleon had his policy to carry out, and England was beside herself with a passion for war, and a craving for adventure.

Immediately on receipt of the news of the raising of the siege of Silistria and the retreat of the Russian army, the Duke of Newcastle, then war minister of England, proposed that the allied armies should go and attack Sebastopol.

Sebastopol, as every one knows now, stands at the southern extremity of the peninsula of the Crimea, and is a port on the Black Sea. The Emperor Nicholas had made it a great naval station. He had built there an immense arsenal, and had filled the place with stores and munitions of war, in case of needing them in any advance into the Turkish territory, because they could thence be conveyed to almost any point by sea. It was of immense strength, especially in its outworks, and the Russian fleet, which had destroyed that of the Turks at Sinope, lay under its guns. The Duke of Newcastle prepared his instructions for Lord Raglan to make this important movement, in fact to open the second campaign of the war, and he read this despatch to his colleagues after a dinner at Richmond. None of them objected; so little was known of the Crimea, or of Sebastopol, that there were no grounds for objection. No one dissented from his views. The despatch was forwarded to Lord Raglan. It was very peremptory, leaving him no discretion, and it was backed by similar orders to Saint-Arnaud from his emperor.

There was not an officer in high command in the armies

at Varna who did not disapprove the project. Lord Raglan was opposed to it, as also were the chief engineer officer of the expedition, his fellow in the councils of the Duke of Wellington, the English admiral, and vice-admiral, and Saint-Arnaud. But the latter was at the moment ill, worried, and dispirited. He shook off all responsibility, and said that he should follow the lead of the English commander.

Neither the French nor English had any certain information as to the state of the defences or the strength of the garrison at Sebastopol. Some said that it contained one hundred and twenty thousand men, some seventy thousand, some seventeen thousand. Lord Raglan could obtain no clear intelligence. But the despatch from the Duke of Newcastle was, as I said, very peremptory. It nettled the old soldier. He determined to yield his own military judgment, and to obey orders.

"I cannot help seeing," wrote the Duke of Newcastle, in a letter of reply to one from Lord Raglan, "I cannot help seeing through the calm and noble tone of your announcement of the decision to attack Sebastopol, that it has been taken in order to meet the views and desires of government, and not in entire accordance with your own opinions. God grant that success may reward you, and justify us!"

It was, however, imperatively necessary to remove the armies from Varna as speedily as possible. The French had brought cholera with them to the Dardanelles. It first showed itself at Gallipoli, and now in the swamps at Varna it grew terrible. General Canrobert's division of the French army, which was marched into the low country round the mouths of the Danube, was decimated by it. In one day's march, and in the space of a few hours, hundreds of men sometimes dropped down in the sudden agonies of the disease; and out of one battalion it was said that, besides the dead, there were five hundred sick carried along in wagons. By the middle of August out of three French divisions ten thousand men lay dead or ill from cholera. The English admiral ran his ships out to sea, hoping that in untainted air they might escape infection, but the disease attacked the sailors with especial virulence. Then was shown the feeling and humanity of British officers, and the childlike trust felt in them by their men. "Partly by cheering words," says an eye witness, "and partly by wild remedies, invented in despair of all regular medical aid, the officers really did sometimes succeed in fighting the disease, or made the men think they did."

The generals at last could not but feel that to go to the Crimea was better than "to linger among the atmospheric poisons of the Bulgarian coast; besides which they knew that bitter would be the disappointment of the people of England to see the army sent back to Malta, and forced to give up the conflict for the bare reason that some of the men were in hospital, and that the rest, without being ill, were miserably weak."

On August 24, 1854, the operation of embarking the allied armies began. The English embarked sixty pieces of field-artillery with their horses and equipments, twenty thousand infantry, and one thousand cavalry. But embarking cavalry horses is a difficult and tedious business. It cannot be done in a rough sea, and it was some days before the English men and horses were on board ship, without, however, the loss of a single man. It had been intended that in order to make the descent on the Crimea a surprise to the Russians, the allied armies should get there as quickly as possible by means of steam, but the French resources in steam were not equal to the emergency, and it was evident that the expedition would be clogged by slow-sailing transports.

On the 5th of September Marshal Saint-Arnaud decided to set sail with such ships as he had ready, leaving the English to follow with the transports as soon as their horses could be got on board. The French army had no cavalry.

The 7th of September, when the fleet sailed out of Baljik Bay, was a lovely morning. Moonlight was still floating on the waters, when in the east appeared the dawn. The French went out of harbor quickly. Their transports, which were small, seemed a swarm. The English followed in five columns of thirty vessels each, and then — guard over all — sailed the English war fleet, prepared to protect the rest in case the enemy had news of their expedition, and his fleet should sail out of Sebastopol to attack them.

"The Black Sea," says Mr. Kinglake, "is a far better name than the Euxine. It *is* a Black Sea, and no scientific man has been able to account for the difference between its climate and that of the balmy, fertile shores that surround it."

Marshal Saint-Arnaud, who had sailed off with the French war vessels, without waiting to consult Lord Raglan, sailed on day after day into worse and worse weather, till at last, alarmed by his isolation, he decided to sail back again to Baljik Bay and try to rejoin the English and his own forces. He met with Lord Raglan the day after the English fleet left the Bulgarian harbor, and thenceforward there occurred no more ebullitions of petulance, nor did Marshal Saint-Arnaud show any more tendency to break away from his colleague.

That night when the French generals were informed where the expedition was going, a number of them signed a paper setting forth the difficulties that they foresaw in landing at all in the Crimea, and in short virtually protesting against carrying out the scheme. Saint-Arnaud was very ill at the time, — unable to bear discussion. He said he would adopt the decision of Lord Raglan. It may be right to say here that General Trochu (who was afterwards commander of Paris during the siege in 1870) had been placed with Saint-Arnaud as head of his staff, and his confidential adviser. He wholly disapproved of the Crimean project, and was sent by Saint-Arnaud to confer with Lord Raglan. Lord Raglan quietly put aside the paper signed by the French generals, without inviting discussion. He was a real head, and things fell at once into obedience to him.

On Sept. 9 the fleet was off the coast of the Crimea, and on the morning of the 10th, a fair, bright Sunday morning with the bells ashore ringing for church, Lord Raglan first saw the forts, and the ships, and the gayly cupolaed town, that was to become so famous in history. Rounding a cape he next saw two old Genoese forts guarding the entrance to that arm of the sea which divides Sebastopol into two parts. In the distance he saw the heights, the fatal heights to so many who then looked on them for the first time, fatal to both commanders, — the heights of Sebastopol.

Having reconnoitred the unknown coast himself, for the whole country was as strange to French and English as if they had been the Argonauts, Lord Raglan decided to disembark to the west of Sebastopol. He fixed on a broad sandy bit of beach near the bright little village of Eupatoria. By this time Marshal Saint-Arnaud had thrown off his attack of illness, and was himself again.

The Tartars of the country proved to be very willing to open a provision market for the supply of the allied troops. A few Russian coins were obtained from some English travellers, who had not (like the government) forgotten that English sovereigns will not pass current among the peasants of Scythia. In two days the men were landed, but it took four more to get ashore the horses. English horses are not, as a rule, so sensible, obedient, and tractable as American horses. In five days all were on shore, but alas! — the cholera came with them, and the first duty of the soldiers was to dig graves.

The Turks provided for their own comfort much sooner than the French and English, and the English and French officers, who had no tents with them, were glad to find some shelter in those of the Turkish officers.

Soon the head-men of the villages began to come in, and they seemed not unfriendly to the invaders. In the villages, strange as they appeared in most respects to English eyes, officers found here and there houses with pianos, music-books, and other signs of refinement. One main want of the country was water, but the English quartermaster-general caused wells at once to be sunk. The army was accompanied by no camp followers to make mischief among the population, and very soon friendly feelings were established between the English soldiers and the Tartar peasantry, the soldiers helping the women in their household labors. The Rifles, an English crack regiment, were their favorites, and, when the soldiers came to understand something of the speech of the peasantry, it was found that the women designated the Rifles as "heroes stronger than lions, and quieter than lambs." Alas! it was as lions, not as lambs, that the Zouaves subsequently made themselves known to them.

The army landed in the Crimea was twenty-seven thousand English, thirty-seven thousand French and Turks, — in all, sixty-four thousand men. On the morning of Sept. 19 the armies began their march southward. We need not attempt any description of that march. The movement of armies is interesting only if one takes a good map of the country on which to study them; abridged, the narrative becomes an unintelligible mass of dry details. And the same may be said of battles.

The first river crossed was called the Bulganak, and here it was that the Russian soldiers first appeared. The next morning they were found in force in an entrenched camp, prepared to dispute the passage of the river Alma.

Prince Mentzikoff (he who had precipitated the war when ambassador at Constantinople) was in command of the Russian forces. "He was," says Mr. Kinglake, "a wayward, presumptuous man, and his bearing toward the generals under his command was of such a kind that he did not, or could not, strengthen himself by the counsel of men abler than himself. In time past he had been mutilated by a round shot from a Turkish gun. He bore hatred against the Ottoman race. He bore hatred against their faith. He had opened his mission at the Porte with insults, he had closed it with threats, and now he was out on a hillside with horse and foot, empowered to take full vengeance on his enemies, Christian and infidel."

It was Sept. 20, 1854, that the battle of the Alma was fought. The two allied commanders went alone together early in the morning to a hill, and surveyed the field of action. Prince George of England (the Duke of Cambridge) commanded an English division; Prince Napoleon (son of King Jerome) commanded a French one.

"The whole allied armies, hiding nothing of their splendor, or their strength," says Mr. Kinglake, "descended slowly into the valley, and the ground on the bank of the Alma on which they were is so even and gentle in its slope, while the bank on which the Russians were was so commanding, that every man of the invaders could be seen from the opposite side."

For the first half of the day the allies gained little. The heaviest fire of the enemy seemed always directed against the spot where Lord Raglan and his staff were standing. The fire was terrible at some parts of the day. The Highlanders and the Coldstream Guards were mowed down by grape-shot after the river was crossed, and they were advancing up the hill to take the Russian batteries; but the Russian position was carried by storm, and its commanding officer made prisoner.

Here is a sad little story which to most of us will have more interest than mere military details of the battle: —

"Colonel Beckwith was seen leading his battalion of the Rifle Brigade with cool gallantry to the steep ascent, after fording the Alma. He disappeared in an unaccountable manner. His body was not found among the slain. Two days after the battle an ordnance wagon, which had been left behind near the stream, was sent for. Colonel Beckwith was found lying under it dead. He had died of cholera. He was an officer who had served with credit twenty-five years. He had just attained the highest regimental rank; he commanded, and was leading into action, one of the finest corps of men in the army. Had he been shot, a nation would have mourned him; but he was compelled to fall out in the agonies of cholera, to creep under this wagon, and to lie there alone like a dog. It was not long after he had died that he was found. Had help come earlier they might have saved him."

"The brunt of the battle," says a diplomatist who was present, "fell on the English, for the French commander here first displayed his serious intention of giving his army an unfair advantage through Lord Raglan's excess of courtesy. He claimed the right flank on the march from Eupatoria, the right being protected by the guns of the fleet, while the English columns marched with no protection. Thus it happened that the English had to storm the strongest Russian positions, while those attacked by the French were the most weakly defended. No doubt the French would have stormed the Russian positions as well as the English, but their general had assigned them easier ground."

Saint-Arnaud, however, did full justice to Lord Raglan. Writing to his emperor, he says, "The antique courage of the English general was splendid to see." He wrote this, too, without having seen, as so many others did, Lord Raglan sitting in his saddle with placid composure under a tremendous fire of artillery and small arms, quietly conversing with Prince Napoleon, who had dismounted to dodge the shot, "knowing," as some one remarked at the time, "that napoleons were scarce, and what was their value."

It was observed after the battle that the dead were out of all proportion to the wounded, the Russians having reserved their fire till the assailants were at very short range.

When the battle was over, and the Russians were in retreat, Lord Raglan refused to allow any pursuit. He had only his Light Brigade of cavalry, one thousand strong, and he feared to risk its being cut off. No prisoners therefore were taken, except the wounded.

The Russian soldiers, who had shown great steadiness and bravery during the fight, and began their retreat in good order, were seized with a sudden panic after all danger was over, and fancying themselves pursued, when there was really a long distance between themselves and any English or French soldiers, pressed in wild confusion into the river Katschov; and even after they had crossed it a further panic hurried them on toward Sebastopol.

It is said that just at the turn of the battle Prince Mentzikoff, observing some wavering at an important point, galloped off to see if his presence would strengthen the position. The country was very rolling. Having descended an eminence, he could see little before him. As he hurried along the great high-road, he saw coming toward him a solitary man on foot. Nearing him, he found it was Prince Gortschakoff. "You here?" he cried. "Where's your horse, — your staff, — your men?" "My horse is shot, my staff all killed or wounded, my men dispersed."

The news of the battle of the Alma reached Queen Victoria at Balmoral, and caused great rejoicings, mingled with grief for those who mourned for friends; but so totally ignorant was everybody at the time of the true situation of affairs that when a false telegram, based on the loose talk of a Tartar peasant, came the next day, saying that Sebastopol was taken, all the members of the Cabinet believed it, except Lord Clarendon.

The allied armies made brief stay on the left bank of the Alma before continuing their march to Sebastopol. They had no tents, no pack-horses, no provision for winter, no warm clothing. It was already autumn, and the climate was severe. Sebastopol, it was supposed by friends in England, would be carried by a *coup de main*, and the army would be home by Christmas, to be fêted, and glorified, and keep the universal holiday with gladness and good cheer.

CHAPTER VII.

THE CRIMEAN WAR (*concluded*).

GREAT was the rejoicing in the English, French, and Turkish allied armies over what Mr. Kinglake calls "the scramble of the Alma."

It was some days before they could go forward, it being necessary to ship off the wounded to Constantinople. The Russian army under Prince Mentzikoff had fallen back in great disorder to Sebastopol, where it was re-formed, and then marched off, the English knew not whither, — though indeed they had little knowledge of any kind of their enemy or of his movements, and fancied that at least a large part of the army they had fought at the Alma was strengthening Sebastopol.

In 1870 the Germans owed their marvellous and speedy success in their campaign against the French largely to the excellence of their maps and their minute knowledge of the country. In 1854 neither the French nor English generals, nor any one connected with their armies, appears to have known anything about the topography of the Crimea, or the defences of Sebastopol. The authentic military information that they had upon the subject was nineteen years old. The Russians had been unwilling to admit strangers into Sebastopol after it became a naval station, and the best recent account concerning it that the authorities possessed was from that charming writer and enterprising traveller, Mr. Laurence Oliphant, who, however, earnestly advised them either to attack Russia through her Caucasian provinces, or to occupy and defend the Isthmus of Perekop, instead of besieging Sebastopol.

GENERAL TODLEBEN.

Perhaps before going further I had better try to present some intelligible plan of Sebastopol, though without a map it may be difficult to do so. We may fancy the extreme southern part of the peninsula of the Crimea (the Crimea is almost as large as Ireland) shaped like a wolf's head looking southwest with the mouth partly open. The open mouth represents the roadstead, within which there is an inner harbor, where the Russian fleet of eight line-of-battle ships was lying. The roadstead, or rather arm of the sea extending four miles inland, divides the city into two parts. The houses on the southern side are nestled in a little valley. On the other side of the harbor, on the northern bank of the inlet, was a fortification called the Star Fort. It was the only defence of Sebastopol on its northern side, and the harbor or inlet lay between it and the town. Sebastopol had no walls, but was protected by very strong bastions or redoubts. The names of some of these are now very familiar. They were the little Redan, the Malakoff, the Redan, the Telegraph Fort, and three or four others. These all extended from Inkerman west of the inlet toward Balaclava. The country was up-hill and down-dale, rolling and rocky, entirely unwooded, cut up by ravines and gorges. The great high-road to St. Petersburg, a thousand miles away, ran straight, and white, and unobstructed, into the northern part of the city. Balaclava was a small seaport to the east of the town, with a harbor so surrounded by high cliffs, and with so land-locked an entrance, that it looked like a still lake. There was another landing-place which the French made into a port not very far to the south of it. Balaclava was east of Sebastopol, and therefore the allies, who had landed on the western coast of the Crimea, had to cross from the west coast to the east coast to get there. Besides ravines and hilly ridges, the ground was cut up by little mountain rivulets which made swamps in low places, though the rest of the ground was sterile.

The arm of the sea of which I have spoken as dividing

the city of Sebastopol is joined by the little river Tchernaya near the ruins called Inkerman.

This is a very imperfect attempt to give an idea of Sebastopol, its position and its outworks, but it may possibly assist somewhat in conveying a faint conception of the scene of action.

The question between the commanders of the French and English forces, after they had crossed the river Alma, was, At what point should they attack Sebastopol? Lord Raglan wanted to push on at once, take the Star Fort by surprise, and thence, across the harbor, bombard the town; the allied fleets at the same time engaging the Russian fleet, forcing their way into the harbor, and assisting in the attack. But Marshal Saint-Arnaud would not listen to this plan, and in truth it seemed hazardous to many of the best military engineers in the English army. We know now that there was no large Russian army in Sebastopol, as was supposed at the time; and that if Lord Raglan's plan had been carried out, it might have been successful. However, no plan could be followed that was opposed by either the English or the French commander. So a singular and very different plan was proposed by Lord Raglan, and accepted by Saint-Arnaud. This was to attack Sebastopol on what is called the south side, instead of by the Star Fort on what is called the north side,—to march the armies right across the lower end of the peninsula of the Crimea, to seize the port of Balaclava, to which the fleet and transports would move round; to fix batteries upon the heights, and thence bombard the city. This march of the armies from west to east is called in history the flank march, and was extremely perilous. Had Prince Mentzikoff, who was outside Sebastopol, at large in the Crimea, attacked the allies on their march, the consequences might have been disastrous in the extreme. He had quitted Sebastopol, insisting, to the grief and indignation of the naval men in the city, that of the eight beautiful great men-of-war in the harbor, all but one ("The Twelve Apostles") should be sunk across the mouth of the roadstead, and so prove (as they did) a complete defence to the city on the side of the water. The crews were taken on shore, and were set to work the guns that defended the bastions.

The allied armies therefore made the flank march, and the English took possession of the little port of Balaclava. As Lord Raglan, who had been foremost all the way in reconnoitring, sat on his horse watching what seemed to him a still smooth pool of water, suddenly there glided into sight an English ship with English colors flying, between two high cliffs which screened the entrance to the harbor.

It was arranged that the English should hold Balaclava for their port, and that the French should content themselves with a less advantageous landing-place.

The allied armies were in position early in October. Here is an eye-witness's account of the harbor of Balaclava on the sixth day of that month, 1854: —

"As we sailed round the southernmost extremity of the Crimea past Sebastopol, the fine day showed to great advantage the blue scarped masses of the interior. Every second mountain seemed a natural fortress. It was like passing a series of Gibraltars. Sebastopol we reconnoitred at a respectful distance. A jet of light smoke leapt every now and then from the forts. In less than an hour after passing it we were steaming into the harbor of Balaclava, skirted less with shores than walls."

The harbor was strewn with the bloated carcasses of dead horses, which the steam-tugs were dragging out into the open sea. The smell was overpowering, accounting largely for the general prevalence of disease. Our eye-witness goes on to say that the place reminded him of some parts of Ireland where stone is plenty, and nothing else, and where whitewash does duty for repairs. Lord Raglan's abode at Balaclava was not much above the level of the general wretchedness. Before the door paced a sentry, "whose get-up was not at all out of keeping with his surroundings. He had a soiled red coat; its ragged worsted tags were the reverse of ornamental, and its open collar showed neither stock nor shirt. His rusty black trousers gaped vainly here and there for buttons, and were tucked up unceremoniously at the heels to keep them dry. His boots were the color of the dust they trod on, so were his Saxon locks and sun-burnt face. Nevertheless there was that about his quiet, honest bearing which would I think have proclaimed him, even without the distinctive red, a British soldier."[1]

The ships had by this time brought in a few tents, and the greatest activity prevailed upon the heights, where batteries were being erected to attack the Russian outworks; though not a shot was to be fired till all were in position. Everything had to be dragged up the steep hills from Balaclava. All the *arabas*, or country carts, were pressed into the service. Some were drawn by little Tartar horses, some by camels, but most by bullocks. The men who owned them, though prisoners after a fashion, served the English not unwillingly; they were paid twenty-five dollars a month,—to them a little fortune; but Mr. Kinglake says sadly that before the siege ended nearly all of them had died.

The gentleman from whom I have already quoted pushed to the front, that is, to the heights where batteries were being erected by one of the English divisions. There he was asked to dine with the general of the division and his staff, and this is what he saw of camp-life that evening:—

"A single wax candle set in the bare ground lighted the interior. Canvas bags, cloaks, and water-proofs strewed around hid the bare earth, and on them reclined, like the ancients the general and his staff. I was accommodated with the only seat, that is, a portmanteau." The dress of the officers was their fatigue uniform, and each wore his forage cap during the meal.

The English officers had bell-tents, that is, tents with a pole in the centre, and a circular wall of canvas round the bottom. The men had at first no tents at all, or little

[1] Blackwood's Magazine.

"kennel tents," only a foot or two high, under which they crept for warmth and shelter. There were no means of washing, even for the officers, and the eye-witness, who was a young lawyer, exclaims: "Think of the unutterable horrors of a state of things where neither the clothing can be changed nor the body cleansed for weeks on weeks. Think of men, born and trained as our officers are trained, undergoing all this without complaint. The sea is too distant for bathing, and, though there are little springs in neighboring hollows, nobody has anything to carry the water in. The men have tin pans that they use for cooking, and the officers sometimes borrow them for basins, when half a pint of water can be secured."

The coloring of the landscape in October was a uniform drab. No vegetation was visible. There had been some good vineyards on the rocky slopes round Balaclava, but they were sear and grapeless in October. There were no trees of any growth, only scrub oaks and shrubs, — just the brown earth, bristling with bunches of burnt up, star-headed thistles, with not a field flower except an occasional anemone. The English camp was between three and four miles long, stretching from the eastern part of the plateau (divided by a gorge from the old ruins of Inkerman) to a ravine on the south, where the French camp began, and continued the cordon to the sea. Thus it will be perceived that Sebastopol was by no means invested. The great highroad to Saint Petersburg lay open from it into the interior; nothing menaced the Star Fort, nor the peninsula on which it stood, called in Russian books the Severnaya. The English army was distributed in six divisions. The last to arrive was the cavalry, — a splendid corps. The Scots Greys had come out, — heavy dragoons wearing bear-skin caps, and their horses all one color.

The tents, when tents arrived, were so small that the officers stored their spare belongings on the outside, and theft appears to have been unknown among the soldiers. Indeed, throughout the campaign there was very little crime.

But there was plenty of sickness, — cholera and dysentery, scurvy and malarial fever, — and a great lack of hospital surgeons, and hospital comforts. Pillows especially were called for, and had not been supplied. But the two greatest wants were firewood and warm clothing. The men's uniforms had been worn threadbare, and the English government, never having contemplated a prolonged winter campaign in the Crimea, and knowing little or nothing of the Black Sea climate, had not provided for these wants in time. Under pressing requisitions for great-coats, blankets, etc., a quantity were collected in haste, and all shipped on board the "Prince," which reached the harbor of Balaclava just in time to encounter a furious storm on November 5, which tore down the tents, greatly damaged the shipping, and sank the "Prince." Weeks of November and December weather had to pass before the loss could be supplied. The soldiers, subject to these privations and to the prevalence of disease, "could hardly have been recognized" as an officer remarked, "for the same men who had landed at Gallipoli."

On Oct. 17 the French and English batteries were all prepared and the bombardment of the city was begun. The firing all day was tremendous, but during the night the Russians, who had General Todleben, then a young officer, for their engineer-in-chief, repaired all the mischief done by the French and English guns during the day.

On Oct. 25 took place the battle of Balaclava. I do not think it was very much of a battle, if we compare it with such fights as Blenheim, Austerlitz, or even Chancellorsville or Gettysburg, but it will live forever in history and literature as famous for the charge of the Light Brigade.

The Russian army outside the walls of Sebastopol was under the command of General Liprandi, who had replaced Prince Mentzikoff. He came creeping up behind the English and French positions, and attacked them just where the two armies came together, and where there was a battery of six guns that had been intrusted to the Turks.

The Turks fired one volley, and then fled, to the intense disgust of Lord Raglan who hated Turks at all times, and of his whole army. The Russians captured the six cannon, and sang a Te Deum over them that night in Sebastopol. The battle would have been almost entirely an artillery fight, had it not been for two cavalry episodes, the charge of the Heavy Brigade (that is, the Dragoon Guards and the Scotch Greys) and the Light Brigade, under Lord Cardigan, colonel of the 10th Huzzars.

Lord Cardigan in his earlier days had been an officer who gave considerable trouble to the Horseguards. He quarelled with one of his officers Captain Harvey Phipps Tuckett, about a bottle of sparkling Moselle brought to the mess-table in the original black bottle. Captain Tuckett resigned his commission, and then challenged his late superior officer. They fought a duel, and Lord Cardigan was tried before the High Court of Peers. The trial was short, however, for an error was discovered in the indictment, where Captain Tuckett's middle name had been omitted. But Lord Cardigan for some time subsequently was not on good terms with many of his officers.

Many years after Lord Tennyson's "Charge of the Light Brigade" had become universally popular, the poet was induced to celebrate in verse the charge of the Heavy Brigade at Balaclava, but the poem never can attain the popularity of its predecessor.

"There was a tremendous charge of Russian cavalry, which came over the crest of the ridge that separated the armies, down into the valley between them. Those on the heights, both Russians and allies, looked down upon the spectacle, unobscured by cannon-smoke, which is unusual in a battle. It was as if they were spectators in an arena gazing upon a fight of gladiators. The Scots Greys advanced first, impeded however by the drains and picket lines of their own encampment, but, soon extricating themselves, they were mingled among the Russians, their red coats, fur caps, and gray horses making them conspicuous. Then came up the fourth and fifth regiments of Heavy Dragoons. For a moment sword-cuts and lance-thrusts were exchanged, then the Russians turned and fled confusedly over the slopes, pursued for several hundred yards by the whole force of the heavy cavalry. The Greys, broken before their comrades came up, rallied in time to join in the pursuit." [1]

That is the story of the Heavy Brigade.

The story of the Light Brigade, which was a body of cavalry made up of parts of several regiments, we all know partly. While the Heavies were engaged, the Light Brigade had advanced to the edge of the slopes, whence they could look down on the Russians as they rallied on their own side of the valley. On the slope the Russians had planted a battery flanked by two others, to repel any attack that might be made on them. Captain Nolan, a brave Irish officer, who had written a book on tactics, brought an order to the commander of the Light Cavalry to charge the enemy, and to take their cannon. To do this with only cavalry seemed desperate, but Nolan asserted the order to be peremptory, and joining in the charge which presently took place, he was struck by a shell in the breast, and fell dead.

"Never did cavalry show more daring to less purpose. Received in front and flank by a fire which strewed the ground for half a mile of the distance which separated them from the enemy with men and horses, they nevertheless forced their way between the guns, and slew the gunners. Their gallantry availed them nothing. The whole Russian force was before them. A body of Russian cavalry interposed to cut off their retreat across the valley, and, assailed on every side by every arm of the service, and their ranks utterly broken, they were compelled to fight their way back, and to regain their position under the same artillery fire that had crashed into their advance. Singly, or in twos or threes, these gallant horsemen returned, some on foot, many wounded, some supporting a stricken comrade. The same fire that had shattered their ranks had also reached the Heavy Cavalry, now rallied on the slope behind, who also suffered severely. The English loss would have been greater but for the timely charge of a body of French cavalry, which, descending from the plateau, advanced up the Russian heights, where they silenced a destructive battery."

[1] Blackwood's Magazine.

Such is the story in the words of a staff officer who wrote his narrative a few hours after the battle. "Never did cavalry show more daring to less purpose," he says; and a Russian officer, speaking of it afterwards called it "magnificent folly." And yet can *we* say that it had not its use and its lesson, — its encouragement, and its purpose? Whose sense of the duty of unquestioning obedience is not stirred when he says the words, "The Charge of the Light Brigade"? It is one of the world's great feats of arms, one of all soldiers' great military lessons. It will act as a trumpet-call, as long as wars may last, to all English-speaking soldiers. It is almost the best good England, or the world, gathered from all the toils and sufferings of that Crimean War.

The Light Brigade — that thousand men Lord Raglan had cherished so carefully from the time of his landing at Eupatoria — had in less than a month shrunk to the Six Hundred who made the charge. Of that six hundred, two hundred and seventy-eight were killed, wounded, or missing; of these, twenty-one were officers; and three hundred and thirty-five horses were destroyed. The Heavies lost over one hundred and sixty men, ten of whom were officers, and forty horses.

Lord Tennyson's first version of his poem contained a verse which he amended afterwards to soothe the feelings of the family of Captain Nolan, but he did not improve his poetry, or his facts, by the alteration. "'Take the guns,' Nolan said," and "Some one had blundered," add immensely to the spirit-stirring effect of the poem.

Lord Raglan was bitterly grieved by the blunder committed, and its consequences. A controversy on the subject subsequently sprang up between Lord Lucan, Lord Cardigan, and the commander-in-chief, which was carried into Parliament, and was not ended for several years.

This charge of the Light Brigade pretty much ended the battle of Balaclava. The Russians kept possession of all that they had won for some hours. The battle began before dawn, and the English fought fasting until after dark, when rum and biscuit were served out to them.

The Russians retired that night, having gained nothing by their battle. They had intended to surprise the English, and to force their way between the two parts of the allied army. All the advantage they had gained was gained over the Turks.

The next day an attack (called sometimes the first battle of Inkerman) was made upon the English, but the Russians were repulsed.

On November 5 the Russian army, having been joined by the czar's sons, the Grand Dukes Michael and Constantine, made another supreme effort. This is called the battle of Inkerman, and is the last of the great battles fought around Sebastopol. Thenceforward the military operations were those of bombardment rather than of battle.

This battle of Inkerman began also before the gray dawn of a November day (the day of the great storm which wrecked the " Prince "), and it was fought fasting by the English. But the surprise intended by the Russians failed. Their loss was enormous. The battle was fought by both French and English serving together; indeed the French in one brilliant charge were led by an English general. By half-past three it was all over, and the whole force of the Russians had retired beyond the Tchernaya, the river which empties into the estuary on which Sebastopol is situated. Eight thousand English and six thousand French were engaged in the battle of Inkerman; the Russian force was estimated by Lord Raglan at fifty thousand.

It was said that the Russians killed wounded English soldiers on the field. This being represented under a flag of truce to the authorities in Sebastopol, the reply was "that it could only have been done in individual instances, and that it must be remembered that the Russians were much exasperated by the destruction during the bombardment of one of the churches in Sebastopol."

Meantime a change of commanders had taken place among the French. Poor Saint-Arnaud had been desperately ill, as we have seen, on the voyage to Eupatoria. On landing, his extraordinary power of conquering bodily pain enabled him to seem to many as well as ever.

After the camp was formed he was attacked by cholera. Of this he was cured, but it left him no strength to stand the next attack of his chronic malady. On leaving France the Emperor Napoleon had given him General Trochu as chief of staff to advise him, Saint-Arnaud having had no experience in the command of a large army. But the emperor was secretive, and loved hidden ways. He had also given General Canrobert a commission (which was to be kept a profound secret until necessity called for its disclosure), appointing him to succeed Marshal Saint-Arnaud, in case that commander should be disabled.

The day before landing at Eupatoria, Canrobert, believing his chief to be dangerously ill, told him of this commission. Saint-Arnaud acquiesced in silence. When his next terrible attack came on it was necessary that he should have a conference with the English commander. He braced himself rigidly in his chair, and went through the interview with fortitude; but Lord Raglan, as he left him, remarked to a staff-officer that the French commander was dying. The next day he was too ill to do more than say: " Send for Canrobert."

Canrobert took the command. The dying marshal was carried on board a French man-of-war, a priest attending him. He had been on board only a few hours when he breathed his last. "He died *en chrétien*" said his spiritual adviser, and it was true that, reckless and dissolute as had been his life, he had never been a scoffer. He had also tender family affections. His last act on the morning of his embarkation had been to send his carriage and horses as a present to General Bosquet who had been his personal enemy.

General Canrobert had commanded the French troops Dec. 2, 1851, in the massacre on the Boulevard, but this was the only stain upon his reputation. He was red-faced, blunt, and soldierly, — a great contrast to the Parisian type of the Frenchman in Saint-Arnaud. " Poor Saint-Arnaud! I shall miss him, and regret him," said the kindly Lord

Raglan; "he was always friendly and pleasant in his intercourse with me."

And now, all the battles being over, nothing remained for the armies but the bombardment, the bleak winter, the chilling winds, the scanty fuel, the insufficient clothing — endurance, and still endurance, with work in the deep mud of the trenches, and the never ending roar of the round shot and the shells.

This terrible suffering from sickness, starvation, bitter cold, and over-work, lasted from October, 1854, to the end of February, 1855. By that time stores and supplies had come in in great quantities, and a railroad from Balaclava to the heights, carried them up to the English encampment. After this the foes to be contended with were the Russians, the mud, and the climate of the Crimea.

We must never forget that the French were so posted that their supplies could be landed near their camp. Besides which, the English army lay between their army and the Russians. The French could not be attacked until the English line was pierced. Therefore all attacks fell first upon the British.

"As soon as a change of temperature checked the ravages of the cholera," says the staff officer already quoted, "the wet set in, bringing a new train of diseases. Horrible cramps seized those exposed sometimes for nights in succession in the trenches. In their ragged garments and with feet almost bare, the soldiers paced the wet mud, or, wrapped in a single blanket, lay in holes, which they dug behind the batteries, shivering the livelong night. When relieved they crept back, not to the comfort of warm fires, and hot coffee, and sound sleep, for fuel was so scanty that it had to be searched for by the soldier, and sometimes brought miles in his arms before he could cook his ration; and the coffee was issued unroasted, and unground, so that it was perfectly useless. All the wearied soldier off duty had to seek was the bleak shelter of his tent."

In December and January the sick in the English camp

numbered as many as thirty-nine hundred in one day, and was never less than two thousand; besides all those who were in hospital at Balaclava, or Scutari, or had been sent home to England. No wonder work fell heavily on those who were not sick; no wonder that since the trenches must be held at any cost, the same men sometimes had to man them night after night because there were no others.[1]

A force of working men was collected in England to labor in the trenches and to lay the railroad about six miles from Balaclava to the English position. Before this work could be accomplished all necessaries had to be brought painfully from Balaclava. Day after day men and horses, enfeebled by hardship, traversed the roads clogged by mire and snow, to and fro between the seashore and the encampment. Sometimes the soldiers walked there and back, twelve miles, to get their rations, and did not break their fast till late in the day. The cavalry had to bring up their forage on their horses. A horse could carry a truss of hay, a wagon five or six trusses, but it required ten horses to draw it loaded, owing to the depth of the mud.

"Let the reader," says the staff-officer, "imagine in the coldest days of an English winter, the poorest family he has ever known, whose food is just sufficient to sustain existence, whose fuel is mere stubble and trash picked up upon neighboring commons and hedges, who lie down hungry and cold at night to shiver till cheerless morning, and then remember that to all these privations must be added want of shelter from drenching rain and sleet and frost, and he will be able to realize the condition of the troops in front of Sebastopol after the end of October."

[1] It was in this service that Capt. Hedley Vicars was killed, the Christian hero whose biography stirred many hearts in England and America. The public also was greatly interested in a book called "English Hearts and Hands," an account written by Miss Kate Marsh, daughter of a well known rector of Leamington, describing mission work among the navvies collected at Sydenham to be sent out to the Crimea and relieve the soldiers from the work of digging in the trenches. — E. W. L.

The blame for this lies chiefly with that press and that public which forced the ministry of the day to oblige Lord Raglan, against his better judgment, to undertake an enterprise of which no one knew the hardships, and for which his army was entirely unprepared. Every one in England had expected that the gallant armies would carry Russia as it were by a *coup de main*, and by Christmas, after a glorious peace, be safe home on their own shores. Therefore no preparations had been made for winter comforts or for winter clothing. Even the men's overcoats were lost in the wreck of the ship that carried them; many were without drawers, flannel shirts, or new clothes till January, when these articles began to arrive in a profusion almost as embarrassing to the commissariat as their absence; for by this time the poor horses had so died off that to get stores to the camp seemed beyond their powers. The ships lay in the harbor with clothing to warm and huts to shelter the perishing troops, — succors no more available than if they had been a thousand miles away.

"Our troops," the staff-officer continues, "are paying the price of being Englishmen in this terrible winter. They are brave and indomitable, and will therefore be victorious; but few and ill-provided for war, and therefore sorely distressed."

Three large hospitals had been established by the English on the coast of Asia Minor, nearly opposite Constantinople. To these hospitals were sent Miss Nightingale and her staff of nurses. On her arrival at Scutari she found at first absolutely nothing, — no beds, no comforts; and vessels were in sight bringing the wounded from the battle of the Alma. There were plenty of medical stores, but they could not be procured without orders from the proper officer; and he was away. Then came in her power as a woman. She took the responsibility. She ordered a party of soldiers to break open the doors, stood in the entrance, and saw everything distributed herself, and, by the time the sick were landed, all was ready for them. Miss Par-

FLORENCE NIGHTINGALE.

thenope Nightingale and Miss Florence Nightingale were born respectively at Naples and at Florence. Miss Parthenope married Sir Harry Verney, the papers of whose family she recently edited. Long before the Crimean War these ladies were known as foremost in good works. Men, themselves distinguished in philanthropic efforts, reverenced and admired them.[1]

I think the general idea of lady nurses in military hospitals or in the rear of armies is that they nurse the sick and tend the wounded. These duties belong generally to hospital stewards; the ladies are rather the housekeepers, the administrators, the care-takers. Theirs is the feminine place in the hospitals. Like their less distinguished sisters, they " rule the house." They see to the cooking, they see that each man gets what the doctor has ordered for him.

[1] I feel myself permitted to transcribe a letter written in those days to an American friend by Miss Parthenope Nightingale:—

EMBLEY PARK, ROMSEY, November 20, 1854.

MY DEAR MRS. B——,—It is very long since we have had any communication; but I cannot help, now that my sister has set forth on what one of her friends calls the true crusade, writing you a few words. Has it reached you across the Atlantic that government has sent her out on a mission to the hospitals at Scutari? I think it will be shortest to send you Mr Herbert's letter, and a little sketch of her, written we know not by whom, but very correct. The letter was published without our leave, but it saves me so much explanation that I must send it, for I am overdone with writing We have been organizing a second detachment of nurses in case she writes for them; and the quantity of offers of all kinds (old linen, books, money, knitted things, etc.) to any amount have been extraordinary; as also nurses of all grades and kinds,— 367 was the last number I set down. From the highest to the lowest, the enthusiasm for her has been something wonderful; even the railroads refused to be paid for her boxes. We have refused to give her picture to the newspapers; but they say that fancy portraits have been made of her, so that we shall perhaps repent ourselves; but we did not like putting her as it were into the glare of day. Dear Mrs. B——, I ought perhaps to excuse this monotheme; but I feel sure you will be interested about her. With the united kind regards of my father and mother to yourself and Mr. B——,

Believe me yours sincerely,

PARTHO NIGHTINGALE.

They keep the supplies of comforts under their care, and see to their proper distribution. The laundries are under their supervision. They have everything ready for the arrival of the sick; they see that every convalescent goes away comfortably provided. They perform all offices of kindness for men who are sick or dying, cheer them, write letters for them, stand by them, if necessary, in supreme moments, direct everything in obedience to the doctors, see that nothing is left undone. Probably, when Miss Nightingale reached Scutari, there was no organization among her nurses. There were about forty women with her. Eight were Protestant ladies, ten were Sisters of Charity, and the rest were attendants, or professional nurses, who had had experience.

By the end of January there were five thousand sick in these three English hospitals. Each day in the largest hospital about sixty died. The dead were sewed up in their blankets, laid in the dead-house, carried in country carts to the burial ground, where each day's dead were laid in one pit, and the English chaplain read the burial service over them.

The hospitals were well heated, for that winter of 1854–1855 was especially cold. It seems as if the Winter King was always on the side of Russia. Hospital supplies too were abundant and of the best kind.

"In the great kitchen of the great hospital," says one who visited them, "rice pudding, manufactured on a large scale, was transferred, smoking, by an enormous ladle to the destined plates; beef tea and mutton broth were being cooked in large caldrons such as the witches danced round in Macbeth, and flocks of poultry were simmering into boiled fowls or chicken broth."

It is pleasant to look upon this picture after thinking of the privations in the camp before Sebastopol. Some convalescents were sent back to the army; but, alas, few of them that winter supported a renewal of their hardships, and nearly all died.

In the middle of March a most surprising piece of news reached Lord Raglan at Sebastopol. "The Emperor Nicholas is dead. Reliable," was all that was said by the telegraphic message. The English commander could not believe it; but the next day came the same news to General Canrobert.

He was gone, — the Agamemnon among European kings, — taller by head and shoulders, bodily, than the rest, and taller metaphorically. He was a man who, until his unhappy quarrel with England, had aimed to stand before the world as a man of honor. His mighty heart had been broken. He may not physically have died of a broken heart (few people do); but he died of the war, its disappointments, its anxieties, its worries.

The feeling of the mass of the Russian people toward the Emperor Nicholas was almost the awe and reverent affection mankind might feel for a demigod. His nobles chafed under the sternness of his administration; but to Russians in general he seemed a kind of divine personage, whose will could not be disputed without impiety. There was no nobler moment in the life of Nicholas than that in which he braved a howling mob who were accusing the Poles and the doctors of being the authors of the cholera. He went down into the midst of them, and suddenly throwing back his large cloak, exclaimed in his commanding voice: "Wretches! down on your knees, — down every one of you, and pray the Father in heaven to pardon those sins that have brought the pestilence upon you; for it is those sins that have brought it into your homes!"

His courage never forsook him. His mind was vigorous to the last; but his physical powers gave way under the accumulation and complication of his responsibilities. He was head of the Greek Church in Russia, and he conscientiously believed himself to be the heaven-appointed protector of Greek Christians in the land of the Infidel. To him the war with Turkey (and the Crimean War itself) was a holy war, and with this feeling he inspired his people.

Throughout the whole of his arduous career he was actuated and upheld by a sense of duty. He lived and died in harness. He sacrificed himself continually to the position in which he thought he ought to move. If there was a fire in his capital the first man there upon the coldest January night would be the emperor. Never does he seem to have bestowed a thought on his own comfort as a man when it came in the way of what he considered his dignity as the czar of Russia.

He rose regularly at seven o'clock in all seasons, and took a cold shower-bath; then he slipped on an old military overcoat which he used as a dressing-gown, and looked over his papers. That done he took a cup of *café noir*, dressed, and walked round the palace in a sort of tour of inspection. In his own country no man ever saw him out of uniform. The only relaxation of dress that he ever permitted himself was sometimes in his study to take off his epaulets, or to unbutton the tight collar of his coat. At ten o'clock he always visited the empress, and passed half an hour with his family. He was faithful to the motto: "Punctuality is the politeness of princes." No one ever found him one minute behind time, but he allowed five minutes' grace to others. At two o'clock he went out, sometimes in a drosky, sometimes in a sleigh, according to the season, but more often on foot, and generally alone, wrapped in the large gray cloak worn by Russian officers. Many were his adventures in the streets, though it was forbidden to speak to him.

Smoking he detested and discouraged, and would not allow a cigar on the streets of St. Petersburg; though one judges from the writings of Count Tolstoi that elsewhere the Russian officers smoked like other men.

After dinner, at which he never sat more than half an hour, the emperor played for a while with his children. The only amusements he cared for in winter were the theatre and masked balls, and in summer, walks and drives with his family. He painted well himself in the style of

Wouvermans, but for any such employment he had very little time.

At eleven he usually went to bed, but would never allow himself to sleep until he had looked over every paper laid upon his table. Often at night, even in the coldest weather, he would get up and go out to inspect the guard-house and the sentries.

About the age of forty he was in all the splendor of manly beauty, — "Jupiter and Apollo combined," says one of his admirers. He was considerably over six feet in height, his features were regular, his mouth was by turns severe or sweet, his voice magnificent. His walk was particularly fine. But he had no personal vanity, and it was hard to get him to spend money on his clothes. He said "extravagance meant robbery of the poor." A lady once said to him at a masked ball: "Do you know, Sire, that you are the handsomest man in Russia?" "I did not know it, madam," he replied; "but if I am that is nobody's concern but that of the empress."

He was capable of storms of passion, and also capable of making generous apologies when his anger had carried him too far.

His mother had told him once that he must keep well with England. He did keep well with her for twenty years; and he broke with her unwillingly, I cannot but think under circumstances of exceeding provocation. His great heart broke under the strain. During the last months of his life he was haunted by a dread of hereditary insanity; but although he became nervous and irritable, his mind was unclouded to the last. He made his preparations for death with perfect orderliness and composure. It is said that when the supreme moment approached he requested all those about him to leave his chamber that he might meet the great enemy face to face alone.

He was succeeded by his son, Alexander II., a much milder man, who was sincerely anxious for the welfare of his people. He became the emancipator of the serfs, the promoter of reforms, and was in the end the victim of Nihilists.

"At the beginning of March, 1855, winter in the Crimea seemed to have departed," says my staff-officer; "only a few cold days lingered in scattered order in its rear. The health of the troops was steadily improving. New batteries had been admirably constructed and were connected with others by long lines of trenches, and there were many new and efficient guns."

Prince Mentzikoff died at about the same time as his great master, whom he had so largely helped to bring into the war.

In order to understand the future military operations of the siege it will be desirable, if we can, to get a good idea of the defences. I repeat that Sebastopol is not a walled city. It was defended by redoubts of great strength, the principal of which were the Redan and the Malakoff. These were called by the Russians the Fourth and Fifth Bastions. A little in front of the Malakoff was the Mamelon, a low, round-topped hill. The English had proposed to occupy it, but the Russians got it first and crowned it with batteries.

On Easter Sunday, April 8, Sebastopol was bombarded furiously by the French and by the English, with a view to an assault, as was believed, by the army. But though many Russian guns were silenced and disabled, the bombardment produced very little effect.

Up to this time life in Sebastopol had gone on much as usual. The bands played of an evening on the Parade, the shops were open, the city was not invested. There was free communication by the great high-road with St. Petersburg and Moscow. Letters came and went, and food and reinforcements came in. But after May, 1855, things changed. There was food in plenty, and officers were arriving from St. Petersburg and departing, but the city was in ruins. The hospitals were filled and badly served, so that the sights and smells in them were sickening. The guns in the redoubts were chiefly manned by sailors, the masts of whose ships (those ships in which they had taken such pride) were sticking out of the water at the entrance of the harbor. In each redoubt there were bomb-proofs with underground chambers hollowed out for the officer on duty, and also as sleeping-places for his subordinates. These redoubts were reached from the city through trenches so deep in mud that the men generally preferred walking at all risks on the path above them. The Russians called their enemy "He." The rank and file fully believed themselves engaged in a Holy War, against "Him" for their Greek Church and their beloved emperor.

What we have learned to call Nihilism in Russia exists only among the educated or half-educated classes. It has no hold on the peasantry. The czar has been always considered, — and, to a large extent, is considered still — their father, and their friend.

By the middle of May the English, who had received new cannon which carried farther than the Russian guns, were doing terrible execution in Sebastopol. "'He' is firing straight through everything," said one Russian soldier to another. "His shells even go over us into the bay." With all the horrors of war in the foreground, in the background the bay had hitherto lain calm and in peace, with its forest of masts, the English and French fleets in the offing; and in Sebastopol itself were the white batteries, the barracks, the aqueduct, the public buildings.

Touching pictures of life in Sebastopol during the siege may be found in a little volume written by Count Lyof Tolstoi immediately after the time treated of, but translated into English only a few years since, and not, I imagine, very widely known. The book is called simply "Sebastopol," and is the first work that brought Tolstoi into notice in Russia.

I have said little as yet of the change of commanders. Perhaps the most surprising thing about the Crimean War was its lack of generalship. The soldiers of the allied armies were brought face to face with heights, redoubts, divisions of the enemy, and told to assault them, to repulse them, or to cut their way through them, and they did so; but no English general showed generalship, though Lord Raglan had many other noble qualities. No French general showed generalship. General Bosquet (afterwards displaced) seems to have been the ablest among them. Still less did any of the Russian generals distinguish themselves, (if we except their young general of engineers, General Todleben, who was a German). The most distinguished looking general was General La Marmora, who with his five thousand Sardinian soldiers, arrived early in the spring to join the allied army.

The Sardinians were not fighting from any hatred to the Russians. They were there to win for their little Piedmont a place among the nations of western Europe. Their valor was to form a stepping-stone for regenerated Italy. They commanded general admiration, but their ranks were sorely thinned by the cholera. Among its victims was the beloved elder brother of their general. The Turks were made far less account of than the Sardinians. Even Omar Pasha, who came with his gallant little army from the Danube in this spring of 1855, was thrust into the background. Lord Raglan could not fail to remember that Turks, in his first encounter with the Russians before Sebastopol, had lost him six guns.

But to return to the generals. Saint-Arnaud died in November, 1854. He was succeeded by General Canrobert. Canrobert was not general enough for the place. The Emperor Napoleon III. had tried to get back some of the grand old African generals whom he had insulted and outraged in 1851 by imprisoning them at Mazas; but they one and all replied that they would not serve him against a foreign foe, though if ever he needed their swords to defend France he might count upon their willingness to draw them.

Canrobert, after some months of experience, arrived at

the conclusion that the commander-in-chief of the allied armies should be one and indivisible. He returned to France in the spring of 1855, and expressed this opinion to his emperor. Lord Raglan therefore retained the supreme command; no new French commander-in-chief was appointed, but General Pelissier, the same who had distinguished himself in Africa, both by his fighting qualities and by smothering his enemies, was made general of the French forces. Canrobert had returned to Paris shortly before Queen Victoria's visit to the French emperor in the spring of 1855; we read of him as sitting next to her at dinner, having just come, as he said, "from the trenches," and telling her stories of her soldiers, whom he greatly admired, and of the vicissitudes of the war.

The Mamelon, as I have said, was a little round green hill, five hundred yards in advance of the Malakoff redoubt, with which it was connected by trenches. On June 7 an attack was made upon it by the French. "The Zouaves," says an English officer, "went up like hounds." In seven minutes and a half they were inside the works, but were driven out again. They attacked it a second time. Then the Russians spiked their guns and retired, as it were, by the back door. It was not until daybreak that the French could feel sure of their prize. The next day there was an armistice to bury the dead. Here is an account of it as told by Count Tolstoi. His account is very nearly the same as that by Mr. Russell, the English war correspondent, which, however, is not so picturesque as that by the Russian writer: —

"White flags are flying on our fortifications, and on the French intrenchments. In the blossom-covered valley mutilated bodies clothed in blue or gray, with bare feet, lie in heaps, and men are carrying them off to place them in carts. The air is poisoned by the odor of the corpses. Crowds of people pour out of Sebastopol and out of the French camp, to witness this spectacle. The different sides meet each other on this ground with gifts and courtesies, and kindly curiosity. 'What a miserable work we are carrying on,' says a Russian to a French officer; and eager to carry on the conversation, he continues, 'It was hot last night, was it not?'— pointing to the corpses. 'Oh! monsieur, it is frightful. But what fine fellows your Russian soldiers are! It is a pleasure to fight such fellows as that.' 'It must be owned your fellows are up to the mark too,' replies the Russian cavalry-man, with a salute. Yes! flags float over the bastions, and on the intrenchments, the brilliantly shining sun is setting in the blue waters which ripple and sparkle beneath its golden rays. Thousands of people assemble, look at each other, chat, and laugh. People who are Christians, who profess to obey the great law of love, are looking at their own work, and do not think of falling on their knees to repent before Him who gave them life, and with life has implanted the dread of death, and the love of the good and beautiful. They do not embrace each other like brothers, and shed tears of joy and happiness. Well, we Russians must at least take consolation in the thought that we did not begin the war, and are only defending our country! The white flags are lowered; the engines of death and suffering thunder again. Once more a flood of innocent blood is shed, and groans and curses again rise up from earth to heaven."

The great attack on the Malakoff and the Redan, the two most important redoubts was to take place on June 18, the anniversary of the Battle of Waterloo. The English were to attack the Redan, the French the Malakoff. The French, having taken the Mamelon Vert, were much nearer to the Malakoff than the English to the Redan.

The English attack was led on by Colonel Gwilt, a brave and gallant officer, but scaling ladders had not been provided. The attack failed on the Redan; the French failed too at the Malakoff.

The disappointment in the camp was bitter. All the English had been sure that a sudden attack would carry the Redan. It was evident that it had not been battered enough, or enough disabled. The only thing to be done was to batter it some more.

But the failure of the attack on the 18th of June broke Lord Raglan down. He had been vehemently assailed in Parliament all winter, and harassed and hindered in every way. It would seem as if he had had enough to do to take Sebastopol, but to this was added the necessity of keeping up relations of amity with the French, of combating imperative and impracticable ideas sent out by the emperor Napoleon (who at one time was vehemently urged by his wife to go out to the Crimea, and himself command his army), and the necessity of parrying attacks at home, and of bearing the pressure put upon him by the home ministry.

He was taken ill on the Tuesday after the 18th of June, and died on the Thursday following of cholera, but his death was really owing to an exhausted frame, incapable of resisting an attack of illness. His death caused sincere grief to the army. His body, with all military honors, was carried on board the "Caradoc," and the command devolved upon his chief-of-staff, General James Simpson, a commonplace, meritorious, well-meaning officer.

As the summer advanced sickness increased among the men, and the mortality among the generals, French, English, and Sardinian, was very great. Wet weather seemed to bring cholera; heat, dysentery. Miss Nightingale came to Balaclava and there reorganized the hospitals. In one day the surgeons made requisitions for six tons of hospital supplies.

The next event was the small battle of the Tchernaya. The allies won the battle, and the Sardinians distinguished themselves.

All July and August the cannonading and the sickness, and the work in the trenches went steadily on. One of the great torments of this time was the plague of flies. The hard-hearted Pharaoh and his people could not have been more beset by them. They did not, like other flies, go to rest at night, and the sick suffered terribly from this plague, while the well were all night distracted by it.

Lord Palmerston was by this time prime minister of England, and he sent out a sanitary commission to report upon the state of the encampment. But it was "a far cry" from sending a commission three thousand miles to report, and the means of getting the evils it reported remedied. However, the improvement in everything had been great since the winter, and heat may more easily be borne than cold.

When one thinks of the state of things in the Crimea it is sometimes hard to say who were the besiegers, which were the besieged. The allied armies, especially the English, lay hemmed in between the fortifications of Sebastopol and a Russian army. This army held the heights of Inkerman and all the north side of Sebastopol or Severnaya, with its great Star Fort. Severnaya was connected with the city by a bridge of boats.

On Sept. 5, 1855, the allies again attacked the Redan and the Malakoff. With their superior cannon they had succeeded in destroying many of the guns in those redoubts, and in shattering much of their masonry. All summer the French had been pushing their lines of trenches from the Mamelon nearer and nearer to the Malakoff, so that by Sept. 5 they were only two hundred yards from it. The English had a very much longer distance to charge over in the open to reach the Redan, and that distance was commanded by batteries placed in certain stone quarries, which were held by the Russians. For that reason, and because of the stony nature of the ground, it had been impossible to advance the English trenches nearer to the point of attack.

We all know the result. The French captured the Malakoff; the English did *not* take the Redan. They were preparing to renew the attack the next morning when they found that there was no enemy to oppose them. Sebastopol, — that is, its southern portion — had been abandoned during the night. General Todleben did not choose to waste life in defending a place no longer tenable. He had stolen away across the bridge of boats. All the army of Russia was now concentrated at Severnaya. Never was anything more masterly. But Count Tolstoi, who was there, shall tell us about the attack on the Malakoff and the midnight retreat, which surprised the Russian soldiers as much as it did the allies: —

"Two Russian officers in the middle of Sept. 5 stood on Telegraph Hill, a high spot within the Russian lines in the Northern quarter of Sebastopol. The sun gleamed down on the bay, the sea was covered with ships at anchor, the water rippled and danced merrily under the sun's rays. A light breeze filled the sails of small boats plying in the harbor. There stood Sebastopol seen from the heights, apparently little changed by all it had undergone during the siege, with its unfinished church, its monuments, its quay, its boulevard, which looked like a band of green passed over the hill, its elegant library building, its little basins in the harbor, its forest of masts, its picturesque aqueducts, while over all floated clouds of bluish tint made by the powder-smoke, which from time to time were lighted up by the red flame from the firing. On the horizon, where the smoke of a steamer traced a black line, white lines of cloud were rising, precursors of a wind-storm. Along the whole line of the fortifications, but especially on the heights toward the left, spurted swift vivid flashes of light, though it was broad daylight, followed by plumes of white smoke, which assuming various forms, rose, extended, covered the sky with sombre, hazy tints. These jets of smoke came forth on all sides, — from the hills, from the hostile batteries of the allies, and from the city. The noises of the firing shook the air with a continuous roar. Toward noon these smoke-puffs became rarer and rarer, and the changes of color in the haze less frequent. 'Do you notice that the Second Bastion is no longer replying?' said the huzzar officer on horseback to his comrade. 'It must have been silenced. It is terrible!' 'Yes; and the Malakoff has slackened fire,' the other answered. He was looking through his field glass. 'They are firing straight on the Kornikoff battery, and *that* too is not replying.' 'You will see,' said the other, 'I was right; toward noon they will cease firing. It is always so. Let us go down to breakfast.' 'Wait — hush!' the other man replied, with agitation in his voice, still looking through his glass. There was a movement in the trenches. 'They are advancing in close column!' he cried. 'See there! — see! how they come out of the trenches!' Both officers could in fact see with the naked eye black spots going down the hill into the ravine, and proceeding from the French batteries toward the Russian bastions. In the foreground, in front of the French 'batteries, black spots, very near their own lines, could be seen by the Russian officers. Suddenly from different parts of the Malakoff spurted white plumes of smoke, and vivid flashes, while a lively fusillade could be heard, like the patter of heavy rain on window panes. The French lines advanced toward the Malakoff wrapped in smoke, drawing nearer and nearer. The fusillade increased in violence, the smoke belched out at shorter and at shorter intervals, extending rapidly along the line in a long light-lilac colored cloud. All noises mingled together in one continuous roar. 'It is an assault,' said the officer, pale with emotion, as he handed his glass to his companion. Cossacks and officers on horseback were seen galloping along the road, preceding the commander-in-chief in his carriage. All faces expressed painful emotion. 'It is impossible they can take the Malakoff!' cried the officer on horseback. 'God in heaven! Look now. See the flag!' cried the other, taking his eyes from the glass. 'The French flag,' he exclaimed, choked with emotion, 'is flying from the Malakoff!' 'Impossible!' exclaimed the other."

The attack had been a surprise to the soldiers in the Malakoff. Those who had been all night in the trenches were resting in the stifling bomb-proofs of the redoubt, while the sailors worked the guns.

"Toward eight o'clock in the evening," continues Count Tolstoi, "all the soldiers and all the inhabitants of Sebastopol were crossing the harbor, some by the bridge of boats, and some in steamers. The firing had ceased everywhere. Stars sparkled in the sky as they had done the night before, but a strong wind was blowing and the bay was rough. From some of the redoubts flames flashed up close to the earth, preceding explosions that shook the ground, and sent stones and black objects of strange shapes into the air. Something near the docks was on fire, and a red flame was reflected on the water. The bridge of boats, covered with people, was lighted by fires from the Nicholas battery. A great sheet of flame seemed to spread over the water; it lighted up the under side of a cloud of smoke which hovered over it. As on the preceding evening, the lights of the hostile fleet sparkled far out to sea, calm and defiant. 'See! they have burned our barracks!' cries a soldier, sighing. 'How many of our people are dead, — and dead to no purpose, for the French have got possession!' 'Do you think they will long enjoy it? Do you think they will lead an easy life there?' cries another soldier. 'Wait a bit; we will take all our redoubts back again. We may lose more men, but, as sure as God is holy, if the emperor orders it, we will get back everything. Do you think things have been left as they were in Sebastopol? They will find nothing but naked walls. The fortifications are blown up. *He* has planted his flag on the Malakoff, it is true, but he won't dare to go into the city. Give us time! Give us time!' Along the whole line of the defences of Sebastopol, where for nearly twelve months ardent and energetic life had been active, there was not left one single living soul. The walls, the works, the timbers were all falling with a din. Torn by a recent explosion, crushed bodies of French and Russians lay under broken beams; heavy cannon, overturned into the moat by terrible force, lay half-buried in the earth, forever dumb. Bombs, balls, splinters of beams lay everywhere. The bomb-proofs were rent open, and corpses, in blue or gray overcoats, were lighted up by the red explosions that every instant shot into the air. The army of Sebastopol, like a sea whose liquid mass, agitated and uneasy, spreads and overflows its banks after some great commotion, moved slowly in the midnight into the impenetrable gloom, undulating over the bridge that crossed the bay, proceeding toward Severnaya, leaving behind the places where so many brave men had fallen during eleven months' defence against an enemy twice as strong as the garrison of the besieged city,[1] in obedience to an order, received that very day, to retire without more fighting. The first impression made by this order weighed heavily upon the Russians' hearts; then fear of pursuit became their dominant feeling. The soldiers, accustomed for so many months to fight in the strongholds they were abandoning, felt themselves without shelter as they quitted them. Uneasily they crowded together in masses at the entrance to the bridge, which was lifted up and down by violent gusts of wind. Though the attention of each man was distracted by a thousand details, the impulse of self-preservation was now strongest everywhere, the desire to fly as soon as possible from that fatal spot. Arrived at the end of the bridge each soldier, with very few exceptions, removed his hat and crossed himself. But besides this feeling was another, deeper, more poignant, a feeling akin to repentance, to shame, to hatred; for it was with inexpressible

---

[1] Count Tolstoi makes no account of the Army of the Crimea which hemmed in the besiegers on the land side.

bitterness of heart that each man sighed, and uttered threats against the enemy, and as he reached the north side cast a last look upon abandoned Sebastopol."

All this happened on the night of September 5, 1855, and with the abandonment of Sebastopol the war may be said to have been over. It had been the intention of the Russians to blow up the whole city, but happily the destruction was less than they had planned.

There was no armistice until February 28, when a month's truce, while plenipotentiaries deliberated on terms of peace, was given. The allied armies, under Generals Pelissier and Simpson, went again into winter quarters. They did not dare to encamp in Sebastopol, for it was all in ruins, and for many a day after it was deserted it was liable to terrible explosions. The moment the last soldier or inhabitant had crossed the bridge of boats to Severnaya the boats had been disconnected and floated away. About sixty drunken soldiers were made prisoners in Sebastopol, and a considerable number of sick and wounded were in the hospitals in a dreadful condition. Of course, skirmishing went on all winter, and the Russians in their turn from the Star Fort bombarded Sebastopol, but little was done except by a naval expedition sent to capture the forts that guarded the Isthmus of Perekop, which unites the Crimea with southern Russia. There was also the brilliant episode of the defence of Kars in Asia Minor, where the Turkish garrison was commanded by a young English officer, Captain Williams.

Peace at last was signed in Paris.

The last Englishman killed in Sebastopol perished while trying to escape after firing a mine that was to bring down an unsafe building; the last Frenchman was killed in a duel with a brother officer.

The last corps of English embarked at Balaclava July 12, 1856; the last Frenchmen a few days later. The armies had accumulated the incredible number of twenty-eight thousand camp followers, for whose transportation their governments had also to provide.

Queen Victoria reviewed and decorated her returned soldiers. It was a campaign of glory to soldiers, not to generals, and few of the latter received any honors. The most brilliant officer, I should say, had been Sir Colin Campbell, afterward covered with glory at Lucknow; and Chinese Gordon was there, a very efficient officer but as yet unknown to history. General Pelissier was made marshal of France, and Duke of Malakoff, and was subsequently appointed ambassador to England by his emperor.

It is said that when England goes into a war and comes out of it victorious her first act is to surrender to somebody else all that she had fought for; and very small were her gains in the Crimean War, in comparison to her losses and expenses. Russia was compelled to demolish her fortresses on the Black Sea, to open that sea to the trade of Western Europe, to agree that no war vessels should pass the Dardanelles or Bosphorus; and Turkey made promises (on paper) that Christians should be admitted to equal rights with Mussulmans in her European dominions. But the signature of a sultan or his representative is powerless against the set of public opinion, the ancient traditions of a haughty race, and the authority of the Koran. The autonomy of Wallachia and Moldavia was confirmed, and they were made into a principality, with Prince Charles of Hohenzollern as their ruler.

The Sardinians gained the recognition and the position they had fought for. The French emperor gained the English alliance, and his complete admission into the circle of European royalties, to which it may be said Queen Victoria introduced him as her good friend and ally. But England — what had she?

Russia was weakened, and the dangerous classes have profited by that weakness to make her the festering sore upon the body politic of Europe. She was left isolated and angry, and ever since has been making such advances in Asia that when she is ready some day she may harass

England in her Indian possessions. As to France, she looks now-a-days to Russia as her ally, and should the often predicted war with Germany break out, it will be France and Russia, against that very Austria and Prussia who refused to take sides in the Crimean War.

CHAPTER VIII.

THE EMPEROR-LIBERATOR, AND HIS REFORMS.

THE Emperor Nicholas, notwithstanding his stern character and all the hard names it was the fashion in England to call him, was a true lover of his country. He said on his deathbed to Alexander, his son and heir: "Save your country. All my care, all my efforts have been directed to the good of Russia. I desired to take upon myself all the dangers, all the difficulties, so that I might leave you an empire tranquil, well-organized, and happy. Providence has decided otherwise, for at what a time, and under what circumstances, am I dying! You will find your way difficult!"

He had indeed left to his country a heritage of woe. He had tried to gather the fruit he coveted, and it proved beyond his reach; he had miscalculated obstacles; he had relied on a military organization that had proved imperfect, and he had met a fall almost as disastrous for Russia as Sedan was afterwards for France. His empire, exhausted by the war, was morally as well as materially a wreck; his treasury was empty; his navy self-destroyed; hostile war-vessels were cruising in his waters. An hour of great darkness had fallen on the empire when Alexander II. mounted the Russian throne.

As soon as possible Alexander, with the prudence shown afterwards by M. Thiers, made peace with the invaders. Nor were the terms very hard. England's demands on a brave foe are never excessive. The Emperor Napoleon III. was weary of the war, which had lasted too long to please one whose policy was based upon surprises; and the moment peace was made, the new Russian emperor devoted himself to the task of consolidating and regenerating his empire. It is said that his desire to reform had been stimulated by his perusal of the early novels of Tourguenieff.

Russia was at that time "filled with antiquated ideas and absurd traditions, conflicting prejudices, and opposing interests. She had millions of serfs and but few schools, miserable high-roads, and only six hundred miles of railroad."

At home and abroad everything was in ruins; not only the military system, but the administrative system of the State had given way under the strain.

The Emperor Alexander II. was born in 1818, one year before Queen Victoria. His father, the Grand Duke Nicholas, shortly before his birth had been in England, and had charmed the Princess Charlotte by his good looks and his good manners when he visited her at Claremont.

At the time of Alexander's birth neither his father nor himself had any prospect of ascending the Russian throne. Alexander I. had had no children, but his next heir was his brother Constantine, whose renunciation of hereditary royalty that he might marry a Polish wife no one could have anticipated.

Alexander II. far more resembled his uncle Alexander "the Blessed" than the stern autocrat his father. It is said that his mild disposition was a great disappointment and annoyance to the Emperor Nicholas, and that it cost him many a whipping from the imperial hand. His next brother, Constantine, was made of sterner stuff, and ventured, when they were grown to manhood, to flout and to annoy his elder brother.

There is an anecdote told in the books of the time of how the Emperor Nicholas was roused one day from his writing-table by a noise in the nursery, in the midst of which he could distinguish the words "Oh, don't!" and "Have mercy!" He found his heir the czarevitch on his back, and

EMPEROR ALEXANDER II.

his brother Constantine tightening a string around his throat, while the other four children stood around. On inquiring the meaning of this scene, he was told that they were playing at the murder of their grandfather the Emperor Paul. Nicholas at once punished the younger ones for any such amusement, and the czarevitch for having shrieked for mercy, which he said was unbecoming in a future czar.

Alexander, for thirty-seven years of his life, was treated as of no political importance. He was put into the army when a mere babe, and at ten years of age was made Hettman of the Cossacks. From that time his education was entrusted to the strictest disciplinarians that could be found among the officers of the guards. Only once did he obtain a tutor to whom he could attach himself, and *he* was soon removed for "liberalism." His other instructors treated him with such severity that he cherished a dread and aversion for them, even after he had grown to manhood and was married.

His marriage took place when he was twenty-three. His bride was the princess Marie of Darmstadt, aunt to the Prince Louis, who was husband of the Princess Alice of England. Princess Marie was a good woman, who bore her husband several children, but after the death of her eldest son the Grand Duke Nicholas she fell into such bad health that she found it impossible to live or breathe in St. Petersburg.

Till Alexander was thirty years old he was absolutely nothing but his stern father's aide-de-camp. His duty was to follow him wherever he went, at home, abroad, in the night-time to a fire, in the daytime to a review. When the Grand Duke Michael died (the Emperor Nicholas's youngest brother, who was very much of a savage) the czarevitch succeeded to some of his posts, among others to the superintendence of the military colleges. In this position he soon made himself greatly beloved by the boys, though old men of his father's school shook their heads at every relaxation of the severity of military discipline.

The love that Alexander acquired in those days by his acts of consideration and kindness stood him in good stead when engaged in his reforms; for, though the old military officers were against him, he had with him the younger men.

A writer in the "British Quarterly Review," speaking of Alexander a few years before his death, says:—

"The slightest, almost imperceptible breach of regulation in military uniform often led under Nicholas to the cashiering of a meritorious officer, while almost the first thing Alexander did on ascending the throne was to allow smoking, and to make the military dress as comfortable and as easy as possible. Nicholas used to interfere in the smallest details connected with everybody in his dominions; an officer or official wishing to marry was bound to write to his emperor. The smallest sentence of a magistrate had to be submitted for his approval, and every trifling item of local news in St. Petersburg was each day reported to him. Alexander put an end to almost all these absurdities as soon as the necessary reverence to the memory of his father would permit. When he had made up his mind to introduce a reform of any kind he summoned a committee of old and new men to consider it. If they could not agree he would send them an order to be quicker, or would fix a date by which time the work was to be done. But he expected it would be finished in a way to follow out his own ideas. There were times when he could take a sterner attitude. He had a way of letting his ideas (which were those of modern progress) Russify themselves, if we may coin a word; and in the beginning of his reign all young Russia was wildly enthusiastic and hopeful as to the changes he inaugurated. In the end many were disappointed, when the great reforms failed to produce such immediate results as they had hoped."

Nevertheless, during the twenty-seven years of his reign a marvellous amount of reform was set on foot, though most of it, thus far, has apparently failed to accomplish its desired end.

"Alexander was a despot, he could not be otherwise, but he was a kind-hearted, liberal-minded man. There was a great contrast between him and the stern, stiff, sergeant-major-like bearing of his father. Every inch of him bespoke the well-bred nobleman, very rich, very good-tempered, affectionate to his children, a man fond of a good dinner, of shooting, of hunting, and of making everybody comfortable, himself included."

But to return to the first days of his reign, and his earliest reforms. "No Russian," says a Russian writer in 1881, "asserts that the work of reform in Russia is complete. Of course there is still very much to be done. One reason for which we deplore Nihilist outrages is because they postpone reforms."

As soon as peace had been declared, and the war in the Crimea was brought to a close, the emperor issued a manifesto to his people, one sentence in which contained the keynote to his policy. He hoped, he said, that "by the combined efforts of the government and the people, the public adminstration would be improved, and that justice and mercy would reign in the courts of law."

It was the first time in Russian history that the people had been, even verbally, associated with the government.

A year later, on a visit to Moscow (the ancient capital of the empire), in an address to the Marshals of the Nobility, a sort of representative body chosen by the nobles themselves, he spoke first on the subject of serfage. "If serfdom is doomed," he said, "it is better that the necessary reform should come from above rather than from below." He therefore urged them freely to discuss the question with their brother nobles. "Every one seemed pleased, and there was no end," says a Russian, "of animated discussions and of brilliant plans."

In 1861 the Emancipation Act was completed, and received the emperor's signature. It gave liberty to twenty-three millions of serfs belonging to the nobles, in addition to thirty millions set at liberty on lands of the crown.

Great was the rejoicing throughout Russia, especially among the more enlightened classes. They were proud of their country, proud of their emperor, proud of their own spirit of self-sacrifice.

The Civil War in the United States began in April, 1861; the Emancipation Proclamation in Russia preceded it by about three weeks.

" Including crown peasants, nearly half the population of Russia were serfs; yet, without a sword being unsheathed, the great work was accomplished; by the simple mandate of the emperor serfdom ceased to exist within the limits of the empire."

This was not done without expense to the government. The cost has been estimated at five hundred million dollars. This is one reason of the present poverty of the State Treasury. I am assuredly no apologist for the horrible condition of Russian prisons, as reported by Mr. Kennan, but it is only fair to remember that orders for new prisons, and for better arrangements for exiles travelling to Siberia, have long ago been given, and would have been executed but for want of funds.

To emancipate the peasants would have done them little good had they been left without resources. We remember the day when it was said that every negro looked to the Federal government for "ten acres and a mule." This dream was in some measure realized by the Russian peasantry.

The land system of that country is very singular; and as we cannot understand Russian emancipation nor even Russian history without knowing something about it, I attempt an explanation.

Russian government is official, and as such centralized. It is communistic, and as such exactly the reverse. As official it is founded on German precedents; in the latter case, on old Slavonic customs and ideas.

Throughout the East of Europe the patriarchal idea prevails. The head of the family is all-powerful over his own household. The same idea created the commune. Each village or commune has its government, — its Mir. The Mir is composed solely of peasants; no nobleman or gentleman is admitted. Its headman is called a Volost.

The Mir holds meetings (much like vestry meetings) whenever it thinks proper, and the head of every family can vote and speak in them.

To each village has been allotted a certain quantity of land for the use of the former serfs, its inhabitants. The official tax-collector for the government looks to the Verlost of each Mir for the amount of taxes due by the commune to the State. The Mir distributes the communal land among the peasants, and may redistribute it at its own pleasure. It also pays an annual sum to the old proprietor, intended to purchase the land on the instalment principle. The Mir supplies the quota of conscripts to be furnished by its village to the army. It designates the time when ploughing, planting, and hay harvest may begin. It settles disputes, and in small matters administers justice in the village. It has power to send any unsatisfactory villager to Siberia.

It is easy to see that these powers may become very burdensome to all parties. The Mir *must* collect the taxes, whatever may be the consequences to the community, and it is not easy to get seventeen dollars a year (which is the amount of the government tax) out of every peasant landholder. Moreover if the headman should lose, squander, or embezzle the money he collects, the peasants, when the official tax-gatherer comes round, may have to pay it over again. If there should be a deficit, any peasant's horse or cow may be seized to make it good.

Again, every married man, or widow, in the commune *must* hold land. If he or she did not the taxes would fall more heavily upon the others. If any one wants to leave his village he must make arrangements for paying his share of the taxes in some way satisfactory to the Mir. If his payments fail he will be summoned home by the village authorities, and if he refuses to obey, he will be sent home by the government police. Sometimes this is done simply to black-mail a man who prospers in the cities.

Courts for the trial of persons guilty of minor offences

can be held by the Mir; but it is said that as a rule decisions can be purchased by a treat of strong liquor.

Over the commune are larger provincial assemblies composed of both peasants and nobles. They began by being dignified and well-conducted; but they had so little power that they fell into disrepute, and at last into disuse.

No man likes to hold office in the Mir. It involves too much annoyance, unpopularity, and responsibility. The better class of peasants shirk office altogether. The communal offices, therefore, fall to the worthless who are willing to accept them.

It will thus be seen that the land held by the emancipated peasant is not an absolute possession. After he has improved and manured his holding, he is liable, on a re-distribution of the land, to have it fall to somebody else, while he may get for his next allotment a barren waste, several miles from his village. Besides this, family expenses have increased under the new system. In serf-times large families of several generations dwelt together; now, as every man *must* hold land, he commonly feels himself compelled to live within reasonable reach of it.

Horses are indispensable to a cultivator, especially when the proprietor may be under the necessity of going a great distance to his daily labor. If a peasant's horse dies, or is stolen, or misfortune or unthrift break in on his resources, he was formerly compelled to go to the Jew money-lender (we have as yet no means of knowing to whom he resorts now). From him he could obtain money to buy another horse, or to pay his taxes. The security was so uncertain that the usurer demanded ruinous interest, sometimes thirty per cent; and this in a great measure laid the foundation of the bitter hatred to the Jewish race felt by peasants in Russia.

Russia, with reference to the nature of its soil, is divided into three districts: the forest, or northern part; the black soil; and the steppes.

In the black-soil zone, which is fertile, populated, and

provided with roads, emancipation seemed, for twenty years after it was granted, to work well; in the other two, badly. The causes for this may be found in Mr. Wallace's book on Russia published in 1879; but it is well to know something about conditions of peasant life so different from ours, when we read the books of Tolstoi, Tourgenieff, Gogol, and Henri Gréville.

In reading Mr. Wallace's account of the proprietor's views upon emancipation, and indeed in reading Russian stories that describe the country life of a Russian proprietor, one is reminded of what was taking place almost simultaneously on plantations in our own country, while the transition from the Old South to the New South was in progress. Almost the same difficulties seem to have beset the Russian proprietor and the Southern planter. But wealth has poured into our Southern States, and a large and industrious population; while no such good fortune befel the Russian landowner. The Southern planter supplied himself, as soon as his means would permit, with agricultural machinery, while in Russia there seems to have been little attempt to pursue new agricultural methods, and a feeling, too often experienced in our kitchens, that "modern inventions" are wasted upon those who have not the perseverance or the ability to understand them.

Again, when we compare Russian with Southern life, — that is, with life as it existed on the farms of old Virginia, — we are struck by three radical differences: First, the brutality of Russian manners toward inferiors, in contrast with the courtesy and kindness always enjoined on children in good families in the Southern States, in their intercourse with household servants, whom it was never considered good taste to call "slaves." Secondly, we are struck by the drinking and gambling of Russian masters, and the brutal beastly drunkenness that prevailed (and prevails still) among the laboring class, whether peasants or serfs. Our Southern gentlemen drank more toddy and more juleps than were good for them, and once in a while there was an incorrigibly drunken negro, but drunkenness was the exception, not the rule, as it appears to be in Russia. Lastly, in every Russian book one is struck with the hopelessness of life in Russia. It is as if Pandora had shaken out her woes upon the land, but forgot to add the gift that was hidden at the bottom. The negro, constitutionally light-hearted, looked forward to his Sundays and his holidays, to his Whitsuntide and Christmas, to say nothing of the frolics after night-fall in the quarter. The same spirit of looking forward to "a good time coming" pervades his songs and hymns. The Russian evidently takes no hopefulness from his religion, — it teaches him endurance; his enjoyment is solely in sleep and in *vodka*. He appears too lost to hope to be capable of aspiration.

Mr. Wallace, writing in 1875, says: —

"The great majority of educated Russians are at present suffering from the effect of shattered illusions. During the time of the emancipation they indulged in the most immoderate expectations. They believed, with an ardor of which only neophytes are capable, that Russia had discovered a new path of progress; that in securing to the peasants the land they actually enjoyed, and in developing the communal institutions in the direction of self-government, Russia laid, so they argued, a firm basis for her future prosperity. Grave doubts might be entertained as to the future fate of the landed proprietors; but there could be none, it was imagined, as to the future of the peasants. They would at once change 'from head to foot.' Their new position would work in them wonders. As soon as they felt themselves free they would strive to better their condition. Agriculture would be improved, the numbers of cattle would be increased, the old vices that had been created and fostered by serfage would disappear, and new institutions would develop a healthy local life. In a word, it was expected that the emancipation would produce instantaneously a complete transformation in the life and character of the rural population, and that the peasant would become at once a sober, industrious, moral agriculturist. These expectations were not realized. One year passed, five years passed, ten years passed, twenty years have passed, — and the expected transformation has not taken place. On the contrary, there have appeared certain very ugly phenomena which were not in the programme. The peasants, it is said, began to drink more and to work less, and the public life which the communal institutions have produced has not been of a desirable kind. The natural consequence of this is that those who had indulged in exaggerated expectations sank into a state of inordinate despondency, and imagined that things were much worse than they are. This despondency exists still, and tinges strongly the commonly received opinions regarding the present condition of the peasantry."

Mr. Wallace's own idea appeared to be that men must have patience with the experiment; that the new institutions forced on the people from above were not those they had grown up to, and that it might take a generation or more to discover how far the new order of things works for good or for evil.

The proprietors speedily complained bitterly of the difficulty of making the peasants keep their contracts. At the moment of harvest, or whenever their services were most needed, they were apt to go off in a body to work elsewhere, or to keep saints' days, or to attend fairs, or were incapable of work because of a night's drunkenness. As I said, love of drink is the Russian's worst enemy. Some one has spoken of Russia as a land in which there are but two classes, — those who sell drink, and those who consume it.

By a system too complicated to explain here, it was arranged that a peasant might acquire his land after a number of years. But few appear to have availed themselves of the chance of doing so. How far a peasant's acquisition of his own land would alter his relations to the Mir, I do not know.

After the Emancipation many proprietors wholly deserted their country houses, and went to live in cities; but the greater part of them soon resumed their former life; and in Russia, as elsewhere, the relations between employer and employed depend largely on the character and behavior of the former.

According to theory the self-government of rural Russia consists : —

First: of the village meetings under the Volost.

Secondly: of an assembly of representatives chosen in these village meetings; this forms the Mir.

Thirdly: of a large district assembly where nobles and peasants sit together; and

Fourthly: of a sort of financial committee which presides over all.

The Zemstvo or District Assembly was supposed to attend to hospitals, schools, asylums, roads, bridges, etc.

So far the plan of government in Russian village communities is Slavonic; but over all stands the bureaucratic system, with its agents, the police, imported from western Europe. The emperor is at its head, supported by a perfect army of officials, besides military officers who abound, and everywhere seem to have a species of authority. Russia is said to possess eight thousand generals.

I have already said that as the possession of a share of land entails its proportionate share of taxes, the peasants are often by no means willing to be burdened by a large communal allotment; and Mr. Wallace in an article on Russian village communities in "Macmillan's Magazine," gives a scene as enacted at one of the village assemblies, "whose meetings are held generally on Sundays after service, in front of the church or before the *starosta's* house (or volost's house), or in some convenient place where there is plenty of room and but little mud " : —

"'Come now, Ivan,' says an elderly peasant, who has evidently an air of authority, to one of the bystanders, 'you are a sturdy fellow, and you have a son there, a fine youth, who can do the work of two; you must take at least three shares.'

"'No, I cannot,' remonstrates Ivan. 'By God, I cannot. My son — praise be to God! — is strong and healthy; but I am no longer what I was, and my old woman is quite without force, fit for nothing but to put the cabbage-soup into the oven. By God! I cannot.'

"'If the old woman is weak, your daughter-in-law is strong, — stronger than a little horse !'

"A giggle in the outskirts of the crowd shows that the young woman referred to is among the spectators.

"'In truth it is not in my power,' pleads Ivan.

"'There is nothing to be said,' replies the old man, in an authoritative tone. 'Somebody must take the remaining *souls* (shares). You must take three shares.'

"'Lay on him three shares and a half!' shouts a voice from the crowd.

"This proposal evokes a confused murmur of 'ayes' and 'noes,' till the noes gain a decided majority, and the ayes are silenced. A general shout of 'Three! Three!' decides the matter.

"'It is the will of the *mir*,' remarks Ivan, scratching the back of his head, and looking down with a look of mingled disappointment and resignation.

"'And now, Prascovia, how such are you to have?' asks the old man, addressing a woman standing by with a baby in her arms.

"'As the *mir* orders, so be it,' replies Prascovia, turning down her eyes.

"'Very well. You ought to have a share and a half.'

"'What do you say, little father?' cries the woman, throwing off suddenly her air of subservient obedience. 'Do you hear that, ye orthodox? They want to lay on me a soul and a half! Was such a thing ever heard of? Since Saint Peter's day my husband has been bedridden — bewitched it seems, for nothing does him good. He cannot put a foot to the ground. All the same as if he were dead; only he eats bread.'

"'You talk nonsense,' says a neighbor; 'he was at the gin-shop last week.'

"'And you,' retorts Prascovia, wandering from the subject in hand, 'what did *you* do last parish *fête?* Was it not you who got drunk and beat your wife till she roused the whole village with her shrieking? And no further gone than last Sunday — pfu!'

"'Listen,' says the old man, sternly cutting short the torrent of invective. 'You must take at least a share and a quarter. If you cannot manage it yourself, you can get some one to help you.'

"'How can that be? Where am I to get money to pay a laborer?' asks the woman, with much wailing and a flood of tears. 'Have pity, ye orthodox, on the poor orphans. God will reward you;' and so on and so on."

Thus it will be seen that the possession of land under the commune is not an unmixed boon to the peasant proprietor. He is tied to his allotment hand and foot. Formerly he was serf to a proprietor; now he is surf to the commune. How he can extricate himself from his obligations in days of pestilence and famine — who can say?

It is hardly too much to add that corruption reigns everywhere, and with corruption comes of course injustice. The peasant is untrustworthy in matters of contract, and in his relations with others looks to his own interest alone; the merchants in the cities think lightly of fraud; and the venality and faithlessness of Russian officials is the stock subject in books of travel and in their own novels.

Justice made great strides in the law courts under Alexander II. Trial by jury in open court was allowed; but the country juries are composed of peasants, who, like Judge Lynch formerly in our far western States, are severe upon horse-stealing, but lenient to other kinds of crime.

The schools, so long as the reform movement lasted, made great progress, but that progress had begun before Emancipation; for in the years between 1860 and 1870 the number of recruits who could read had increased five-fold. But the teachers were very poor in the provinces, being for the most part young foreigners with advanced and crude ideas, while in the universities distinguished professors were distrusted by the government, for fear they should prove "Liberals."

By degrees the mineral wealth of Russia (enormous, especially in Siberia) was becoming turned to profit in Alexander's reign. Great coal-beds and oil-wells were beginning to be worked, and railroads and telegraph wires were stretched over the land.

Do we realize that the emperor of Russia rules over one seventh of the earth, and over more than ninety millions of subjects; or that Russia is forty times as big as France, if we include her Asiatic possessions?

Among Alexander's reforms was the abolition of the knout, and of corporal punishment in the army and navy.

I fear I may have been wearisome with these details, but in general we only think of Russia in connection with her projects in India, her designs on Constantinople, and her exiles in Siberia. We overlook the marvellous changes taking place, notwithstanding the obstinate conservatism of her lower classes, although attention has been called to them in the novels of Tolstoi.

One of the first events of Alexander's reign was a rising in Poland in 1863. That unhappy land, which has neither a middle class nor a frontier, which finds sympathy everywhere but no allies, made another attempt at insurrection, failed utterly, and the rebellion was stamped out ruthlessly, even by Alexander, who is said always to have cherished a personal antipathy to the Poles. I need not tell the particulars of this sad rising, which, taking place when all our thoughts, and the attention of all Europe, were concentrated on our Civil War, is very little known to us. The Polish peasants were in general not unfavorable to Russia. The Polish patriots were among the land-owning country nobility, and the educated professional class. These were divided into two parties, — Extreme Radicals and Conservative Patriots. They had no leader of ability, no efficient organization, either political or military. They had built hopes upon assistance from France, but the Emperor Napoleon III. had the affairs of Italy and Mexico upon his hands at the moment, and, in spite of the strong sympathy for the cause of Poland freely expressed by the Empress Eugénie, he was not disposed to engage in another enterprise of intervention. The rising was a mere sacrifice of generous lives. There is an interesting paper on the subject in Laurence Oliphant's delightful book, " Gleanings in a Life of Adventure, or Moss from a Rolling Stone." It is said that the emperor in his dealings with Poland desired to show Europe, as well as his own subjects, that he too, on occasion, could be stern.

A Frenchman writing of Alexander II. says: "He was tall, though he had not the majestic height of his father, the Emperor Nicholas. He was well made, more so than his father, whose legs were too thin for his immense *torso*. His blue eyes were tender and soft. His smile was charming; his hair short and fair; his moustache long and thick, as were also his whiskers. His voice was flexible and very fine."

Such was Alexander when he ascended the imperial throne at the age of thirty-seven. He wanted to make every one about him happy, and his domestic life, until broken up by his son's death and his wife's ill-health, was extremely happy. The young czarevitch, whose name was Nicholas, died in 1865; and from the sorrow of his death his father and mother never recovered. He expired at Nice, where his mother was then staying. Some time before he had been injured in a wrestling bout, some say with his cousin, Prince Nicholas of Leuchtenburg; some say with Alexander, his athletic brother. At any rate no injury of any consequence was apprehended at the time, and he was betrothed to the beautiful and amiable Princess Dagmar of Denmark, sister of Alexandra, Princess of Wales. When alarming symptoms showed themselves his father hurried across Europe without stopping, to reach the death-bed of his boy, one of whose last entreaties was that the czarevitch who would succeed him, his brother Alexander, should take to wife the Danish princess who was shortly to have become his bride. He had been brought up with the greatest care that he might be qualified for his *profession*, as king Victor Emmanuel used to call kingship.

Alexander II. felt his son's death the more severely because he considered him in every way qualified to make a noble and enlightened ruler, and to carry out his plans. The intellect of his next son, Alexander, he by no means valued so highly, and it is said that had it been possible he would have made his third son, the Grand Duke Vladimir, his heir. Alexander was, however, at once put under military training, and eighteen months after his brother's death was married to the Princess Dagmar, who, on being baptized into the Greek church took the name of Maria Feodorovna.

Marie of Darmstadt, the wife of Alexander II. was gentle, amiable, and cultivated, but she was at first not disposed to Russianize herself. In the early years of her married life she had carefully abstained from taking any part in politics, and it excited some surprise when she — a convert to the Greek Church — suddenly became in 1877 an enthusiast for the Turkish war. She believed in it as a holy war; she lent it her utmost support. She outdid the old Muscovites in their horror of the Infidel.

She particularly disliked the French, and in her court circle was a model of rigid propriety. In private life, however, she could be gay and engaging. A good wife and a devoted mother, she caused her sons to be educated in all the accomplishments of gentlemen, instead of their being drilled soldiers as had been the case with the generation before them. The young Czarevitch Nicholas was in every way accomplished; to Alexander, who had no taste for learning, she seems to have communicated her religious enthusiasm for the church of her adoption, while the Grand Duke Vladimir became one of the most accomplished musicians in Russia, a patron so far as possible of artists and authors. The last years of her life were clouded by illhealth, by her son's death, and by gloomy forebodings as to the future in store for her family amid the dangers of Nihilism. When she died her husband made a morganatic marriage with the Princess Dolgorouka, by whom he had had several children. It is said that in the last years of his life he practised strict economy in order to provide them with fortunes. The connection with the Princess Dolgorouka was greatly disapproved by the present czar.

When Alexander II. and his empress were crowned at Moscow in 1856, just after the Crimean War, Napoleon III. sent a brilliant embassy, headed by his kinsman, the Duc de Morny, to represent him at the ceremony. The equipages of the French ambassador were marvels of magnificence; the liveries were white and gold with scarlet waistcoats. The English and Austrian carriages were next in splendor; and as for Prince Esterhazy, the Austrian ambassador, he was literally covered with diamonds and pearls.

The illumination that night in Moscow must have seemed like a scene in the Arabian nights. The principal buildings were covered with lights from their foundations to their gilded domes. The emperor and empress appeared in the streets in an open barouche, without an escort. The crowd pressed round them with cries of affection and joy. Alas! twenty-five years later the same czar lay shattered and dying by a bomb, thrown under the direction of a young and beautiful woman, after having escaped many other attempts at assassination.

The first attempt on Alexander's life struck him with even more surprise than consternation; and it is said to have produced a deep and lasting impression on the mind of his son the present emperor. He was shot at while walking in the gardens of his palace at Saint Petersburg in 1866 by a man in peasant dress named Korakasof; the czar saw, or thought he saw, a peasant standing near throw up the pistol, and it went off in the air. The assassin was at once arrested, and, being asked why he sought to kill the czar, replied, because the estates of the nobles were not sufficiently divided among the peasantry. Under his peasant's dress, however, he wore the clothes of a student, and on his person were found papers connecting him with secret societies, and making it plain that to him had fallen by lot the task of killing the emperor. He was tried and sent to the mines of Siberia, where he may be to this day. The peasant who saved the czar's life hardly met a better fate. The czar gave him a palace, and wealth, and made him a baron; but the man was little better than a brute, so addicted to drink that finally he was sent as a lieutenant to a regiment campaigning in the Caucasus, and there committed suicide. In the following year a second attempt by a Pole named Berezowski gave Alexander infinite pain. He had tried to think that the crime of Korakasof was an isolated case of regicidal mania; this one of Berezowski inaugurated a series of such horrors, which never ceased till they had accomplished their purpose, and which continue to be directed against the life of his successor to the present day.

In 1867 the emperor visited the Paris Exposition as an act of courtesy to Napoleon III., through whose dominions he had passed without stopping two years before, when hurrying to the death-bed of his son at Nice. The king and crown prince of Prussia were there, and a crowd of other royal, ducal, and illustrious personages. Some one on the occasion remarked that the French emperor "looked like a man who had invited an incongruous set of guests, and did not know how to amuse them." He was uneasy himself, for the prince imperial was seriously ill; the king of Prussia was not well pleased that higher honors were offered to his nephew than to himself, and the czar, to every one who saw him, seemed out of spirits. On June 6, after a review on the Champ de Mars, the royal and imperial guests returned to Paris, through the Bois de Boulogne. Napoleon III. and the Emperor Alexander, with the czarevitch and the Grand Duke Vladimir on the back seat, occupied one carriage; the king of Prussia and the Empress Eugénie were in the next, and the carriages of other notabilities followed. The crowd was great and the carriages moved slowly. Suddenly a Pole named Berezowski fired a pistol at the czar. The shot struck the nostril of an outrider's horse, causing it to rear violently, scattering its blood over the czarevitch and his brother. The assassin fired again, but his pistol burst in his hand, and he fell to the ground with a shriek. The correspondent of a London newspaper wrote: "For a moment when the czar saw blood upon his sons he looked alarmed. Napoleon got up, waved his hat, and then said to the czar, 'Sire, we have been under fire together.' Calmly the czar replied: 'The lives of kings, as of their subjects, are in the hands of Providence.' Next day a Te Deum was sung in the Russian Church, where the grand dukes embraced their father, and showed much feeling."

When Berezowski was put upon his trial it turned out that his father and brother had been exiled to Siberia for participation in the Polish insurrection of 1863, and this fact saved him from the guillotine. The jury brought in a verdict of "guilty with extenuating circumstances," and he was sent to New Caledonia. The government of National Defence in 1870 granted him a pardon. M. Thiers revoked it, and it seems uncertain what has become of him. There can be no doubt, however, that his crime did his fellow-countrymen a great deal of harm.

And now perhaps we may approach the subject of Russian Nihilism. Yet who can understand it with its ramifications which run through what is called in Europe the International Society; and our Anarchists in the West, who are imported chiefly from Germany and Norway, are said by Western men to be more numerous than the general public in the Eastern cities is willing to suppose. Even Nihilists are said not to understand Nihilism, but to yield it a blind obedience. And first we may say that while there is probably hardly a peasant in Russia who is a genuine Nihilist, there is probably not a genuine American who is an Anarchist.

Nihilism means — *Nothing at all*. It comes from the same root as *annihilate*. It proceeds on the supposition that *whatever is, is wrong*. Its avowed object is destruction. Everything that exists having been destroyed, men may begin to think of building up again.

It destroys, not from aversion to an individual, but because his or her death may help the cause. The Nihilists do not call their deeds *murder*, any more than the sheriff who hangs a man, or a soldier who shoots one, call their killing by that name.

The first plot of the Nihilists was the one that was ripening when the Emperor Alexander I. died. He had been told of the discovery of a plot to assassinate him a few days before his death, and it had greatly discomposed him. His brother Nicholas's first step on coming to the throne was utterly to crush out this Nihilism in his dominions. Alexander had had no personal enemies. His sacrifice was to be for the good of the cause. That "cause" Nicholas set himself to destroy, both root and branch; and thoroughly and mercilessly he prepared himself to do it. He thought, as his reign went on, that he had accomplished it. He walked fearlessly among his people all his days; to be sure, it was forbidden to speak to him. On one occasion he met in his park the first tenor of the Italian Opera, and exchanged a few words with him; the moment the czar was out of sight the tenor was arrested. The czar attended the Opera that evening, when after some delay the manager came forward and announced that the first tenor could not be found. The czar started, guessed what had happened, and sent an aide-de-camp to the police. The singer was released and the play went on. A few days after, the czar, meeting him again, began with an apology: "I was very sorry—" "May I implore your Majesty," cried the Italian, "not to speak to me. Your Majesty will compromise me with the police."

There is a Nihilist song in circulation which describes the good time coming as the day in which there will be no God and no czar!

Here is an article published in one of the Nihilist organs in Switzerland on the subject of political assassination:—

"A few trifling assassinations committed by us have induced the Russian government to proclaim a state of siege, to double the political police, to place Cossacks in all directions, and to redouble the vigilance of the gens d'armes. By a few resolute acts we have brought to these exaggerated measures of desperation an autocracy that years of agitation, and centuries of agony, the despair of young men, the groans of the oppressed, the curses of thousands murdered by exile, tortured to death in Siberian deserts and mines, — could not have effected. Who says that assassination is not one of the most powerful means by which we may carry on successful warfare against Russian despotism?"

Another address that lies before me, after proclaiming that the murder of a sovereign can only be punished with death like any other murder, goes on to speak of the necessity of clearing away everything that exists, — government, religion, family ties, patriotism, and so on. "Then," it cries, "will spring to life a new generation, pure from routine! Then a new dawn will light up this old earth! All will be happy till abuses re-accumulate, and our great grandchildren do over again the things that we have done. Thus from struggle to struggle human society, after centuries of combat, will reach perfection, and become itself that which you call God! Follow me, brothers! Follow me, and conquer for yourselves divinity!"

Poor creatures! In these ravings we hear the voice of our common humanity as it looks forward to the Great Day of the Lord, — the "time of the restitution of all things," the time for which "the whole creation" "groaneth and travaileth together" in expectation. And to think that that time could be hastened by blood-guiltiness — by assassination!

If this statement of the views and aims of Nihilism, culled from its own documents, published in its own newspapers, should seem exaggerated, we have only to compare it with Tourgenieff's account of Nihilism in his novels, especially the one called "Fathers and Sons." The great novelist sustains every word I have said upon the subject.

Only those are permitted to become influential Nihilists who have personal reasons for hating the government, or have some vengeance to wreak on some *employe*, or have received a revolutionary education, or have the revolutionary temperament with which some men and women appear to be born.

The Nihilist army is ruled by a central committee, which is ruled by what some secret societies call a Grand Centre. But none know each other; none communicate directly with the Grand Centre, nor even know who he is. Some accounts say that Nihilists are divided into companies of five, ten, or fifteen, each with an officer over them, who does not communicate directly with the Central Committee, still less with the Grand Centre, but only with a delegate or sub-delegate of the committee.

Tourgenieff was always insisting that the national defect of the Russians is want of *will*. The easiest thing to them, he says, is passive obedience. He considers that the power of Nihilism lies in making use of this spirit of passive obedience. Every man beneath the Grand Centre gives up his private judgment, and for " the good of the cause " does simply what he is required to do.

Every treason, disobedience, or undue exhibition of curiosity is punished with death, — death as sudden as a thunderbolt.

As all members are bound to help the rest, the power of the society is enormously increased, and all members become, as it were, each other's accomplices.

Corruption is employed to get state secrets, etc., out of public *employés*, non-commissioned officers, the police, etc. Sometimes money, sometimes the wiles of women, sometimes intimidation are employed.

I said there were probably few or no peasants among the Nihilists, and the peasant class comprises five sixths of the population of European Russia: —

" A stolid, ignorant, utterly unprogressive mass," says one who knows them, "they have received in gift to their communes half the empire for their own use, yet in many cases the gift has ruined them. Still they cling to the soil, and dread all change, fearing it may endanger that coveted possession. A dense, solid stratum of conservatism thus constitutes the base of Russian society, and above it lies the most corrupt set of officials to be found in the whole world, kept in order neither by a public press, public opinion, nor civil service customs. The middle and upper classes are often full of ardent wishes for the advancement of society, and the reform of the State. Their views of action are generally of the wildest and most terrible description: but their objects are anything but unreasonable. They desire to share in political power and the government of their own country, as is the privilege of every other nation in Europe, and they hope to do something for the seething mass of ignorance and misery around them."

It is from this educated class — professional men, college students, and the younger members of the nobility — that the society of Nihilists recruits itself. When the Emperor Alexander II. opened new colleges and public schools he had not the means to invite distinguished professors from other countries; he had to content himself with men who could be had for a small salary, — young men, for the most part, whose unsettled opinions were a bar to their getting on elsewhere. These, coming into Russia just as a social revolution was inaugurated, pressed progress to its extreme, and inspired the young people under them, male and female, with the wildest aspirations after liberty and revolution.

Newly adopted ideas, as we all know, produce fermentation; and fermentation will produce explosion. Young men and young women of the higher classes, having received a college education and the germs of revolutionary ideas, on returning to their homes from the university commonly find nothing to do, nothing to interest them, nothing to call out their higher feelings; and they are attracted to Nihilism, misled by patriotic sympathies, and the charm of mystery and secret power.

All accounts tell us that, while Russians are most punctual in devout observances, heart religion in their country is at a low ebb. As it was in ancient paganism, when religion consisted in due offerings to the gods, due vows performed, and hecatombs sacrificed, — so the religion of the Russian peasant seems to consist in an unquestioning submission to the decrees of fate, and devout adoration of the sacred *ikons*, without any thought of personal relations to God. He brings home nothing from his church that will enter into his daily life but blind submission.

The imagination of the Russian, always gloomy, seeks its outlook, among the educated, in wild schemes of patriotism and philanthropy, to be preceded by destruction, — while the peasantry (like our own people on sandy shores or in mountain districts, where the imagination has nothing to feed it but what it can derive from crude notions of religion) run into the wildest, wickedest forms of piety, if we may so term their religious beliefs.

About forty years ago an educated fanatic on the eastern frontier of European Russia, disgusted with the wickedness of the world around him, retired into a forest, determined to make an end of this life of sin and ignominy. He did not attempt to proselytize, but his views soon found acceptance among his neighbors, and numbers flocked to him in the woods crying: "Antichrist is raging round! Let us escape by dying of hunger!" The women made graveclothes for themselves, their men, and the little children. The men dug their graves. They renounced Satan, and they pledged themselves never again to taste food. The children's sufferings, after two days, so moved two of the male fanatics that they escaped from the dreadful sight. Then the leader, fearing other desertions, called on them to massacre each other. The children were killed first, then the women. At last only the leader and three more were left alive; these fell into the hands of the police, who had been summoned by the fugitives.

This mania for suicide, and indifference to death, is a national characteristic of the Russians. In 1812 all the inhabitants of a village flung themselves, for the glory of God and the salvation of their own souls, on to a funeral pyre. In 1860 fifteen men for the same reason devoted themselves to death in one family. On the very day I write these lines a newspaper telegram informs us that hundreds of peasants have flung themselves before the train that was carrying the Emperor Alexander III. to the Crimea.

The same state of nerves and of excited feeling that induces such things in the ignorant, produces Nihilism in the educated classes. In one place eighty-four persons made a frantic attempt to burn themselves alive in a cavern, crying, "We die for Christ!" as they perished in the flames.

Some sects advocate all that is *natural*. They will not shave nor cut their hair; they do not smoke, nor drink spirits. The consequence of those two last peculiarities is that they grow rich as those around them grow poor. Men, they say, should make for themselves all that is necessary, and never trade nor buy. They preach free-love, and discard marriage. They are called Negators. They recognize no rights of property, no social institutions. The government has been always very severe on dissenters from the orthodox Russian Church, and even in the time of Alexander II. numbers of such extravagant fanatics were sent to Siberia.

Some sects forbid any amusements; some are "jumpers;" others enjoin their members to live alone; some allow two wives to a believer; some are socialists as well as religious fanatics; some might be described as Russian Quakers.

But this is enough. It was Taine who said that when a people has no proper outlet for its imagination (a gift which is inevitably bestowed on some persons in every community, however prosaic and commonplace) it will assuredly result in wild, uncouth misconceptions of religion.

According to Mr. Kennan's articles in the "Century," over one hundred and fifty thousand convicts were sent to Siberia in six years (from 1884 to 1890), but of these not more than one in a hundred was a political exile. Of the political exiles the larger part, according to Mr. Kennan, are simply men who hold (or are supposed to hold) advanced political opinions, without belonging to the secret organization which preaches bombs and dynamite. How far Mr. Kennan's testimony is true remains to be proved by corroborating or rebutting evidence. There can be no question that the Russian police, all on the *qui vive*, is ready to make arrests upon the slightest suspicion, and that one half of the exiles have been banished without trial, a large part of them by their own communes, expelled as unruly members, or as defaulters in their taxes, — private spite having probably, in a good many instances, considerable to do with their misfortunes.

When Alexander II. came to his throne Russia, exhausted by the Crimean War, had only paper money, few factories, only old methods in agriculture, six hundred miles only of railroad, and hardly any other tolerable roads over its enormous territory. The emperor applied himself to the peaceful work of reform, and carried it out with a skill, tact, and above all with an ease which a foreign public is hardly able at present to appreciate, but which may some day excite the wonder of those who are able to grasp the magnitude of the task he attempted and in part performed.

In less than twenty-five years an amount of work was performed in Russia that it has taken a century to accomplish in other lands. Into every large town in Russia now runs a railroad, well managed and well appointed. Steamers ply on all the rivers, even those of Siberia ; produce is brought westward from the remotest provinces ; and, alas ! wherever Russian civilization establishes itself corruption and petty oppression seem to spread.

I do not think I can better conclude this paper than by slightly abridging the sketch Mr. Wallace has drawn for us of a landed proprietor of the old school under the new conditions : —

"Somewhere about sixty years ago [Mr. Wallace is writing in 1876] Ivan Ivanovitch was born in the country house where he still lives. His first lessons he received from the parish priest, and afterwards he was taught by a deacon's son, who had studied in a theological seminary to so little purpose that he was unable to pass the examination. Under both these teachers he was suffered to learn as little as he chose; and he was still very slightly acquainted with the elementary rules of arithmetic when his father one day declared that as he was eighteen he must enter the service. His father's project that he should enter a cavalry regiment as a Junker, or volunteer, under an old colonel, a former friend, did not at all please Ivan. He had no love for military service, and possibly disliked the prospect of an examination: so, while seeming to bow implicitly to his father's authority, he induced his mother to oppose the scheme.

"The Marshal of Nobility, who happened to call one day, helped him out of his difficulty by offering to inscribe him as secretary in the office of a certain court, where his duties could be filled by a paid secretary. This plan exactly suited Ivan Ivanovitch, and in seven years, without having done a stroke of work, he rose to a civil rank corresponding to that of a captain in the army, by gradual promotion.

"By this time it was decided he must marry. His courtship did not even cost him the trouble of proposing. The whole affair was arranged by his parents, who chose for their son's bride the daughter of their next neighbor. The young lady was only about sixteen, and was not remarkable for beauty, talent, or any other peculiarity; but she had one very important qualification,—she was the daughter of a man who had an estate contiguous to their own, and who might give as dowry a certain bit of land they had long desired to add to their own property.

"Though the bridegroom had received, rather than had taken to himself, a wife, and did not imagine for a moment he was in love, he had no reason to regret the choice that was made for him. Maria Petrovna was exactly suited, both by nature and education, to be the wife of such a man as Ivan Ivanovitch. She had grown up at home in the society of nurses and servant-maids, and had never learned anything more than could be obtained from the parish priest and from Mam'selle, a person occupying a position between a servant-maid and a governess. The first years of her married life were not very happy, for she was treated by her mother-in-law as a naughty child who required to be frequently snubbed and lectured; but she bore the discipline with exemplary patience, and in due time became her own mistress, and autocratic ruler in domestic affairs.

"The daily life of this worthy couple became singularly regular and monotonous. In summer Ivan Ivanovitch gets up about seven o'clock, and puts on, with the assistance of his *valet de chambre*, a simple costume consisting principally of a faded, plentifully stained dressing-gown. Having nothing particular to do, he sits down at the open window and looks into the yard. As the servants pass he stops them and questions them, and then gives them orders or scolds them as circumstances demand. Toward nine o'clock breakfast is announced, and he goes into the dining-room, a long, narrow apartment with bare wooden floor, and no furniture but a table and chairs in a more or less rickety condition. Here he finds his wife with the tea-urn before her. In a few minutes the younger children come in, kiss their papa's hand, and take their places round the table. As the meal consists only of bread and tea it does not last long, and then all disperse to their several occupations. Ivan Ivanovitch smokes several pipes, and then, if not too warm, goes forth to visit the stables and farm-yard, but soon returns to his place by the window, and remains wrapped in contemplation.

"Maria Petrovna spends her morning in a more active way. As soon as the breakfast-table has been cleared she goes to the larder, takes stock of the provisions, arranges the *menu* for the day, and gives the cook directions and the necessary materials. The rest of the morning she devotes to her other household duties.

"Toward one o'clock dinner is announced, and Ivan Ivanovitch prepares his appetite by swallowing at one gulp a wineglass full of home-made bitters.

"No sooner has the last dish been removed than a deathlike stillness falls upon the house for about two hours. Master, mistress, children, servants, dogs, are taking their siesta. In about two hours they awake. The *samovar* is brought, and they have tea. Then Ivan Ivanovitch makes the tour of his fields in a drosky, consisting of two pair of wheels joined together by a single board on which the driver sits astride. In the evening often a group of peasants comes into the yard and asks to see the master. In reply to his question, 'Well, children, what do you want?' they tell their story in a confused, rambling kind of way, several of them speaking at a time, and he has to question and cross-question them before he can find out clearly what they desire. If he tells them he cannot grant it, they probably resort to supplication: 'Little father! Ivan Ivanovitch! be generous. You are our father — we are your children,' etc.

"The family leads a very isolated life, but they have one bond of connection with the great outer world. Two of the sons are officers in the army, and they write home occasionally to their mother and sisters.

"During the Crimean War Ivan Ivanovitch half awoke from his habitual lethargy, and read the papers. He was a little surprised that no great victories were announced, and that the army did not at once advance on Constantinople. Some of his neighbors told him that the army was disorganized, and that the whole system of Nicholas had proved worthless. Well! — that might be true. He did not understand politics. It would all come right in the end. And so it did, after a fashion, but ere long he was startled by rumors more alarming than any rumors of war. The emancipation of the serfs was in question. For a long time he would not believe it. When he was forced to do so he was somewhat alarmed at the prospect of losing his authority. He had never been a cruel master, but he had not spared the rod when he considered it necessary, and he believed birch twigs to be a necessary instrument in Russian agriculture. When he found that the peasants were to receive a large part of his estate for their own use, he considered himself ruined.

"These dark forebodings have not been by any means realized. His serfs pay him annually a considerable sum, and they are at hand to cultivate his fields for a fair remuneration. His yearly outlay is now considerably greater, but the price of grain, when it has risen, counterbalances the increased expenditure. The administration of the estate is much less patriarchal; much that was formerly left to custom and tacit understanding is now regulated by express agreement. More money is paid out, but a good deal more comes in. There is less authority in the hands of the master, but he is relieved from much of his responsibility. Ivan Ivanovitch would have great difficulty in deciding whether he is now a richer or a poorer man. He has fewer horses, and fewer servants, but he has still more than he requires, and his mode of life has undergone no perceptible alteration. Maria Petrovna complains that she is no longer supplied with eggs, chickens, and home-spun linen by the peasants, and that everything is three times as dear as it used to be; but somehow the larder is still full, and abundance reigns in the house as of old."

CHAPTER IX.

FOUR SULTANS.[1]

WE may fill up the interval between the Crimean War and the Russian invasion of Turkey in 1877 by some account of the three sultans who ruled during that period, and of the fourth who in 1876 ascended the throne. It is not always easy to intertwine the threads of narrative while telling the story of two countries, and it is sometimes necessary to retrace our steps over already trodden ground.

Mahmoud II., the destroyer of the Janissaries, died in 1839, leaving three sons, two of whom, Abdul Medjid and Abdul Aziz, subsequently mounted the Turkish throne. By Mohammedan law the sons of a deceased sovereign who has no brothers, succeed each other, till on the death of the youngest the heirship reverts to the sons of the eldest brother. As Sultan Mahmoud had no brother, he was succeeded by his son Abdul Medjid, who came to the throne during one of those crises in the Eastern Question which convulse Europe about once in fifteen years. On this occasion, as we have seen, Ibrahim Pasha, the bold son of the viceroy of Egypt, had conquered Syria, and was threatening Constantinople. Russia had volunteered her protection to the Porte, and the balance of power was disturbed.

The reign of Abdul Medjid lasted from 1839 to 1861. Turkish history has no record of any other sovereign so

---

[1] For this chapter I am largely indebted to Count E. de Kératry, who in 1878 published a book called "Sultan Murad V.," from which I made by translation and abridgment an article published in the "Living Age," No. 1787. — E. W. L.

humane, so fond of order, so much inclined to accept the refinements of modern civilization; but the systematic opposition of his pashas, that oligarchy of office-holders who aspired to be the actual governing power in Turkey, rendered his reforming *hatts*, or edicts, of very little avail. In vain did Abdul Medjid and his successors promulgate decrees in favor of non-Mussulmans; neither Jew nor Christian dared seek protection from such documents in opposition to public opinion.

As a reformer Abdul Medjid had to keep his eye upon all public officers, provincial governors, and judges; in matters of religion his task was to build up a liberal party among the interpreters of the Koran; and the struggle to accomplish these things without support proved too great for him.

The Crimean War, too, notwithstanding its avowed aim of protecting Turkey, brought two new elements of decay to hasten the disintegration of the empire.

Up to 1856 Turkey had been free from foreign creditors. The opening of the Dardanelles brought commerce, and a foreign loan, and on the steps of indebtedness followed extravagance, speculation, and national bankruptcy.

Besides this, the great Powers, by the Treaty of Paris, forbade the interference of Russia in the internal affairs of Turkey, and at the same time renounced all right to intermeddle themselves. This "self-denying ordinance" cut off from Abdul Medjid a great source of strength. He became no match for his conservative pashas, and most dreadful massacres in Syria were the first fruits of the new system of diplomacy.

Finding his solicitude for his subjects barren of good results, Abdul Medjid, during the last years of his life, gave himself up to self-indulgence, especially in wines and in the pleasures of the table. He limited his reforms thenceforth to his harem and his household. To his courtiers he was an amiable and considerate master, and he was ever a tender, loving husband to his wives. The death of one of his favorites, to whom he is said ever to have borne himself as knight to lady, brought on an attack of melancholy which hastened his end.

If we look back to the reign of his father Mahmoud we shall see how Abdul Medjid redeemed at least court life from barbarity, and softened the brutal element in Oriental manners.

Mahmoud made no scruple of strangling his pashas without forms of law; he massacred without pity or remorse his whole corps of Janissaries; and his wives, if any offended him, were never pardoned. Abdul Medjid, unlike his father, loved justice and mercy. Devoted as he was to his own son Murad, he never dreamed of delivering himself of his brother Abdul Aziz in order to open the succession to this beloved son. Ottoman custom, from the earliest history of the race, has, as I said, fixed the succession to the throne and the caliphate, not by hereditary descent from father to son, but successively to every living son of a dead sultan. For this reason every sultan from Bajazet to Ahmed I. had been guilty of fratricide. But Abdul Medjid refused with horror all suggestions of that kind, and treated his brother Abdul Aziz with a persistent kindness and consideration, which Abdul Aziz, when subsequently upon the throne, did not return to his nephew Murad.

Mahmoud II. transmitted to neither of his sons the daring nor the strength of will that made him great. Their mothers' characters came out in them. Abdul Aziz cared nothing for the welfare of his subjects; he hated the civilization of Europe; he was a true Turk of the old school. In person he was more like his father Mahmoud than his elder brother, and he displayed the savagery of the destroyer of the Janissaries without his noble qualities. His mother was a daughter of the Kurds, and he inherited the temperament of her race. She exercised over him a fatal influence, being a woman of low, vulgar type, fit only to develop his bad passions. She used to laugh when she saw him amuse himself by plucking live birds in his boyhood, and applauded him when upon one occasion he tore to pieces with his hands a tame dove belonging to his brother Abdul Medjid. It is said that when he was about sixteen she made him a present of a young Bulgarian slave-girl. This poor creature having offended her young lord, he tore her, as he had done the dove, limb from limb. His Kurdish mother, without blaming her "young lion," as she called him, had the body sewn up in a sack, and sunk in the Bosphorus, forbidding all who knew of it on pain of death to say anything of the matter to Sultan Mahmoud or Prince Abdul Medjid. Abdul Aziz cared nothing for study, — reading and writing wearied him; but he was fond of active sports, and was a muscular Mohammedan. He destroyed the pretty theatre erected by Abdul Medjid at the Dolma-Baghtché Palace, but he built a private circus near his own apartments, the entertainments in which consisted of a number of slaves being forced to feign sleep till a pack of hounds were let loose upon them. The terrors, struggles, sufferings that ensued were inexpressibly delightful to the sultan, and he expected every one present to share his enthusiasm. It was by flattering him on this point that the Armenian Seraf Abraham Pasha (brother-in-law to Nubar Pasha, the minister of the khedive) gained his favor, and retained it to the end of his reign.

With his natural love for killing and savagery, it is fortunate that the history of Abdul Aziz does not exhibit a long list of horrors; but a public opinion against wanton cruelty had been formed under Abdul Medjid, and ministers such as Fuad Pasha, and Aali, who were by turns the grand viziers of Abdul Aziz for eleven years, would not have countenanced open brutality. By the ascendency of strong minds over the weak they held in check the ferocity of the savage. Abdul Aziz frequently endeavored to get rid of his two great ministers. In 1863 he peremptorily dismissed them, and offered the place of grand vizier to his chief buffoon. The man, however, had more sense of propriety than his master. He declined so high a post, and contented

SULTAN ABDUL AZIZ.

himself with one equally unsuitable, — that of minister of public instruction.

Fuad Pasha accompanied Abdul Aziz on his visit to the Paris Exposition in 1867, and to the courts of western Europe, but he drew upon himself the displeasure of his master by his attempts to make him conduct himself with civilized decorum. The imperial barbarian brought back from western Europe a hatred of civilization, founded most probably on secret envy. He was bitter against Fuad, and also against his heir-presumptive, Prince Murad Effendi; for that young prince, by the graces of his person, the modesty of his deportment, and his accomplishments, had made himself a great favorite, especially with the future Emperor William, then king of Prussia.

Abdul Aziz, from the first moment of his return to his own capital, cherished a project of changing the old law of succession, and setting aside the late sultan's son. According to the customs of the seraglio, the infant children of the reigning race, unless born to the sultan himself, must be destroyed. Abdul Aziz had succeeded in saving one son, Yussef Izzeddin, born in 1854, who was doubly excluded from inheritance, both by the law of succession, and by his having been born before his father's accession to the throne.

This project occupied the attention of Abdul Aziz for the remainder of his reign. He tried to create a precedent by permitting the khedive of Egypt to set aside the legal claim of an uncle and a cousin to the vice-regal throne; but Fuad and Aali refused resolutely to favor their master's views. Yussef Izzeddin was a spoilt boy, educated by his grandmother, and inheriting his father's ferocious passions, while the true heir, the son of Abdul Medjid, showed all the noble qualities of his dead father, and gave promise of becoming a sovereign open to all the good influences of civilization. Abdul Aziz dared not set himself in open opposition to his distinguished ministers, but with bitter resentment waited till death or opportunity should dispose of them. Meanwhile he did his best to thwart their ideas of progress and of policy. In vain did Fuad and Aali exert themselves to promulgate edicts for the protection of Christians; the sultan himself led the opposition against them. They were worn out with the struggle. Their edicts remained inoperative. They died within a few months of each other.

Both Fuad and Aali were aware that reforms in law and politics should be preceded by reforms in education and manners. Each had but one wife, and on one occasion, only one, they induced the sultan to sit at the same table with other persons, — the Prince of Wales, the foreign ambassadors, and his own ministers. It was the first time that the Commander of the Faithful had eaten meat with any man, the rule being that the head of the Moslem faith (like the pope) must always eat alone.

Railroads and schools were projected and patronized by Fuad and Aali; but the trunk line of railroad between Constantinople and Belgrade was opposed by the Servians, till at last the contractors threw up the work, having only completed short lines of unconnected railway in places where the right was conceded to them.

The schools fared little better, — only one, for boys of all religions, came into successful operation; but the navy was improved, the soldiers were better armed. This was, however, all that Turkey gained from its enormous foreign loans. Vast sums went into the hands of middlemen and speculators, among them the sultan himself, who speedily learned all civilization could teach him of the *modus operandi* of the stock exchange.

Money once obtained, the sultan spent it in absurd building projects. He was fond of jewelry, and spent vast sums on precious stones, particularly diamonds. He had no knowledge of painting, but had a passion for buying indifferent daubs. Sculpture is an art forbidden by his faith, but he took a fancy to set up an equestrian statue of himself in Constantinople. The work was executed at Munich, but when it reached his capital it was such a cause of scandal to the *softas* (a class answering to the scribes and lawyers of the New Testament) that it was hidden away for several years, and recast into cannon on the death of its original. His personal expenses were enormous. He had a nervous horror of fire, and one of his freaks was to destroy all the beautiful furniture in the Dolma-Baghtché Palace, and replace it by iron-work. One of his devices for raising money was frequently to command his vassal the khedive, to visit him at Constantinople, well knowing that he dared not present himself before his sovereign without magnificent gifts. On one of these occasions, in July, 1873, the present to the sultan amounted to three million and a half of dollars, besides *backshish* distributed to his princes and ministers. Looking to future favor the khedive offered on this occasion six hundred thousand dollars to the heir of the Turkish throne, but Prince Murad refused it, saying: "My dignity will not permit me to receive your money as a gift; still less would I take it as the price of a protection which ought neither to be bought nor sold."

At that moment the young prince was pecuniarily embarrassed, owing to his relations with his uncle Abdul Aziz; and this leads us to speak of his early life more particularly.

His mother was a Circassian. He was born Sept. 21, 1840. His father early removed him from the pernicious influences of the harem, and placed him under manly and able tutors. Abdul Medjid superintended his boy's education himself, and was often present at his lessons. He called him, affectionately, "Muraddin," or "my Murad;" and twice a week a report of the boy's progress was sent in to him.

Docile, patient, and gifted with a good memory, the child soon learned to read and write his own language. A talent for composition developed itself as he grew up, and his poems, though not numerous, were remarkable for their delicate taste and elegance of diction.

Besides Turkish and Arabic, he studied Turkish history,

arithmetic, geometry, and drawing. When he was fourteen he began to study French. His teacher was the future grand vizier Edhem Pasha, who had been the instructor of Abdul Medjid.

The history of Edhem is a curious one. He was born of Greek parents, and saved from the massacre of Scio in 1822. He was then sold as a slave in Constantinople, and bought by the grand vizier, who sent him to Paris, whence he returned a bachelor of arts, and one of the best pupils at the École des Mines. He was advanced to high dignities, was several times minister, and was made grand vizier, Feb. 5, 1877, after the unjust dismissal of Midhat Pasha.

Murad soon learned to read, write, and understand French, but he never could speak it fluently. Still, during his journey in western Europe in 1867 he made himself understood in the courts he visited, and his conversation made everywhere a favorable impression. One reason why he made no great progress in languages (the most important accomplishment for a sovereign) was that his whole soul was absorbed in a passion for music. He not only played the most difficult music well, but he solaced himself with musical composition, frequently setting his own words to his own airs. All his music was, however, plaintive; it seemed to breathe a presentiment of his own sad destiny.

Subsequently Murad developed a taste for architecture, less hurtful to his temperament than his love for music, but more dangerous to his purse; for during the latter years of Abdul Aziz's reign his love of building brought him great pecuniary embarrassment.

He was constitutionally sweet-tempered, and was beloved by those about him; but he appears to have been deficient in that strength of character which no Turk, if it be not his by nature, can acquire under the enervating conditions of his domestic life. Abdul Medjid emancipated his brothers and his sons from that law of Mohammedan etiquette which confined all the princes of the blood-royal to the bounds of the seraglio.

Great was the grief of Abdul Medjib's children when that enlightened sovereign and kind parent, at the age of thirty-eight, was gathered to his fathers of the race of Othman. Reschid (or Richard), the third son, now heir presumptive of his brother Abdul Hamid, was on the point of committing suicide. Murad alone accepted his changed position with composure, protecting and comforting his younger brothers.

Abdul Aziz, who had promised him many favors on his accession, by no means kept his word. In 1863 Ismail Pasha, who had succeeded his uncle Said as viceroy of Egypt, came to Constantinople to receive his investiture as khedive. In gratitude for the permission to leave his throne to his own son, according to the European law of succession, he offered a magnificent steam-yacht to his suzerain. Abdul Aziz was delighted with the gift, and instantly embarked for Egypt, taking with him Murad, whom he appeared afraid to leave behind. On their return from this excursion he manifested great jealousy of his young heir, whom he was always suspecting of conspiracy. On one occasion he confined him for a year to the boundaries of the seraglio. In 1867 Abdul Aziz visited, as we have said, the Paris Exposition. The origin of the troubles of 1876 and 1877 in Bosnia and Herzegovina was, it is said, the burthen of the increased taxes imposed to pay the expenses of this journey. Abdul Aziz was accompanied by his own son, Yussef Izzeddin, and his two nephews, Murad and Abdul Hamid. Before reaching Marseilles, however, his anger against Murad broke out afresh, and he was anxious to leave him on board the yacht, or send him back to Constantinople. Fuad Pasha here interposed, objecting that the sovereigns of Europe would not understand such treatment of the heir presumptive.

Under this pressure the sultan was obliged to yield, but everywhere during their journey he found fresh occasion to be jealous of his handsome nephew. He was continually complaining of his conduct, which appeared to others to be marked by tact and good sense in every particular. He took it extremely ill that Queen Victoria, Napoleon III., and the king of Prussia, should show more attention to a young man of twenty-seven, the heir-presumptive of the Turkish Empire, than to his own ill-conditioned son. When they got back to Constantinople Murad had to pay for his popularity in London, Paris, and Berlin. He was kept like a state prisoner in his own apartments in the Dolma-Baghtché Palace, or in his country house of Kourbalidere. But his servants frequently connived at his escape for a few hours. On these occasions he would always make his way to the house of a French friend at Pera. "Now then," he would cry, "for a visit to the French Theatre!"

Such visits were very dangerous both for the prince and his accomplice. The disguise of a false beard and a felt hat might easily have been penetrated by the eyes of some old pasha; and frequently the prince, becoming alarmed for his companion's safety, would say: "Let us go home to your house. I will play and sing for you, and then we can talk philosophy."

He is said to have been a good converser. He had, of course, not what would have been called a liberal education for a European, but he could talk agreeably on a large variety of subjects, and put questions like a man who wants to know and understand. He was tolerant and liberal both in religion and politics, — almost too liberal perhaps, for his French friends seem to have been men of very advanced ideas. He often expressed his earnest hope that when he came to the throne he might be able to promote self-government among his people.

He once employed a French lawyer in Constantinople to draw him up a constitution, but the draft was never finished. Murad himself, however, composed a paper in which his wishes on the subject were set down.

No foreigner was allowed to visit him openly. Even Sir Henry Elliott, the English ambassador, was denied access to him. A Frenchman, however, by the aid of one of the prince's tradespeople, made his way to his country place, and has left an account of the interview: —

"We reached the *tchiftik*, or country seat, of Kourbalidere," he says, "which was surrounded by a high white wall with an enormous entrance gate. 'We must go in by a little door,' said my cicerone, pointing to a wicket. He rang; a black eunuch opened it with due precaution, but on recognizing my companion he welcomed him politely, and led the way to a summer house in a beautiful garden. There, in a room luxuriously furnished, Prince Murad stood, expecting our arrival. Without permitting us to complete our Oriental salutation, he held out his hand smiling, and invited us to be seated. He wore an English morning suit of light gray cloth, the only sign of the Turk about him being a fez. He was small, but well-made. He looked in good health, and had a clear complexion. He was thirty-three, but looked younger. His eyes were bright and soft, intelligent and tender.

"The conversation turned on Europe, which gave him the opportunity of speaking of his travels. The city he most admired was Paris; the country he liked best was England; the sovereign who had most impressed him was the king of Prussia.

"'When we were staying at Potsdam,' he said, 'I left my room early one morning, and went into the garden. I saw some one at a little distance talking quite familiarly with a sentinel. My surprise was great when I recognized the king of Prussia. When he saw me he came toward me, quitting the sentinel with a few parting words and a kind nod. "Ah!" said I to myself, "now I behold a model king, without pride or pretension." I gave him at once my affection and esteem.'"

Murad then asked the visitor about his own travels, and appeared particularly interested in his account of the United States. "If I am ever sultan," he said, "I hope to see Mussulmans and Christians, Jews and idolaters (if there be any in my dominions) sitting on the same bench, and learning to look upon each other as brothers."

The conversation lasted an hour and a half. It appeared to give great pleasure to Murad, who requested his French guest to correspond with him. This led to a series of letters on the affairs of Europe, which lasted several years. Several of Murad's letters upon Turkish politics were published anonymously by his correspondent in one of the French papers.

"You cannot imagine," said Murad to another friend, "what disgust and weariness I sometimes feel when surrounded by the women of my harem. The abject submission that prevails among them withers the germs of love. I get so tired of this domestic life that it is the cause of my taking more wine and *mastic* (the Levant brandy) than is good for me."

Alas! this taste, which had hastened his good father's end, was to wreck the career of a prince endowed by nature with every good disposition. It was also unfortunate that Dr. Capoleone, who had been assigned to him as his physician, was an ignorant, low-minded Italian, who cared more to minister to his patient's weaknesses than to help him to overcome them.

A Greek doctor of a different stamp, Dr. Mavroyéni, had been assigned to Abdul Hamid. That prince's mother had died of consumption, and his constitution was delicate. He, too, had inherited a taste for drink, but Dr. Mavroyéni assured him it would be his destruction. "Then I will never touch wine or liquor again!" said Abdul Hamid, and he kept his word. Murad might have made a similar resolution had his doctor been a man who could have inspired him to make it. Italian, Greek, Jewish, and Armenian doctors have often played important parts in Turkish history. Dr. Mavroyéni contributed largely to Abdul Hamid's elevation to the caliphate. Dr. Capoleone, on the contrary, by his ignorance and malpractice, led to the sad fate of the elder brother.

After the deaths of his great ministers Aali and Fuad Pasha, Abdul Aziz had no check upon his passions. He had eight grand viziers in five years, the worst of whom was Mahmoud Nedim Pasha, who, like his master, was bent on increasing his own wealth by every means in his power. To this end he became a creature of General Ignatieff, the Russian ambassador, and was guided by his advice in all matters of government. He belonged neither to Young Turkey nor the old school, but was influenced solely by self-interest and cupidity. In three years, under his administration, the Turkish debt increased nearly four hundred millions of dollars. The substitution of Yussef Izzeddin for Prince Murad as heir presumptive was a point on which the Russian ambassador agreed with the sultan and the grand vizier. He urged, however, that the change in the law of succession should be effected without violence, and wear the appearance of a salutary reform. A proclamation to that effect had been several times on the point of being promulgated, but was postponed on each occasion in consequence of the opposition of England, the court astrologer, and the *sheik-ul-Islam*, or chief interpreter of the Koran, who utterly refused to issue a *fetva* contrary to the spirit and the letter of the *cheri*, or Turkish unwritten constitution.

In 1876, however, the hesitation of the Sultan Abdul Aziz came to an end. The proclamation was to take place on the 25th of June. Murad was sounded as to his willingness to resign his rights, and peremptorily refused the offers made to him. He also refused with horror the offer of some Greeks to create a disturbance while the sultan should be at public prayers, and in the confusion to kill Abdul Aziz.

"If I am raised to the throne because my people wish me to reign," he said, "so be it. But no violence shall be offered to the person of my uncle. I should detest a throne that had cost a murder. I shudder at the bare idea of such a crime." "But suppose," said one of those about him, "that there was no alternative between his death and yours?" "Then let me die," was the prince's answer. There seemed no little probability of this event when the eight male descendants of Abdul Medjid received a command to move into the Dolma-Baghtché Palace, and there await the sultan's orders.

At that time all classes in Constantinople seemed ripe for revolution. Abdul Aziz had made young Yussef Izzeddin commander in the army, and had placed a younger son, just ten years old, at the head of the navy; but such appointments did not compensate the soldiers or the sailors for arrears of pay. Young Turkey was indignant at the banishment of some literary men, who were its leaders. Old Turkey was opposed to impious changes in the law of succession. Old Turks and young Turks agreed in hating Russia, and blushed to see the subservience of the Commander of the Faithful to his hereditary enemy.

Jews, Greeks, and Armenians had all causes of complaint against the government of Abdul Aziz. Even his court and household despised him. He was known to be dishonest whenever he could see a chance to gain. When not roused by temporary fits of savage anger, he was grim, torpid, and abusive. Yet two women in his household loved him, — his mother, who, with all her faults, was devoted to her son, and his third wife, or more properly the third woman who had borne him children; for, by Mohammedan custom, no legal marriage is possible to a sultan. This girl was a Circassian. . She loved him with such fervor that her end was hastened by his death. She died, partly of lung disease, and partly of grief, only a week after him. She was sister (or near relative) to Hassan, who avenged her death, and that of the master she had loved, by a wholesale massacre.

In the spring of 1876 the question of succession had produced a struggle between English and Russian influence in the affairs of Turkey. England favored Murad and the legitimate succession; Russia lent herself to the views of Abdul Aziz, and was anxious to see Yussef Izzeddin proclaimed heir to the throne. The English fleet was ordered to Besika Bay, at the entrance to the Dardanelles, and the Russian government promised the sultan material support in case of difficulty.

The most influential adherent of Murad at this period

was Midhat Pasha, a statesman on whom had fallen the mantles of Aali and Fuad Pasha. Midhat planned at this crisis a revolution. He had great influence with the *softas*, the students and interpreters of the Koran, of whom there were from thirty to forty thousand in Constantinople. His chief task in the affair, however, was that of buying the neutrality of the Grand Vizier Mahmoud Nedim Pasha. This end Midhat successfully accomplished, and the first fruits of the negotiation were that the grand vizier declined Russian assistance in the event of an insurrection. A rising of *softas* and of workingmen employed by the government soon after took place. The sultan becoming alarmed, sent to the mosqes to inquire what were the demands and desires of the *softas*. He was answered, the immediate dismissal of his grand vizier and the *sheik-ul-Islam*, and the substitution of Midhat Pasha and Haïrullah Effendi.

The sultan yielded immediately. He only stipulated, in deference to Russia, that Ruchdi, and not Midhat, should be nominated grand vizier, and that Midhat should content himself with a subordinate position, while Hairullah should take charge of the religion of the State.

Ruchdi was a man amiable and undecided. In politics he was, what is called in western Europe, a conservative. He was willing, however, to swim with the current, and at this crisis his appointment was acceptable to Midhat Pasha. The sultan, as if to make up for his grand vizier's want of will, nominated Hussein Avni, the incarnation of energy, to be war minister. By this time there was serious revolt in the provinces of Bosnia and Herzegovina.

The history of Hussein Avni is a curious one. He was born in a district of Asia Minor, known as Sparta, because peopled originally by a Spartan colony; and he exhibited all the daring, courage, and pertinacity which distinguished the comrades of Leonidas among the people of Greece. When he was sixteen he went forth to seek his fortune at Constantinople. He entered a mosque as student in law and theology, having an uncle who served as *khodja* there, that is, as teacher and preacher. But he soon found he had mistaken his vocation. He obtained an appointment to the Military Academy, and remained attached to it till he was thirty-three, first as student, then as sub-professor, with the rank of major. During those years he translated several French books upon tactics, which brought him into notice, and opened to him a career. He distinguished himself in the Crimean War, and was chief of staff to Omar Pasha. At one time he was made grand vizier, because both Abdul Aziz and the *valide* believed that he would lend himself to their scheme of substituting Yussef Izzeddin for Murad as heir to the Turkish throne; but Hussein was too good a patriot to favor Russian views.

When he lost the grand-viziership, on the restoration of Mahmoud Nedim to the favor of the sultan, he set out on a tour to western Europe, where he was particularly delighted with England and her institutions; but he was suddenly recalled. The sultan flattered himself that a man of Hussein's energy and determination would easily, as *seraskier*, or general-in-chief, control the revolutionary element, and hold it down with an iron hand. He had not miscalculated the energy of his war minister; but he was mistaken in the direction of the iron hand.

An understanding speedily took place between Midhat Pasha and Hussein Avni. A plan of reform was drawn up, combining equality of all persons before the law, a parliament, which should control the public purse, the responsibility of ministers, and greater freedom of the press. On the 31st of May the *softas* and others were to meet in one of the grand mosques, and send a delegation to request the proposed reforms from Ruchdi, the new grand vizier. If the sultan consented, giving substantial guarantees for his good faith, the revolution would be accomplished. If he refused or hesitated, he would be dethroned, and his next heir would be proclaimed by the title of Murad V.

Up to this point Prince Murad was kept informed of all that was going on, notwithstanding his state of close seclusion. He approved all the projects of reform, and consented to accept the throne if offered to him, but on condition that his dethroned uncle should be treated honorably, and that no indignity should be inflicted on him except the loss of his power and prerogatives. But a mine was being dug beneath this project of a popular revolution, — Hussein Avni was determined to forestall it by a *coup d'état.*

Midhat, Ruchdi, Ahmet Kaiserli (the head of the navy), and Hairullah Effendi the *sheik-ul-Islam,* all gave in their adherence to the plan of Hussein Avni. His Spartan spirit made him despise mixed multitudes, and a high-handed movement was far more to his taste than the underhand intrigues of the originally projected revolution.

Already the *sheik-ul-Islam* had prepared a *fetva* to authorize the deposition of the Commander of the Faithful. It was in these words: —

Question. If the Chief of Believers gives proof of derangement, or of ignorance in public affairs, if he employs the public revenues for his own personal ends to an extent ruinous to the nation and the State, if he causes confusion between things spiritual and things temporal, and if his continuance in power is hurtful to the State and to the nation, may he be deposed?

Answer. The law of the Prophet says: Yes!

Written by the humble Hassan Haïrullah, to whom may God be merciful!

Neither Hussein Avni nor Midhat thought it best to inform Prince Murad of this change of programme.

On the night of Monday, May 30, 1876, the minister of war and the director of the Military Academy had their troops under arms, ready to march, as they were led to believe, into Bulgaria. At the appointed hour they were led to the palace, whose water-front was already guarded by the boats of the ironclads.

All this took place after midnight. The night was dark and rainy; the sound of the waves upon the beach concealed slight noises. All in the palace lay asleep. Murad was sleeping heavily, when a quarter before three the *seraskier*, Hussein Avni, entered his chamber. He shook the prince's arm and begged him to rise and dress himself. Seen unexpectedly at that hour and under those circumstances, the stern and bearded countenance of Hussein Avni inspired Murad with nervous terror.

"What is the matter?" he asked, his first thought being that his uncle had discovered all, and had sent this man to murder him.

"The palace is surrounded by soldiers. Abdul Aziz cannot escape. At break of day he will be told that he has ceased to reign, and that his lawful heir, Murad V., has been proclaimed sultan."

These words in a harsh voice frightened the prince, who unhappily during the suspense and excitement of the past few days had been taking wine too freely. He refused to get up, saying: "I had rather be murdered in my bed."

"And so you will be if you do not rise and come with me at once," was the stern answer; "but to allay your suspicions take the revolver hanging at your bed's head, and at the smallest sign of treason shoot me through the brain."

At last, half reassured, Murad got up, took the revolver, and followed Hussein Avni. As they were leaving the palace they were stopped by a sentinel. The *seraskier* had forgotten the password. With great presence of mind he opened his cloak, and showed his breast covered with orders. Then roughly pushing the sentry aside, he said: "Fool! cannot you recognize your commander-in-chief and his aide-de-camp?" The man drew back, and they passed out, — the one bold and self-possessed, the other suspicious and unnerved.

A *caïque* was waiting for them; they entered it with a few followers. Murad was to cross the Golden Horn and so reach Stamboul, but Hussein Avni, who had some orders to give the fleet, insisted on passing under the stern of an ironclad. This put fresh apprehension into the heart of the new sultan. He thought that the steamer was to be his prison, and took no pains to conceal his great alarm.

SULTAN MURAD V.

Fortunately, the *caïque* was detained only a few moments, and those in her landed safely, without further adventure, on the beach at Constantinople. Thence they drove to the war-office, — the *seraskieriat*.

All the members of the divan, including Midhat Pasha, the *sheik-ul-Islam*, and the sheriff of Mecca, were awaiting their arrival. There were several *ulemas*, and several Christian dignitaries in the assembly. The act of the deposition of Abdul Aziz was then read, after which that which proclaimed Murad his successor.

When a salute of one hundred and one guns announced what had happened to the public, there was a general explosion of enthusiasm. No regrets were expressed for the fall of Abdul Aziz. Western Europe and Turkey were of one accord, but it is said that when the Emperor Alexander of Russia, at Ems, got a telegram with the news from General Ignatieff he sat for ten minutes without uttering a word.

From the war-office Murad drove to the water-side, through an enthusiastic crowd of his new subjects. He embarked in a *caïque* with forty-eight oars, which rowed him back to the Dolma-Baghtché Palace. On his way he met a smaller boat with his uncle on board of her. Murad's mind had been diverted from the terrors of the night by the excitements of the morning, but this spectacle filled him with deep pity. He shed tears, and shedding tears re-entered the imperial abode.

Murad, on his arrival at the Dolma-Baghtché went through the ceremony of *biat*, equivalent to the hand-kissing of European monarchies. The same name is still applied to the same ceremony at the Spanish court, and to official receptions in the South American republics of Spanish origin. The levee was altogether informal, — more like a presidential reception at the White House than a court held by the representative of the dynasty of Othman; and Murad was well pleased to see court etiquette and dignity disappear. The next day he put forth his first proclamation, announcing a policy of reform; he had himself drawn up the first draft, which was by no means approved by his advisers, and the document as it appeared was very far from expressing his views.

On Friday, June 2, 1876, took place his first *selamick*. Ill or well, a sultan is obliged to go publicly to prayers each Friday in the mosque. This ceremony is called the *selamick*. If it be omitted for two weeks the empire, according to Mussulman belief, is in the greatest danger. The national prosperity depends upon these public prayers of the Commander of the Faithful.

Another ceremony ought to have taken place that day, equivalent to the Christian ceremony of coronation; but the officer whose hereditary right it was to gird the sultan with the sword of Othman in the mosque of Eyoub, was unfortunately absent in Asia Minor. He was summoned by telegraph, but did not arrive in time to accomplish his duty on that Friday. Week after week he waited in Constantinople, but the important rite could never on any succeeding Friday be performed. Perhaps, had Sultan Murad been solemnly girt with the sword of sovereignty, there might have been more hesitation in setting him aside.

On the triumphal day of his first *selamick* he rode smiling and happy to the mosque of St. Sophia; by a strange coincidence it was the feast-day of Saint Constantine. The enthusiasm of the multitude was excessive. He was saluted as "the called for," "the desired," "the beloved." *Softas* raised Korans in their hands; women flung flowers in his path. Several times the Greeks tried to take the horses from his carriage. Forgetting the restraints of Oriental etiquette, Murad bowed to right and left like Western sovereigns.

On his return home the *seraskier* was announced. The sight of Hussein Avni had been painful to the sultan ever since the night of his accession.

After a military salute the minister grimly observed that a wise and venerable custom forbade sultans to respond to the acclamations of a multitude. Already, under pretext of imaginary conspiracies, Hussein Avni was keeping the palace guarded by his soldiers, and was refusing admittance to the sultan's oldest and most intimate friends. He himself slept for three nights in the palace, and the unfortunate prince, so long a prisoner during his uncle's reign, found himself in closer captivity than ever.

This was ill calculated to calm his nerves, already unstrung by his terrors on the night of his accession. His physician, a true Dr. Sangrado, prescribed copious bleeding, the most mistaken treatment for a man in his condition.

On the morning of Saturday, July 3, the new sultan held his first council. His ministers were Ruchdi, Midhat, Ahmet Kaiserli, Haïrullah, and Hussein Avni. It soon appeared that their views, especially in the great matter of public instruction, differed essentially from those of the reforming sultan. Feverish, excited, and discouraged, Murad left the council, and the next day he received news of the unhappy fate of Abdul Aziz.

That dethroned prince had been removed to the ancient palace of Top Kapou, whence he addressed a letter to Sultan Murad on the second day after his deposition:—

"Next to my trust in God, my hope is in your Majesty. I congratulate you on your accession, and I regret I could not serve the nation as it desired to be served. I trust your Majesty will not forget that I laid the foundation of those means that will preserve the empire and protect its honor. I call your attention to the fact that soldiers armed by my own hand have placed me in this situation. As I have always had the merit of being ready to help those who were in distress, I implore you to let me be removed from the melancholy and narrow residence in which I find myself, and to assign me a more suitable place of abode. I congratulate you that the power has now passed into the family of Abdul Medjid."

This letter was in the ex-sultan's own handwriting. It was written with red ink, such as in Turkey is only used by sultans. In a postscript he begs his successor to send him twenty thousand Turkish pounds which he had left behind him.

Murad's reply was likewise an autograph. In most suitable terms it tried to calm, console, and reassure his uncle, and he gave orders at once that he should be transferred to that wing of the palace of Tcheragan that he himself had formerly inhabited. But Hussein Avni put off the removal for three days, under various pretexts, really because he wished the new sultan to understand thoroughly that his orders must be subject to his own control.

At last, when the *seraskier* could no longer refuse obedience to the reiterated commands of his master, backed by the remonstrances of other members of the cabinet, he ordered Abdul Aziz and his family to be transferred from Top Kapóu to Tcheragan. But he would do nothing to discover and restore the twenty thousand pounds that the ex-sultan had left behind him.

The new residence of Abdul Aziz was guarded by three lines of soldiers, and he was desired to confine himself to his own rooms. Without paying any regard to these orders, Abdul Aziz went out at once upon the terrace that overlooks the Bosphorus, and proceeded to walk up and down there. The sentry on duty requested him to go indoors. "Rascal! who am I?" cried the ex-sultan. "Abdul Aziz Effendi," was the answer.

This curtailment of his titles highly exasperated the dethroned sultan, and the sentry, uncertain what to do, went in search of his colonel. That officer, approaching the ex-sultan, remarked that he had better avoid the night air. This interference still further exasperated Abdul Aziz, who, drawing a small revolver from his breast, fired at the colonel. The officer fortunately was bowing at that moment, and the ball passed over his head. He drew back, and brought up a party of soldiers. Seeing these the captive monarch turned away, and went back into the palace; but not being able to sleep, he came forth again in the dark, and wandered unmolested in the gardens and on the esplanade, still guarded by the soldiers.

In his agitation he talked aloud, and was heard saying, "Have I no one to defend me? Where are the men I have loaded with favors and kindness? Where are my sons? To one I gave my army, to the other my navy. Where are your regiments? Where are your ironclads? Why does not that noble vessel I see yonder blow up my enemies with its mighty cannon?"

When day broke his frenzy gave way to utter prostration. Sometimes in a tone of command he gave orders to his fleet, or broke out into reproaches addressed to Hussein Avni. Sometimes he resumed his dignity, called for his ministers, and questioned them as if they had been present.

Toward evening an aide-de-camp arrived to request him to give up his revolver. Abdul Aziz was himself at that moment, and he said, with irony: "What for? Why does my dear nephew want my revolver?" "He is afraid your Majesty might wound yourself." "Take it, then, out of my bosom." "No man may place his hand upon the person of your Majesty. Will you be pleased to give it me yourself?"

Abdul Aziz drew the revolver from its hiding-place, and gave it to the aide-de-camp, who, saluting most respectfully, was about to retire, when the sultan called him back again. "Fool!" he exclaimed, "why do you take the pistol, and leave hanging on the wall my sword and dagger?" "I have no orders concerning anything but the pistol," replied the messenger. But a few hours after the household of the ex-sultan removed the weapons.

The *valide* and some other women of the harem spent all Saturday with Abdul Aziz endeavoring to calm and comfort him. They succeeded in producing some effect, but during the night, in which he could not sleep, he became greatly agitated. Once he broke out fiercely against the *valide*, who was sitting beside him. "It is you," he cried, "*you*, you vile creature, who are the cause of my misfortunes." Was he alluding to his mother's intrigues, or to the evil education she had given him? After this he strode wildly up and down the hall, with many windows overlooking the Bosphorus, stopping from time to time to gaze upon its noble waters, and growing calmer as his eyes rested on the glorious scene. At sunrise, in an armchair, he fell asleep. He woke about eight o'clock, and sent for his reader, whom he ordered to read to him the Turkish papers. After listening to these for half an hour, he turned calmly to Faker Bey, his favorite chamberlain, and ordered him to bring him a small looking-glass, and a pair of scissors, as he wished to trim his beard.

The chamberlain went and told the *valide*, who gave him the scissors. They were a small pair with sharp points used for embroidery. "Now leave me by myself," said Abdul Aziz. He was accustomed to shut himself up alone when dressing or trimming his hair.

A few minutes after the chamberlain left him, some of his women peeped at him through a window in an opposite wall, and saw him cutting his beard, and apparently absorbed in the occupation.

Sitting on a chair near a window which commands one of the finest sea views in the world, Abdul Aziz with his right hand must have severed an artery in his left arm, and then must have used the weakened left hand to serve the right arm in the same way. It is hardly to be supposed he had ever heard of Seneca, but he imitated the great suicide unconsciously, dying with equal courage and with less parade. Weakened by loss of blood, he slipped from his chair upon the floor. The noise of his fall was heard by some of his women. They gave the alarm to the *valide*. Already a stream of blood was trickling from beneath the door of his apartment, which was fastened on the inside. It was forced open, and Abdul Aziz was found still alive. He was able to say to his mother, "I have killed myself," and in a few moments expired. It was nine o'clock in the morning. Two physicians were already in the house; they hastened to the spot, but could only declare that the dethroned prince was dead. Loud wails arose from his bereaved mother and

his women. Hussein Avni hastened to the palace. He
instantly ordered the body to be brought down to the lower
floor. There it was laid, all bloody, on the pavement. His
next care was to hold an informal inquest, — to examine the
valide, and to take other testimony. He also gave orders
to call in at once the seventeen chief physicians of Constantinople, including those attached to the British and
Austrian embassies. All came immediately, and by eleven
o'clock had drawn up a paper which they all signed. It
contained these paragraphs : —

I. The death of Sultan Abdul Aziz is due to loss of blood
caused by severance of veins in the left arm.

II. The instrument shown us is capable of having produced these wounds.

III. The direction of the wounds and the nature of the
instrument convince us that it was a suicide.

At the word " suicide " all Europe smiled incredulously.
The medical journals of London and Paris expressed grave
doubts upon the subject. A paper in the " Lancet "
brought out Dr. Dickson, the physician to the English
embassy at Constantinople, who had the reputation of being a good physician and an honest man. He acknowledged that, when first sent for to assist in the *post mortem*,
his expectation had been that he should behold the victim
of a murder. " It was not until we had thoroughly examined the facts brought before us," he concludes, " that I
became convinced that the death of Abdul Aziz was by his
own hand, as is stated in the report of the physicians."

But for some time the public impression in Constantinople and in Pera was that the case was one of murder.
It was said that early in the morning Hussein Avni, aided
by Redif Pasha, had committed the crime, and that they
had slain two victims, — the ex-sultan and his third wife,
the sister or near kinswoman of Hassan, the Circassian,
who had lost her life attempting to defend her husband
and sovereign. This romance may make a future plot for
a sensational novel ; but in sober truth the Circassian wife

of Abdul Aziz lay dying of consumption; and her end, which was indeed hastened by her grief, did not take place till some days afterward.

Murad himself believed that Hussein Avni was his uncle's murderer. The story was told him without any precautions, and in the excited state of his nervous system it had the worst effect upon him. "They have covered me with shame!" he cried. "I promised him his life! Those wretches have murdered him! How horrible! How horrible!"

His excitement brought on an attack of frenzy. His medical attendant was wholly incompetent to deal with the case judiciously. It virtually brought to its close a reign which, though it lasted three months and one day, according to history, was limited to six days' actual sovereignty. When Abdul Aziz raised his hand against his life, he slew two sultans. His madness was the cause of his nephew's loss of reason. Abdul Aziz had indeed shown previous signs of insanity. In 1862 his furious conduct had so much alarmed Mehemet Ali Pasha, his brother-in-law, that he one day sent in haste for Dr. Mongeri, director of the insane hospital at Scutari, who prescribed sedatives, change of air, and frequent yachting.

According to Mohammedan law, a dead body must be buried before sunset. The remains of Abdul Aziz were therefore washed, perfumed, and wrapped in a shroud immediately after the departure of the physicians. They were then placed in a steamboat, and taken to the Sanctuary of the Mantle of the Prophet at Top Kapou. Here the funeral services took place in the presence of almost all the ministers and certain other official personages. The body was then borne to the splendid mausoleum of Sultan Mahmoud, where father and son lie side by side.

Fully persuaded that his uncle Abdul Aziz had been murdered by the war minister Hussein Avni, Sultan Murad, during the fatal Sunday, June 4, 1876, spoke of the event again and again with horror. Sometimes he grew wild with indignation, sometimes he wept, sometimes he sat in melancholy silence, from which no one could rouse him. None of his European friends were suffered to approach him at this crisis. He was left to the care of an incompetent physician and an ignorant, weak-minded *valide*.

His reign was now over. Hussein Avni, the head of the conspiracy that had placed him on his father's throne, now governed in his stead. The official organ continued to inform the public each day that his Majesty had transacted business with his ministers or his grand vizier; but he was no longer capable of attending to affairs. He ceased to care for food; he talked wildly to himself. Sometimes he walked restlessly until exhausted; sometimes no persuasion could arouse him. Yet he had lucid intervals, when he would cry: " I will give in my resignation as sultan! Let me find an asylum in France or Italy. Let my successor be called to the throne."

Such was his condition for ten days. At the end of that time a dreadful tragedy cut short the career of the powerful dictator, Hussein Avni.

Hassan Bey, brother or cousin of the fair Circassian, the best beloved wife of Abdul Aziz, belonged to the indomitable race of Caucasian mountaineers, whom the Russian government expatriated, sending about five thousand of them over the frontier, to find an asylum in Turkey. Hassan's father had been Ismail Bey, a noted chief, who as head of a small colony in Roumelia contrived to prosper in spite of the hardships which beset his fellow exiles. He was sufficiently well off to send his son Hassan to the Military Academy, which he quitted with the grade of lieutenant. A brilliant future seemed in store for this young man, whose near relative already occupied an important position in the sultan's harem, being mother to his third son, Prince Mehemet Selim Effendi. Hassan rose rapidly in his profession. In a few months he was made a captain, and then aide-de-camp to Prince Yussef Izzeddin. His advancement was due to influence; for as a scholar he had never been distinguished, and he was a very insubordinate and indifferent soldier. Though a married man, his life was disorderly. Every night he might be seen in the disreputable singing-gardens of Pera, gambling and drinking in low company. Indeed his reputation was so bad that suspicion rested on him as the probable murderer of two disreputable Armenian women. His tall figure and his martial bearing made him everywhere conspicuous. But his high cheek bones showed the Tartar blood in his veins, and his stern, cruel look, rough manners, and quarrelsome disposition did not dispose people in his favor, though they treated with respect the sultan's brother-in-law.

After the *coup d'état* all aides-de-camp of the court of Abdul Aziz were ordered to report themselves in garrison towns in Asia. Bagdad was assigned to Hassan, who, however, continued to linger in his old haunts, openly accusing the *seraskier* of regicide.

For this he was put under arrest. The next day, June 11, the young widow of Abdul Aziz died. On the 15th Hassan declared himself humble and penitent, and promised to set out the next day for Bagdad. On giving this promise he was set at liberty.

That evening he presented himself at the residence of Hussein Avni, and was informed that his Highness had gone to dine with Midhat Pasha, at whose house after dinner a cabinet council was to be held. He next crossed the Golden Horn in a *caïque*, and entered a restaurant, where he tossed off several glasses of *raki*. After this he made his way to the house of Midhat Pasha, — a mansion standing in a garden exposed to public view. On the ground-floor was a large vestibule, on which opened the servants' rooms and offices; above were the reception-rooms, one looking toward the sea, the other toward Constantinople. The ministers were assembled in the one overlooking the city, where a chandelier with forty lighted candles hung over an oval table, on which lay handsomely bound French books. The furniture consisted of sofas placed in each corner of the apartment, and large armchairs covered with red silk-damask in the most modern style. The other saloon (empty at the moment) was larger. It had blue silk furniture, and doors leading into the harem. It was lighted by two chandeliers, whose soft light fell through folding-doors into the red reception-room.

The ministers present were: Midhat; Ruchdi, the grand vizier; Hussein Avni, minister of war; Ahmed Kaiserli, minister of naval affairs; Raschid Pasha, minister of foreign affairs; four other members of the cabinet, and an ex-sheref of Mecca. Besides these there were two other high officials, Mahmoud Bey and Said, who was secretary to the grand vizier, — twelve in all. They had begun business about ten o'clock, but had paused for half an hour to eat ices, and partake of other refreshments. The council was going on again when an unbidden guest appeared among them.

At half-past ten Hassan Bey had presented himself in the vestibule. An aide-de-camp asked him what he wanted. "I leave for Bagdad to-morrow morning," was the answer; "and want to make an important communication to his Highness the *seraskier*."

He was invited to sit down, and refresh himself, and await the rising of the council. He preferred, however, to walk up and down the hall, where some of the aides-de-camp were asleep, and some engaged in card-playing. By degrees they ceased to notice him, and he quietly passed up the stairs; in an antechamber at the head of the staircase he found the grand vizier's servant, and two footmen of Midhat Pasha. Addressing the former he said that he was anxious to speak to the *seraskier*. The man politely offered to go below and send up a servant of Hussein Avni's.

When he departed Hassan half opened the door of the reception-room. "It is forbidden!" cried the servants. But Hassan had had time to see how the guests were distributed. The grand vizier was on a sofa near a window talking to the *seraskier*, who was seated at his ease in an armchair. Near them were Ahmed, Kaiserli, Raschid, and another. Nearer to the door on the same side of the room was Midhat, with the secretary and Mahmoud Bey, leaning over a small table on which were writing materials. The other side of the room to the left was occupied by the other ministers.

In a few moments, without heeding the prohibition of the servants in the anteroom, Hassan a second time opened the door and entered, wrapped in his military cloak, with his martial stride. He made his salutation in a grave, respectful manner. Then drawing a revolver from his sleeve, he cried, " *Seraskier*, do not stir !" and pointed his pistol at Hussein Avni. The weapon went off. What next passed it is difficult to describe, all present having been too excited to recall particulars. Almost all rushed in a body to the blue reception-room, but Kaiserli sprang to his feet, and seized the murderer. Hassan, however, freed himself, and struck him with a dagger in the face. Meantime Hussein Avni, who had been shot in the breast, had just strength to reach the door. Hassan ran after him and plunged the poniard into his stomach, making repeated wounds. There remained in the red room only one minister, — the minister for foreign affairs, Raschid Pasha, who had fainted in his chair. Hassan, disregarding him, rushed to the door of the blue room, crying, " Kaiserli ! Kaiserli !" Then he fired into the folding-doors. He evidently no longer knew what he was doing. Seizing an armchair he flung it against the chandelier, and with a lighted candle that dropped upon the floor he tried to set fire to the curtains. At this moment a brave young Anatolian page of Midhat's, a lad of singular beauty, rushed into the room. He at once threw his dagger at the head of the murderer, wounded him slightly and tried to pinion his arms. But Hassan, shaking himself free, stretched him dead at his feet. He then turned on Raschid Pasha, and fired through his skull; he died without having recovered from his fainting-fit.

Nearly half an hour had thus passed, and one man remained master of the battle-field in a house crowded with others.

The ministers, supposing that they were attacked by a band of brigands, intrenched themselves in the blue reception-room, waiting for succor, which a servant was sent through the garden to obtain. But that no servant but the brave young page should have come to their assistance seems very singular. It could not have been from cowardice, for no people are braver than the Turks. They probably believed that the blow was struck by order of the government, and dared not interfere with an accredited official.

Fortunately, near Midhat's house was a post of *zaptiehs*, military police. They reached the scene of blood, somewhat leisurely, about midnight, and their officers — a major and a lieutenant — summoned Hassan to surrender. He half opened the door and fired twice, wounding both of them. Their men, being then reinforced by a picket of soldiers from the war-office, broke in the door, and, notwithstanding a fierce resistance, overpowered Hassan. In the struggle an aide-de-camp of the grand vizier lost his life.

Mohammedan justice is speedy. Hardly six hours elapsed between the murderer's fourfold crime and his execution. After a brief examination, in which he said that he was sorry for Raschid's death, and for that of the brave young Anatolian, he was hung up to a tree in an open space before the *seraskiat*, his face bare, but his body wrapped in a kind of white shroud, with a writing on his breast describing his crime and its punishment. He remained hanging until sunset.

His victims were buried the same day. No one regretted Hussein Avni; and yet at that crisis the life of a general so energetic and so stern might have been of great service to the Ottoman Empire.

Raschid was a man of a very different spirit, — timid, prudent, and reserved. He had been educated in France,

and spoke French like a Frenchman. He seemed made
for an ambassador. He was, besides, strictly honest. He
was in his forty-seventh year. Hassan, his murderer, was
twenty-five.

For more than two months afterward the country was
governed by a triumvirate, — Midhat, the grand vizier, and
Haïrullah, the *sheik-ul-Islam*. These continued to deceive the public as to the true condition of Sultan Murad.
It was given out that he had had a sharp attack of illness,
that he suffered from fever and from several boils. Every
Friday he went to public prayers in the mosque, but he
proceeded thither in a *caïque* or a close carriage. "It is
because of his boil that he always hides his face," said
some; but others answered, "There is something worse
than a boil." At that time the whole Turkish Empire was
in commotion, and needed a strong hand to control both
its arms and its diplomacy. The wholesale massacre of
Christians in southern Bulgaria had roused the indignation
of all Europe. Bosnia and Herzegovina were in open
insurrection; Servia and Montenegro, assisted by Russian
officers, were at open war with the Porte; and the Russians
were massing troops on the frontier of Roumania. General
Ignatieff threatened to withdraw the Russian embassy from
Constantinople until a sane sovereign should occupy the
throne. Abdul Hamid, Murad's next brother and presumptive heir, was asked if he would undertake the regency.
He replied that a regency was not recognized by the law
of the Prophet, but that he would accept the throne if quite
convinced that his brother was incurably insane. After this
Dr. Liedersdorf was sent for from Vienna. He was the
director of an insane hospital in that city, and had been
already summoned to attend other crowned heads. He
wholly disapproved the lowering treatment of Dr. Capoleone,
recommended salt bathing and yachting, and far from considering the case hopeless is reported to have said in
private: "If I had Sultan Murad under my own care in
Vienna I would have him all right in six weeks."

This opinion was not what had been looked for, nor was it satisfactory. Indeed after improving under the new treatment Murad suffered a relapse, his nervous system being shaken by the thunders of a salute from the great guns of his own iron-clads as he was passing them in a *caïque* on his way to the mosque. But he could not be set aside without the approbation of the *sheik-ul-Islam*, who after a little hesitation issued the following *fetva*: —

Question. If the Commander of the Faithful be attacked by mental insanity, and if the objects for which he holds his functions cannot be attained in consequence, may he be deposed?
Answer. Yes.
Written by the humble Hassan Haïrullah, on whom may God send peace.

On Thursday, therefore, Sept. 1, 1876, Murad V. was formally deposed; Sultan Abdul Hamid II. was proclaimed, and the next day he was girt with the sword of Othman in the mosque of Eyoub.

Murad was unconscious at the time. His mother, unlike the savage Kurdish mother of Abdul Aziz, submitted to the change with a good grace. She was complimented by a promise that she should suffer no loss of dignity, but that she should be the adopted *valide* of the new sultan. Dr. Capoleone, in whom she had great confidence, assured her that her son's malady was incurable, and that his days were numbered.

Abdul Hamid had had ill-health in his youth, and had received little instruction. From a young Belgian seamstress, Flora Cordier, whom he converted to Mohammedanism, and placed in his harem, he had acquired some slight acquaintance with French, but he showed little of Murad's eager love for knowledge. Before his accession he did not care for much intercourse with foreigners, nor did he ever give ear to Young Turkey's liberal ideas. He was very fond of agriculture, and during the reign of Abdul Aziz had amused himself by cultivating a model farm. The *softas* and *ulemas* flocked around him. He was well versed in the Koran, and loved disputations in theology. To his mother, an Armenian from Georgia, he owes a quality very rare in the family of Othman, — the spirit of economy. He never exceeded his income before he came to the throne, and even laid by money.

At first he was disposed to treat his brother Murad with great consideration. "If his reign had only lasted a few years," he said in his speech after his inauguration, "I should have had the example of his virtues to walk by." But it soon appeared that the existence of a dethroned sovereign, — a state of things unparalleled in Turkish history, — gave his successor an uneasy throne.

Murad was rigidly secluded, and has been so up to the present time. No European friend was allowed to visit him; even his kinsfolk were denied access to him; and it was soon understood in his household that to acknowledge he was better was looked upon as a sort of treason to the brother who occupied the throne.

The *valide* soon associated with Dr. Capoleone a dervish, whose charms and verses from the Koran were probably a great improvement upon the Italian's leeches and hot water. But Murad in his first lucid interval refused to have anything to do with either of them, and from that time continued to improve. It was hard, however, to emancipate himself from the *valide's* fancies. She continued to fumigate his rooms, and to go through various barbarous and disgusting ceremonies to drive out, as she asserted, the demons and afrites.

His health might possibly have been restored by a journey to western Europe, but it is a great affair of state for any member of the house of Othman to quit the soil of the Ottoman Empire, — the law of the Prophet forbids it; and when in 1867 Abdul Aziz went to the Paris Exposition he was obliged to compromise by having the soles of his shoes daily powdered with dust from his own dominions.

About a twelvemonth after Murad's deposition a French-

SULTAN ABDUL HAMID II.

man succeeded in passing three days with him in the palace of Tcheragan, before he was removed to the old seraglio of Top Kapou. He found the ex-sultan to all appearance in good health, and exhibiting, so far as he could see, no sign of mental derangement; but his beard and hair, which were coal black on his accession, had become white as snow. Seeing his visitor's astonishment, Murad remarked: "I suppose you think that my hair has grown suddenly white from grief, like Marie Antoinette's, or that it has been blanched by the severity of my captivity. Not so. Some months before my uncle's death I found myself getting a little gray. I was rather pleased with my white hairs, but my mother objected to them. Not long before my elevation to the throne she purchased in Pera some marvellous hair-dye, with which she rubbed my head several times. The gray hairs disappeared, but shortly after I became subject to intense headaches, which Capoleone attributed to another cause, but Dr. Liedersdorf said they came from nitrate of silver, and such ingredients in the hair-dye. Since I have given it up my hair has grown snow-white, but the headaches have disappeared."

CHAPTER X.

THE TURKISH WAR OF 1877. — GENERAL SKOBELEFF.

IN order to understand the attitude of western Europe in reference to the Eastern Question, we must keep in mind the system of European police which maintains what is called the balance of power. The United States are happily preserved thus far, by their traditional policy, from taking any part in this matter, but more or less it concerns not only the continent of Europe, but the whole Eastern Hemisphere.

By the Congress of Vienna in 1815 it was laid down as a law of Europe that there were five Great Powers, namely: England, France, Russia, Prussia, and Austria. Of these, Prussia was then the most feeble. There were seven second-rate powers, namely: Spain, Portugal, Naples, Turkey, Holland, Sweden, and Denmark. Besides these there were third-rate States more or less dependent on the five Great Powers.

It was agreed that no one of the five Great Powers was to aggrandize itself (except as regarded colonies) without giving the other four a right to take something to their own advantage, that would keep even the balance of power.

If any two Great Powers went to war the other three had liberty to negotiate, or if need were, to intervene by force of arms, provided there was a chance that the balance of power would be disturbed.

Each Great Power had certain minor Powers under its protection. England, for instance, had Portugal; Austria had the Italian princes; Prussia, the northern States of

Germany. It was much like the system in an English public school, where a boy in the sixth form has one or more little boys under his protection.

But there was one country that refused to come under such protection, or to accept the obligations protection would have laid upon it. That country was Turkey. More than half the population of Turkey in Europe was Christian. Russia claimed a right to protect Greek Christians, and England claimed the right to uphold the Turkish government. From 1821 to the present day this question has been the most troublesome one in European international politics. It has given rise to three great wars: that of 1828, terminated by the Treaty of Adrianople; the Crimean War in 1855 and 1856, terminated by the Treaty of Paris; and the war of 1877 and 1878, when the police policy of Europe was put upon a new footing by Beaconsfield and Bismarck at the Congress of Berlin.

After the Crimean War, Turkey, in acknowledgment of French and English help, had to make great concessions. Her two Danubian provinces, Moldavia and Wallachia (wedged in between Russia and Hungary), were made autonomous; that is, they had a prince of their own and were only nominally a part of Turkey.

South of the Danube were two provinces, Servia and Bulgaria, with the river for their northern boundary. Servia secured autonomy under her own prince, but Turkey kept a garrison in the strong fortress of Belgrade, and received tribute.

To the west of part of Bulgaria, and south of Servia, were Bosnia and Herzegovina, with the little Black Mountain principality (Montenegro) lying between Bosnia and Albania.

The chain of mountains called the Balkans ran through what in 1876 was called Bulgaria. It now separates the Bulgarian principality from southern Bulgaria, better known under its new name of Eastern Roumelia.

The dance of death in 1875 was led off by Herzegovina.

It began by local quarrels between peasants and a Turkish tax-collector. Besides a tithe tribute on everything produced by agriculture, the Christian peasant had to pay poll-tax, land-tax, and a heavy tax upon his earnings, besides being subject to a strict *corvée* of forced labor on the public roads. Laws for the protection of the Christian population in Turkey have been repeatedly made and promulgated. After the Crimean War England and the French emperor insisted that a *hatt*, or royal ordinance, should be issued giving equal civil rights to Christians and to Mussulmans; but though such reforms were conceded to diplomacy, they remained entirely unenforced. Indeed, who can regulate the local oppressions of the landlord and the tax-gatherer?

The result of these oppressions, and of the scorn and contempt with which Christians were treated by Mohammedans, was that in 1875 a general insurrection broke out in Bosnia and Herzegovina, when the leaders of the rising put forth a pathetic appeal to the Great Powers to come to their help in one of four ways: either to give them leave to fight their quarrel out with their oppressors; or to assign them some land to which they might all emigrate; or to form an autonomous State of Bosnia and Herzegovina, to be ruled by some foreign prince under the suzerainty of the sultan; or lastly, to send foreign troops into their villages till the homes, honor, property, and religious liberty of Christians should be secured to them.

I have not space to describe minutely all the oppressions from which eight millions of Christians in Turkey in Europe suffered. These oppressions in Bulgaria by no means annihilated the prosperity of a very thriving population of Christians, but in Bosnia and Herzegovina their case was harder. The best way, perhaps, of giving some idea of the state of things will be to tell an anecdote taken from the note-book of a newspaper correspondent in 1875, and to give a copy of the usual official certificate issued to permit the burial of a Christian.

"I had," says the correspondent, "a *zaptieh*, or Turkish rural policeman, who accompanied me in many of my wanderings. The man was kind-hearted and gentle, and I saw many a kind act of his when he was with me, but it never occurred to him that it was wrong for a Turk to appropriate the property of a Bulgarian. One hot day, after a dusty ride we found ourselves on the top of a hill on the sides of which were vineyards full of fruit. Presently, as I sat on the ground, I found my *zaptieh* and the horses had disappeared. In vain I called; there was no response for some minutes, then he returned and beckoned me to follow him. To my amazement he had turned the horses loose to eat up the little vines, and had picked thirty or forty great bunches of grapes, which he was carefully stowing away in his saddle-bags, having reserved the best for me, and was preparing to ascend a peach tree, and to strip that also. When in imperfect Turkish I refused to participate in his act of robbery, I shall never forget the look of amazement with which he held up the grapes I had refused, gazed at them for a moment, then putting them into his saddle-bags mounted in solemn silence, and rode down the hill. It was an hour before he spoke, and then it was to express a fear that the heat of the sun had affected my head. 'For,' said he, 'if the Chelleby Effendi would hire a cart we might go to that vineyard to-morrow, and take away as many grapes as we could sell for ten dollars!' Now this man was one of the best of his class, as gentle as he was brave; but his education had taught him that what belonged to a Christian was his as a Moslem, and this idea had all his life been built up in him by what he saw around him."

"Had the Bulgarian proprietor," adds the reviewer who relates this story, "resisted this spoiling of his goods, this kind and gentle policeman would probably have slain him without compunction, and would have considered any man a fool or a madman who had suggested that he had committed a crime."

Here is the form of burial certificate which was given under Turkish rule when a Christian required interment:—

"We certify to the priest of the Church of Mary that the impure, putrid, stinking carcass of Sardeh, damned this day, may be concealed underground."

Bosnia is a country divided from Servia by the river Drina, and from Herzegovina by a mountain chain. The population of both countries is Slavonic, like that of Servia. Turkish Croatia and Herzegovina would have bordered on the Adriatic but for the decision of the Congress of Vienna in 1815, which gave Austria a narrow strip of territory running along the coast, and the beautiful Bay of Cattaro, which with her possession of Venice at that period gave her command of the northern part of the Adriatic Sea.

By 1876 the revolt begun in Herzegovina was exciting the hopes and sympathy of the Christians in Bulgaria. At the close of that year a hideous massacre of the Christian population took place south of the Balkans. The indignation of Europeans and Americans was roused to the highest pitch, and Russia prepared to invade Turkey on behalf of the Christian population.

When Russia had finally subdued Circassia, the Circassians, who were Moslems and unwilling to submit to a Christian yoke, were by the advice of England invited to take refuge in Turkey. The sultan colonized them in his own dominions, especially in southern Bulgaria, making them form small settlements or village communities. These people were cordially hated by the Christian peasantry; endless quarrels went on between them. The Circassians robbed; the Bulgarians retaliated. Among all the Christian populations of the Porte there were none at that time so industrious, ingenious, artistic, and progressive as the Bulgarians. In spite of oppression, these qualities made them prosper. Carpets, embroidery in gold thread, silver filigree work, and *repoussé* work were their chief industries. Politically and socially they made progress under great disadvantages, and they paid some attention to education.

When Bosnia and Herzegovina revolted, and Servia went to war with Turkey, it was determined by the Porte to take away all arms from the Christians in Bulgaria, and at the same time to arm, at the sultan's expense, all the Circassians and other Moslems in the province, besides bringing into it a large force of Kurds, Bashi-Bazouks, and Asiatic barbarians.

Before long Salonika (the Thessalonica to which Saint Paul wrote two Epistles), a noble port on the Ægean Sea, was the scene of a massacre which included two European consuls. This brought down an English fleet to threaten the place, and to demand reparation. But the Turkish government was very soon satisfied that, whatever might take place, the cause of the Porte would not be deserted by England. At once thousands of Bashi-Bazouks and savage Circassians were let loose on the unhappy Christian population of southern Bulgaria. More than one hundred towns or villages in this part of Turkey were destroyed; men, women, and children were slaughtered, — not only slaughtered, but in many cases tortured. It was the massacre of Scio, that had taken place fifty years before, over again. In one instance a large school of children were killed at once, and the bodies of the victims, together with the schoolhouse, were burned by the destroyers. About forty thousand Bulgarians were thus massacred in the month of June, 1876. Children made captives were sold in the large cities. Who can wonder at the passionate excitement that pervaded Russia on receipt of this intelligence?

Alexander II. was in the main a man of peace, but he took arms to insist on the fulfilment by the Porte of the Hatt-i-Heymin granted after the Crimean War, which gave protection and civil rights to Christians. This *hatt*, as I have already said, had remained a dead letter, and possibly, as its provisions were in opposition to all Mussulman feeling, it was out of the power of the sultan and his government to enforce them.

Everywhere Russia was hailed by the Christians of Bulgaria as their deliverer. Their belief was that Russia, and she alone among all the nations of the earth, could feel for them and would help them.

The war the year before, when Servia attacked the Turks, had brought many Russian officers across the Danube as volunteers. There were many also in Roumania, which although nominally under the suzerainty of the Porte, considered itself under the protection of Russia.

The Russian armies marched therefore through Roumania, and concentrated at Gourgievo, a Roumanian town on the left bank of the Danube. Before them lay the river, two miles wide, its course broken by a muddy islet near the Turkish shore. On this shore lay a Turkish army with strong redoubts, and below these, also on the Turkish side, was the town of Rustchuk. There was also a strong Turkish fleet in the river.

A story to be interesting should always have a hero, and the hero of this Turkish war was General Skobeleff. By following his history we shall obtain all the principal points of the war, which was a brief one, its actual operations only lasting from June, 1877, to February, 1878.

Mikhail Dimitrivitch Skobeleff — the "white general," as all called him, — the "intelligible general," as some of his soldiers named him, was, when the war opened, about thirty-three years old.

As so much Russian literature is read at the present time, it is probably superfluous to explain the Russian system of nomenclature. A Russian has but one baptismal name, but as a middle name he always takes his father's baptismal name with *vitch* added to it. A woman does the same thing, but adds *ovna*. Servants in Russia, instead of addressing their mistress as Ma'am or Madame, or even by her married name, would say: "Here is a letter for you, Elisaveta Ivanovna," or to their master, "Some one would like to see you, Alexander Vassilivitch." It is in Russia as it was in Greece in the Homeric days, when it was not courteous to address a chief without adding his father's name to his own. Agamemnon, in a crisis, warns Menelaus to give no offence by neglecting this piece of propriety.

Skobeleff's father was therefore Dimitri Nicolaivitch Skobeleff, and the son became Mikhail Dimitrivitch. His great-grandfather was said to have been a Scottish immigrant named Scobie; but he himself cared to go no farther back than his grandfather, a peasant, who went into the Russian army and rose to be a general.

Skobeleff's father was a gruff old gentleman, with a harsh voice. Many esteemed him miserly, but he was a brave and distinguished officer, and devotedly fond of his son, who delighted in playing boyish tricks on him. Both father and son were tall and very handsome. Mikhail Dimitrivitch indeed was six feet two. The old general placed his boy, who was too young to enter the army during the Crimean War, in the hands of a German tutor, who, if he implanted nothing else, inspired his pupil with a hatred for Germany. "He was an unjust, mean, rough fellow," said Skobeleff to a friend in after years. "I hated him as much as one human being can hate another. Once he struck me, — a boy of thirteen, — in the presence of a girl whom I admired immensely, struck me without the slightest provocation on my part. . . . I forgot what I was doing. I sprang upon him, seized him, and remained petrified. Do you know what that fellow tried to teach me? He taught that Germany was everything to Russia; that everything in Russia had been done by Germans, and that Russia must either obey Germany or perish. There was no universe, there was nothing but Germany. And I hated those things in my heart. My father dismissed the German, and I was sent to Paris, to a tutor named Girardé. What a contrast! I love Girardé — love him more than my own relations! He taught me to love my country. He showed me that there is nothing on earth higher than one's country, and said that every citizen should carry his country's name with pride. After having experienced a course of hard words, abuse, and blows, I now met with gentleness, attention, delicacy. I am deeply grateful to that man. He made me study, and instilled into me a love of science and of knowledge."[1]

---

[1] Much of this account of General Skobeleff is taken from a charming book by Alexander Verestchagin, "At Home and in

And this love of science and of knowledge was with Skobeleff to his dying day. He always said that men must grow in knowledge till they die. Not only was he always increasing his own vast stores, but he was constantly trying to stimulate others. The young men under his influence he taught to acquire knowledge, and to enjoy it. He could speak five languages fluently. Wherever he went he could find time for new books and reviews; he loved poetry and quoted it beautifully.

After leaving Paris he went to a Russian University. He seems there to have indulged in a good deal of extravagance, so he was put into the army and sent to Turkestan. In Turkestan he acquired great credit, received the cross of Saint George, the highest reward of bravery, and was made a general.

At one time in his career he outranked his father, and was delighted to tease the old gentleman by his official seniority.

His successes in Turkestan made many men at St. Petersburg about the court jealous of him. When he joined the Russian forces at Gourgievo he was not at first given a command, but was attached to his father's staff. There he was virtually in command. The arrangement, however, was not destined to last long. Even the envious could not ignore his merits, and he soon became the favorite of the commander-in-chief, the Grand Duke Nicholas, the brother of the czar.

The great strength of Skobeleff lay in his power over his private soldiers. Accustomed to abuse and blows, they found nothing of the kind in Skobeleff, who would have no flogging in his division, and twice threatened to break officers (one of them a colonel) for striking their men. In other parts of the Russian army (except in the Cossack

---

War." I am indebted also to an article in the "Fortnightly Review," by a war correspondent, Mr. W. K. Rose, also to lives of Skobeleff, by Dantchenko and Novihoff, and to miscellaneous articles in French and English newspapers and reviews.

regiments) blows from an officer were considered part of the discipline. Alexander Verestchagin relates that when he joined the Cossacks at Gourgievo he was cautioned at once by his brother officers to be civil to his men.

Skobeleff was never weary of seeing that his soldiers were well-fed, warmly clothed, and comfortable. He was their comrade as well as their officer. Innumerable are the anecdotes told of the ways in which he gained their confidence and affection, — how he would take a wounded soldier beside him in his carriage, or fling his cloak over another as he lay upon the ground; or how he has been known to dismount from his white charger, and march with a weary regiment, reviving its spirits with gay talk as the men toiled on. To all suffering he was generous and full of sympathy.

I said his soldiers called him "the intelligible general." This was because he explained to them his orders. For example, when, early in June, 1877, they were to cross to an island in the Danube to support the boats which were laying torpedoes in the river, the following scene took place. The officers were on the point of proceeding with their men when Skobeleff stopped the infantry. "Wait," he said, "you must not go off like that; the soldier should always know where he is going, and why he is going there. The soldier who knows what he has to do, and understands the purpose of the expedition is a thousand times more valuable than an unconscious instrument. The Cossacks I have already talked to. Good morning, my good fellows. Do you know where you are going?" "To Parapan, your Excellency." "What for?" "To thrash the Turks." "That's right. What's your name?" "Ergoroff, your Excellency." "You are a smart fellow. I see that you will soon get the Saint George. Only we are not going to thrash the Turks just yet. We have another job before us just now. We want to cross the river, — do you understand?" "Yes, your Excellency." "Mind you do. We have got tired sitting of here among the Moldavians, where we can't do anything without money. There is little work for soldiers here." " Exactly so, your Excellency." " Well, we have come here to fight, but the enemy over yonder won't come to meet us. He is too snug over there, so we must beat him out of it. Let us go and turn him out, my eagles!" This was met with a cheer. " But to turn him out we must first cross the river. That is where we shall catch it! As soon as we begin to cross over, the Turk, who is no fool, will set his monitors at our pontoons and our flotillas. You have seen how those monitors can puff and blow?" "Yes, your Excellency." " He will try to drown us, but we are more cunning than he. We are going to put such mines in the river that he will be unable to pass them. As soon as he gets over one of these mines it will explode and blow him up. We mean to cross the river under his nose." " He is quite different from the others," said the soldiers among themselves, " he is a clever general, and *intelligible*."

In June, 1877, when only a small detachment of the Russian army had crossed the Danube, and the pontoons which had transported them were being worked into a bridge, Skobeleff undertook to test if it were possible to swim cavalry across, by himself making the attempt. He pushed his white charger into the river, and here is an account of the scene, written by Mr. Rose, who watched him breathless from the bank, standing beside the rough old father: —

"He wound his way down the scarped clay cliffs at Zirnitza, across a small bridge which spanned a creek, to the island of Ada, and then, entering the river, the gallant horse, guided by Skobeleff's skilful hands made for the farther shore. . . . With his binocular the gray-haired father followed the progress of his son and his charger through the swift current. Then his arms began to shake, and his hands refused to hold the glasses to his eyes. He who had headed eight hundred troopers in a fierce onslaught upon five thousand Turks was unnerved by the sight of so venturesome a deed. Prince Tzeretleff, who was standing by his side noting the slow course of his comrade in his unequal struggle with the moving waters, in response to the earnest appeals of the old general, reported every circumstance of the exciting adventure. At one time Skobeleff was forced to fling himself from his saddle and to swim beside his horse. Emotion choked the voice of the father as this was reported to him, and he exclaimed ever and anon, 'Oh! my brave boy! Is he drowned yet?' And when young Skobeleff touched the little shelving bay below Sistova in safety, a ringing cheer was given by the Russian soldiery who had witnessed the rash exploit, and the group which surrounded the gray-haired general, echoed his 'Thank God!' as much for *his* sake as for the sake of an undertaking almost unparalleled in its temerity."

When the passage of the Danube was made finally on the pontoon bridge, Skobeleff shouldered a musket like a private soldier and marched over with the men.

He was put into command of a division; every officer under him was devoted to him. He treated them all when off duty as friends and comrades; but then every one of them was expected, when occasion came, to lay down his life as an example to his men. "Fear," he has been heard to say, "must cease when a man reaches the grade of captain."

"Skobeleff's friendship," says Verestchagin, "meant responsibility and increased danger. The friend of Skobeleff was expected to follow his own example. When a stranger might be excused or pardoned, there was no mercy for a friend."

The army, having crossed the Danube, was in Bulgaria. The Turks retired before it. Plevna, on the high-road to the passes of the Balkans, was the strong place they had determined to defend. There lay Osman Pasha with his gallant little army. The works of defence (in which the Turks excel) were very strong. Three times the Russians attacked the place, and were repulsed, — twice in July, and the third time on the 11th of September. On this last occasion Skobeleff's duty was to take a redoubt on a certain Green Hill, which he regarded as the key to the Turkish position.

He always rode a white horse, and wore a white coat, that he might be conspicuous to his own men during a a battle. With the usual address to his soldiers, he despatched them to the redoubt. He knew well that he was sending numbers of them to death. They knew it, too; but they advanced right up to the Turkish cannon with unflinching bravery. One company, however, gave way. In their disorder they were encountered by Skobeleff on his white charger. "Follow me!" he cried; "I will show you how to thrash the Turks! Close up there! Follow me, my men! I will lead you myself. He who deserts me should be ashamed of himself! Now then, drummers, — look alive!"

Meantime — for there was no quarter on either side — the Turks were seen torturing the wounded before despatching them. This roused the spirit of the Russian soldiers. They pushed on with fury. Probably no engagement was ever so bloody in proportion to the men engaged; but Skobeleff's soldiers won the Green Hill and the redoubt, and planted two Russian flags upon it. All the Turks were driven out or slain. Then Skobeleff on his white horse (two that day were killed under him) started off to headquarters to secure reinforcements. The battle was going against the Russians in other places.

"Major Gortaloff, you will remain here in charge of the redoubt," he said. "Can I depend on you? You must remain in this position at any price!" "I will remain or die, your Excellency!" "Possibly I shall be unable to send you any reinforcements. Give me your word that you will not leave the redoubt. This is the key to the enemy's position. Yonder they may not understand this yet. I am going to convince them of it. Give me your word that you will not leave the redoubt." "My honor is pledged. I will not leave this place alive." The major raised his hand as if taking an oath. Skobeleff embraced him. "God help you! Remember, my men; there may be no reinforcements. Count only on yourselves. Farewell, heroes!"

But as he took his last glance at the finest troops of his division, he sighed. "Consecrated to death!" he said, and thundered down the hill.

All his efforts at headquarters were in vain. He could not obtain a man to reinforce his position. He burst into tears. In vain he represented that the redoubt that he had won was the key of the position. There was nothing for it but to draw off his men from the Green Hill, and retreat. The colonel of one of the regiments of Cossack infantry, however, without orders, put his men at Skobeleff's disposal to cover the retreat of the heroes, and bring as many of them off safe as possible.

"They must all die, — my heroes, my lions!" cried their commander, rising in his saddle, and raising his cap. The Turks were swarming again into the fortress, mounting its walls on a rampart of dead bodies. The little garrison, defending themselves with their bayonets, began to despair. At last, through the fog which that day obscured everything, they saw comrades coming to their assistance, — Skobeleff and the Cossacks who had volunteered to follow him. There seemed to be one line left, by which they could retreat. "Will you order me to lead the men off by it?" said a lieutenant to the major. "We must save the flags," replied the old officer. "Wait! some one is coming! It may be reinforcements. Can you see what it is?" "Yes —no! It is Skobeleff! But he has only one battalion with him. I think he wants to cover our retreat. With so small a force the Turks cannot be beaten off."

There was no hope. The old major gathered his men around him, and looked earnestly in their faces. "Comrades, go!" he said. "Open your way with your bayonets. This place can no longer be held. God bless you, my children! Forward!" And bowing his head, he reverently made the sign of the cross over his men. "And you, father?" they exclaimed. "I stay with our dead," he answered. "Tell the general I have kept my word. Good-by, children!" They watched him as they turned their heads in their retreat. They saw him standing on the rampart waving to them. Then the Turks rushed in, and surrounded him. They saw the struggle. They saw his body uplifted upon Turkish bayonets.

An English war correspondent describes Skobeleff that evening as he turned from headquarters, when he could obtain no help for those he called his "lions." "He was in a fearful state of excitement and fury. His uniform was covered with mud and dirt; his sword was broken; his cross of Saint George was twisted round his shoulders; his face was black with powder and smoke; his eyes haggard and bloodshot. He spoke in a hoarse whisper. I never before saw such a picture of battle as he presented."

"I have done my best," he said in the hearing of another Englishman. "I could do no more. I blame nobody. It is the will of God."

But Skobeleff never recovered from the suffering of that day. He had sacrificed his men to win the battle; and the battle was not won. "Until the third battle of Plevna," he said to a friend, "I was young; but I have come out of it an old man. Not, of course, physically or intellectually, but I feel as if years had elapsed since I conquered at Lovichska, and after that our defeat at Plevna. It is a nightmare that may tempt me to suicide. The recollections of that place of slaughter are too terrible. I tell you honestly I sought death there. If I did not find it, it was not my own fault."

After the army retreated from Plevna, he retired for a week or two to Bucharest, the capital of Roumania. There he met General Todleben going to the front. The two men were attracted to each other. Todleben, the great engineer officer, who had planned and superintended, twenty-one years before, the defence of Sebastopol, was now going to plan works which should take Plevna, not by assault, but by starvation.

By the middle of October, 1877, Skobeleff was back again at the seat of war with his division, about forty thousand men. Plevna was then closely invested, and he was in possession of formidable redoubts and a long line of trenches. The place to which his division was assigned was called "the works of Zelony Gory."

But he had no longer with him the "lions" and the "eagles," who had perished in September, and whose fate, so long as he lived, he so bitterly mourned. Half his force consisted now of new recruits, whom he had to train.

On several occasions, when he observed them waver under fire, he rallied them, and marched them back where bullets were flying fast, and put them through their drill as on a parade ground ; after which he dismissed them to their work, and there was no more faltering.

Akh Pasha, as the Turks called him — the White General — went everywhere on his white horse in his white coat exposing himself. His soldiers believed him invulnerable. One wounded soldier solemnly assured a Sister of Mercy that he had *seen* the bullet that shattered his own arm pass through the body of his general. That general *would* make his own reconnoissances, his personal representations at headquarters, his personal inspections of everything, especially of all that concerned the food and comfort of his men ; remonstrances were useless. And he was only twice wounded, on which occasions the wounds were slight, being severe contusions. "I must show my men how badly the Turks aim," he said once when standing as a target to the enemy. "I know how to cure him of exposing himself," cried a soldier in the trenches to his comrades. "The first time he jumps up on the rampart above the trench let us all jump up after him." They did so, men and officers, and Skobeleff, who could not bear needlessly to expose his men, took the hint, and for once retired.

On the heights of Zelony Gory he lived several weeks in the trenches. He forbade his soldiers to rise to salute him as he passed, saying he was constantly on his rounds, and it would wear them out unnecessarily.

"I am going to get into an awful scrape at headquarters," he said one day to a friend. "I have been guilty of flagrant disobedience of orders. No one is permitted to pass out of Plevna, where Osman Pasha is anxious to get rid of useless mouths. There came this morning half a dozen carts full of Bulgarian women and children into my camp, and I passed them on in safety. I shall catch it!" "Perhaps," said his friend, "they won't hear of it at headquarters." "Oh! but I reported it myself," was the quick answer.

That same day a poor old Bulgarian woman escaping from Plevna, entered the Russian camp in another direction. The general commanding there ordered his Cossacks to scourge her with whips back to the town.

At last Osman Pasha was starved out and surrendered. As soon as the city fell Skobeleff was appointed its military governor. The Roumanians in the Russian army had already begun the plunder of the city. When Skobeleff remonstrated their officers replied: "We are the victors, and the victors have a right to the spoils." "In the first place," answered the general, "we were never at war with the peaceable inhabitants of this place, and consequently cannot have conquered them. But, secondly, please acquaint your men that I shall have victors of this kind shot. Every man caught marauding shall be shot like a dog. Please bear this in mind. There is another thing. You must not insult women. Such conduct is very humiliating. Let me tell you that every such complaint will be investigated, and every case of outrage punished."

A French gentleman who was at Plevna with the officers of the commander-in-chief's staff, speaks thus of what he saw of Skobeleff: "He is a magnificent looking soldier, almost as tall as the emperor; so that he has to stoop to enter any tent, and when he is in he cannot stand upright. He has a fine head, keen blue eyes, commanding forehead, and long whiskers and moustache, fine, soft, and golden. He is careful in his dress, especially when going into action, and dainty in his personal habits, loving shower-baths and perfumery. On the battle-field he is as brave as a lion, — too brave perhaps, for he has been known to engage when he was required to remain inactive."

This assertion I am disposed to think a calumny; for he was very angry if his soldiers disobeyed him in the same manner.

"When ordered to retreat," continues the Frenchman, "he sheathes his sword, sends his white charger to the front, and remains on foot, the last man in the rear, saying: 'They may kill me if they like, but they shall not harm my horse unless he is advancing against the enemy.' He has never quitted a battlefield without carrying off his wounded, nor has he ever, after a battle, gone to rest without making an address to his men and writing his own report to the commander-in-chief. He is adored by his soldiers. It is a common saying that if Skobeleff were killed every Russian soldier in the army would give a *kopek* to raise his monument. He is highly educated and a sincerely religious man. 'No man can feel comfortable in facing death,' he has been heard to say, 'who does not believe in God and have hope of a life to come.' Each evening in the camp he stood bareheaded, taking part in the evening service which was chanted by fifty or sixty of his soldiers."

This evening prayer struck our French observer [1] as very touching. "If people in Paris," he says, "who shed tears over the Miserére in the Trovatore, could hear these simple soldiers in the presence of death, addressing prayers and praises to the Almighty Father with their whole hearts, they would find it far more moving. Skobeleff is as distinguished for his modesty as his bravery," he continues. "He never alludes to his own deeds of valor. 'My children,' he says to his soldiers, 'I wear these crosses, but it is you who have won them for me.' He is a brilliant and amusing talker, a man calculated to be the idol of society,

---

[1] Supplément Littéraire du Figaro.

and to shine among those who are best skilled in the arts of making themselves agreeable."

One little trait alluded to by this writer I must further notice. Skobeleff was devoted to his horses, which were bred on his own estates, of an Arab strain. Cruelty to a horse was almost as abhorrent to him as brutality to a man; and he had a warm and loving heart for little children.

After Skobeleff the favorite Russian generals were Radetsky (I know not what relation to the old Austrian general) and Gourko, who is still living. He was said to be always ten leagues in advance of where you would have expected to find him. Todleben had aged since the Crimean war, but to him was due the capture of Plevna. The other generals had exhausted their troops in direct assaults upon the works. Todleben on his arrival said: "No more attacks upon the works. Let us raise intrenchment against intrenchment; let us dig; let us put our guns into position, and in a few weeks Osman Pasha will be starved out, and will fall into our hands." Todleben knew many languages, especially those of the East. He was also a great reader. As Osman Pasha slowly starved in Plevna Todleben found plenty of leisure for the improvement of his mind. Every week a great box of books reached him from St. Petersburg. He said his books enabled him to wait patiently till the Turkish commander was ready to surrender.

As to Osman Pasha, a man who cost the Russians many thousands of lives, he had after his surrender no greater admirers than the Russians themselves. When he was brought into their camp wounded and a prisoner, everybody tried to get an opportunity to compliment his defence of the city. "I am proud," said Skobeleff, "to make the acquaintance of the brilliant Turkish general, whose valor and genius I have so much admired." Osman replied, "The Russian general is yet young, but his fame is great. He will soon be the field-marshal of his army, and will prove that others may envy *him*, but that he has no reason to envy others."

Before the war the Emperor Alexander was respected by the great mass of his subjects, but when its successes began there was no end of the adoration all Russia felt for him. He had not been anxious for war, but he had been led into it by the circumstances of his situation. In his first address to his army he said: "While you are fighting I shall pray for you;" but he soon felt that his true place was on the Danube, and he quitted St. Petersburg for the army in spite of the remonstrances of his generals. When he reached the seat of war he assumed no command, but he endeavored to inform himself about everything. His presence seemed to animate his soldiers, who found him kind, compassionate, simple, and easy of approach.

The first three failures before Plevna moved him greatly. His whole expression changed. He became silent, sad, and thoughtful. He felt himself compromised by such a run of ill-success. How could he return to St. Petersburg an unsuccessful sovereign? But he never uttered a word of reproach against his generals. To more than one who had suffered defeat he said, taking him by the arm: "My poor friend, we must not be discouraged; we shall do better next time." Several times he was heard to say: "If we lose I will never return to Russia. I will die here with my brave soldiers." He was always ready to expose himhimself to danger. His escort was fifty Cossacks and his staff officers. With these he went everywhere. The Bashi-Bazouks might have carried him off twenty times had they known of his being near them.

Mr. Archibald Forbes says of the emperor: —

"He is a true patriot, earnestly striving for the welfare of his country; but he toils amid obstacles: he struggles in the heart of gathered and incrusted impediments, the perception of which on his part must, it seems to me, kindle wrath which is unavailing, and bring about misgivings which must awfully perturb, and induce a despair which must strike to his very heart."

Of the Russians Mr. Forbes remarks: —

"The rank and file are splendid soldiers. The Russian officers are courteous and gentlemanly. They are delightful comrades, always good-tempered and cheerful, commonly humane, and very frequently generous, and they never decry an enemy. The Russian private is astonishing on the march for his powers of endurance, and of carrying weight. He is handicapped, indeed, by many pounds more weight than any other soldier in the world. Patient and capable of unlimited endurance, devoted to his faith and to his czar, the only thing the Russian soldier needs is a gallant leader. He is destitute of perception when left to himself; somebody must do his thinking. But even if this fails him he remains true to his instincts, and stands up to be killed in 'noble stubbornness of ignorance,' rather than retire when there is no one left to give him orders. The Turk, on the other hand, is a born soldier, capable at any time of acting for himself in the absence of any officer."

But with high admiration for the Russian military force, Mr. Forbes cannot speak strongly enough of the corruption that prevails in every department of Russian administration and paralyzes the operations of a gallant army. Contractors who made money out of our own war seem honest patriots beside the Russian functionaries employed by the government to superintend the contractors. Skobeleff got rid of them all by having nothing to do with the commissariat. His men were fed, and well fed, by the care of their captains. But their arms were defective and their boots wretchedly poor. Each man in place and power, from the lowest to the highest, had some man higher than himself to favor and sustain him. Everything hinged on favoritism, even a boy's examination at school; and favoritism of course led to intrigue. Then, too, few Russians high in office (or indeed elsewhere) have any relish for responsibility.

"The Turks," said Mr. Forbes, "in my opinion, committed two military blunders. One may surely be remembered to their honor, and it was probably due to the indignation excited against them throughout Christendom by the atrocities committed eighteen months earlier on Bulgarians, south of the Balkans. When the Russians crossed the Danube into Bulgaria, the Turks fell back, leaving that rich province to the occupation of the Russian army. All Turks who were resident in its towns and villages were ordered to retire south of the Turkish lines, while the Christian Bulgarians were left entirely free to welcome and provision the invader."

Then, being barbarians, "the Turks, in a military point of view," thinks Mr. Forbes, "might have taken their stand as being such, and have warned all Christendom that they meant to make war accordingly;" instead of which "they tried," as he phrases it, "to profit in actual warfare by their barbarian instincts, and yet plough with the heifer of civilization. The Bashi-Bazouks might be seen after every battle torturing and slaughtering the Russian wounded. This mode of fighting had its inevitable result upon the Russian soldier."

And who were the Bashi-Bazouks, who distinguished themselves by their inhumanity? They were irregular and most banditti-like cavalry, who wore the Turkish dress, but were recruited from the scum of every nation. They served rather for permission to plunder than for adequate pay. During the Crimean War some of them were officered by Frenchmen, and served with the allied army. They nearly wore out the lives of their officers by their irregularities. Finally they were paid off and dismissed. Their officers, travelling the same road through a friendly country, along which they had passed a few days before, were horrified by reports of the atrocities they had committed.

And now to return to Mikhail Dimitrivitch Skobeleff, made governor of Plevna. The Emperor Alexander, on arriving there, sent him word that he was coming to take luncheon with him. He came, with his staff. Skobeleff was prepared to wait, as host, on his illustrious company, but the emperor made him sit down with him. Nothing was said by which Skobeleff could divine the purpose of this visit. He thought indeed that it betokened the imperial displeasure, when the emperor, suddenly rising, asked him to show him his house. The staff rose also. "No, gentlemen," said Alexander, "the general and I will go alone."

Skobeleff conducted the emperor through his apartments,

when Alexander turned suddenly and kissed him. "I thank thee, Skobeleff," he cried, "for all that thou hast done! For thy good service, many, many thanks!" And he kissed him again.

This was well done on Alexander's part. Such a mark of favor shown publicly would have brought down enmity and calumny on Skobeleff, and might have increased his unpopularity among courtiers and generals.

The month was November, and the weather north of the Balkans was growing bitterly cold. Skobeleff foresaw that the Russians must soon cross the mountains, and he was deeply solicitous about the equipment of his men. He bought up all the sheepskins, boots, and other necessaries he could find in Plevna. He changed their heavy knapsacks for bags of linen. He was particularly desirous they should have the comfort of fur coats. There came a dealer from Russia with a consignment of such articles. Skobeleff went to the old general his father, and invited him to ride with him to inspect them. The garments were satisfactory. The two generals saw them packed and sent off to young Skobeleff's division. As the generals were mounting their horses the dealer asked to whom he should send the bill. "Oh, to my father," replied Skobeleff, pointing to the old general; and then, turning quickly to his escort, he said: "Children, thank my father. He gives all the regiment fur overcoats."

In vain old Skobeleff fumed and remonstrated. He had to pay the bill. It is just to him to say that although he was penurious, the very lavish habits of his son had brought him in from time to time large debts which he had to settle satisfactorily.

At Plevna young Skobeleff kept open house. "His dinner table was surrounded," says one of his friends, "by the most variegated company." "I call it an eating house," said the old general one day, as he entered the dining-room.

When the time came for resuming the march, in the

middle of December, Skobeleff's divison was to cross the Balkans by a pass in the Tscherna Gora range leading to Senova. The main army was to take the Shipka Pass. One precaution the general took which caused much amusement among his brother officers. Each man of his division was ordered to carry a log of wood with him. "What will he think of next?" said some. "If Skobeleff has ordered it," said the Grand Duke Nicholas, "he has some good reason."

He had, indeed, good reasons. He always insisted that his men under all circumstances should have three hot meals a day. He knew that there would be no firewood on the summit of the Balkans. In consequence of his precautions not one man of his division arrived disabled or frozen on the other side of the mountain range. Not one had straggled. The only men that the division lost were two who slipped and fell over a precipice.

The soldiers who crossed the Shipka Pass suffered frightfully. Alexander Verestchagin, who passed over it a week or two later in a carriage, relates that he saw pile after pile of frozen Russian corpses, many of them young men of the Imperial Guard. They could not be buried. They were piled up to await the thawing of the earth and the melting of the snow.

Skobeleff's passage to Senova, though safely accomplished, was an awful journey. The men had to break their way through snow-drifts. They had to put their cannon upon sledges, and drag them along by hand.

On the third day they debouched into the Valley of Roses, which lies between the greater Balkans and a lesser chain. This valley is a little paradise in summer, devoted to the cultivation of roses for the attar of roses, which the Turks so much prize.

Here Skobeleff and his division fought their great battle of Dec. 28, 1877, and here Turkey lost her last army.

"I congratulate you, my men," said Skobeleff, when they were drawn up in order of battle; "throughout this war the 28th has been to us a day of good fortune."

Skobeleff always made his bands play when going into action. He said that martial airs wonderfully kept up the courage of the soldiers. Radetsky and his men shared the honors of the day with Skobeleff, much as Blucher and his Prussians shared the honors of Waterloo. They descended from the mountain into the valley as the battle was being won.

I need not describe the battle. It is enough to say that the Cossack cavalry were very effective, and that regiments kept coming down the Shipka Pass as the battle raged, and went immediately into action. There was a great deal of hand-to-hand fighting in the earth-works thrown up by the Turks. In such encounters the Russians would never look full in their foes' faces, it being a superstition that the glance of a man you kill will always haunt you.

At last the Turks put out two white flags. The Turkish pashas in command surrendered themselves and their whole army.

Skobeleff's first order was: "Let the Turks' property be sacred to us. Let not a crumb of theirs be lost. Warn the men I will shoot them for stealing."

"I shall never forget," says Mr. Kinnaird Rose, "a solemn service for the repose of the souls of the dead that was held on that battle-field of Senova by the general and a score of companions. Skobeleff's chaplain chanted the mass, with a simple dragoon for clerk. Every head was uncovered. The party stood in respectful groups around a monumental column with its cross, the general to the right of the priest.... As the service progressed the general wept like a child, and among the small but deeply moved congregation, there were but few dry eyes."

Thirty-five thousand men, and one hundred and thirteen guns were surrendered. "The scoundrels!" muttered Skobeleff, — "to give up with such a force, and with such a position!"

With the two Turkish generals, as soon as they became his prisoners, Skobeleff rode, accompanied by three or four Russians only, and a number of Turks, to a distant part of the field to stop the fighting. "No wonder," cried the Turks, "that we were beaten; for the Russians were commanded by Akh Pasha, and it is impossible to overcome him!"

Every kindness was shown the prisoners. They mingled with Skobeleff's men, and shared the porridge from their camp-kettles. The next day they were sent over the mountains, and on the journey their sufferings were terrible. Verestchagin met parties of them on the mountain, and saw many frozen corpses lying where they had halted.

"Skobeleff's care for his men," writes one who loved him, "grew greater and greater as time advanced. His heart bled for them; every insult, every injustice to the private he felt keenly. It was as if the insult had been aimed at him personally. He would grow pale with rage when he was told how in one division the men were starved, how in another they were flogged, and how in another their lives were sacrificed in useless reconnoissances in force."

On Jan. 1, 1878, the third day after the battle of Senova, Skobeleff's division was on its way to cross the Lower Balkans. It was a forced march, thirty and even fifty miles a day, — the infantry, encouraged by their general, keeping well up with the cavalry. The Turkish pashas stood aghast at the rapidity of his march on Adrianople; and after a fight with Suleiman Pasha, whose men fled to the mountains, the victorious little army entered the second city of the Turkish Empire.

The soldiers were billeted in the houses of the inhabitants, strictly ordered to behave well, and not to appear in the streets for two days. By the end of that time they had made friends with the population. The shops were reopened. There was not one instance of theft or burglary, — not a street row. When Skobeleff left the city it was occupied by other divisions, and all this was changed.

"And now God grant," said Skobeleff, speaking of the success of his forced march, and relating how he had entered Adrianople without one man sick in his division; "God grant that we may soon be in Constantinople!"

"Adrianople (which the Turks call Edirmè) seemed to me," says the writer from whom I have just quoted, "like a poetical dream. It is a beautiful town, crowned, as it were, by the Mosque of Selim with its four beautiful minarets. Its fortifications are wonderful. Skobeleff was anxious to know the engineer. He saw him afterward in Constantinople, and found him an entirely self-educated man, neither bright nor prepossessing, but with a genius for fortification."

The house Skobeleff occupied in Adrianople belonged to a renegade, a famous leader of Bashi-Bazouks, a scourge of peaceful citizens. It was a marvel of luxury, — tropical plants in winter gardens, marble halls, poetical fountains, every appliance for self-indulgence. Skobeleff chose the plainest room he could find, and his staff occupied those more magnificent.

He governed Adrianople as he had formerly governed Plevna. "Everybody," said a Turk, "thinks it an honor to serve Akh Pasha. There are no generals like him. The Koran says we must obey him." "How do you make that out?" said his questioner. "The Koran says: 'Be subject to your conquerors; there is no power greater than the sword.'" "Let the White Czar make thee ruler here," said others to the White Pasha; "we desire nothing better."

In about a fortnight Skobeleff's division was marched to the borders of the Sea of Marmora, only a short distance from Constantinople. Peace negotiations were already in progress; and soon was signed the Treaty of San Stefano. The treaty was not all that the Russians had hoped; but such as it was, almost all its provisions in their favor were set aside by the European Congress at Berlin; for the police policy of Europe interfered, and the czar had either to risk a European war, or have the settlement of the Eastern Question taken out of his hands.

Skobeleff raged when he found the Russian army was not even to enter Constantinople. There were moments when he debated with himself whether he would not on his own responsibility take the city without orders, and break the meshes of diplomacy.

GENERAL SKOBELEFF.

"I would hold a congress in Constantinople — *here!*" he said, "and would myself preside, if I were emperor, with three hundred thousand bayonets to back me, — prepared for any eventuality. Then we could talk to them!"

"But suppose all Europe should oppose you?"

"There are moments when one must act, — when it is criminal to be too cautious! We may have to wait centuries for so favorable an opportunity. You think the bull-dogs would fight us? Never! It should be our duty to defend this — our own city — with the last drop of our blood!"

The English in Constantinople admired Skobeleff immensely when, like other Russian officers, he went into the city in plain clothes. "I must tell you, general, honestly," said an English lady, with more candor than good-breeding, "that I hate the Russians." "And I only see a beautiful woman before me," replied Skobeleff, "and, without asking what nation she belongs to, must do her homage."

We see by this how deep is the Russian desire to possess Constantinople. It never slumbers; and in our present century it breaks out about every fifteen years.

Skobeleff was one of those who dream of a Pan-Slavonic federation. He thought the Slav States could be federated like those in the German Empire, strong to oppose outside influence, but internally at liberty to govern their own affairs; and Russia was to possess the power in this federation that Prussia has in Germany. But the Great Powers are wholly unwilling to favor any such aggrandizement of Russian power and influence.

For a time after the war ended Skobeleff remained governor of Bulgaria; and he governed it admirably as a Russian province, until he resigned it into the hands of Prince Dondoukoff-Koursakoff, and thence was transferred to Alexander of Battenberg.

The Congress of Berlin was assembled to set aside the

Treaty of San Stefano and to diminish as much as possible the influence of Russia in the Eastern Question. Lord Beaconsfield and Prince Bismarck took the lead in it; and all the other leading European statesmen were present. The treaty as amended by the Congress was signed July 13, 1878.

In brief it contained six stipulations: —

I. Bessarabia, torn from Russia after the Crimean War, was to be returned to her.

II. Bulgaria was formed into a principality; but only that part lying north of the Balkans.

III. Servia and Montenegro were to receive additional territory, and to pay Turkey no more tribute.

IV. Greece received a better boundary line, giving her more of Macedonia.

V. Bosnia and Herzegovina, unprovided for by the Treaty of San Stefano, were placed under the protection of Austria.

VI. Russia received some towns and territories in Asia Minor, and Batoum, an important sea-port on the Black Sea.

By a secret stipulation, England was to receive from Turkey the Island of Cyprus, as a set-off against Russian acquisitions in Armenia.

No one can admire the corrupt and brutal Russian administration, nor the organization of its police, — which, by the way, Skobeleff hated so cordially that he would never have anything to do with any officer or soldier who had served under him, if he disgraced himself by joining it, — but one cannot but feel that Russia was most ungenerously treated by the Congress. Hers had been the blood and the money that had been expended; and what did she get in return?

"No great power shall have Constantinople with my consent," said the first Napoleon; and this view has guided the police policy of Europe to the present day.

Skobeleff's opinion was that a great European war was not far distant, and that it would begin by a struggle for life or death between Russia and Germany. He hoped to be in it, and yet he expected an early death.

In 1880 his father died, leaving him, to his great surprise, an enormous fortune. He was at once full of plans for doing good with it to old or disabled soldiers. I do not know whether his intentions have been carried into effect.

In 1880 he requested the command of an expedition to subdue the Tekké, — the Russian name for Tartar robbers, who persisted in attacking the Russians in Turkestan. These people had a mountain fastness called Geok Tepi. It had resisted all attempts to take it, and had utterly discomfited other Russian commanders.

Skobeleff felt it to be, as he said, "a difficult business — very difficult. A large army," he continued, "cannot be taken there. The thieves have cost Russia quite enough money as it is; and if we do not give them the *coup de grace*, all our Turkestan possessions will find themselves in a precarious state." He had grown older and sadder and more discreet before this expedition, in which he was brilliantly successful, — not more in his storming of Geok Tepi than he was in winning the confidence of the Tekké, and in punishing and circumventing the deliquencies of officials in the commissariat.

He was less excitable, less lavish than he had been. In all else he was the same as ever. When he came from the East, he went to Paris; and there, and at Warsaw, he made Pan-Slavist speeches, the sentiments of which were disavowed by his government, and created considerable stir in diplomatic and journalistic circles. It was the first time he had taken any part in politics. He had said that "in the field it was his duty to be only a soldier."

A friend, who saw him after he returned from the East, was struck by his air of depression and despondency, and got him to talk about his campaign. "It is not the expedition," said Skobeleff, "which has had such an effect on me, although there were some terrible moments. My army was small — but what of that? I have faced worse foes than the

Tekké. The death of my mother, however, has been a very great blow to me. Her murdered body seems always before me. And who did it but one who owes his all — positively his *all* — to me! I went about like a madman for the first few days. Her image is still before me as if she were calling me. Do you know, I think I have not long to live."

This mother — so dear to him — was extremely beautiful. He was always, to her, "her boy." When her husband died she went into Bulgaria, and found comfort in her bereavement in the organization of schools, hospitals, and orphanages. Her son had detailed, as her guard and attendant, one of his own aides-de-camp, a young Russian whom he had literally out of compassion raised to the position he then held. This scoundrel formed the diabolical plan of murdering Madame Skobeleff and robbing her of her jewels and twenty-five thousand dollars she was carrying with her for distribution to her various charities. He effected his object on a journey from Philippolis to Sofia. Skobeleff received the news in Turkestan; and the deep emotion it caused him, from which he never recovered, may have had its influence on his own fate.

"On Skobeleff's last visit to Moscow," writes one of his friends, "he invited me to dine with him two or three days ahead. On the morning of the day I was to do so my man ran into my room, crying, 'The general is dead!' 'What general?' 'General Skobeleff!'" The man burst into tears. I hurried to the hotel. A crowd thronged the street, weeping and praying for his soul. The body had been brought from his bedroom into a small antechamber. Only the evening before he had been gayly chatting with some of his old staff officers. He died, the doctors said, of heart disease. He lay, when I arrived, not yet dressed in his uniform, his body covered with a pall of cloth of gold. Loud sobs were audible all around. The light fell full on his delicate, handsome face, on his long golden whiskers combed out on each side, which stirred occasionally in the breeze as if he were living. Two sentries soon appeared, to stand beside him. Discipline forbade them to raise their hands to their faces, but one man's tears were trickling down his beard."

There still hangs deep mystery over the cause of the death of Skobeleff. Recently the Figaro called on any of its readers who knew anything authentic on the subject to answer the question: "Are the circumstances of General Skobeleff's death sufficiently known to enable us to disentangle fact from fiction?"

The question produced two answers: one from Madame Juliette Adam, Skobeleff's especial friend and admirer; the other from M. Ivan de Wœstyne, the only newspaper correspondent who was in Moscow at the date of Skobeleff's death.

Madame Adam had already published a pamphlet on the subject, in which she exposed her reasons for believing that he was foully murdered by two German adventuresses, paid for the crime out of the Guelph fund.

M. de Wœstyne's communication is as follows: —

"I affirm that the idea of foul play in the death of the late illustrious general at the age of thirty-nine must be laid aside. I had visited Skobeleff the morning before his death, and he had asked me to breakfast with him the next morning.

"By chance I met him about four o'clock in the afternoon in the Tverskaia, the great avenue which leads to the Park.... He stopped his carriage, and asked me to go with him. I declined, and saw him no more till the next day, when he was laid out in full uniform in the apartment on the ground-floor of the Hotel Dussaud, occupied in 1878 by Mademoiselle Stella, the singer.

"I had a full account of his death from an employé of the *chancellerie* who lived just over the room on the ground-floor where he was carried off by a congestion. This apartment was in a house at the end of a courtyard, the front of which was occupied by a French hair-dresser and a Russian liquor-dealer, people always ready to talk.

"I telegraphed all I learned, in four languages, to the 'New York Herald,' hoping by this means to escape the censorship.

"At one in the morning I was awakened by the head of the telegraph office, who told me Prince Dolgorouki, the governor-general of Moscow, wished to see me.

"I went at once to the palace, where the prince, after shaking hands with me, laid before me three of my despatches.

"'Did you telegraph that?' he asked.

"'Yes, general.'

"And then, as the excellent old man seemed greatly disturbed to think that I had done so, I added at once: —

"'I sent another dispatch to New York, saying: "Now that you have all details in your possession, I think, seeing the great celebrity of the person they concern, you had better withhold them from the public, and simply announce his death."'

"When the prince heard this, he seemed overjoyed, and insisted I should sit down to supper with him.

"The 'New York Herald' withheld its information, but some years after, annoyed by all sorts of irrational and contradictory reports, I published what I knew in the 'Gaulois.' But I am not inclined to tell a second time a story for relating which I have been reproached by some of my very good friends among the Russians."

Thus it will be seen that over the death of Skobeleff still hangs a mystery.

His funeral procession from Moscow to his estates was such as could only have been given to one whom all men loved. All over Russia and in Bulgaria masses were said for him. "He was one of our own," said the peasant and the soldier.

CHAPTER XI.

THE ASSASSINATION OF ALEXANDER II.

THE remaining three years of Alexander II.'s life after the conclusion of the Turkish war were very miserable. Indeed we can hardly conceive of any human being of whom it might so truly have been said: "Without were fightings, and within were fears,"—fears, less for his own life, for life could hardly have been dear to him, than for all those whom he treated with confidence, or who surrounded him. Not only were his ministers killed under orders of the Revolutionary Committee, but policemen and Cossacks who were placed about his person for his safety. Society in St. Petersburg would not buy tickets for the Opera when it was known that the emperor was likely to attend the performance, fearing some dynamite explosion; office-seekers were discouraged by the perils of an official position; daily black-bordered letters threatening the emperor's death were found among his clothes, or among his papers. On one occasion his handkerchief was filled with some explosive powder, which injured his sight for a time; on another a box of pills sent him as a remedy for asthma proved to contain a very small but very powerful infernal machine. No wonder that though only fifty-nine years of age he grew haggard and pale, that his hair was blanched, his form shrunken, and his nerves unstrung. He suffered, too, from sleeplessness, from overwork, and the continual strain of anxiety.

The causes of his unpopularity with Nihilists and Pan-Slavists were manifold. By the peasantry his memory is still adored, as I should think it still must be by all who can appreciate what the aim of his life was, and can echo the words of Mr. Gladstone : "The sole labor of a devoted life was, with the deceased sovereign, to improve his inheritance for the benefit of his subjects and of mankind."

He had undertaken a work too vast for him, — a work for which he had at hand no fitting materials ; and it resulted in lost illusions, and in disappointments visited by others on himself; for it is one of the penalties of autocracy that the emperor is held responsible for everything, — bad harvests, pestilence, or the abuse of power by officials who are supposed to have little individual responsibility.

The new conditions of existence opened to the peasants after the Emancipation had not worked as popular enthusiasm had anticipated. The peasants retained their devotion to their czar, but they had practically only exchanged one form of serfage for another. For three years there had been bad harvests throughout Russia, and the taxes and responsibilities imposed upon them by their new condition filled them with discontent. The army, and all those who had lost friends in the Turkish war, were beyond measure outraged by the Treaty of Berlin. They had thought their emperor was too moderate in the Treaty of San Stefano ; but when that treaty was set aside, and Armenian Christians in the East, and Macedonian Christians south of the Balkans were delivered over again to the tender mercies of the Moslems, their wrath fell upon the czar who had consented to such sacrifices. The Pan-Slavists who hoped that the result of the war would have been a Slavonic federation, found themselves further than ever from the realization of their dream, since the new kingdoms and principalities torn from the Turkish Empire were given over to German rulers, supposed to be inimical to Russia ; then, too, the crop of young men and women educated in the new schools and colleges founded by Alexander, without sufficient precaution as to the moral qualifications of the professors, had just come upon the scene, boiling over with excitement and revolutionary fervor, eager to be doing something, and furious at finding all outlets for their activity closed. Besides this, the foreign newspapers never ceased their attacks upon Alexander. They said he was past work. They opened their columns even to Nihilistic writers. The old Emperor William remained faithfully attached to his nephew, but Prince Bismarck fully recognized the strong anti-German feeling in the Russian Empire, and did not scruple "in ways that were dark" to take revenge upon the Russians and their czar.

Alexander himself felt painfully the incompleteness of his work, and his own inability to deal with forces that were too strong for him. In a speech made in 1879 he said: "We have great tasks yet before us. Those to be attended to at once are the reduction of our expenses; the regulation of our currency; further reorganization of our army; and improvement of the sanitary conditions of our country. There is more to be done, which must wait till the existing passions are appeased. If I must die before such reforms are accomplished I trust they will be carried out by my successor."

During these latter years of his life the emperor's unhappiness was aggravated by the condition of his wife, who was dying slowly of consumption, and whose sufferings from apprehension for the safety of those she loved were intense. To no one in Russia had the insufficient success of a war into which she had put all her heart, and a great portion of her means, on behalf of oppressed Christians, been more full of disappointment.

Alexander had not been a faithful husband, — but he endeavored to make up to his wife for his *liaison* with the Princess Dolgorouka, by whom he had three children, by devoted personal attention during her illness, and by his tender solicitude.

We must not forget that the motto of true Nihilism is that "whatever is, is wrong;" and must also remember that the political exiles in Siberia are very far from being all Nihilists. The Russian police, in chronic dread of Nihilism and its plots, lays hands ignorantly and indiscriminately on any man suspected of liberal opinions; and when arrested he has no redress, because, unless accused of a *crime* he has no trial, but is sent off to Siberia as a precautionary measure, by what is called "administrative process," lest his opinions should "take root downward and bear fruit upward" in some dangerous way.

The headquarters of the Nihilists outside of Russia were in Geneva. Their leaders sat there like spiders in the centre of a web.

In February, 1879, when the Nihilists, exasperated by the results of the Turkish War, had worked themselves into frenzy, Prince Krapòtkin,[1] governor-general of Kharkoff, was assassinated by a Nihilist agent, a Jew named Goldenburg, who, after dogging him for some days, fired at night into his carriage window, and escaped arrest in the darkness.

In April a young Nihilist, Solovieff, fired at the emperor. Goldenburg had solicited the post, but was rejected by the Nihilist Central Committee on the ground that the czar's murderer must be an orthodox Russian. The attempt was made on Easter Monday, April 14, a day considered fatal to rulers by the Nihilists, because on that day of the month John Wilkes Booth had succeeded in assassinating President Lincoln.

In June, 1879, the Nihilists held a convention and resolved to use dynamite, to destroy the governors-general of Odessa, Kieff, and St. Petersburg, and to leave no means unemployed to kill the czar and his heir-apparent. In 1878 they had succeeded in killing General Menzenzel, chief of police, and Baron Heykin of Kieff. The successors of General Menzenzel — Drenteln and Trepoff — barely escaped death, and the latter was severely wounded. To become one of the czar's ministers in those years was as dangerous as leading a forlorn hope.

The first result of the agreement to use dynamite, and of

[1] Brother of Prince Krapòtkin, Nihilist and exile, author of much magazine literature.

the plans fixed upon for introducing it into Russia, was the mining of three railroads, beneath which dynamite was placed for the purpose of blowing up the czar and those about his person. One mine, however, proved useless, the emperor having changed his route at the last moment; one failed to explode, probably from want of skill in its management; but the history of the third mine, which exploded, and killed or wounded very many persons, though not the czar, is worth relating.

A house on the railroad not very far from Moscow had been purchased by one of the conspirators. He took possession of it with several other men, and two women; others were lodged in the nearest town, and came sometimes to visit their friends. Without tools, except two shovels and a grocer's scoop, they proceeded to mine from the house under the railroad, placing boards, tent-fashion, as they went along. On reaching the railroad track they bored holes upward with a large auger and inserted iron pipes, which communicated with dynamite stored below. Their greatest difficulty was how to dispose of the earth they dug out of the mine. At first it was spread out smoothly and trodden down in their yard; then they began to fill the cellar with it, and finally the larder. They were greatly embarrassed on one occasion by the persistency of the wife of the former owner of the house, who insisted on going into the larder in search of some pots of preserve she had left behind.

When the day and hour of the emperor's journey were announced, Sophia Perovskya, the most enthusiastic of the women, was appointed to stand on the track, and give the signal by waving her handkerchief. The imperial train was always preceded by a pilot train to see that the track was clear, to avoid accidents. This train passed safely; and in it was the emperor. The other train was wrecked when, as had been expected, it pulled up at a water-station.

Some of the conspirators were arrested; but the chief man among them, a German called Hartmann, escaped.

He had Nihilist friends all along his route, pledged to assist a brother Nihilist. Had he been an ordinary thief, he could not have evaded the police; but at every stage hands were held out to help him; disguises were provided for him, and he was passed from one Nihilist agent to another. Sometimes he travelled on foot; sometimes in peasants' carts with ox-teams; while those who were hunting for him were systematically put off his track. He passed the frontier of Russia without difficulty, reached Berlin, and telegraphed to his fellow-conspirators at Geneva, who at once set about hatching another and, unhappily, a more successful plot. Before, however, this was executed, there were intermediate horrors.

On Feb. 5, 1880, the czar was to entertain at dinner Prince Alexander of Hesse in the Winter Palace, where the czarina (the prince's sister) was lying very ill, — almost at the point of death.

Prince Alexander ought to have been punctual; but for some reason he was late. Had it not been for this delay, the whole imperial party would have been blown up at their dinner-table. While they were proceeding to the dining-room along a corridor, a tremendous explosion took place. Officials rushed wildly about the lower story of the palace under the impression that the heating apparatus, or the gas, had blown up. The alarm bell of the *corps de garde* rang frantically; and above the confusion rose the shrieks of the dying and the wounded, who struggled from beneath the *débris* of the demolished guard-room. There were in all sixty-seven victims.

In the midst of the confusion one of four carpenters who had been employed for four months in the Winter Palace was found to be missing. Dynamite had been stored in a tool-chest in his room. He was a Nihilist leader, who had feigned himself a workingman. He was never found after that day; and, for aught we know, he may be living in America.

Two days later the body of a policeman was found on

the ice of the frozen Neva, pierced with many wounds. Pinned to his breast was a paper denouncing death to every governor-general, except Loris Melikoff, who had succeeded the murdered Krapòtkin as governor at Kharkoff.

It was to Loris Melikoff that in that terrible hour of distress Alexander II. turned.

Loris Melikoff was born of a noble Armenian family in the Caucasus; and his appearance showed his Oriental origin. His complexion and his glance were Asiatic; his expression of quick intelligence was European. Nubar Pasha, the great Egyptian statesman, had the same origin.

Loris entered the Russian military service young, and until he became a major-general, in 1856, his career had been wholly provincial. In 1877 he was placed at the head of the Russian army in Asia, and distinguished himself greatly in the taking of Kars, which had been brilliantly defended by the Turks under English officers. In the spring of 1878 he made his first appearance 'at St. Petersburg. He had lived principally with books; but the charm of his conversation was irresistible. All felt that there was something different in him from the ordinary courtier, — different from the usual type of a military man. After he had been a few months in St. Petersburg, the plague broke out in a remote part of the Russian dominions. He was appointed governor of the province. He hastened to his post, and applied vigorous sanitary measures; the plague disappeared, and he became the idol of the people. On his return to St. Petersburg, in April, 1879, he found the city in the greatest excitement. Solovieff had just fired five ineffectual pistol-shots at the emperor; martial law was proclaimed in the chief cities; and Melikoff was sent to Kharkoff, — a very hot-bed of Nihilism.

In a few weeks he was the most popular man in all Russia. Every one contrasted his methods of government with those of other governors. The true liberal party began to think of him as its leader. He was stern to genuine Nihilists, but on him were fixed the eyes of true reformers; and when, after the explosion in the Winter Palace, in 1880, the government knew not what to do, Alexander called around him all his governor-generals, and offered to abdicate, if they thought his abdication could in any way restore peace and order to the empire, — a resolution was taken to make Loris Melikoff for six months dictator of Russia. He was not dictator in name; but he had a dictator's powers.

The empress died June 1, 1880, and was buried with the usual funeral ceremonies, which in the case of a member of the imperial family are of great pomp and long duration. It is said that preparations had been made to blow up the bridge over the Neva, as the hearse passed over it, followed by the emperor and all his sons on horseback; but that a storm and freshet, which caused the waters of the river to rise, drowned out the preparations.

Not long after the death of the empress Alexander was morganatically married to the Princess Dolgorouka, the witnesses present being the czarevitch, the Grand Duke Michael, and the emperor's trusted friend, Count Adlerberg.

In the last speech made in public by the Emperor Alexander he said that "he was greatly occupied with plans of reform: that he desired to abolish the poll-tax, first instituted by Peter the Great; to perfect a better system of allotments, which would benefit the peasantry; to make the examinations less severe for military or civil service, — believing as he did that many who had failed were driven by disappointment into the ranks of his enemies; to make the railroads less expensive to the State; and to abolish the heavy imposts laid on the estates of Polish nobles to defray the expenses of the insurrection of 1863."

The twenty-fifth anniversary of Alexander's emancipation proclamation was at hand. The day had been dreaded as one on which there would probably be an outbreak of Nihilists; but it passed off quietly. The appointment of Loris Melikoff, — the forlorn hope of utter helplessness — was apparently crowned with success. The minister of public instruction, Count Dimitri Tolstoi, obnoxious for his oppressive measures, had been dismissed. The Third Section (in other words, the Russian star-chamber) was abolished; the hated tax on salt was given up; restrictions on the freedom of the press were removed. To use the words of a Russian, " A regenerating breath seemed to pass over the land, and to bring back the air of life to the lungs of panting millions."

Finally, in February, 1881, when the rule of Loris Melikoff had lasted a year (for at the end of his dictatorship he continued to govern as minister of the interior), it was rumored that the czar was about to grant a constitution.

That document was the summoning of a species of States General, deputies to which were to be elected from the Zemstovos, or Provincial Councils, and to offer their advice to their sovereign. They were not to have the same functions as our Congress or those of the Reichtag or the English Parliament, which hold power by control over the finances, but it was an immense step in advance to associate the Russian people in any way with their general government.

The paper was signed on March 12 (according to our calendar) the czar making over it the sign of the cross, and remarking to Melikoff as he did so that it seemed to him like the calling of the States General by Louis XVI.

The paper lay on his desk ready to be sent to his council the next day, but it was never sent; the hand of Fate was on Alexander. Ever since power had been conferred on Melikoff his sovereign had objected to the harassing precautions taken to ensure the safety of his person. He persisted in taking his daily walk upon the Quai. He *would* drive in a drosky with his coachman and one Cossack in the streets of St. Petersburg. He refused to be attended, as several of his ministers were, by a guard of Cossacks, saying: " Only Providence can protect me, and when God no longer sees fit to do so, these Cossacks cannot possibly help me."

On the morning of March 12 Melikoff came to tell him that a man connected with the explosion on the Moscow railroad had been arrested, in whose possession were found plans for a new plot, and entreated him not to expose himself.

But on Monday, March 13 (or March 1, according to the old style used in Russia) the emperor went early to mass; then with his brother he reviewed his household troops, and an hour after he was brought back to his palace torn in pieces, and bathed in blood.

I said that Hartmann, when he made his escape the year after his attempt to kill the czar and all about him on a railroad, reached Berlin, and telegraphed to Geneva. He telegraphed also to a young Russian student named Trigoni to meet him in Paris. This man, after due instructions from Hartmann, was sent back to St. Petersburg. We have no means of knowing what he did there, but he was arrested by the police a few days before the fatal morning when Alexander was assassinated. It was this arrest that induced Melikoff to implore his master not to go to the review upon that fatal morning; but the danger seemed very vague, and the emperor would not be deterred.

Geneva in 1879 was full of Nihilists, all in a state of great excitement and activity; and there were plenty of Russian spies watching them.[1] About the time when Melikoff came to the head of affairs Hartmann, on demand of the Russian government, was expelled from France, and disappeared, going no one knew whither; but it was conjectured that he had gone back to Russia, where rumors of a new plot were beginning to be rife. In consequence of these rumors the chief of police under Melikoff withdrew the spies of his predecessor from Geneva, and concentrated them on home service, leaving the Nihilists in Geneva unwatched to work their will.

It was proposed by some among them that the czar

---

[1] This account is principally from an article in the "Gentleman's Magazine," 1888, by J. E. Muddock.

should be poisoned. By all it was agreed that his son must perish with him. In the event of this double murder being successful, a rising was to take place simultaneously in Moscow and St. Petersburg; barricades were to be raised, the palaces seized, and a new government in the name of the people was to proceed to make a constitution.

It is hard to know what is meant in Russia by "the people," — the small middle or professional class, it is to be supposed, recruited by disappointed young men who are younger members of the old nobility. It can hardly include the lately emancipated peasants, the army, or the enormous staff of office-holders under the government. It was from the middle, or literary and professional class, that the Nihilist ranks were chiefly recruited; also from the various universities, where highly "liberal ideas" were considered "good form," and a "little" knowledge of political economy, without balance, proved a "dangerous thing" to its possessors. We may add to this what is known to all those who have lived under the repressive tyranny of a local police, that the very fact of being forced to be secret stimulates the desire for conspiracy.

It is not that the fundamental ideas of Russian revolutionists are wrong. They are the ideas that govern our own country, and all the countries of western Europe; but the ideas of liberty, equality, civil rights, universal suffrage, and the rest, must have a foundation of experience in self-government to rest upon. If they have not there must be a counterbalancing power somewhere in the State to keep things steady. The working of self-government in Russian village communities does not encourage us to place much reliance on the present fitness of the nation for experiments of the same kind on a larger scale. The Russian peasant, like the Russian soldier, seems only to desire to be kindly, sympathetically, and wisely governed. A few thousand Skobeleffs in civil life might solve all difficulties.

Among the leading Nihilists were women of rank and cultivation. A woman who once passes the barriers that restrain her sex is apt to stop at nothing. She will go straight on to her end, no matter what she destroys, nor how high may be the obstruction that she has to leap over. Her very highest qualities may be enlisted in the cause of evil, — self-devotedness, energy, perseverance, and even tender-heartedness, though one-sided. Such a woman was Sophia Leooffa Perovskya. She was in 1880 about twenty-five years of age. She had been well educated, she was handsome, winsome, and fascinating. By birth she was noble, and her father had been many years governor of St. Petersburg. Unhappily, during her babyhood he had cast off his wife and banished her to Switzerland, leaving their daughter to grow up in ignorance of her mother's being alive. Sophia when she learned all this burned to revenge herself upon her father for what she considered his brutality, and on the government, of which, in her eyes, he was the representative. She entered into various Nihilist plots, one of her objects being to bring disgrace upon her father.[1] Her beauty and her high connections gave her great power. She could go where meaner plotters could not tread, and men of rank and position about the court fell victims to her fascinations. She possessed a wonderful power of drawing men on to reveal to her their secrets, and in this way she was able to learn all the movements of the court, and all the precautions taken by the police to secure the czar's safety. To obtain this information, that she might impart it to her fellow conspirators, was the object of her existence. To effect her purpose she felt no scruple in leading the life of a woman of lost character. After breaking from her father she had at one time joined her mother in Geneva, and there associated with the leading Nihilists.

The poisoning plan did not find favor with the Revolutionary Executive Committee. They said that the death of the czar was to produce what they called "*a great moral effect;*" and that that *moral effect* would be lost by vulgar poisoning, — indeed that the matter would be hushed up, and

[1] Cosmopolitan Magazine, September, 1891.

that the Nihilists would not get the credit for it that they deserved. "Their idea was to startle the world with the performance of a tragic drama, that should have a vast multitude for audience, so that there should be thousands of living witnesses that Nihilism was irresistible."

A student in the School of Chemistry in St. Petersburg sent to the Nihilist committee in Paris a recipe for a very formidable compound for filling bombs. He stated that two drachms of the devilish agent being exploded would kill every living thing within twelve yards.

What became of this inventor is not known. He is thought to have drowned himself in the Neva. An ex-divinity student in St. Petersburg constructed the bombs. The explosive matter to fill them was made up in France. Every precaution was taken. Every chance on either side was calculated beforehand. To make assurance doubly sure, a cheesemonger's shop was opened on a street leading to the palace, and a mine was constructed from it under the roadway; while the bombs were to be thrown at the emperor if he drove home along another street leading from the Catherine Canal.

The mine was very carefully prepared. It was filled with dynamite, and had it been fired, it would have wrought terrible destruction as well as have blown up the czar.

Sophia Perovskya was not the only woman concerned in the conspiracy; there was a Jewish girl named Hesse Helfman. Hesse was openly the mistress of one of the conspirators. Sophia's derelictions, which she used to promote her political purposes, were not so well-known. The police obtained some information which, on the 10th or 11th of March, caused them to attempt the arrest of Hesse Helfman's lover, who at once shot himself; but a great deal of information was found in the girl's house; and this caused Loris Melikoff, as I have said, to remonstrate earnestly with the emperor about exposing himself. It does not, however, seem to have moved the police to take especial precautions for his safety.

It has always been a mystery to the world and the police how the materials used in the manufacture of the new explosive were brought from Paris into Russia. Even the tea that came over the eastern frontier on the backs of camels had for the past year or two been carefully searched; furniture and carriages imported from western Europe were often rendered worthless by being pulled to pieces by the police to examine their stuffing. All travellers were minutely searched, and women were required to take off all their clothes, often in the presence of gendarmes. Any one coming by sea or railroad to St. Petersburg could not engage a cab to take him to his house or a hotel without permission of the police; and yet the very thing to exclude which all these precautions were daily taken was brought, into the country.

It is supposed that an old Jew carried it from Paris to Geneva in a leather travelling case; and that a woman transported it thence to Frankfort, whence it was despatched by various ways and in small quantities to St. Petersburg.

As the day for the regicide approached, the conspirators worked incessantly. The bombs were ingeniously constructed. The explosive compound looked like golden syrup, and was sweet to taste. If a drop or two fell on a hot stove they produced instantaneously a brilliant sheet of flame; but it made no smell and no noise.

Sophia Perovskya meantime kept the chief plotters well informed, and was soon able to announce that on March 13 the emperor was going with his brother, the Grand Duke Michael, to inspect his body-guard. It was then decided to destroy him as he drove back to the Winter Palace. The attempt was probably hastened lest the discoveries made by the police at the house of Hesse Helfman should frustrate the conspiracy. The first design had been to select some occasion on which the emperor and the czarevitch would be together.

Sophia had a lover high at court; and from him she probably obtained all the desired information. She did not know, however, which route the emperor would take. If that by the Sadoveya (one of the principal streets of St. Petersburg), he would pass over the mine, which would then be exploded; if he went by the Catherine Canal, the bombs were to be thrown at him.

Everything was ready. Sophia drew plans to assist the bomb-throwers, and volunteered to signal the approach of the emperor's carriage. She had two men under her especial orders, — Resikoff and Elnikoff, the latter a young man completely fascinated by her beauty.

Resikoff threw the first bomb. It exploded with a tremendous report, slightly wounding the horses of the emperor's carriage, and killing on the spot a baker's boy and the Cossack footman. The coachman was unhurt, and he implored the czar not to get out of the carriage, but to let him drive him swiftly out of the gathering crowd. But Alexander had seen that somebody was hurt, and insisted on getting out that he might give assistance. As he set foot on the pavement, Elnikoff flung his bomb at him. It exploded at the czar's feet; but though the explosion was tremendous, and men, standing many yards away, were thrown down by it, only two men were killed, — the emperor and Elnikoff. The latter died almost immediately; the emperor lingered some hours in frightful pain. His lower limbs, and the lower part of his body, had been blown to pieces.

There were eight men and two women concerned in the execution of this plot. Of these, one shot himself; one was killed by the explosion; two, who were brothers, made their escape; and four, together with the women, were sentenced to execution.

Men intimate with Sophia, from whom she had extracted information, were greatly alarmed lest she should betray them. She, however, held her peace. Owing to her rank, the young Czar Alexander III. had himself to sign her death-warrant. This he was very reluctant to do; and she would possibly have been spared had it not been for the earnest representations of courtiers, who feared that their indiscreet revelations to her might be brought to light. Hesse Helfman was not executed; but Sophia Perovskya was hanged with the four men in the presence of a crowd, who seemed to think that hanging was "too good for them."

The rising that was to have taken place immediately on the czar's death failed to be accomplished. The Nihilists made nothing by their crime. The czar was no sooner dead than the cry was raised: "Long live the czar!" — and "the dropped crown of Alexander II. was immediately taken up by Alexander III."

For some time Nihilism was scotched, but not killed. It revived again, however, and holds the sword of Damocles over the emperor's head. His nerves, it is said, have been greatly shaken by the continual apprehension in which he lives; but he is happy in the deep devotion of his wife, Princess Dagmar of Denmark (in Russia the Empress Maria Feodorovna), and occasionally, while visiting *en famille* her parents, the good Danish king and queen, he can throw off the terrible cares that oppress him.

The plan for a species of constitution to be given to Russia fell to the ground. Prince Ignatieff, who had returned from his embassy to Constantinople, and was high in the young czar's favor, and Katkoff, the Russian journalist, remonstrated earnestly with the new sovereign against its being carried into effect. The Nihilists had destroyed all hopes of liberal institutions.

Loris Melikoff felt that his hour was past, and that his mission was over. He and his colleagues resigned. A few days later he set out for his old home in the Caucasus. But soon he felt himself ill at ease in his retirement, and his health gave way.[1] His malady was slow consumption. He went to Nice, where he lived in strict retirement, keeping an attentive eye on the public affairs of his own country. He never spoke of the past with

[1] Revue des Deux Mondes.

bitterness, though he commented sometimes on the present with severity.

He died in the winter of 1888, aged sixty-three, and is buried at Nice in the same cemetery as Léon Gambetta. The time had been when the names of those two men rang loudest throughout Europe; now they sleep in neighboring graves, and by the world outside of Russia Loris Melikoff, one of the most remarkable men of his times, is almost forgotten.

The tragedy of 1881 taught the Russian authorities the lesson that "eternal vigilance is the price of safety;" and grieved as we may feel at the sad stories of administrative justice (or rather injustice) to men of cultivated minds and genuine patriotism, we can hardly wonder at the panic precautions of the police department, when we remember that among the real Nihilists there are still men and women who will stop at nothing that will enable them — as they call it — to regenerate their country.

CHAPTER XII.

ALEXANDER III.

AS I have said, Alexander III. in the first hours after his father's death might possibly have carried out the late czar's purposes, and have promulgated the *ukase* authorizing an advisory council chosen by the Zemstvos (assemblies elected by the people). But he was restrained by advice from Ignatieff, the diplomatist, and Katkoff the journalist, which advice indeed coincided with his own feelings and his most cherished opinions. It was no time for further concessions to the spirit of democracy. Alexander II. had tried what were called reforms, and he lay a mangled corpse as the result. The policy of the Emperor Nicholas was best for his grandson to follow. From that moment the desire and design of Alexander III. was to counteract the reforms set on foot by his father.

We read in our newspapers upon one column an account of the charming manners, the free enjoyment of domestic life, the kindliness and the courtesy shown by the present emperor during one of his visits to Denmark; on the next column we read horrible accounts of cruelties perpetrated under his orders against Lutherans, Orthodox Dissenters, Polish Catholics, and Jews. We are at a loss to understand the contradiction. Yet both accounts are true. Alexander III. appears to the world in a double aspect. Born to be simply the Grand Duke Alexander Alexandrovitch, he was a man of somewhat narrow intellect, but with fine moral dispositions, great tenacity of purpose, strict honesty and conscientiousness, and real kindness of heart, — all which qualities would have made him in private life a happy and

EMPEROR ALEXANDER III.

most estimable man. Fate made him the autocrat of all the Russias, arbiter of the destinies of more than one hundred millions of his fellow-creatures; and God having called him to this "state of life," he has valiantly and conscientiously taken up its onerous duties, and endeavors to fulfil them according to his lights, in obedience to what he conceives to be the welfare of his country and the will of Heaven. He has no personal ambition, no selfish aims. He has taken his grandfather's motto for his guidance: "Orthodoxy, autocracy, and nationality." On these, if Heaven seconds his wish that they should be established in Russia, he builds large hopes for her influence and prosperity. In visions he sees her in future years all-powerful in eastern Europe, and mistress of the Mediterranean, dominating the world by her influence, proving to the perfect conviction of all men of sense that the Orthodox Faith, having exterminated all dissent, all atheism, and all Church rivalries, is the one and only form of Christianity suited to our race; that autocracy is the only government that can repress the devilish aspirations of democracy; and that Slav civilization — or, as one Russian writer triumphantly expresses it, "Slavonic barbarism" — is meant to dominate the world.

Alexander III. is not a man of the nineteenth century. He hates what we call progress. French ideas, both social and political, are repugnant to him. English constitutionalism he believes will bring the British Empire to ruin; German hair-splitting and discussion he has no patience with. His ideas are those of sovereigns and ecclesiastics of the seventeenth century.

In all the ordinary relations of life no man can sustain a more estimable character. But while no man is probably strong enough to deal decisively with the problems of Russian life and government, if any such man exists he is not the Emperor Alexander.

The murder of Alexander II., like that of President Lincoln (and indeed like most other murders), was not only a crime, it was a blunder.

"Nothing has put Russia further backward," says the great Danish critic, George Brandes, "than this occurrence, which was pregnant with misfortune. It immediately prevented the formation of a sort of parliamentary constitution, which had just then been promised; it frightened the successor to the crown back from the paths his father had entered upon at the beginning of his reign; and it seemed to justify the rulers in oppressions and persecutions of every kind."

Ivan Aksakoff, the friend of Skobeleff, also wrote thus at the close of the first ten months of Alexander III.'s reign:

"Misunderstanding and mistrust have spread like a blight over Russia. They have marred the proportion, form, and color of all the manifestations of our life. Between the nobility and the people, the government and society, the educated and the ignorant, nay, even between members of the same classes of society, exists distrust and harrowing misunderstanding. Everything is out of joint, everything has lost its foundation, discontent is everywhere."

Along with the dread of new revolutionary crimes arose the fear of blind reaction, and the fear of fear.[1]

The Orthodox Russian Church has added an additional sacrament to those in the early Church, or in its Latin sister. To baptism, holy communion, confirmation, matrimony, orders, penance, and extreme unction, it has added *coronation;* and the devout spirit of Alexander III. fully believed that especial grace to govern would be conferred upon him by that ceremony. It was more than two years, however, after his father's death before he braved the dangers of being crowned. The ceremony of course was to take place at Moscow in the Kremlin.

A kremlin is, properly speaking, four high walls with towers at their corners, originally built up in the centre of a city, as a place of refuge in case of an attack by marauding Tartars. Many Russian cities have kremlins, — but the kremlin *par excellence,* the one known to all the world, is the Kremlin of Moscow.

[1] Russia under Alexander III. 1893.

Moscow has been called the Muscovite Rome. It stands on seven low hills. It has been partially burnt down more than once, and as houses of different styles of construction rise after each burning, the effect is extremely picturesque. The houses and roofs are of many colors; on gala days brilliant carpets and tapestries are hung from the windows.

May 22, 1883, was the day appointed for the public entrance of the imperial family into the Kremlin, where etiquette prescribed that they should pass some days before the coronation.

Before daylight the line along which the procession was to pass for four miles was lined with soldiers. In order to ensure the emperor's safety the police had taken possession of the back doors of all the houses looking on the route, and in most cases had nailed them up, that no one in the press while the emperor was passing might suddenly rush out and throw a bomb.

"The streets leading to that which was the line of the procession were barricaded, and guarded by large bodies of soldiers. Only persons provided with an especial passport ticket, and a privileged number of chosen peasants who stood behind the double line of soldiers, were allowed to remain on the street.

"The procession started at two P.M.; as it did so, from all churches along the line of march came forth priests in robes of cloth of gold, who, on altars erected in the street, offered prayers for the imperial family, the deacons waving incense, and all the church bells (Moscow is famous for its church bells) ringing merrily. There had been a rumor that no window was to be opened along the line of the procession, and no balcony occupied, but this proved untrue. Probably it was thought too strong a measure, and one that would too openly exhibit the alarm felt by the authorities.

"First came the magnificent *Gardes à cheval*, in new white tunics, shining cuirasses, and silver casques, surmounted by gilded double-headed eagles. This corps, the emperor's body-guard, was the one that suffered so fearfully six years before in crossing the Balkans, when many frozen dead bodies were collected in stacks beside the road.

"Deputations then followed from many guilds and many

towns; and then a group of colored men in fantastic dresses, styled Arabs of the household of the empress. Then came two bodies of imperial huntsmen, palace officials, equerries, etc., in open phaetons.

"Midway in the long stream was the emperor, wearing the uniform of a Cossack general, with a Cossack Astrakhan cap. He was mounted on a white horse."[1]

"The pale man on the white horse," says a writer in the London "Spectator," also present on the occasion, "who as his people shout their devotion, and all the world bends in reverence, feels chiefly the necessity of fortitude to await what may meet him at the next turning, rides on expecting, though probably not fearing, instant execution."

"The emperor rode a little in advance of his two sons and the Duke of Edinburgh, his brother-in-law. Behind them came all sorts and conditions of princes, generals, and aides-de-camp, among them the English general, Lord Wolseley, fresh from his Egyptian campaign, conspicuous in his scarlet English uniform.

"Then followed deputations from all the tribes of Central Asia that owed fealty to the czar. They rode splendid Turcoman horses, and were clad in every color under heaven, green, the color of the Prophet, predominating. They had bright eyes, and gypsy features, and a peculiar *nonchalance* of manner, which seemed to say that, though they rode in the procession, they owed allegiance to no one. The strangest head-dress was that of the men of Khiva, which was, first, a very high cap made of brown sheepskin, and on top of that a black and red pointed hat, like the hat in children's picture-books of Goody Two Shoes.

"After the czar's procession, but at some distance, followed the czarina's. The carriages were all glass and gilding, like the fairy coaches for queens we dreamed of in our childhood. The czarina's carriage was drawn by eight perfectly white horses in gold harness, each horse held by a groom in blue velvet, with a casque and white plumes. There sat the empress and her little daughter Xenia, eight years old, who was dressed all in white, and sat up looking very pale and astonished at the homage paid

---

[1] From the "Monthly Packet," December, 1883 — an article by Mrs. Trench, wife of the military attaché to the English embassy.

them. The empress was arrayed in imperial splendor, and wore the official insignia of state. She was very pale. But on her bright and animated face there was a smile for every one as she bowed right and left. As the procession approached the altars, the priests held up the cross, to which all bowed as they drew near.

"Poor woman! Poor empress! Poor wife and mother! It was well known to those behind the scenes that that very morning several anonymous letters had been received both by the emperor and empress, telling them to prepare for the worst if they persisted in going in procession to the Kremlin. Yet there sat the empress with a brave smile on her face, though not knowing at what moment some desperate attempt might be made on the lives of her husband and her sons! Not only did she and the emperor receive such letters that morning, but many of the attendants who were to form part of the procession, and the little pages and postilions who accompanied the empress's chariot received separate letters, warning them that they would never reach the Kremlin alive.

"About a dozen gold state carriages followed, filled with ladies of the suite, and with grand duchesses. When the emperor had entered the Kremlin a gun announced it to the multitude. Then the line of soldiers broke up behind the procession, and the streets filled again."

This public entry into the Kremlin was, however, only preparatory to the coronation. The dangers of the imperial family were by no means over. Every few yards of the ground covered by the Kremlin was guarded by a policeman or a soldier.

The Kremlin in Moscow is not, like almost all the other kremlins, a square, but a triangle, two miles in extent, and surrounded by a handsome red wall. It has five gates; over each is a shrine, and worshippers are at all times to be seen kneeling before them in the open air. Within the Kremlin are cathedrals, convents, arsenals, and palaces. In the inner court indeed there are three cathedrals, none however as large as our ordinary city churches, but each has five golden domes.

On Sunday, May 27, 1883, the actual coronation took place. The Kremlin was carpeted with red cloth, as it had been for the coronation of Alexander II. Four spaces were railed off for spectators. Two were for soldiers; one for peasants; and the other for mechanics, trades-people, and their wives. All these had previously had their characters thoroughly investigated by the police.

The Church of the Assumption, in which all emperors are crowned, was one glitter of gold. In Russian churches there are no seats for worshippers; so the *corps diplomatique* and their ladies had to stand five hours. The procession of the emperor was led by the queen of Greece and the young czarevitch, followed by the Grand Duke George and his little sister, Xenia. Then came the emperor, very pale, in uniform. The choir sang, "Justice and mercy shall be the strength of thy throne," etc. The empress was very much agitated. "I could see," says the lady whose account I am following, "that her chest was heaving with emotion; and she was nearly as white as her silver dress. Her pallor was heightened by her black hair, which was simply dressed, with two long curls falling on her shoulders, without a single ornament."

The service began by a Te Deum, exquisitely sung by more than one hundred voices, the choristers all clad in gold and purple. The czar received the coronation-robe from the metropolitan of Moscow, who gave it with the words: "Cover and protect thy people as this robe covers thee."

The emperor crowned himself. The crown was brought him on a yellow satin cushion. The archbishop said: "In the name of the Father, and of the Son, and of the Holy Ghost."

"It was with much admiration," says Mrs. Trench, "that I watched the calm and thoughtful dignity with which the emperor lifted the crown from the cushion, and held it for a few moments in his hands as if he must reflect, and then, turning it round slowly, raised the massive pile of diamonds to his head."

No wonder! It was to the emperor a solemn moment.

It was to him a sacramental rite. Not only did he believe the crown conferred upon him heavenly grace, but it made his person sacred; and that sacredness was the source of his prerogative. The czar is patriarch of the whole Russian Church as well as sovereign of the Russian millions; and in his consecration a religious function is performed, which, in the eyes of the Russian people, is the most important of all rites: and as other ceremonials are slow, costly, and magnificent, it must be slowest, costliest, and most magnificent of all.

When the crown was on the emperor's head the beautiful diamond collar of the Order of Saint Andrew was put on him; and when the orb and sceptre were handed to him he was invested with all the symbols of his sovereignty.

"There was a moment's silence which well suited the occasion; for there could not have been any one present whose heart was not moved, or whose spirit did not breathe a prayer that to the monarch who had just put on the crown — the mighty crown of diamonds, yet a very crown of lead, bringing with it colossal responsibilities — might be given a double portion of grace, wisdom, and power, to enable him to fulfil the duties which his high position demanded of him."

Then the emperor beckoned to him his wife, who approaching knelt down before him on a crimson cushion. He lifted the crown from his head, and just for one moment placed it upon hers. Her ladies then fastened on a smaller crown of diamonds. She continued kneeling, her head resting in the flowing robe of her husband's mantle. When she rose, it was observed that she looked calmer.

The three imperial children, the czarevitch, the Grand Duke George, and little Xenia, then pressed around their father and mother with congratulations and embraces. After them came in turn the whole imperial family.

"Prayers then began again, — an exhortation, and the anointing, done with a brush of gold and precious stones. The emperor afterward received the Communion for the first and only time as a priest, — that is, the bread and wine from the paten and the chalice. In Russia the laity receive only bread soaked in wine.

"Then the procession quitted the Cathedral of the Assumption to visit all the other churches within the Kremlin, a magnificent baldequin being held over the emperor and empress, composed almost entirely of yellow feathers mixed with black and white plumes."

A banquet and a reception followed. Then the emperor and empress dined alone on a raised dais. After they had sat an hour at their table, with nothing to eat, the viands were brought in, which was the signal for the departure of their guests.

During the evening magnificent balls were given. The empress and the Russian ladies all wore the national costumes of velvet, pink or blue, the bodice with a long point, the sleeves very long and wide. Over the head was worn a raised bandeau of velvet, embroidered with pearls and hiding the hair. To the bandeau is fastened a long veil. It must be something like the head-dress worn by Homeric women. At the court ball tnere was no dancing, — only a procession with partners, called a Polonaise.

A few days after the coronation some members of the English embassy went to the top of a curious structure, called Ivan the Great's Tower. Ivan the architect, not Ivan, who had entertained the ambassadors of Queen Elizabeth. It consists of five stories, in each of which bells are hung. In the first are about thirty bells, the number diminishing as they go up, till in the fifth there are only two silver bells. From this tower they looked down on the imperial kitchen, where cooks in white caps were preparing dishes, while soldiers stood on guard around them as a precaution against poisoning!

The fêtes closed with a review of forty-five thousand men on the 9th of June, 1883, having lasted two weeks without any *contretemps.*

It is said that the Nihilists about this time offered to engage not to destroy Alexander III. if he would grant a constitution. The emperor, however, refused to enter into the agreement; he had already determined on his course, and was at once too brave, too honest, and too obstinate to make terms with his enemies.

There are in the Russian Cabinet ten ministers and five assistant-ministers.[1] These are not servants of the public as are ministers in other countries; they are the czar's personal servants; and their duty is to carry out in their departments his personal will. When a law is to be made, custom and the statute book require that it should be submitted to a committee of ministers; if approved by them, or rather by a majority, it is passed on to the Imperial Council; and if it there secures approval, it is laid before the czar, who signs it or not, as it meets his views. But sometimes these formalities are dispensed with altogether, — generally, when the enactment in question is one not likely to secure the approval of a majority of the ministers or the council. Such, for instance, was the edict expelling the Jews from Moscow, which was decreed without asking the advice of ministers or the Imperial Council. It was promulgated after a report handed in by the minister for foreign affairs, who had been encouraged to take this step by the Grand Duke Sergius Alexandrovitch, brother of the emperor, — in some respects a reproduction of the Grand Duke Constantine Paulovitch of a preceding generation.

Again, the measure that has done most to undo the reforms set on foot after the Emancipation has been that which effaced the Zemstvos, or Provincial Assemblies, and in their place set over the village communities what are called district commanders. This measure, which has produced a radical transformation in the entire internal organization of the empire, as established twenty years before under Alexander II., was signed and made law by Alexander III. in opposition to the votes of his ministers and his council.

[1] E. B. Lanin, Leisure Hour, 1892, — Statesmen of Europe.

The district commander must inevitably be an hereditary noble. He is appointed by the government, nor need he be in any way connected with the district he is to govern. His functions are both those of administrator and judge. His duty is to see that no Mir deviates from the way in which it should act to suit the emperor's policy. The agents of the district governors are the police. It is the reintroduction of a system of centralized bureaucracy into the rural districts, and sets over the emancipated serf two masters, the Mir and the commander of the district, in place of his hereditary master and the headman of his village.

Strictly honest himself, the czar has aimed to surround himself with men of respectability. A man whose moral character will not bear investigation rarely can find favor with Alexander III. Talent or administrative capacity are secondary considerations. Ministers need not agree with each other's views, and are never called upon to act as a cabinet, but each minister or imperial councillor must adopt and carry out his master's views upon three subjects: orthodoxy, autocracy, and nationality. That "Russia must be for the Russians" is a favorite maxim; therefore there must be in Russia (which unhappily includes many nations, races, and religions) only one faith, the Orthodox Russian Church, of which the emperor is the anointed Head. Autocracy (which means the czar's will, as set forth by his *ukases*, and carried out by the army of officials through which it percolates to his people) must be absolute and paramount. Nationality implies that by any means, however arbitrary, all the various peoples who dwell under the czar's rule are to be forced to surrender any national institutions they have inherited from their ancestors, and are to become Russified. To this end the Mir, the Slavonian village system, has been forced upon the Poles, the Finns, and the inhabitants of the Baltic Provinces. To this end the Jews are to be as speedily as may be wiped out of the empire. Lutherans, Catholics, and Orthodox dissenters are to be made to feel that they can no longer live comfortably in Holy Russia. It is to be a Slav Empire. Already men whose names denote that they are not Slavs by descent, even if they have been born Russian subjects, are being weeded out of the army and the public service. It is a new crusade against modern progress, and Alexander III. has taken the cross, and said *Dieu le veult*, as sincerely as any monarch, knight, or baron in the Middle Ages.

As I write these things they seem incredible, but they are literally true. Western progress means to the Emperor Alexander the social immorality of France, her political unrest, and her detestable liberalism; it means the subjection of the head of the State in England to such fluctuations of public opinion as regulate the action of the British Parliament; it means the religious antagonisms of Christian sects and churches; it means interminable discussions (which the czar hates); it means experiments with things too sacred to be touched, — a swift rushing toward the weltering gulf of atheism and anarchy. While *we* look upon Russia as a country that has already become effete, and is on the point of retiring from the page of history, the czar, and those who think with him, consider that its destiny is to devote itself to its historical mission of destroying the culture of the West, and so averting what at present seems the doom of the world.

This would be history all over again, and in the twentieth or twenty-first century a new Gibbon would find materials for a new "Decline and Fall."

In Russia there is no public opinion either to oppose or to support the emperor's views, and were this not the case Alexander would be wholly indifferent to public opinion. He intends to do his duty as he sees it; to die if need be as a martyr to his duty, which is to enforce on Russia the three things already mentioned, — "autocracy, orthodoxy, and nationality," in which he sees the will of God, and salvation not only for his own country, but possibly hereafter the regeneration of the world.

As there is no representative body in Russia to divide

politicians into parties, and in point of fact no politicians to divide, it is very hard to classify the different shades of thought pervading society, but rarely finding public expression within the limits of Russia. Perhaps they may be roughly divided into six classes: peasant opinion; Nihilism; liberal opinion; Slavophilism; Pan-Slavism; and the opinion of the emperor.

All our information about Russia seems so very vague that modern writers do not even agree as to its population. Some estimate it at one hundred and ten millions, some at one hundred millions, some at ninety millions, some at eighty millions. All these statements I have found in writings apparently speaking with authority upon the subject, in the last five years. But whatever the millions more or less may be, it is probably an overestimate to say that not more than ten millions of the czar's subjects have any political views. The mass of the people believe in the czar, obey his police, grumble at their condition when misfortune seems to come upon them from local injustice on the part of their communities, but whatever appears to have come upon them directly from the hand of God, or the will of the emperor, as manifested through his representatives, is accepted with submission.

Secondly we have Nihilists, bound together in a secret society to effect destruction. Their doctrine for the future, so far as they have set it forth, is universal brotherhood. Their motto might be "Liberty, Fraternity, — or Death." Love for country, love for family, rights of property, are among the things to be done away. Their number cannot be very great, but their works are deeds of darkness; and not being restrained by laws of conscience, such as regulate the hearts and lives of other men, they are dangerous unspeakably. A counter organization was at one time formed among the young nobility of Russia, to which Prince Demidorff (the husband of Princess Mathilde) contributed large funds. It was a secret society intended to detect Nihilists, and to circumvent their plots, but it was soon found that amateur detectives fell into such mistakes that the Emperor Alexander III. put an end to it.

Thirdly, there is a class of liberal thinkers who cannot be classed with Nihilists, — men who would have been followers of Loris Melikoff, and have labored for reform; but who now, driven to secrecy, groaning under their own impotence, and resenting repression, have among them those who carry liberal theories to an impracticable extreme, and find occasion to express their feelings in intemperate language through the press of foreign countries. They suffer themselves abroad to be classed with Nihilists, and share the fate of Nihilists at home when they fall into the hands of the police. Their sentiments range from those of the statesman and reformer to those of extreme demagogues. All forbidden fruit has for them an attraction; and, alas, fruits the most wholesome, as well as the most poisonous, are forbidden in Russia. Among these liberals may be classed those who hold eccentric, communistic, philanthropic opinions, like Count Leo Tolstoi, who owes his protection from the police to the interest the emperor is said to take in his writings. The only novel of his that the emperor has disapproved was the " Kreutzer Sonata," which he placed under the ban. He subsequently removed that ban, and repented it afterward.

Fourthly, we have those who are called Slavophils, — fanatics for the restoration of old Muscovite Russia. Their stronghold is Moscow, the ancient capital. They look on Peter the Great as the worst enemy of his country, he having introduced into it Western culture and Western ideas. They have no sympathy with Slavs outside of Russia. They care nothing for the Russification of outlying provinces. Slavs must be born, not made, is their motto. They would like to see the old Russian dress resumed, and old Russian manners. They care nothing for foreign literature or for the classics. Old Russian literature alone is to be cultivated.

Fifthly, there are the Pan-Slavists, who desire to unite all

Slav races into one federated empire, of which Russia shall be the head, as Prussia is of Germany. A Slavophil, Ivan Aksakoff, writes thus of the Pan-Slavists, and their notions: "I and my relatives do not believe in Pan-Slavism, — nay, we consider it impossible; firstly, because it would require the adoption of a single faith by all the Slav races; and the Catholicism of Bohemia and Poland would bring a hostile foreign element into our community, which could not be amalgamated with the orthodox faith of the other Slavs; secondly, because the individual elements of the Slavonic nations must previously be dissolved and fused into a differently characterized, more powerful, more united, and mighty nationality, — namely, the Russian; thirdly, because a large part of the Slavonic races is already infected by the influence of barren Western liberalism, which conflicts with the spirit of Russian orthodoxy. Russia is far more to me than all the Slavs. We have been reproached with indifference to all Slavs outside the Russian kingdom; nay, outside Greater Russia." To this the Emperor Nicholas appended an autograph note on the MS.: "And he is right; for everything else is madness. God alone can determine what is to happen in the far future. Even if every circumstance should combine to lead up to this (the Pan-Slavic) union, its accomplishment would be the ruin of Russia."[1] Nevertheless, Pan-Slavism has great hold on the mass of educated Russians; but it is not the idea of the emperor. His opinions, and those who follow him, we class as sixthly. He has no wish to govern over a federation of Slav peoples, of whom the greater part would be little in sympathy with Holy Russia, and who, like the people of our own States, would have constitutions, legislatures, laws, and customs of their own. He wishes to be autocrat over all Russia, — to Russify his outlying provinces, to extend his power to the Pacific Ocean, to strengthen orthodoxy. "Russia for the Russians," — is a maxim he

---

[1] Russia under Alexander III.; translated from Von Samson-Himmelstierna.

believes in; and he is wholly disinclined to admit non-Russians, even if they may be Slavs, into what he desires should be a close corporation, as exclusive as Dr. Francia made Paraguay, or Cotton Mather and Winthrop would gladly have made their colony in New England.

The private habits of Alexander III. are of the simplest kind. Discussion or representations, I have said, he particularly dislikes; and his intercourse with his ministers is largely carried on in writing, chiefly by brief remarks made on the margin of the reports submitted to him. These reports, he requires, should be very brief. The only persons who feel it likely they can obtain a hearing, when offering him opinions in opposition to his own, are his connections, the Danish king and queen. The queen made repeated attempts to influence "Uncle Sasha" in favor of the Lutherans in the Baltic Provinces; "she might have spent her time as profitably in reasoning with the Egyptian Sphinx." On one occasion, after her Majesty and her consort had exhausted their eloquence and their stock of facts, the czar replied dryly: "I, a born Russian, find it a difficult task to govern my people from Gatchina, which, as you know, is in Russia; and now do you really fancy that you, who are foreigners, can rule them more successfully from Copenhagen?"[1]

The same writer tells us: —

"Those who accuse the emperor of cruelty wrong the man, and misconstrue his acts. . . . His intentions have never been called in question by those who are competent to sit in judgment on his conduct. He has granted their lives to many men who risked them in dastardly attempts to take his own; and there are depths of tenderness in his soul which even most of his ministers do not suspect; and if his people are none the better for them, the fault cannot be entirely laid upon his shoulders, but must be added to the mountains of wrong that may never be rightly apportioned. . . . Alexander III. has never regarded his kingly office as anything but a heavy burden, which personal inclination, as well as common prudence, imperatively urged him

[1] E. B. Lanin, Contemporary Review.

to shake off; and he richly deserves all the credit attaching to the mistaken sense of religious duty which makes him disregard his own happiness, and the manly courage which he has opposed to considerations of his own safety."

The person whose indirect influence has been of most importance to the emperor has been his former tutor, M. Probédonostzeff. He has elevated this gentleman to an office which corresponds to that of minister of worship in France, and has given him a seat in the Cabinet. "His influence," says the writer who has described all the statesmen of Europe in a series of articles in the "Leisure Hour," "almost overshadows the throne. More than half the existing ministers owe their nomination, more or less directly, to his influence." Without being in the least "a religious enthusiast, he is convinced that he has been called of God to save Russia from that breaking up into rival creeds which exists in the rest of Europe. To him Russia is a church; she is primarily a religious communion, and only secondarily a secular community. He holds that the Church saved Russia in the past, and that the sacred duty which history has bequeathed to the Russian government as the first of all its duties is to safeguard the orthodox Church against anything that should menace its security and unity." Imbued by such ideas, and supported by the emperor, he has in his new office every opportunity of carrying into effect the religious persecutions undertaken at his instigation; "and never has superstitious religion, as distinguished from real religion, been so rife in the empire as it is now."

The czar lives principally at Gatchina, having a great dislike to residing at St. Petersburg, where what little liberty he can enjoy in his well-watched country-home is curtailed by the precautions of the police. When at St. Petersburg he occupies apartments in the Anitchkoff Palace, avoiding the Winter Palace, the scene of his father's death and of several explosions. When residing at Gatchino, where he has selected for himself the worst suite of rooms in the palace, "he rises at seven, takes a quiet stroll in the uninteresting grounds of the park, returns to early breakfast, and engages in some severe manual labor as preparation for the official work of the day." He is unusually strong, having been known in his young days to bend a bar of iron across his knee. He is so much a prisoner that all forms of exercise taken for healthful amusement by country gentlemen are denied him, and he has to invent bodily labor for himself. "He unhesitatingly puts his hand to any kind of work that has to be done; but his usual occupation is to fell trees, to saw them into planks, to plane them, and generally to prepare them for the cabinet-maker. In winter the gardeners have strict orders not to clear away the snow from the avenues and walks of the park, which is invariably left for his Majesty, who, attired in a short gray jacket, shovels it up into enormous mounds, and then transfers it to a cart. It occasionally happens, when he cannot complete the task he has set himself within the time at his disposal, that his children lend him their assistance and cart away the snow to a remote part of the grounds." [1]

Alexander dislikes horseback exercise; and, indeed, it would expose him to too many dangers. He is said to be nervous even when driving; and no wonder, for regicides have commonly found their best opportunity when their victim was in a carriage.

Alexander III. takes great interest in Russian history, particularly in what relates to its romance, and has even established in his palace an historical society, which meets several times during the winter, and of which he is president. The amusement he takes most pleasure in is the opera. For martial manœuvres he has little taste. As czarevitch he did conscientious service at the head of a *corps d'armée* in the war of 1877; but the "pride, pomp, and circumstance of glorious war" have little attraction for him. This greatly impairs his popularity with his army, which is said to be not wholly well affected to its sovereign.

[1] E. B. Lanin, Contemporary Review.

Indeed, in March, 1887, on the same day of the year and on the spot where his father had been murdered, some young Cossacks of the Don were arrested, who were about to throw a bomb under his carriage as he was returning from a mass held for the repose of his father's soul. Very recently a mutiny among the Cossacks in southern Russia has been reported in our newspapers; but the details of all such outbreaks and of attempts on the czar's life are now withheld from the public as much as possible.

No wonder that sad experience has taught the czar to distrust human nature. Here are a few facts reported by an already quoted writer: —

"Having put his trust in a minister who was also a soldier, he had the chagrin to discover, later on, that to that apparently frank soldier truth was stranger than fiction.[1] He made a companion of another general, with whom, during the Turkish War, he had been wont to play interminable games of chess; and scarcely had he placed the crown upon his head than he was called upon to sign the sentence banishing that same general to Siberia, for having, at the very time when he used to play chess with his future sovereign, taken an active part in an infamous conspiracy to starve the wretched soldiery, and put the money intended for their rations into his pocket. . . . He has seen a trusted minister, whose solid reputation rested on his zeal to spread Orthodoxy and root out Catholicism, convicted of robbing widows and orphans of the millions destined to alleviate their lot, and then commit suicide to escape from justice. . . . He has absolute confidence in no man, and for the objects of his trust must look to God and to the narrow circle of his own immediate family."

In judging Alexander III. we are apt to forget that he is a born Russian, — nay, that there is much of the *moujik* in his composition. He partakes the national characteristics of his people, — their fatalism, their spirit of submission to the divine will, their stolid apathy, which is seldom aroused except by religious emotion. But sobriety and honesty are virtues all his own.

[1] Probably General Ignatieff, the diplomat, whose nickname in Turkey was "the Father of Lies."

EMPRESS OF RUSSIA.

The empress devotes herself to her duties as a mother and a wife. Her duties as an empress seem to consist chiefly in giving a tone to good society. On her devolve the social obligations of the crown. To promote frivolity among the upper classes of St. Petersburg is to turn away their thoughts from dangerous things. The emperor dislikes all kinds of social "functions." His State Balls must close some hours earlier than those given by his subjects. He himself always takes an early dinner, unless obliged to entertain guests at his table. When he drives out, the empress almost always accompanies him, preferring to share his danger rather than anticipate it at home.

The imperial pair have five children: the Czarevitch Nicholas, the Grand Duke George, the universally praised and admired Grand Duchess Xenia, who is now grown to womanhood, Michael, and Olga, who are children still. None of these young people have yet been married; but the czarevitch has been betrothed to Princess Alice of Hesse-Darmstadt, granddaughter of Queen Victoria. It is said that the health of the elder grand dukes gives their parents cause for uneasiness. There is consumption in the family through their grandmother, Marie of Darmstadt.

The other members of the imperial family are the Grand Duke Michael Nicholaivitch, uncle of the emperor, and his wife, a princess of Baden. He has a family of seven children, — six sons and a daughter, — but takes no part in political life. He made at one time an excellent governor in the Caucasus.

His brother, the Grand Duke Constantine Nicholaivitch, now dead, was a man of considerable accomplishments, who will be missed at St. Petersburg in artistic and literary circles. He died of a lingering and painful illness a few years since, and left three sons. The two younger, Constantine and Dimitri, are the emperor's aides-de-camp; the eldest is the young prince who some years ago made a scandal by stealing his mother's jewels that he might bestow them on an American courtesan. He has been banished to a military post in the Caucasus, whence he is not likely to return.

The emperor's sister is Marie, Duchess of Edinburgh. His brothers are the Grand Dukes Vladimir, Sergius, Alexis, and Paul.

Both Vladimir and Sergius married ladies who were not of the orthodox Church. The Grand Duchess Maria Paulovna, a princess of Mecklenberg, retains her Lutheran faith; but the wife of the Grand Duke Sergius, *nee* Princess Elizabeth of Hesse-Darmstadt, daughter of the lamented English Princess Alice, has succumbed to the pressure put upon her, and joined the national church of Russia.

The Grand Duke Vladimir keeps aloof from political affairs. The Grand Duke Sergius, who is at present governor of Moscow, is a bitter persecutor of the Jews,—a man of notoriously brutal character, and unfaithful in his conjugal relations.

The Grand Duke Alexis is unmarried. He is in the navy, and a few years ago came to the United States, where he made himself extremely popular, especially among the ladies. He lives as little as possible in Russia, and takes no part in political affairs. The Grand Duke Paul, who was very young at the time of his father's death, married his cousin, the Grecian Princess Alexandra, who has died recently.

NOTE. — Since this chapter was written, the emperor, in June, 1893, has appointed Sergius Julevitch Witte his minister of finance. This gentleman was born in the Caucasus in 1849, where his father was a member of the Caucasus Government Council. Witte has been in the public service since the age of twenty-one, and wherever employed has distinguished himself by ability, honesty, and great success in achieving reforms in various branches of administration. A Russian writer is reported to have said of him: " He is of strong character, and has by his bluntness gained the czar's confidence. Practically he has the reins of government in his own hands."

CHAPTER XIII.

SIBERIA. — CENTRAL ASIA. — THE BALTIC PROVINCES. — THE PERSECUTION OF THE JEWS.

THERE have been no picturesque events to brighten the reign of Alexander III. All is gloomy, hopeless, painful, as indeed seems to me the character of Russian religion, Russian history, Russian life, Russian literature, and Russian art. Besides what I have related there remains to tell something about Siberia and its exiles; something about the Russian advance in Central Asia; something about the two stupendous railroads which before the close of this nineteenth century may connect St. Petersburg with the Pacific; something about the Russification, political, social, and religious of the unhappy Baltic Provinces, with brief allusions to the recent famine and the persecution of the Jews.

None of these are cheerful subjects, if we except the magnificent conception and execution of the engineering work across the continent of Asia, but our story would be incomplete if they were left without allusion.

The subject connected with Russia that has probably for every foreigner the most interest is the condition of the exiles of Siberia; and popular interest in it has been recently stimulated by the papers published in the "Century" by Mr. Kennan, and the lectures he has given in various cities.

Mr. Kennan is a gentleman who, after some years residence in Russia and acquaintance with its language, formed the idea in 1879 of writing upon exile in Siberia. His first papers, like those of an American clergyman who about the same time visited the Russian penal colonies and prisons, were to the effect that the horrors of the subject had been greatly exaggerated. In this spirit he made a report to the New York Geographical Society, which paper disposed the Russian government in his favor, so that he received letters from Count Dimitri Tolstoi, then minister of the interior, which enabled him and an artist, Mr. Frost, to travel, unmolested by the police, through Siberia, to examine its prisons, to talk freely with the officials and the exiles, and to bring back to readers in the Western world the fullest information.

In considering this subject we must first disabuse ourselves of several ideas which we have probably held from infancy, — to begin with, that Siberia is a land of perpetual snow and ice, barren and inhospitable. "You could take," says Mr. Kennan, "the whole of the United States, from Maine to California, from Lake Superior to the Gulf of Mexico, and set it down in the middle of Siberia without touching its borders. You could then take Alaska, and all the countries of Europe, except Russia, and fit them in like pieces of a dissected map round the edges of the United States as it lay in the middle of Siberia, and you would still have left more than three hundred thousand square miles of Siberian territory."

In this vast region there is every variety of climate, from arctic to tropical; the beauty of the scenery, the magnificence of the rivers, and above all, the wonderful brilliancy and variety of its flowers, continually strike wonder and admiration into travellers. It is a land full of raw materials for wealth, and is being opened up rapidly by steam navigation, and by railroads.

Another usual idea is that the exiles of Siberia are all political exiles. This is very far from being the case. Each village community — the Mir (now presided over by the district governor and the government police) — has a right to banish to Siberia any member of its community whom it wishes to get rid of. A man incapable of work through drunkenness; a man who does not pay his share of the commune's taxes; a man who has become a bad character, or made himself in any way obnoxious to his commune, — may by its decree be banished to Siberia; and his wife and children may go with him, partly at the expense of the government, partly at that of his village. There is no appeal. If the Mir decides to banish him, go he must.

Another class of persons sent to Siberia, and the most numerous, are criminals convicted in local courts of various offences. They are treated with more rigor than those simply exiled from their villages, are not given land on their arrival in Siberia, and, if great criminals, they are sent to the mines.

A third popular idea is that all the political exiles are Nihilists. This is by no means the case. They are divided into two classes: those condemned for crimes in connection with politics, who have been tried by juries; and those exiled by what is called administrative process, namely, persons arrested without trial, without crime, on mere suspicion of holding opinions that may become dangerous to the peace and order of the State. The political *criminals* go to the mines, far away in Eastern Siberia, where no pains described in the Inferno can exceed their wretchedness. If any become utterly unmanageable, they are sent to the Island of Saghalien lying north of Japan; and no one, so far as I am aware, has ever escaped from that prison island to tell its secrets to the Western World.

Those arrested by administrative process are settled in various villages, and allowed to enjoy personal freedom, though closely watched by officials; and they are generally very poor. Some have their families with them; some are young girls who have imbibed heated notions from their unripe higher education. These are the exiles with whom Mr. Kennan chiefly associated, and whom he found mostly cultivated and agreeable gentlemen and ladies.

Noblemen are a privileged class, even in Siberia. They travel in carriages, while the ruder exiles march chained, and on foot. Boats are now being constructed to mitigate the hardships of this journey, *en attendant* the completion of the Siberian railway. By these boats it is hoped to transport the exiles from some port on the White Sea to the great rivers Obi, Yenesei, or Lena, which, after traversing Siberia, empty into the Arctic Ocean. Some persons who have seen these boats in process of construction have been shocked to find a large part of their decks converted into a great cage, but this seems a far more humane method of transportation than the land journey. The plan of having barges similarly constructed and towed by steamers has long been adopted on the Volga, and Messrs. Kennan and Frost, as they approached Siberia by the great city of Nishni-Novgorod, met many parties of exiles, for the most part banished by the Mir, and accompanied by their families.

From Nishni-Novgorod (not the city of the Norsemen who founded the first civilized empire in Russia) the travellers proceeded to Perm at the foot of the Ural Mountains. There, taking the Ural railroad they found excellent stations and European cookery. As they reached the summit of the Ural Mountains — snow-covered and dreary as we all have imagined them — "the sun was shining brightly in an unclouded sky, the morning air was cool, fresh, and laden with the odor of flowers and the resinous fragrance of mountain pines; a cuckoo was singing in a neighboring grove of birches, and a glory of early summer was over all the earth. . . . As the train swept on it passed over miles and miles where there was not a sign of human life, then past placer mining camps, where men and women were washing for gold. Sometimes we came out into beautiful park-like openings, diversified by clumps of graceful silver birches, and carpeted with turf almost as smooth and green as an English lawn. Flowers were everywhere abundant. Roses, dandelions, violets, wild strawberries, and lilies of the valley were in blossom all along the track, and occasionally we crossed a glade in the heart of the forest where the grass was almost hidden by a vivid sheet of yellow lilies." Such passages as this abound in Mr. Kennan's narrative.

The imperial ukase commanding the construction of the trans-Siberian railroad was signed May 19, 1891. The railroad was at once commenced at both ends; the western end has reached the River Tobol, a branch of the Obi, while the eastern end, in March, 1893, starting from Vladivostok, a place so strongly fortified as to be a sort of Sebastopol on the Sea of Japan, has been completed to Graffskaya on the Amoor, a distance of four hundred versts, or about two hundred and twenty-five miles, at a cost of sixty thousand roubles a verst, or about thirty thousand dollars per mile. The discovery of large fields of coal, both bituminous and anthracite, much of it of very fine quality, and some of it smokeless, will be of inestimable advantage to the new railroad. The coal is being rapidly mined, and much of it is within easy reach of Vladivostok. The Russian government has already expended vast sums on the most improved coal-mining machinery; for this supply of fuel is not only of vast importance to the railroad, but to the war-steamers on the Pacific. Before this century closes we may see a line of steamers in the merchant service, running from Vladivostok to San Francisco, touching at Japan and at the Sandwich islands, and opening new channels for trade. "Over six thousand men are steadily employed on the railroad at its eastern end, only four hundred of whom have been imported from Russia; eight hundred are criminal convicts from the mines, four hundred and fifty are exiles under police supervision" (in other words. banished by administrative process), "two thousand are Chinese laborers, and two thousand five hundred are regular Russian soldiers."[1] But there has been trouble among the laborers, the soldiers have refused to work with the criminals. The imported Russians clamored for more pay. The convicts escaped in considerable numbers, and formed

[1] Cosmopolitan Magazine, M. Gribayédoff. March, 1893.

predatory bands which roamed the country, and kept the governor's hands fully employed in hunting them down.

In June, 1885, however, Mr. Kennan and Mr. Frost, after crossing the Ural Mountains had to proceed on their journey in a *tarrantas*, a sort of boat on wheels. It had no thwarts, and they sat on their luggage. Soon they began to pass parties of exiles on the march. More than one hundred and seventy thousand had travelled that road since 1878, and more than half a million since the beginning of the century.

The prisons, and the *étapes*, or stations where the exiles were halted on their march, were found to be *awful*. The great receiving prison at Tieumen was built to hold eight hundred; when Mr. Kennan saw it it contained one thousand seven hundred and forty-one. As we read his terrible accounts of the filth, the sickness, and above all the smells, we have only the consolation of reminding ourselves that *perhaps* to the Russian peasant these things are not so intolerable as they would be to an American.

In the year 1885 fifteen thousand seven hundred and sixty-six persons passed the boundary of Siberia as exiles; of these, fifteen hundred were criminals, or hard labor convicts; twenty-six hundred and fifty-nine had been convicted of minor offences, and were not sentenced to hard labor in the mines; about six thousand were banished men and women, of whom thirty-seven hundred were exiled by the Mir; seventeen hundred and nineteen were deported as being tramps; and five hundred and fifty (of whom seventy-eight were were women) were banished by administrative process as political exiles. Besides these, there were fifty-five hundred and thirty-six men, women, and children accompanying their relatives. The exiles by administrative process were, however, not all political offenders. Many were exiles, who, having finished their first terms of banishment, were refused reinstation in their village communities, and were sent back to Siberia by the police.

In 1885 the long journeys on foot involved terrible suffering, especially to women and children. Among the political exiles Mr. Kennan and his friend found many who had apparently been exiled through pure misunderstanding. The police, often ignorant and full of restless zeal, turned anything into a dangerous proof of disaffection; and no doubt there is abundant disaffection in all the educated classes in Russia. With Nihilists plotting all kinds of atrocities, it is very hard to blame the rude zeal of ignorant officials; yet Skobeleff we know so hated and despised the government police that he always turned his back on any man who had entered it out of his own division. Mr. Kennan relates many sad stories; many instances of flagrant injustice and oppression. One of the exiles whom he met had been a lieutenant in the navy, who accompanied the Grand Duke Alexis when he visited this country. In a basket on his table were cards of invitation to many of the best houses in New York, where, a year or two before, he had danced gayly and enjoyed himself.

Some of the administrative exiles were literary men; one was a novelist whose works have been translated in America; some were young girls who had been studying medicine; some were editors, reviewers, and professional men.

They lived in log cabins very poorly furnished, but most of them had books. Mill, Darwin, Buckle, and Spencer were apparently great favorites, and were read in the original.

The exiles have been described by a Russian official as "quiet, orderly, reasonable human beings. We certainly," he added, "have no trouble with them here. Our government treats them with great kindness and consideration, and, so far as I know, they are good citizens."

The governor of Archangel in 1883 reported to his government that "from the experience of previous years, and from my own personal observation, I have come to the conclusion that administrative exile for political reasons is much more calculated to spoil the character of a man than to reform it. The transition from a life of comfort to a life of poverty, from a social life to a life in which there is no society, and from a life of activity to compulsory inaction, produces such ruinous consequences that not unfrequently we find the political exiles going insane and committing suicide. There has not been a single case in which a man suspected with good reason of political untrustworthiness, and exiled by administrative process, has returned from such banishment reconciled to the government, convinced of his error, and changed into a useful member of society and a faithful servant of the throne."

Escape, to a certain extent, seems frequent, — but few of those who escape ever get alive beyond the bounds of Siberia. As a soldier said to one who was recaptured: "The czar's cow-pasture is large, but there is no getting out of it."

From time to time French, English, and American magazines give accounts of exiles who have escaped from Siberia; these seldom complain of personal ill-treatment from Siberian officials; on the contrary, the higher officials seem to exhaust themselves in making reports, probably far from agreeable to the czar, advising better accommodation in the prisons, better clothing, better hospitals, etc., — reports which, when they reach St. Petersburg are rarely attended to. Let us trust that improved means of transportation will diminish the worst horrors of the system.

If we look at the matter from the point of view taken by political malcontents, who can blame them for aspirations after better things, — though where the materials for political betterment are to come from, who can say? And when driven frantic by the oppressions of the police, by the imprisonment of friends, and all the rest, who shall blame them if they look on Nihilists with a more lenient eye than we can? As a Russian, tried in 1881 for one of the attempts on Alexander II.'s life, said of a comrade: "He was not very well inclined to the terrorizing system, and had but lately joined it, moved solely by a revengeful and embittered feeling toward the government, in consequence of a long series of cruel persecutions, which had impressed him the more deeply that some of those who had suffered were his associates and friends."

We may indeed thus palliate the criminality of such acts, but nothing can mitigate their unwisdom. The men and women who destroyed the emperor-liberator shattered the dawning hope of better days for their own country. Russia indeed at the time of Alexander's death seems to have been politically and socially in a state of wild disorder; but we all know by experience that when we begin to set our house in order the first result is dust and general confusion.

I will close this part of my subject with what a Russian lady says of the possible ultimate fate of some of these political exiles, so deeply and so justly pitied by Mr. Kennan, and through his representations, by ourselves. It throws a somewhat brighter light upon a lurid picture:[1]

"Let us follow those whose doom is heaviest. Few of them, probably none, will end their allotted time at the mines or the State factories. An untimely death will doubtless end the sufferings of many before the tardy hand of mercy can reach them. Yet, wonderful to say, many more survive the horrors of the first years than would seem possible for men of gentle nurture and unhardened body. If they are resigned, and quietly behaved, they will, after a while, — three, four, or five years, — instead of the fifteen or twenty of their sentence, be brought under one of the so-called 'gracious manifestoes' which are always being issued on occasions of birthdays, marriages, etc., in the imperial family. They will then be transferred to some one of the convict colonies, from which in due time they will be released in like manner, and allowed to live within some particular rural district at a great distance from any city or town, and under strict surveillance of the local police. Gradually the range widens till it comprises district towns, the surveillance is lightened; at last the capital of the government itself is opened to the half-pardoned convict, and with it society, and resources of every kind. It now depends in a great measure on himself, on his good sense and abilities, to shape his further fortunes. Men of education, and scientific or technical attainments, are in as

[1] International Review.

great demand (and for the same reasons) in the Far East of Russia as in the Far West of America; and when, by the end of ten or twelve years, as is generally the case, and after having been previously transferred to the more populous and civilized western governments, the political convict is restored to his rank and privileges, freed from all disabilities and finally recalled from banishment, it is by no means rare to see him return to the shores of Lake Baïkal of his own free will, to settle there for life. I have known such,—lawyers, physicians, engineers, miners, able and energetic men.... One young lawyer in particular I remember. He was a little over thirty, sturdy of frame, and keen of look. He had come to St. Petersburg to assert his newly recovered rights and to transact some business, but all his thoughts were centred on a speedy return to Irkoutsk, where he had left a promising practice, some half-started ventures in a mining enterprise, and, as he almost hinted, a fairer attraction. Such political exiles as are not deprived of their liberty have of course all the more chances in their favor. The intercession of friends at home also does much to shorten their term and hasten their return to cities, or more favorable regions, if they behave judiciously, and have not the ill-luck of exceptionally falling under the rule of some of those ignorant and wantonly brutal officials whose number is diminishing every year. My object is by no means to palliate the horrors of the penal sentence known as 'hard labor in the mines.' The removal from the midst of civilization, from all old ties, and intellectual communion, the civil death which it entails, the rigid climate, the unwonted physical labor and coarse food, the daily, hourly association with real malefactors, many of them hardened wretches sunk to the lowest depths of degradation, — all these are features doubtless terrible enough; but it should be borne in mind that this heaviest penalty is but sparingly inflicted on 'politicals,' and that the victims are not debarred from hope in better times."

All the world knows Russia's passionate and not unreasonable desire to reach the sea. The Baltic can be closed to her ships by the Scandinavians, her outlet by the Black Sea is blocked by Constantinople. The Arctic Ocean is shut in by ice. She has only the eastern coast of Siberia, with which the great trans-Siberian railroad will connect her; and it is supposed that if she cannot get Constantinople she is aiming to indemnify herself by gaining communication with the Persian Gulf. But Russia proceeds warily. In Central Asia in eight years "Russian soldier-engineers have taken a bold flight through tracts which it was asserted they could never reach, and have laid down nine hundred miles of rails, uniting Krasnovodsk on the Caspian with 'silken Samarcand.' They have crossed the sand steppes to the north of Persia, skirted the northern slopes of the mountain ridge that forms the northern boundary of Persia, reached Merv by rail, a place that twenty years ago was considered inaccessible, and whose history goes back into pre-Christian times; they have planted their rails upon the quivering, shifting sands which almost fill the horrid space from Merv to the Oxus, thrown a bridge over its yellow floods, and passing near Bokhara 'the holy' have prolonged the path of the 'devil's cart,' into the heart of a country once rich and prosperous, and have set up their terminus at Samarcand near the tomb of Timour."[1]

Between Persia and British India lies Afghanistan, a "land of the mountain and the flood," — the Highlands of India. In Afghanistan are three chief places forming a military triangle, and strongly fortified, — Herat, Cabul, and Candahar. Of these, Herat lies to the west, not far from the Persian border, and is on the direct road to Bushire, the principal seaport on the Persian Gulf.

Afghanistan lies both north and south of the great chain of mountains running across Central Asia. We know them chiefly as the Himalayas, the Hindoo Koosh, and the Paropamisus, a low range lying at the western edge of the great chain between Persia, Afghanistan, and what fifty years ago was known in our school-books as Independent Tartary.

This Turkestan, or Independent Tartary, in which lies the Aral Sea, and which is bordered by the Caspian, is watered by three great rivers, the two principal of which are the Oxus and Jaxartes, so known in history, but now

[1] London Spectator, 1888.

called by Russians the Amu Darya, and the Sir Darya. The whole country was in prehistoric times an inland sea, of which the present Caspian and Aral seas formed part. It was dotted with large islands which are now oases in the midst of sand. These oases are many days' journey from each other. Until a late period each was governed by its khan, and the oases collectively are called the Khanates. They were five: Khiva, Merv, Bokhara, Tashkend, and Khokand. The Oxus and Jaxartes were formerly mountain streams falling into the great sea. When it dried up they made their way, the one into Lake Aral, the other into the Caspian. But some centuries ago the men of Khiva built a dam across the Oxus and directed its channel so that it flowed into Lake Aral. Ever since Peter the Great's time the Russians had been planning how to destroy the dam, and turn the waters back into their old channel, when a few years ago a great freshet came to their assistance, and without the need of engineering the Oxus, or Amu Darya, now flows into the Caspian.

This territory, once a great inland sea, is now a bare, sandy desert, with the exception of its oases, its northern part lying between the Caspian and Aral seas, its base resting on the undefined frontier of Afghanistan, whose ameer claims suzerainty over tribes beyond the mountains; to the east it is bounded by deserts and mountains, and on the west by Persia.

Peter the Great had some plans, which he never carried out, for the subjugation of Khiva. In 1839 an expedition from Russia was sent against it, but such were the hardships of crossing the deserts that the expedition had to retreat, having lost two thirds of its troops, and multitudes of camels and horses. Any one who has read poor Captain Burnaby's "Ride to Khiva" will not wonder that troops carrying their own supplies, broke down under the fatigue of the sandy march, the horrible heat of the desert, and its equally horrible cold.

About 1860 another advance began. The Sea of Aral

was reached, and the Russians then marched down the banks of the Amu Darya toward Khiva. But the farther they advanced the more opposition they encountered from the tribes of Tekkés, or Independent Tartars. "We must of necessity go on," said Prince Gortschakoff, "until we reach the settled States, with whom we can enter into peaceful commercial relations, profitable to both parties. And there and then we shall stop."

By 1865 the Russians had acquired all northern Independent Tartary, and then they took Tashkend and Khokand, which brought them near the khanate of Bokhara, while over the mountains in an outlying district of the Empire of China, lay Kashgar and Yarkand, places whose names we read in newspapers with ignorant indifference. In 1868 Samarcand and Bokhara were placed under a Russian protectorate. Bokhara had always been a place of refuge for Afghan deposed princes. In 1840 it was governed by that unspeakable wretch the Emir who imprisoned Captains Stoddard and Connelly, and finally thrust them into a dreadful pit, to be eaten alive by insects kept there for the purpose; from which death one is thankful to think they were released, on some sudden alarm, by the sword of the executioner.

Khiva and Merv remained independent, but in 1873 three Russian columns marched against Khiva. One perished of thirst and heat, one came near doing so, but one succeeded. Khiva fell without a struggle, and its khan, like the other khans, became a Russian feudatory.

Russia has therefore in suzerainty a quadrangular mountain and desert region in Central Asia.

One of the officers employed in this war against the Tartars, as we used to call them (Turcomans and Tekkés the books name them now), was the future General Mikhail Dimitrivitch Skobeleff. He early conceived the idea that the conquest of this country would be to Russia the conquest of a road to India through Afghanistan; that some day, if England continued to oppose the acquisition of

Constantinople, Russia through Afghanistan could threaten her Indian possessions, and keep her armies employed for their defence, or might make a bargain with the English government promising to give up her designs on India, and relinquish all alliance with Afghanistan, provided England would consent to her designs upon Constantinople.

The Turkish War of 1877 broke out, and Skobeleff was sent to the Danube. The English government, having ventured some remonstrances about the Russian advances in the East, was answered somewhat roughly by Prince Gortschakoff that while he "had a whale to look after he would not trouble himself about little fishes." But he very seriously troubled himself about the "little fishes" notwithstanding; an embassy was about to be sent to Cabul to propitiate the ameer; and if the Treaty of Berlin had proved wholly unsatisfactory to the Emperor Alexander, or had he been one of those monarchs who "delight in war," those plans would have been carried out which were already made for an advance on India, for stirring up the native population against the British, and taking a position of strong influence, if not of authority, in Afghanistan. At that time Skobeleff had his scheme fully drawn out for an invasion of India, by taking possession of the Afghan passes, — the Khyber and the Bolan. He seems to have changed his mind, however, afterward, and to have considered that the best way to attack India would be by crossing the Paropamisus Mountains near the Persian frontier, and taking possession of Herat.

This is not the place to relate the history of Afghanistan, or the story of the second Cabul massacre, which ended by the present ameer of Afghanistan, the stern and cruel Abdurahman, being placed upon the Afghan throne. He has maintained himself upon that throne for twenty years; and on the whole has been faithful to his alliance with the English. But his life is an uncertain one. He suffers severely from gout, he is always exposed to assassination, and many men have with him blood-feuds for the unjust slaughter of their relatives. His authority over his mountain chiefs, their strongholds, and their followers is as precarious as that of any King James or King Robert in Scottish history over Highland chieftains and their clans. When Abdurahman dies, or comes to grief, there will be a fresh struggle, either by arms or by diplomacy, between England and Russia.

The English within the last few years have established a protectorate over Beloochistan. Not that Beloochistan is worth anything, — for it is as sandy as the bed of the ocean, — but it contains a place called Quetta; and Quetta is supposed to be a back door to the possession of what is called the key of India, — namely, Herat.

Who shall have Herat is now the great question to be decided between the Russians in Central Asia and the British in India. The English have no desire to occupy Herat. Their wish is to have it in the hands of an ameer of Afganistan, who is faithful to their interests, and who will oppose its falling into the power or under the influence of Russia.

Herat lies on the edge of northwestern Afghanistan, not far from the frontier of Persia and south of the Paropamisus range of mountains. All great military authorities (Skobeleff in his latter years among them) seem to agree in regarding Herat as the key to India. Past Herat all conquerors of Hindoostan, except the English, have come, — Alexander the Great, Timour the Tartar, Yengis Khan, Nadir Shah, and all the rest. "It is a city," says a Persian geographer, "that has been fifty times taken, fifty times destroyed, and fifty times has risen from its ashes." Though the orientalism of the statistics of the Persian makes his statement in substance untrue, it is true in spirit.[1] It was in the Middle Ages the route of all caravans from the west to the east, as well as of all armies. Seven hundred years ago it contained, according to the records of that period, twelve thousand retail shops, six thousand public baths, caravanseries, and water-mills, three hundred and fifty schools and Moham-

[1] Cf. Blackwood's Magazine.

medan monastic institutions, and one hundred and forty-four thousand occupied houses. The country surrounding it is marvellously fertile and beautiful, particularly rich in apple and plum orchards. Herat is no longer what it was; but it still commands the only easy road running through a fertile country to India. This road passes along a narrow strip of land lying between deserts. An army that sets out from Herat may cross Afghanistan to the Bolan Pass, without experiencing difficulties.

Before 1879, when the second Cabul massacre took place, and before Abdurahman was placed upon the Afghan throne, it had been a great object with the English to put resident agents into Herat, Cabul, and Candahar. Shere Ali, then ruler of Afghanistan, believed in a coming war between England and Russia, and sat on the fence prepared to drop down upon the winning side. Meantime Skobeleff was again in Tartary, this time with a view of taking Geok Tepi, — a stronghold in which the Tekké-Turcomans had shut up themselves and their families. This place had successfully repulsed one Russian army; but Skobeleff was not to be resisted. The account of the siege, the assault, and the sack may be found in that very interesting book, — Alexander Verestchagin's "At Home and in War." Among the followers of Skobeleff was a young man of Asiatic birth, Ali Khan by name, who entered the Russian army and Russianized himself into Alikhanoff. He had been a favorite with Skobeleff in the war of 1877; but one day, having lost his temper in a quarrel, he challenged his superior officer, was reduced to the ranks as a punishment, and was sent as a private to Turkestan. Already when Skobeleff took command in that country he had begun to rise again.

Alikhanoff's deeds are celebrated in that war; and the great ability and unscrupulous audacity he showed in connection with the taking of Merv, have made him a brilliant figure among Russian military heroes.

Alikhanoff may be said to have captured Merv almost

single-handed for the Russians; and now outside its gates is a railway station. To that point the trans-Caspian railroad runs south, and then branches off to take a course as directly east as possible to Samarcand. From Samarcand it is thought probable it may eventually skirt the Chinese frontier, and enter southern Siberia.

Be that as it may, Merv lies only three hundred miles north of Herat.[1] The Russians are endeavoring by every means to encroach on the undefined frontier of Afghanistan north of its mountains; and most probably the time is not far distant when the Russian border will reach the Paropamisus range. This range is not difficult to cross. It was formerly supposed to be so; but experience has proved that it consists at its western end of gently sloping hills. By this road Russia, when she is ready, can approach Herat, and (Herat in her hands) can march toward British India. An army could be carried from St. Petersburg to the Volga. Down the Volga, with its navy of steamboats, the troops could float two thousand miles to the Caspian Sea. Things have changed upon the Caspian since 1879, when Skobeleff had his army ferried across it in barges. There is now an immense fleet on the Caspian, called into being by the petroleum wells of Baku. These wells have come into knowledge just in time to supply fuel for the great Central Asiatic railroad.

In 1888 the railroad was opened to Samarcand. It is stupendous to think of it, — a city in which Queen Scheherazade placed her fairy-land ! The Tartars of that district used to say that, unless the Franks could fly faster than their horses, and could bind down the sands of their deserts, that region could never be subdued. But both these things have been done. Nine hundred miles of rail connect Krasnovodsk on the Caspian with fairy Samarcand, which is now within ten days' journey from St. Petersburg. Already commerce has availed itself of the new means of transportation. The merchant of the interior no longer

[1] Cf. The Russians at the Gates of Herat.

travels across sandy deserts with his merchandise on camels, exposed to dangers from heat and cold and shifting sands, and above all from bands of robbers and the exactions of local rulers. An immense trade is now carried on between Central Asia and Batoum, — a port on the Black Sea, ceded to Russia by the Treaty of Berlin, to which there is a branch railroad, connecting it with the trans-Caspian.

In a very interesting paper published in the "Nineteenth Century," 1890, by Arminius Vambéry, the distinguished Hungarian traveller, linguist, and professor, he comments on the changes that have taken place in Central Asia since, in 1863, he visited the regions, now traversed by the railroad, in terror of his life, and in disguise. He was then lame, or he would have been undoubtedly captured by robbers, and sold as a slave. He travelled in a pannier slung on a camel's back, and on the other side, to balance him, was a buffalo calf. He tells appalling stories of the slave trade in 1863 carried on by the Tekké-Turcomans. The slaves were principally Persians, heretics in the eyes of their captors. All wore heavy chains. The domestic slaves had collars by which they were pegged down at night, and the tents of the Turcomans were full of them.

A Turcoman poet living at the close of the last century, in one of his poems on the end of the world, made this remarkable prediction: "Russia will be the power that will destroy the Moslem, and finally Antichrist shall annihilate Russia."

"So isolated was the region through which I travelled in 1863," says Vambéry, "that on my return the shah of Persia and his ministers made the most anxious inquiries of me, — Central Asia seeming to be to them as unknown as Japan or China. . . . Boundless is my wonder when I consider the changes."

And yet, among the things introduced by "civilization in a Russian dress," are three that were unknown in 1863 among the "Man-Stealers" (the Russian name for Turcomans): liquor, gambling, and official corruption.

The Russians are not bad masters at first to the nations they annex or conquer. It being impossible at once to Russify them or to convert them to orthodoxy, they are suffered to retain their own manners and customs, and as much as possible to govern themselves. The Russians never try to ameliorate the condition of the working class, or to correct abuses. What is custom in a place they let alone, however bad it may be. Their system is policy, not philanthropy, and they do what is rarely done by the English, they assimilate the leading men and make them Russians. The Russian army is full of Asiatics, officers and gentlemen, who are still Mohammedans, but they wear the Russian dress, their breasts are covered with Russian orders, and like Ali Khan they Russianize their names. Under English rule no Asiatic becomes an Englishman.

I cannot leave the subject of Russian railroads without alluding to the terrible experience of the imperial family on October 29, 1888, while making a tour in southern Russia. They had left the town of Borki behind them, and were in the midst of what seemed an interminable desert. There were several carriages on the train, one filled with guards, others with servants and officers of the household.

Suddenly — from some cause that the public has never distinctly known — a terrible wreck of the train took place, perhaps by accident, perhaps by design. The members of the imperial family were not seriously hurt, but twenty-one persons were killed, most of whom were soldiers or railroad employees.

It must have been a fearful scene to the empress when she found herself standing in that desolate waste, in the midst of the dead, wounded, and dying, — the little Grand Duchess Xenia clinging to her father with cries of, " Oh ! they are coming to kill you ! They will kill us all ! " And indeed, had that been the purpose of hidden enemies they might doubtless have accomplished it, as the czar and his family stood helpless and shelterless in the midst of death and desolation.

No wonder that members of that most unhappy race never feel themselves, those dear to them, or those surrounding them, safe from the destroyer.

This continual apprehension of a danger "that walketh in darkness" is upon all of them, and has a deplorable influence on the sensitive nervous system inherited by the Romanoffs from generation to generation.

It need not surprise us that the emperor, seeing a young officer approaching him with his hand in the breast of his uniform, at once thought of the assassin who had thus ridden up to his grandfather in the great Square of St. Isaac, and drew his own pistol.

Can we wonder that he flees from the harmless stranger who lies in wait for him with a camera; or that the first impression of the boy czarevitch when a Japanese fanatic sprang upon him was that his assailant was a Nihilist convict, escaped from Saghalien?

We read frequently in our daily papers about the designs of Russia on the Pamirs. The Pamirs are great plateaux in that part of the Himalaya Mountains where they are joined by two other ranges, the Beloor and the Kien-Lun. This spot has been called, poetically, the Roof of the World. The Kien-Lun and Beloor mountains form a crescent round the western portion of the Chinese Empire, the territory called sometimes Eastern Turkestan, and known in earlier geographies as Chinese Tartary.

An outlying portion of Thibet, called Little Thibet, a region infested by fierce and lawless tribes, lies in a narrow valley between the Kien-Lun and Himalaya mountains directly north of British India.

By looking at a map of British India, we shall see that Hindostan runs to a point at the north, where it is bounded by mountains which shut it off from Afghanistan, Little Thibet, and Eastern Turkestan. Directly north of the Kien-Lun Mountains, shortly before they reach the meeting-point of the Roof of the World, lie the khanates of Kashgar and Yarkand, near neighbors to Bokhara, which is now in the possession of Russia. At present Kashgar and Yarkand owe a doubtful allegiance to the emperor of China, but Russia advances claims to them as former possessions of Bokhara.

England, Afghanistan, and China are all united in resisting Russian encroachments in this direction; if she obtains possession of the Pamirs (vast steppes in the heart of that meeting-place of mountains) she will have great advantages in any attack she may plan on Afghanistan, on China, or on British India. By entering Afghanistan on the northeast she could, if she were at war with England, and had secured possession of Herat, have two roads which would lead her to the Khyber Pass or the Bolan by which to enter Hindostan.

Russia, by her possession of Bokhara; China, by her possession of Yarkand and Kashgar; England, by her possession of Cashmere, Afghanistan on her northern boundary, and the strip of land called Little Thibet, — seem to meet almost at the same point on the northern frontier of British India. All that in case of war would separate the English and Russian outposts is the narrow line of land north of the Hindoo Koosh, claimed by Afghanistan, and inhabited by turbulent tribes who pay to the ameer a doubtful homage. This is why Russia and China are contending for possession of the Pamirs, and why England and Afghanistan look on Russia's success in that direction with a jealous eye.

We come now to what seems to me the most flagrant abuse of Russian power, even worse than the revival of the policy of the Middle Ages in the persecution of the Jews. Comparatively it has attracted little notice in Europe. The Jews have at least some protection from their co-religionists, who can retaliate on their oppressors in the money markets of the world; but there is no one apparently to lift up a voice of remonstrance for the Baltic Provinces. Not that any voice of remonstrance from the West would be of service. The czar, as we know already, takes refuge in the firm conviction that Russia and her institutions are destined to override all western Europe, and meantime intrenches himself behind that dangerous maxim: "May I not do what I will with mine own?"

The Baltic Provinces needed no coercion to confirm them in their fidelity to the czar. Their inhabitants were among his most loyal and attached subjects; but all methods are being resorted to to establish orthodoxy and nationality among them; the government is resolved to suppress "their Protestant faith, their German laws, and their national customs: and to supplant them by the faith of the orthodox Church, the Russian language, and above all by the peculiar system of the village tenure of land which prevails among Slavonic peoples."[1]

The Baltic Provinces consist of three distinct nationalities: Finland, which was once Swedish; Courland, Livland, and Esthland, which were German; and Lithuania, which was Polish. Together they form the western boundary of the Russian Empire; until Russia acquired them she was simply Muscovy, a barbaric semi-Asiatic power. But these provinces, each with its own laws, language, history, and customs, are as strange to each other as they are to the race that has incorporated them.

The three provinces, Courland, Livland, and Esthland (or Courland, Livonia, and Esthonia) were called Hanse Provinces in the sixteenth century; but three centuries earlier they were colonized by German knights, merchants, and priests, who easily established their supremacy over the native Slavonian peasantry. The knights were of the Teutonic order; before long disputes arose between them and the bishops, while both fought with the inhabitants of the free cities Riga, Revel, and Dorpat. By these quarrels they so weakened themselves that in the days of Ivan the Terrible, when Russia had grown into a formidable power, they could oppose little resistance to an inroad carried on as is implied by the very name of the invader.

[1] Edinburgh Review.

Meantime they had made great progress in prosperity and civilization; but so terrible was the destruction wrought by the Russian invasion that to this day Livland (or Livonia) has never recovered the prosperity she enjoyed up to the close of the sixteenth century.

Sweden and Poland, encouraged by the unhappy condition of the Baltic Provinces when the Russians had retired after their raid, stepped in to take possession of them. Finland had been always Swedish, but south of Finland lay Esthland (or Esthonia) which gladly placed itself under the protection of the Swedish kings. Courland became a vassal duchy of Poland, and retained its quasi-independence till the middle of the eighteenth century, while Livland (or Livonia) united itself by a solemn treaty to Poland, — a treaty by which its people conceived they had secured forever their Lutheran faith, their German language, and internal self-government.

The treaty, however, was made only to be broken. The effect of annexation to Poland was as disastrous as the invasion of Ivan the Terrible; but Polish oppression did not last long. Livland was made over to Sweden, and under the humane rule of its kings, who carefully respected the rights and privileges of their new subjects, it was restored to prosperity and civilization.

This lasted until the death of Gustavus Adolphus; but one of his successors being in straits for money "ventured on a measure which, under pretence of overhauling the defective titles of the nobles of Livland to their estates, confiscated nearly three fifths of the land of the province to the Swedish exchequer." The nobles considering themselves oppressed beyond endurance, sought protection from Peter the Great, who was at once impressed with the importance which the extension of his territories along the shores of the Baltic would afford to his new empire.

Sweden in 1712 yielded Livland and Esthland to her powerful neighbor by treaty. The possession of these provinces was indeed all important to the Russian emperor;

for St. Petersburg, the foundation of which he had laid in 1703, is built upon the soil of Esthland. But by treaty Peter renewed for himself and his successors an engagement that some years before he had entered into with the Baltic Estates to acknowledge and to respect the ascendency of the Lutheran Church, the German laws, and the German language, as well as the hereditary institutions of the land.

After the final partition of Poland, Courland, which until then had been a quasi-independent duchy, was reunited to its more northerly sister-provinces, and under the rule of Alexander I. a new and hopeful epoch for the Baltic Provinces began. For fifty years (from 1795 to 1845) their history was one of continued peace and of advancing prosperity. As knowledge and civilization increased, however, the chains of serfdom weighed heavily upon their peasantry, until, some years before the proclamation of Alexander II. gave liberty to all other Russian serfs, those in Esthland and Livland were voluntarily emancipated by their masters.

"Nowhere in his vast dominions could the czar boast of more faithful subjects than in the Baltic Provinces, so long as the Russian government respected their acknowledged rights and hereditary customs. Their nobility furnished the Russian army and diplomacy with the ablest of their generals and ambassadors. The names of Lieven, Rosen, Pahlen, Brunnow, Krüdener, and others are inseparable from Russian history."

But in the reign of the Emperor Nicholas the triune maxim of autocracy, orthodoxy, and nationality began to make itself felt in attacks upon the peculiar institutions of Finland and the Baltic Provinces.

Under Alexander II., who was personally attached to his Finns, and to the people of his provinces upon the Baltic, they recovered heart and hope. Alexander restored the old Swedish constitution to Finland, and Poland, when he first came to the throne, was granted a provisional government under a national minister. Courland, Esthonia, and

Livonia, however, had not yet shared in Alexander's political reforms, — probably because he was anxious to extend his land-system to the already emancipated serfs, — when the Polish revolution broke out, in 1863, and checked the reforming enthusiasm of the Emperor-liberator. In order to punish the Polish nobility, to depress them as much as possible, and to raise up enemies against them among their own peasantry, the village community system (the Mir) was forced on Poland. An intense hatred of things German became in Russia tantamount to patriotism. The Moscow "Gazette" declared that the time was passed when Russia could play at liberalism and cosmopolitanism. The duty of every Russian was to serve the State. Freedom without a country was an empty phantom. "It is foolish," cried the editor Katkoff, "to speak of the future world-wide sway of a Pan-Slavonic empire, and to break into ruins that State which is the sole representative of Slavonic ideas."

So "Russia for the Russians" was the war-cry, and to be a true Russian it is necessary to belong to the orthodox Church, for not to acknowledge the Russian czar as spiritual as well as temporal autocrat, is, in a Russian subject, treason.

As soon as Alexander III. came into power the cry was: Recovery of the original Russian character of Lithuanian lands, the re-establishment of the Russian peasants in the Baltic Provinces in their rights as legitimate possessors of the soil, of which they were deprived five hundred years before by Teutonic knights and German traders. The whole power of the government has ever since been directed to the annihilation of all non-Russian institutions in the empire, and the establishment of one compact Russian peasant State.

As year after year goes on the pressure becomes stronger against the Lutheran religion, the German language, the political privileges, and the hereditary customs of the Baltic Provinces. And it is especially true that in these provinces the ruthless cruelty and unrelenting perseverance with which subordinates in Russia carry out the designs of their master are best shown. Roman Catholic churches on the smallest pretence have been pulled down, Lutheran churches closed, and Baptist meeting-houses suppressed. To convert an orthodox believer to another faith, or to any heresy, involves deportation to Siberia for the converter and the converted. Those who have joined the orthodox Church, as many peasants in the Baltic Provinces did at one time from interested motives, are, if they relapse, most severely dealt with.

"Edicts," says Mr. Lanin, "have been issued, some clauses of which, if fairly carried out, would banish to Siberia the apostles themselves, — nay, One greater than the apostles, — were He or they to return to this earth and preach in the dominions of the czar. . . . The possession of absolute truth is said by historians to render people intolerant, and what the uninitiated might call cruel. There is no doubt that Alexander III. believes himself in possession of absolute truth, and his religion runs into his politics, his politics into his religion. Besides his persecution of the Jews, he is bitterly severe on Catholics, thousands of whom in Lithuania he has compelled to embrace the State religion on the ground that their grandfathers or great-grandfathers were members of that church, and could never have acquired a right to abandon it. The czar is pursuing the Baptists and the Stundists with a degree of refined cruelty compared with which Louis XIV.'s persecution of the Huguenots, if we closely examine it, was humane. And firmly convinced that all these acts are the embodiment of the will of the Almighty, his astonishment is extreme at the indignation they arouse in the civilized world. . . . Alexander III. is not one whit less obedient to the voice of his conscience than was Archbishop Laud or Oliver Cromwell." [1]

Such being Alexander III.'s feeling against his fellow-Christians, can we wonder at his animus against the Jews? — especially as the persecutors of the Jews, taking advantage of the death [2] of their protector Alexander II. (called in Poland the "Jew Emperor"), broke into riots and outrages immediately on the accession of a new czar.

[1] Contemporary Review.
[2] There were Jews concerned in his cruel assassination.

In accordance with the fourth clause of the will of Peter the Great, which recommends his successors to maintain agents who shall intrigue in foreign courts and among foreign peoples to promote the interests of Russia, there are Russian political missionaries at work wherever Slavonic ideas are likely to take root if planted. Those who do this work are officially called missionaries. They are not unknown even in the United States, where men out of favor with their government have been sent from time to time to earn their pardon by creating a public opinion favorable to Russia. But the chief fields of this "missionary" work are in Servia and the Balkan principalities, in the outlying Slavonic appendages to the Hungarian kingdom, and among the Slavs (or Czechs) of Bohemia. The unrest that we read of in these countries, and among the Afghans and Armenians, is due in large part to the efforts of these agents to impress on all malcontents that they have a sympathizing friend in Russia. One duty of these "missionaries" for the past dozen years has been to create strong popular feeling against the Jews.

From what we have already said of the present Emperor Alexander we can feel at once how sincere must be his desire to rid orthodox Russia of an alien nationality and an unorthodox religion.

The murder of his father, who was supposed to protect the Jews, was soon followed by outbreaks of peasant hate against them all over the provinces of Southern Russia. National anti-Semitic fanaticism was intensified by hopes of gain; for a report was current, set on foot it is believed by secret agents, that the czar countenanced the plunder of the Jews, and had given his orthodox subjects their property. But loss of property was of little moment, compared with outrages that have been thus enumerated by a correspondent of the London "Times": —

"Men murdered, tender infants dashed to death, or roasted alive in their own homes, girls violated in the sight of their relatives by soldiers, who should have been the guardians of their honor; for during scenes of murder and of pillage the local authorities everywhere have stood by with folded arms, doing little or nothing to prevent their occurrence or recurrence, and allowing the ignorant peasantry to remain under the impression that a *ukase* existed ordering the property of Jews to be handed over to their fellow-Russians. Indeed, in one place the mayor read a copy of the supposed *ukase* to his fellow-citizens, and a riot would have ensued had not the village priest done his duty, and declared his belief that no such *ukase* existed."

In one province, where a flourishing agricultural settlement of Jews had been established for forty years, the mob was led by men dressed as police officers, who produced a document purporting to be the spoliation proclamation of the czar. In this place the farm implements were all destroyed, and five hundred cattle and ten thousand sheep were driven away. In one village " the Jews adroitly turned the supposed *ukase* of the czar into a safeguard. Hearing that the rioters were advancing to the attack, they brought the keys of their houses to their Christian neighbors, saying that if the *ukase* was true it would be better that neighbors should have their property than the rioters; and if the *ukase* proved to be untrue of course their good neighbors would return the keys. The Christians of the village accordingly repulsed the rioters, and in a few days the Jews were again in possession of their property."

By early summer in 1881, a few months after the death of Alexander II., the chief towns and villages of southern Russia were ablaze with violence and riot. Whenever arrests were made, after the work of destruction was completed (never before; for until the rioters had done their worst the authorities do not seem to have interfered with the work that was going on), Jews were among those who were put in prison, charged with carrying revolvers without a permit, to defend their homes.

The excitement spread even to the Caspian Sea and to Siberia. As late as November the myth of the spoliation *ukase* encouraged all outrages.

Not content with riot, the "red cock" that summer crowed over forty-one towns inhabited by Jews, twenty thousand of whom were rendered homeless. The "red cock" is the proverbial expression used by the Russian *moujik* for the work of the incendiary. The value of Jewish property that summer destroyed in southern Russia, by arson and by pillage, has been estimated at eighty million dollars.

These outrages were recorded for us in telegrams twelve years ago, as similar horrors are in 1893. "A violent outbreak against the Jews took place at" Lipsk, Pinsk, or elsewhere. And that is all we hear of them.

"The municipalities," says the "Times" in its issue of Jan. 13, 1882, "with the connivance of the local governments, have added to the misery of the situation. With rough logic they have argued that, as these riots were directed against the Jews, if there had been no Jews there would have been no riots. They accordingly petitioned the governors of their provinces to issue orders for the expulsion of the Jews from towns in which they had no legal right of domicile. The Jews in Russia are only allowed to reside in twenty-eight provinces, often only in certain towns; and the number of persons to reside is (at least theoretically) limited. During Alexander II.'s reign, however, these laws had been somewhat allowed to fall into desuetude; and many Jews had ventured beyond the limits assigned them. But leaving aside the general question, it was a most heartless act to add to the miseries of the Jewish population at the moment when the mob was eagerly scanning the disposition of the authorities to discover to what lengths they might proceed with impunity."

Nevertheless, this was the view taken by the czar's reactionary minister, General Ignatieff, who, as we have seen, was put in office to reverse the policy of Loris Melikoff, and to abridge as much as possible all privileges granted by the late czar. Nothing whatever was done by government to protect the Jews or to suppress the riots; but after May 23, when a deputation of the Jews of St. Petersburg, headed by Baron Gunzberg, waited on the czar, Alexander III.

expressed his intention of dealing with the evil; and the result was that on September 3 the following edict was issued, which simply tended to aggravate the situation. I give the larger part of it intact, because it is the keynote to the policy which has been ever since pursued in Russia, and which has culminated in that expulsion of the Jews about which at present we know so little, but which has filled all western Europe and America with horror: —

"For some time the government has given its attention to the Jews and to their relations to the rest of the inhabitants of the empire, with a view of ascertaining the sad condition of the Christian inhabitants brought about by the conduct of the Jews in business matters.

"For the last twenty years the government has endeavored in various ways to bring the Jews near to its other inhabitants, and has given them almost equal rights with the indigenous population. The movements, however, against the Jews, which began last spring in the south of Russia and extended to central Russia, prove incontestably that all its endeavors have been of no avail, and that ill-feeling prevails now as much as ever between the Jewish and the Christian inhabitants of those parts. Now, the proceedings at the trial of those charged with rioting, and other evidence, bear witness to the fact that the main cause of these movements and riots, to which the Russians as a nation are strangers, was but a commercial one, and is as follows: —

"During the last twenty years the Jews have gradually possessed themselves of not only every trade and business in all its branches, but also of a great part of the land by buying or farming it. With few exceptions, they have as a body devoted their attention, not to enriching or benefiting the country, but to defrauding by their wiles its inhabitants, and particularly its poor inhabitants. This conduct of theirs has called forth protests on the part of the people, as manifested in acts of violence and robbery. The government, while on the one hand doing its best to put down the disturbances, and to deliver the Jews from oppression and slaughter, have also, on the other hand, thought it a matter of urgency and justice to adopt stringent measures in order to put an end to the oppression practised by the Jews on the inhabitants, and to free the country from their malpractices, which were, as is known, the cause of the agitation."

With this view commissions were appointed, and encouraged to report as unfavorably to the Jews as possible on their trades, the extent of their farming, their usury, and liquor dealing.

There is no word of reprimand to those who had indulged themselves (not in isolated cases, but in whole districts) in rape, murder, and rapine. The document showed clearly to the populace that the government shared their prejudices against the Jews.

When the governor of Warsaw was ordered to publish this circular, he at first refused, saying that Jews and Poles had always lived on such friendly terms that no commission to inquire into their relations seemed necessary. He was, however, forced to publish the rescript; and the result was a frightful rising against the Jews at Christmas, three months after. Three hundred houses and six hundred shops in Warsaw were pillaged and devastated, and thousands of victims were rendered homeless, and reduced to beggary.

"In the first place," says the "Times," "the riot at Warsaw was clearly planned, an alarm of fire being simultaneously raised in at least two places, and the mob being directed by men who spoke Polish with a Russian accent. The culpable neglect of the military authorities in refusing to make use of the twenty thousand men forming the garrison, finds its counterpart in the similar behavior of other governors earlier in the year. The behavior of the police, who are described as only interfering to prevent the Jews from protecting themselves, tallies with their behavior elsewhere. And finally the attempts that were made by telegraph officials and others to prevent the true state of the case from reaching the rest of Europe may serve to account for the fact that the enormities of the past nine months have only found the faintest echo in the press of Europe."

And even so it is now. It is impossible to give anything like an historical account of what is going on in Russia in relation to the Jews, or what has been going on there for the past two years; indeed, from the time the document I have quoted was put forth, the government has steadily acted on its spirit. Neither concerning the expulsion and persecution of the three million Jews in Russia, nor of the famine, nor of the cholera, can anything reliable as yet be told. We can only read brief newspaper reports and telegrams; and by the faint light that streams down to us from events that took place a dozen years ago, can form some idea of the present situation.

Under M. Probédonostzeff, now minister of worship, a man whose influence for the past eight years has almost overshadowed the throne, — it is natural to suppose that all religious persecutions undertaken at his instigation will be carried on with redoubled vigor. "It is Pobédonostzeff," says a writer in 1892, "who keeps alive in the czar the idea that he is the anointed of the Lord, the representative of God upon earth; and that the population of his endless empire only exists to obey his will."

Yet the czar has no love for greatness; he conscientiously believes that the duties of his position have been thrust upon him; and sees in himself a Joshua commanded to purge a land that is holy of all but the race to whom its destinies have by Providence been committed. He will exterminate by modern methods all misbelievers in Holy Russia, even as the people of Jericho or Ai were put to the sword.

CHAPTER XIV.

SULTAN ABDUL HAMID.

I HAVE told the history of the war between Russia and Turkey, which had its origin in the Bulgarian massacres, perpetrated during the last months of Abdul Aziz's reign. These massacres were chiefly due to the obstinacy, the supineness, or the incapacity of the grand vizier, Mohammed Nedim Pasha, who, strange to say, was at that very time the close ally of the Russian ambassador, General Ignatieff, and indeed it has always been believed that he accepted pay for his influence in favor of Russia.

It needed no foresight to tell what would be the result of arming all Mussulmans in Bulgaria, at the same time that all men in the Christian villages were disarmed. Nor, when outrages began, would the grand vizier suffer regular troops to be sent into the disturbed districts, where Pomacks, Bashi-Bazouks and Circassians were falling with fury on the defenceless population.

Pomacks are renegade Slavs; the Circassians, as we know, were Mohammedan mountaineers from the Caucasus, to whom in 1869 Abdul Aziz offered an asylum; and Bashi-Bazouks were an irregular corps composed of outcasts of all nations, ready for any deviltry, and keen for plunder. It was not the Turks who murdered their Christian neighbors, but men of alien races, all of whom, however, professed the Moslem faith.

The Turkish Empire is said to be composed of nineteen nationalities, each and all antagonistic to one another; and at the very moment when America and western Europe were filled with excitement, arising from reports of the atrocities in Bosnia and Herzegovina, a revolution was taking place in the palace of the sultan, the details of which have excited very little interest, partly because in the end it proved abortive, and partly because what public attention could be given to Turkey was soon absorbed by accounts of the Russian War.

Something about this project of reform has been related in the chapter called "Four Sultans." Its leader was Midhat Pasha, the third great Turkish statesman of modern times. The two others, Fuad Pasha and Aali Pasha, happily for themselves, died natural deaths in 1871; for Midhat was reserved detraction, disappointment, exile, and eventually poison. He had been appointed by Abdul Medjid governor-general of the province of Rustchuk on the Danube, and he was spoken of to Sir Henry Elliot, English ambassador at Constantinople from 1867 to 1877, in the following terms: "He is a man wholly unlike the ordinary Turkish *vali*. He has been doing all in his power to develop the province, establishing schools, making roads, encouraging industries, and giving security to life and property by a firm and impartial administration of justice."

When Fuad and Aali died, within six months of each other, Sultan Abdul Aziz, who had not dared to rid himself of their control, congratulated himself on being, at last, out of leading-strings.

Midhat was head of what was called the party of Young Turkey, and was a man of so much influence that his rival, Mohammed Nedim did not dare openly to get rid of him. For three years (from 1872 to 1875) a struggle was carried on between them. From time to time Midhat would venture to remonstrate with the sultan, sometimes to some purpose, generally with no effect. By degrees, — at times in power, but more often in disgrace, — he matured his plans. In 1875 he detailed them thus to the English ambassador: —

"The sultan's empire is being rapidly brought to destruction; corruption has reached a pitch that it has never before attained;

MIDHAT PASHA.

the service of the State is starved while untold millions are being poured into the palace, and the provinces are being ruined by the uncontrolled exactions of the governors, who purchase their appointments at the palace; and nothing can save the country but a complete change of system."

The only remedy that Midhat could perceive lay, first, in securing a control over the sovereign by making the ministers — especially as regarded the finances — responsible to a national popular assembly; secondly, in making this assembly truly national by doing away with all distinctions of classes and religions, and by placing the Christians upon a footing of entire equality with the Mohammedans; thirdly by decentralization, and by the establishment of provincial control over the governors.

In a previous chapter I have told all the details of the actual outbreak, a year later, in the autumn of 1875. The word "constitution" was by that time in everybody's mouth, but it being reasonable to expect that the sultan's views on the subject would be obstinate and obstructive, the hopes of the reformers turned to Prince Murad, the heir presumptive, who it was known was prepared to grant a constitution, and to inaugurate reform. We know already how the conspiracy of reform was carried out. On May 30, 1876, when war was going on with Servia, and when Bosnia and Herzegovina were in insurrection, the empire was in the utmost peril. Abdul Aziz was made prisoner and Murad V. proclaimed, amidst general and apparently heartfelt expressions of rejoicing. We know also how Murad's nerves proved unable to bear the strain and excitement of the revolution in his favor, and how his mind gave way when he found himself only a tool in the hands of his ministers.

Having related at some length the story of the suicide of Abdul Aziz, I should not recur to it here were it not that it had subsequently its influence on the fate of Midhat Pasha; and it may be well to draw attention to what has been said of it by Sir Henry Elliot, because in magazine articles up to the present day, doubts have been cast upon the manner of Abdul Aziz's death, and because a trial of two men, a wrestler and a gardener, was gotten up by the *camarilla* that desired the complete destruction of Midhat Pasha, then an exile in Arabia. The wrestler and the gardener confessed that they had been hired by Hussein Avni and Midhat Pasha to slay the deposed sultan. These men, (supposing them to be guilty) were never punished for the regicide; but the death of Midhat, and the closer confinement of ex-Sultan Murad, quickly followed their supposed confession. Sir Henry Elliot says: —

"When, on the morning of June 4, 1877, five days after his deposition, it was announced that Abdul Aziz had committed suicide by opening the veins of his arms with a pair of scissors, there was probably not a person who doubted, any more than I did myself, that he had in reality been a victim of assassination; and my suspicion of foul play was only removed in the course of the forenoon by the report of Dr. Dickson, the embassy physician, who made me acquainted with particulars and details which up to this time (1888) have been to the general public almost, if not entirely, unknown.

"Dr. Dickson was a man of great intelligence, of long experience in many parts of the East, where he had seen much of the secret and dark doings of the harems. He was of a suspicious rather than a confiding character, little likely to shut his eyes to any evidence of a crime; and he certainly would not have concealed it from me, his ambassador, if he had entertained even the remotest doubt upon the case.

"Dr. Dickson came to me at Therapia straight from an examination of the body, and declared in the most positive manner that there was not a doubt in his mind that it was a case of suicide, and that all suspicion of assassination must be discarded. He told me that, early in the morning, he had received a summons from the government, inviting him to go to the palace to examine the body of the ex-sultan, and to ascertain the cause of his death. All the principal medical men in Constantinople had received a similar invitation, which eighteen or nineteen, including those of several of the embassies, with Turkish, Greek, and Armenian physicians, had accepted.

"Besides these, there was another English doctor, an old Dr. Millingen, the same who was with Lord Byron when he died at

Missolonghi, and who had ever since remained in the East, and was a medical attendant on the ladies of the imperial harem.

"He and Dr. Dickson went together to the palace, but found on their arrival that the other doctors had finished their examination; and Dickson told me that he and Millingen, being thus left alone, had made as complete an examination of the body as it was possible to make. He told me that they had turned it over, and looked minutely at every part of it, to see what traces of violence could be found upon it, but there were absolutely none, with the exception of cuts in both arms, partly severing the arteries, from which the sultan had bled to death. The skin, he said, was more wonderfully delicate than he had ever seen in a full grown person, and was more like the skin of a child, but there was not a scratch, mark, or bruise on any part of it; and he declared that it was perfectly impossible that the force that would have been required to hold so powerful a man could have been employed without leaving visible marks. The artery of one arm was almost entirely, and that of the other partially, severed; the wound being such, in Dickson's opinion, as would be made, not by a knife, but by sharp-pointed scissors, with little cuts, or snips, running in the direction that would be expected in the case of a man inflicting them on himself.

"He had therefore no hesitation in accepting as correct the account that had been given of the manner of the sultan's death. The wounds, moreover, if not made by himself, must have been made from behind, by some one leaning over his chair, where no one could have taken up his position without a struggle, of which traces must have remained, or without noise, which must certainly have been heard in the adjoining room, in which the ladies were collected. It further appeared that when the sultan was seated in the chair in which the pools of blood proved him to have bled to death, the back of his head could be seen by the women, who were watching at a flanking window in the next room, and to whom any one getting behind the chair would be distinctly visible.

"From all this Dr. Dickson and Dr. Millingen concluded, as I have said, without hesitation, that the sultan had destroyed himself; and when they went out and joined the other physicians who had examined the body before their arrival, they found that they also were unanimous in arriving at the same opinion. Among them were foreigners whose independence of character was beyond dispute, and who would, without hesitation, have given a contrary verdict had there been reason for it;

but they one and all came to the same conclusion; and several years later Dr. Marouin, the eminent physician of the French embassy, as well as Dr. Dickson, published a statement that nothing had in the slightest degree shaken the conviction originally arrived at by them. Even if the medical evidence stood alone, it would seem to be very conclusive; but it does not stand alone, and taken in conjunction with the statements of the women of the harem, it appears quite irresistible.

"Dr. Millingen, as medical attendant of these ladies, went into the harem, and questioned them, immediately after examining the body. They told him that, in consequence of the state of mind into which the sultan had fallen since his deposition, every weapon or instrument by which he could do himself or others an injury had been removed from his reach; that in the morning he had asked for a pair of scissors to trim his beard, which were at first refused, but afterwards, in spite of the urgent remonstrances of the women, they were sent to him by the order of the sultan's *valide*, who did not like to refuse him; and that, as soon as he got them he made the women leave the room, and locked the door. The women took their station at the projecting side window of the adjoining room of which I have spoken, from whence they could look into the part of the room in which the sultan's chair stood, and could just see the back of his head as he sat in it. After a time they saw his head fall forward, and alarm being taken, the *valide* ordered the door to be broken open, when the sultan was found dead, with pools of blood on the floor, and with the veins of both arms opened. When Dr. Millingen, hearing that the *valide* was in a state of distraction, asked if she would see him, she exclaimed that it was not the doctor, but the executioner who should be sent to her, as it was she who had caused the death of her son.

"Sultan Abdul Aziz had an undoubted predisposition to insanity in his blood. He had, to my own knowledge, been out of his mind on several occasions, the first being as far back as 1863. I had spoken of his insanity in my letters to Lord Derby, reporting that I had been told of it as an undoubted fact by one of the ministers. He was known to hold that suicide was the proper resource of a deposed monarch. When the news of the deposition of Napoleon III. had been brought to him, his immediate exclamation had been: 'And that man consents to live!' If at the time there was no ground for a suspicion of assassination, there was certainly no evidence worthy of the slightest consideration brought forward three years later, at the iniquitous trial, when the ruin of certain important personages had been resolved upon. The men on whose perjured and suborned evidence the conviction of Midhat Pasha and others was obtained, though they declared themselves to have murdered the sultan with their own hands at the instigation of the pashas, were not only not executed, but are believed to have continued in the enjoyment ever since of comfortable pensions."[1]

It is hardly to be supposed that for this iniquitous proceeding — this blot upon an otherwise creditable reign — Abdul Hamid himself is to be held responsible. For the first four years after his accession he was completely in the power of three of his ministers, a triumvirate who would not even allow him a voice in the matter of appointments. As for instance when the sultan, at the beginning of the Russian war, nominated the unfortunate Baker Pasha (Col. Valentine Baker) second in command of the armies of the Sublime Porte, the *seraskier* Redif Pasha flatly refused to give him his commission. Baker objected that the sultan had given him orders to join the army. "No matter," said Redif; "he will revoke those orders, for I refuse my signature to any order that may be given you to leave Constantinople for Shumla."

The three men who composed the triumvirate were, Mahmoud Damat; Redif Pasha, *seraskier* (or head of the war department); and Said Pasha, an excellent man, educated in England, but very timid. He was made *ferik* of the Palace, that is, its chief controller. The sultan was also at that time very much under the influence of his foster sister, the wife of Mahmoud Damat.

Abdul Hamid, who bore the name of his great grandfather, was the third son of Abdul Medjid, and was born in 1842. His mother was a Georgian who died of consumption very soon after his birth. He was then adopted by one of his father's wives who was childless, and who subsequently occupied the position of the sultan's mother or

[1] Nineteenth Century, 1888.

valide, though the office has been somewhat shorn of its privileges.

His health being delicate, he was never urged to make much progress in his studies; but after his visit to the courts of Europe with his uncle Abdul Aziz, and his brother Murad, he acquired a strong liking for European ways of life, and developed a great desire to improve himself in certain branches of learning, especially in geography and topography. He has a large collection of maps and charts, and nothing pleases him better than a gift of photographs of remarkable places. Before coming to the throne, after which for a while all his wishes were made subservient to those of his ministers, he had expressed himself as well aware that the friendly feelings of Europe toward Turkey could not but have been checked by the outrages in Bulgaria; that the credit of the country ought to be restored by economy; that justice should be done to public creditors, and control established over the finances to put a stop to corruption.

On August 31, 1876, Abdul Hamid was proclaimed sultan, and was at once girt with the sword of Othman, the people looking on without any demonstration of satisfaction or enthusiasm. Six weeks later it was announced that a scheme of reform for the whole Ottoman Empire was in course of preparation.

This instrument made its appearance in the following January. It was a much less sweeping reform than Midhat wished, or could have had granted under Sultan Murad; nevertheless it provided for a Senate, and a House of Representatives, which last was to take control of the finances; the system of taxation was to be revised, and better laws were to be enacted for the provinces. Election to the lower house was to be by universal suffrage; for the upper house electors were restricted to two classes: the noble, and the educated.

Abdul Hamid seems cordially to have disapproved of this check on the absolute power enjoyed by his predecessors. He was willing to do justice, and to temper it with mercy; but to be placed in the position of a servant of his people was odious to him. Indeed that very phrase, reported to him as having been used by one of the reformers, poisoned his mind against Midhat Pasha.

At a council held when only his other ministers were present, the sultan asked what should be done with Midhat Pasha. Two of those present answered, "Let him die." But Abdul Hamid has never been bloodthirsty. It was decided to banish him to Arabia, and he was arrested at once, as he was entering the Council Chamber. We have seen how two years later a charge was trumped up against him of having, in conjunction with Hussein Avni, instigated the murder of Abdul Aziz.

There were two sessions of the Turkish Parliament, which conducted itself in a manner that at once filled those who wished well to Turkish reform with admiration and surprise. But the sultan was unwilling to rule as a constitutional sovereign; the pashas, against whose cruelty and corruption most of the reforms were aimed, sided with their sovereign; the triumvirate held the reins of power, and was restive when its acts, pronounced unconstitutional by the Parliament, had to be defended in a manner never before heard of in the Ottoman Empire. A return to the old methods was effected in the old way. By the will of the sultan the constitution was abrogated, and before long the dismission of the ministers who had formed the triumvirate followed.

Since then Abdul Hamid has governed alone. His rare industry, his unexampled economy, his steadfastness of purpose, and his moral courage, have won for him the respect and affection of his subjects, and the commendation of foreigners who visit his capital.

He had been called to the throne in the darkest moment of Turkish history. The State had recently declared itself bankrupt; its finances were in a state of chaos; war was going on with Servia, and was impending with Russia;

besides which all Christian powers were exasperated by the outrages in Bulgaria. Eighteen months after Abdul Hamid's accession, Russian troops had threatened his capital, and extorted the Treaty of San Stefano. The Congress of Berlin, while it tore up this treaty, consulted only the interests of western Europe in the provisions that replaced it, and they greatly reduced the area of the sultan's dominions.

Abdul Hamid accepted the decision of the Congress, — he could not do otherwise, — but it taught him a policy to which he has strictly adhered. He dreads friends as much as enemies. He will enter into no entangling alliances with any Christian nation. He works with an energy that wears out his ministers, but they are only heads of departments; he keeps all power in his own hands. Like Queen Victoria he reads every despatch; and he gives his own orders. This sometimes indeed impedes business, for there are limits to what the industry of any one man can do. He has every day all newspaper articles or paragraphs that appear in European papers and bear upon Turkey, or the general affairs of Europe, translated for him into Turkish; for he is no linguist, speaking fluently no language but his own; and he never has been known to sign a paper without first reading it. He has established a government printing-press, and now, " by imperial command, all the most important literary and scientific works of Europe are issued in translation at Constantinople."

Probably the most trustworthy account of Sultan Abdul Hamid has been given us by the Hungarian Professor Arminius Vambéry. This wonderful linguist and enterprising traveller, was a poor lame boy apprenticed by his parents to a dressmaker. From this employment he ran away, and through unheard-of difficulties, procured himself an education, — learning all the languages of Europe, so that he speaks and writes them like a native. In 1860, he went to Turkey, where he became known as Reschid Effendi. He adopted Turkish manners and Turkish dress; and made his way to Persia. There he assumed the character of a *mollah*, or ecclesiastic, and travelled, in company with a band of dervishes (the Callenders of the Arabian Nights) to Bokhara, and Samarcand. His story is so very interesting that I have long wondered that it is so little known. Not long ago he revisited, by railroad, the scenes of his painful, dangerous, toilsome desert journey; and in the preceding chapter I have quoted largely what he says about the changes which, since 1860, have taken place in Central Asia. He spent some time in Turkey two years since, and while there was admitted on terms of companionship and intimacy to intercourse with the present sultan, whom he had known very slightly more than a quarter of a century before, when the future Padishah, a lad of sixteen, was only Hamid Effendi; but his pronounced Oriental features, his expressive eyes, and his reserved and dignified manner had stamped themselves, even at that age, on Vambéry's memory. As Professor Vambéry is one of the few Europeans whom Sultan Abdul Hamid has favored with his confidence, I can hardly do better than quote what he has said of him in his own words : —

"I must own that the education of Abdul Hamid, like that of all Oriental princes, was defective, very defective indeed; but an iron will, good judgment, and rare acuteness, have made good this shortcoming, and he not only knows the multifarious relations and intricacies of his own much-tried empire, but is thoroughly conversant with European politics; and I am not going far from the fact when I state that it has been solely the moderation and self-restraint of Sultan Abdul Hamid which have saved us hitherto from a general European conflagration. To all pressure from Russia, and central European powers, to vindicate by arms his rights in Eastern Roumelia, he answered with the Arab saying, 'Peace is the best of all judges.' As to his personal character, I have found the present ruler of the Ottoman Empire of great politeness, amiability, and extreme gentleness. When sitting opposite to him during my private interviews, I could not avoid being struck by his extremely modest attitude, by his quiet manners, and by the bashful look of his eyes. He carefully avoids in conversation all allusion to his position as a ruler, and when unavoidably obliged to mention the beginning of his reign, he invariably says, 'Since I came to this place.' He has ever since that time shown himself anxious to do away with the encumbering etiquette of Oriental court life, and he likes to show himself plain, civil, and unaffected to his visitors. He drives himself, even in public; his dress is scrupulously plain. He has discarded the *aigrette*, worn on the fez by his predecessors as a sign of royalty. At his table, though wine is served to European guests, it is not offered to the sultan, or any other Mohammedan.

"His views on religion, politics, and education have a decidedly modern tone, and yet he is a firm believer in the tenets of his religion, and likes to assemble round him the foremost *mollahs* and pious sheiks, on whom he profusely bestows imperial favors; but he does not forget from time to time to send presents to the Greek and Armenian patriarchates; and nothing is more ludicrous than to hear this prince accused by a certain class of politicians in Europe of being a fanatic, and an enemy to Christians, — a prince who by appointing a Christian for his chief medical attendant, and a Christian for his chief minister of finance, did not hesitate to intrust most important duties to non-Mohammedans. Sultan Abdul Hamid is the first Ottoman ruler in whose hospitality, not only European princes and ambassadors and distinguished visitors from the West, but his own Christian subjects, amply partake. He is the first Ottoman ruler who has publicly encouraged the arts of painting and of sculpture, in spite of those arts being strictly forbidden by orthodox Mohammedanism; and during one of my visits he pointed out to me, with a certain pride, two pictures in his *salon* as having been painted by Moslem pupils, brought up in the School of Art in Stamboul; and I can state with confidence that, if the Turks continue steadily on the way inaugurated by their present ruler, and if political complication does not offer any hindrance, they will soon reach a level of culture on which they may secure a firm basis of mental and economical development, and future political existence.

"'It is for this purpose,' said the sultan one day to me, 'that peace is now the object of my desire; peace alone can cure the manifold evils and shortcomings of the past; order and security can only be introduced by civil officers trained and educated in the school of modern social and political life.' In accordance with these views a new spirit seems to have taken hold of the whole people; the language and literature have undergone an essential change; while I am writing this paper I have on my table various Turkish books and treatises on social economy, history, astronomy, geography, etc., which are sent to me for review, and some of which are really admirable. Of course there is much, very much, to be done yet in the way of public instruction, for the great bulk of the people is totally ignorant and neglected; but educational progress does not permit of leaps and bounds, and we are only doing justice to the praiseworthy efforts of Sultan Abdul Hamid in mentioning that he is sincerely bent on the amelioration and mental development of his subjects. . . .

"In reference to the charge of ruthless despotism laid upon Sultan Abdul Hamid, in connection with his abrogation of the charter granted during the first months of his reign, I will also quote his own words. He said to me one day: 'In Europe the soil was prepared centuries ago for liberal institutions; and now I am asked to transplant a sapling to the foreign, stony, and rugged ground of Asiatic life. Let me clear away the thistles and stones, let me till the soil, and provide for irrigation, because rain is very scarce in Asia, and then we may transport the new plant; and believe me that nobody will be more delighted at its thriving than myself.'

"We need not shut our eyes to the deplorable conditions under which Turkey is laboring; we must not lose sight of ruined villages, neglected roads, decaying towns, choked harbors, and an impoverished population; but we can be, nay, we must be, indulgent, and, instead of always finding fault with the Mohammedan Turk, we should begin to discard all political bias in our judgment of an Eastern prince and of his people."

These are the words of a man who knows what he is talking about, who has dwelt with Turks, who speaks their language as well as he writes English, and we find his judgment of their ruler confirmed on all sides. Not only was Abdul Hamid the sincere personal friend of the author of "Ben Hur," which ought of itself to create among Americans a prejudice in his favor, but we have the impressions of the American minister, the Hon. S. S. Cox, who succeeded General Wallace, and who has published his "Diversions of a Diplomat," which, though based on far less knowledge than the writings of Professor Vambéry, confirm his conclusions. Mr. Cox says of the sultan:—

"He is middle-sized and of the Turkish type. He wears a full black beard, is of a dark complexion, and has very expressive eyes. His forehead is large, indicative of intellectual power. He is very gracious in his manner, though at times seemingly a little embarrassed. . . . You may ask how he is dressed. I have generally seen him in a blue-black frock coat, closely buttoned, edged with red cord. He is a graceful rider, and when on horseback, like his fellow-countrymen, he shows to advantage. His title 'sultan' does not signify all the power he possesses as an absolute ruler, but yet it signifies much. 'Padishah' signifies most. It is the chief and favorite title. It signifies 'Father of all the Sovereigns of the Earth.' As caliph he is the Divine representative of Mahomet. His family line runs back with unbroken links to the thirteenth century. . . . He is one of the most industrious, painstaking, honest, conscientious and vigilant rulers of the world. He is amiable and just withal. His every word betokens a good heart and a sagacious head. He is an early riser. After he leaves his seraglio and has partaken of a slight repast, his secretaries wait on him with portfolios. He peruses all the official correspondence, and current reports. He gives up his time till noon to work of this character. Then his breakfast is served. After that he walks in his park and gardens, looks in at his aviaries, perhaps stirs up his menagerie, makes an inspection of his two hundred horses in their fine stables, indulges his little daughters in a row upon the fairy lake which he has had constructed, and, it may be, attends a performance at the little theatre provided for his children in the palace. At 5 P. M., having accomplished most of his official work, he mounts his favorite white horse Ferhan, a war-scarred veteran, for a ride in the park. The park of the palace of Yildiz, where he lives, comprises some thousand acres. It is surrounded by high walls, and protected by the soldiery. Oftentimes, being a fine shot, he tries his aim upon some of the wild fowl which are decoyed on to the waters of the park. He is at the palace for dinner at seven. When without guests he dines alone; when he receives company he dines after the European method. It would be a task to make a catalogue of the gold and silver candelabra and massive *épergnes* which, with their flowers and fruits, decorate the table. When foreigners are present Munir Pasha, his first chamberlain, acts as interpreter, standing behind his Majesty's gold chair. He offers wine to his guests, but *he* indulges only in water. A fine military band plays during the meal. The servants are dressed in scarlet with gold epaulets. You would think they were mutes by the quiet way they serve. It is understood, of course, that the wives of the sultan are never at the table. The wives of others are frequently invited (Americans or Europeans), but on such occasions the sultan does not preside. If the sultan desires to converse with any one, there is a convenient room where cigarettes and coffee assist the conversation. But it is all over by ten o'clock. Imperial carriages for the guests are then at the door."

Abdul Hamid takes particular interest in natural history, and has collections of stuffed animals and impaled insects of all kinds. He is also greatly interested in trees and in fruit raising. Professor Vambéry speaks of having one day been presented with a dish of strawberries laid out in various lines according to the shadings of the fruit, headed by a bit of paper bearing the inscription: "From plants reared by the hand of his Majesty." On another occasion an apple and a peach of extraordinary beauty were similarly sent to him. Several times before the arrival of Mr. Cox the sultan had expressed a wish to receive from America a collection of American fruit-bearing trees, shrubs, and evergreens. He also desired photographic and stereoscopic views of scenery, buildings, and so forth, in the United States. The trees, I believe, have not been sent; but in May, 1886, Mr. Cox had the pleasure of presenting to his Majesty a very fine collection of photographic views of points of interest in America, and likewise a copy of the "Reports of the United States Census for 1880."

"The sultan was delighted with the gift. He selected some of the views from the hundreds before him, and placed them in the stereoscope, on which was inscribed on a silver plate: 'From the President of the United States to His Imperial Majesty, the Sultan of Turkey.' They elicited expressions of delight and wonder. The photographs of the 'Red Men' attracted his eager attention. He asked many questions as to their origin, their movements, and their present numbers, condition, and government. I could see he surmised them to be of that Mongol race which in the cycles of history clustered in

'Tartar tribes' on the territory between the Himalayas and the Mediterranean; out of which came the Seljukian Turks, who almost conquered Europe, as well as a large part of Asia and Africa. He was anxious to know if our Indians amounted to much, and how we provided for them. I explained as well as I could the effects of white raids, whiskey, and 'land-grabbing,' as well as the reservation plan. The towns and houses of the Zuñi Indians attracted his attention; for they are counterparts of certain towns in Asia Minor. The sultan asked curiously, pointing to the minaret of the new mosque visible from the kiosk, if they believed in *one* God? I gave him a brief outline of the natural religion of these people, who have almost ceased to be interesting to ourselves, except in romances, but who, as these photographs showed, are a source of infinite interest to the ethnologist."

There are four palaces of note in Constantinople, — the old palace of Top-Kapou, the original residence of the conquerors of Constantinople; the Tcheragan, where Abdul Aziz died, and where ex-Sultan Murad is now in confinement; the Dolma-Bagtché, a magnificent structure built by Sultan Abdul Medjid; and the old Seraglio, to whose limits Prince Yussef Izzeddin and the other descendants of Abdul Aziz are restricted.

Sultan Abdul Hamid rarely inhabits the Dolma-Bagtché Palace, though it is used sometimes for official receptions. In point of fact residence there is too expensive; it involves providing for six thousand people out of the imperial treasury. The sultan, the first Ottoman ruler ever endowed with a spirit of economy, made it his first business, on coming to the throne, to reduce the expenses of his household. But there are many vested interests connected with a sultan's harem; and though he has consistently discouraged unnecessary expenses, and is said to confine himself to one wife, he cannot escape having at least three hundred ladies in his seraglio, according to the customs of his land and of his dynasty. About one hundred of these girls are married to pashas and great officers of State every year; and each of them is entitled to receive a marriage portion of fifty thousand dollars. As the sultan loathes the whole system, but is obliged to permit each vacancy to be filled, a recent English ambassador strongly advised him to make a stand against it; but was told that this would not be easy, seeing that every cabinet-minister and pasha of note looks upon passing his daughter through the sultan's harem as a simple means of securing her a marriage portion and a brilliant establishment.

The sultan ever since his accession, or rather ever since he took power into his own hands, has preferred to live at Yildiz. This small palace is beautifully situated on the summit of a high hill, about two miles beyond the bounds of Constantinople. The Bosphorus, which it overlooks, is in front of it, and is two miles wide. It runs about a mile below the palace, and then melts into the Sea of Marmora. "Yildiz" in Turkish means *a star*. It is the star which lies between the horns of the Crescent. The park and grounds are of great extent, and are surrounded by a high wall to prevent intrusion.

On Saturday, May 29, 1886, the American minister and his wife were invited to dine at the palace. Several ladies, wives of ministers and ambassadors, had been invited to meet Mrs. Cox, and very distinguished gentlemen and officials to meet her husband. On driving up to the palace, they noticed that the garden wall was one mass of Bankshia roses.

"We were met," says Mr. Cox, "at the vestibule by a grand pasha in uniform and decorations. We walked upon carpets, ascended and descended into the marble entrance, and were there invited to take off our wraps. We were then ushered into a small side-room, where we found the German ambassador and ambassadress with other invited guests, among them Dr. Mavroyéni, the sultan's physician, whose son was subsequently Turkish minister to the United States. Thence in a few moments we were summoned to the upper *salon*, and presented in turn to the sultan by the master of ceremonies. The sultan cordially shook hands with all. When the ladies were seated on the divan, he called up the three princes, — his son, then seventeen years old, and two nephews, who are being educated as his companions. These youths wore military suits, epaulets, spurs, and swords. Each was presented in turn. The sultan accompanied his guests to the door of the grand *salon* (we have seen that he never dines with ladies), gave us a parting salutation, and remarked that he would continue the reception after dinner."

The dining-table was wide and long, with a gorgeous display of flowers, lights, and crystal shades. The American minister and his wife were placed among the princes. One of these lads, Tewfik, was about ten years of age, — a meek, subdued-looking child. He spoke only Turkish. The other two could speak some French. The princes seemed interested in geography. They were curious about Egypt, which their guests had lately visited. They asked also about America. In turn the minister inquired about their amusements, but got little information. Their exalted position apparently gave little scope for amusing themselves.

After dinner all passed into a beautiful green and black tiled coffee-room to take coffee; and there was presented to Mrs. Cox, by order of the sultan, the Grand Order of the Chefekat, — that is, the Order of Good Works. It was a star in brown, gold, and green enamel set with brilliants. It had five points, and twenty-six diamonds in each point. The order had originated in a wish to honor Lady Layard for her services in the hospitals during the Crimean War. Next the ladies were driven round the beautiful gardens, the gentlemen following on foot; but no offer was made to take any one into the harem. "The scene," says Mr. Cox, "was like one from the Arabian Nights. The beautiful lights in the garden and from the windows of the palace, the plashing fountains, and the fragrant air produced the impression of something magical and marvellous."

After that they returned to another *salon*, with a parquetted floor covered with rugs, divans, chairs, and tables. On the shelves were rare books. It was the sultan's library. There he again received them, talking with them through an interpreter. A German violinist, accompanied on the piano by a pasha in attendance, gave some music. The sultan lighted a cigarette, and asked the gentlemen to join him. The ladies, who did not smoke, were offered tea in golden cups and saucers. Then the sultan, rising, took little Tewfik his nephew by the hand, and led him to the piano, saying to his guests: "This boy will give us some music, though he plays only by ear." The quiet little prince played a spirited march, and then some selections from Norma. His father, a younger son of Abdul Medjid, had died when Tewfik was only a few months old, and the sultan had assumed his guardianship and education.

The present heir to the throne by Ottoman law is Mehemet Reschid (or Richard). He is the third son of Abdul Medjid, and the next brother to the present sultan. Abdul Hamid in 1887 had six children, four sons and two daughters; the oldest was the youth Mehemet Selim, presented to the American minister, who was born Jan. 1, 1871. The daughters were named Zekihe, and Naime. Besides Murad and Reschid, Abdul Hamid had three other brothers. These princes and others of the imperial family, with the exception of those confined to their palaces in semi-captivity, " are often to be seen driving or riding about the city, and not unfrequently at the 'Sweet Waters' of Europe, where every class of people congregate. They are of distinguished appearance, and dress in Frank costume, except that each and all wear the inevitable fez."

The great difficulty that besets Abdul Hamid is the lack of enlightened and honest subordinates to carry out his plans for the welfare of his people. Being fully sensible of this, he has had it in view in the enlargement and improvement of the school system. It was remarked many years since by travellers that Turks, however poor, could read and write, but this knowledge was acquired solely by reading the Koran; under Abdul Hamid more useful and more modern attainments can be acquired. He has frequently expressed the hope that improved education may supply himself and his successors with civil officers more upright and intelligent than those he is now able to send into country districts remote from his capital. Probably the worst governed part of his dominions is Armenia. Thirty-three years ago, when Arminius Vambéry first travelled through that country, he found its provincial government was horrible. In an Armenian village, recently plundered by banditti, he asked: "Why do you not get help from the governor of Erzeroum?" "Because," answered the villagers, "he is at the head of the robbers. God alone, and his representative on earth, the Russian czar, can help us." And we may be sure this feeling is kept alive by Russian agents. But the first care of Abdul Hamid, after something had been done to set straight the finances of the empire, which were in utter confusion, was to put down brigandage, — "one of the greatest curses of the Turkish Empire, affording a lucrative, if irregular, method of gaining a livelihood to thousands, and exercising a rule of terrorism and pressure."

The army had also to be organized and better disciplined; and to this the sultan devoted himself with the same energy he had shown in other departments.

It is universally conceded that the men of the Turkish army are admirable soldiers, and almost equally acknowledged that their officers are little competent to command them. But in no army in the world (unless it may be in the British army in India) is there a greater variety of race and hue than in the army of the sultan of Turkey.[1] Up to less than ten years ago uniformity was required in but one thing, — all were expected to be Mohammedans. Christians and Jews were not eligible for military service; they had to pay a military tax instead of serving in the army. Of late years, however, though neither enlisted nor conscripted, they have been received as substitutes.

The best troops in the army that held the Russians in check during the summer and autumn of 1877 were the Anatolian battalions. Turks from Bosnia and Herzegovina

[1] St. James Gazette, 1886.

made splendid soldiers; so did the descendants of the old Turks who had settled in Bulgaria. Strange to say, the Circassians showed little capacity for fight; they and the Pomaks, Bashi-Bazouks, Syrian Arabs, and Albanians were more given to plunder and to outrage than to regular warfare. Still, properly commanded, regularly paid, decently fed and clothed, the Turkish army is thought, by those acquainted with the subject, able to hold its own against almost any army in the world.

"Few sultans," says a writer in the "Leisure Hour," an English magazine which has given excellent articles on eastern European affairs, "have been so beloved by their subjects as Abdul Hamid. Indeed he is to them quite a new type of sultan, and they do not fail to appreciate the novelty. He is a man who does not pass his days in his harem, toying with his slaves. He is a man who takes a real interest in public affairs, and who, far from following the example of his predecessors, and leaving the reins of government in the hands of some clever courtiers, insists on seeing and judging all things for himself." In this way, however, he sometimes causes vexatious delays.

All American or European travellers admitted to his presence remark upon a look of uneasiness in his eyes, and it is known that he takes extraordinary precautions to secure his own safety. In this his prudence, nay, his patriotism, is to be applauded; for he is the sole hope of Turkey, — a change of rulers would certainly produce confusion, and might destroy his cherished projects of reform. What sovereign in these days is not bound to take precautions?

"Abdul Hamid does not feel himself safe even in his own palace. He does not suspect any person in particular, but he is on his guard against every one. He knows too well that palace conspiracies are of frequent occurrence in the life of an Oriental sovereign, and he cannot forget the tragic events that led to his own elevation to the throne."

This account of Abdul Hamid is corroborated by all other accounts that I have read of him, with the exception of that of Count E. de Kératry, published in 1878, when the writer was burning with indignation at the deposition and imprisonment of Sultan Murad, and when the new sultan had not taken the reins of power into his own hands. The ex-minister from the United States, Mr. Cox, from whose "Diversions of a Diplomat" I have already quoted, sums up in eager words his impressions of Abdul Hamid. We should not accept of course the *dicta* of an ex-diplomat, on the subject of the sovereign to whom he has been accredited, without a grain of salt; but, as I have said already, and have taken pains to show in my quotations, his views seem to be fully shared by others, who, speaking Turkish and admitted to personal intercourse with the sultan, have been better qualified than himself to understand him. He says:—

"Since the accession of the present sultan it is apparent that his rule has permeated the empire with a wise and honest sovereignty. I have observed heedfully much of the progress of Turkey during the last three decades, and from what I have seen of it I believe that the sultan, being himself a Turk, is the only man who can give Turkey the proper impulse to overcome the *vis inertiæ* of her laggard progress, so as to bring her forth into the light and liberty of a new civilization. If you question the ability of this people for self-advancement, look for the inspiration of their remarkable race and rule; and you will find an answer in those rare qualities which Gibbon catalogued when he said, 'The Turks are distinguished for their patience, discipline, sobriety, bravery, honesty, and modesty.' It is because of these solid characteristics, and in spite of the harem, in spite of autocratic power, in spite of the Janissary and the seraglio, that this race and rule remain potent in the Orient. It is a good omen that the head of the Turkish government to-day is a man of honest intentions and clear intellect, and that he gives unremittingly his time to the service of his people. He is not merely an amiable and humane prince, but wisely versed in statesmanship. His heart is touched by suffering, and his views lean strongly to that toleration of the various races and religions of his realm which other and more boastful nations would do well to imitate."[1]

[1] See note on page 404.

CHAPTER XV.

THE TWO DANUBIAN KINGDOMS. — SERVIA AND ROUMANIA.

IT seems a distracting task to unravel so tangled a skein as the history of the Danubian kingdoms, provinces, and principalities (namely, Servia, Roumania, Bosnia, Herzegovina, Montenegro, and Bulgaria) during the last half-century. When the Crimean War broke out in 1854 these countries were more or less part of the sultan's dominions. Some enjoyed autonomy, but paid tribute; some were Turkish provinces under the capricious rule of a Turkish pasha; all have now been rent out of the sultan's hand. Two (Servia and Roumania) are independent kingdoms; two (Montenegro and Bulgaria) are kingdoms in everything but name; while Bosnia and Herzegovina have been virtually united to Austria; and heartily as they hated the Turks, they do not seem satisfied with the exchange.

The united wisdom of the Great Powers at Berlin in 1878 endeavored to erect these feeble States into a barrier between Russia and Constantinople. The story to be told in these last chapters is the story of the erection of this barrier, and of the persistent efforts made by Russia to break it down.

The present czar, as we have seen, is Slavonic to the backbone. A Russian Russia is his dream and his ideal. He is not a Pan-Slavist. He is not willing to sacrifice Russia for Slavs, but within the bounds of Holy Russia Slavs are not only to be the dominant race, they are, as far as possible, to be the only one. The idea of a Pan-Slavonic federation is, however, all-powerful among the educated class in his dominions. It is almost as dangerous to the emperor as Nihilism; indeed, it has been thought to result in Nihilistic practices.

The Slav peoples of Europe are the Russians, the Poles, the peasantry of the Baltic provinces of Russia, the Servians, the Montenegrins, the population of Bosnia and Herzegovina, the inhabitants of the restless dependencies of the kingdom of Hungary, the Bulgarians, who, although not pure Slavs, are closely affiliated with them in language and religion, and the Czechs of Bohemia, Moravia, and Austrian Galicia, — a turbulent race, who are at this moment trying the patience of the Austrian emperor.

In the midst of this Slav population lie two nations intensely hostile to Slavs: the Magyars (or Hungarians), and the Roumanians. To fuse these into a Slavonian federation with their own consent would seem impossible; yet to obtain their submission seems indispensable to the realization of the Pan-Slavonic idea.

The Slavs in Europe are said, roughly, to number eighty millions. There are Slavs under the rule of the German Empire; the Reichstag contains a considerable Polish vote, representing German Slavs; the Slavs in Austria are estimated to number thirteen millions; those in Servia a million and a half. In Roumania, Bulgaria, and Eastern Roumelia they abound, and if, as they say, "the Germans have reached their day; the English their mid-day; the French their afternoon; the Italians their evening; the Spaniards their night; but the Slavs stand on the threshold of their morning," powerful empires must go down before them, and the present policy and civilization of Europe must be greatly changed.

But among the various branches of the old Slavonic stock there is no point of unity. "There is no such thing as a Slav language. A Russian does not understand a Bulgarian; a Bulgarian does not understand a Pole; a Servian does not understand a Czech. These various so-called Slav communities have no common grammar; not even an entirely common alphabet. They have each of them a distinct literature, such as it is, a different history, and different traditions." The utmost that can be said in support of their nationality is that far back in history, "even earlier than the days of Herodotus," they seem to have migrated from eastern Asia, — not in one vast horde, like other conquering barbarians, but in tribes and families, settling, as they journeyed westward from the Caspian, on unoccupied plains.

The Servians claim descent from an organized community of Slavs invited by the Emperor Heraclius to people Danubian lands laid waste by the Avars. When they adopted Christianity part joined the Greek Church, and part the Church of Rome. For a brief period, during the reign of one man, Stephen Dushan (from 1333 to 1355), there was a powerful Servian kingdom, including Bosnia, Herzegovina, and other neighboring territories; but after the downfall of Dushan, and the disastrous fight of his successor at Kossova, the component parts of this Servian empire fell asunder. In course of time the Servians and all others of their race along the Danube were conquered by the Ottomans. The nobles, to preserve their privileges, adopted Mohammedanism, and the land became "one of the dark places of the earth, full of the habitations of cruelty."

About the year 1804, when the attention of the world was fixed upon the mighty conqueror in western Europe, and there was little interest to spare for a peasant insurrection in an obscure province of Turkey, "a simple peasant of darker complexion than is usual with his countrymen, and thence Kara George, or Black George, by name, fled to the mountains, a ruined man, leaving a home desolated by the Turks. With a heart on fire for revenge he gathered together a number of men made desperate like himself, and became a sort of Robin Hood." He was, however, far more ferocious than that genial outlaw. By degrees the lawless acts of himself and of his band became extolled as heroic deeds in a righteous cause by the sympathizing peasantry; for to seize and plunder a wealthy Moslem was in their eyes no crime.

At a great meeting in the depths of a dark forest held by Servians ripe for insurrection, Kara George was nominated their leader. "But he stepped out of the crowd and cried: 'Brothers! why do you call for me? A leader of Serbs should be mild and forbearing. I am an angry man, unable to keep my temper. Choose some one else.' 'We need an angry man. We want a man of iron!' was the reply. 'But, by God!' cried Kara George, 'if I order a man to do anything, and he doeth it not, I shall slash off his head!' A shout went up: 'You are the man we want! You are our chief and leader!'"[1]

After this the successes of the patriots under such leadership struck terror into the ruling race. There was a swift rush of the Turks into their fortresses, and for a moment the Servians found themselves a free people, but with a terrible war impending, in which no mercy would be shown. They were not, however, fighting for independence; their struggle was simply for deliverance from oppression. They offered to submit to the sultan on condition that the Moslem military aristocracy should leave the province, and that its government should be administered by a pasha appointed by the sultan himself; that an improvement should be made in the methods of taxation, and only such taxes exacted as had been fixed in 1773 by a firman from the sultan; that courts of justice should be established throughout the province; that towns should choose their own mayors, subject to the approval of the governing pasha; that Christians might build monasteries and churches; and that they might choose themselves a chief through whom should pass all communications between the Sublime Porte and the Servian race.

These terms were not listened to for a moment, and the war was carried on with increasing ferocity till 1812; the Servians not only fighting the Turks, but exhausting their strength by factious squabbles among themselves.

[1] Cf. British Quarterly Review.

Another leader had risen up among them, — Milosch Obrenovitch, "the pig-driver;" and to this day the dynastic quarrel between the descendants of Kara George and the descendants of Milosch Obrenovitch has not been terminated.

When Russia and Turkey signed a treaty of peace at Bucharest on the eve of the French invasion of Russia, it was stipulated that the Servians should be pardoned for their rebellion. The sultan promised reforms in the internal administration of their province, and was himself to fix the amount of their taxation.

Like all Turkish promises made by treaty, these failed in the performance. The Servians again took arms, but the forces let loose on their luckless land were overwhelming. The panic-stricken peasants fled in crowds into Austria. Servia was once more conquered "and lay wounded and bleeding at the feet of Asiatic soldiers."

Kara George fled over the frontier with his people, but Milosch Obrenovitch remained behind. He was kept in the fortress of Belgrade as a sort of hostage, while horrors of Turkish vengeance fell upon his people. Before his eyes the Turkish pasha impaled one hundred and seventy Servians before the walls of the fortress, and tortures of all kinds were inflicted upon prisoners. "Milosch, of course, was an object of intense suspicion, and was in hourly expectation of death. . . . He determined to put himself at the head of another rising; but how to get out of Belgrade was a difficult question. He was rich and offered the pasha a large sum for the ransom of certain Servian prisoners, proposing to pay down half the money if he were suffered to pass over into Austria and raise the rest by selling a herd of swine. The pasha consented, though reluctantly, and Milosch plunged at once into the heart of Servia."

In the spring of 1815, when Europe was gathering together all her strength for the great struggle at Waterloo, an immense assembly of Servians was again held in the dark depths of a forest, and Milosch Obrenovitch, in full fighting costume, waving aloft the flag of Servia (a white cross on a red ground), roused his countrymen to arms, and offered himself as their leader.

Again the war raged; but the Turks at length proposed a peace, addressing themselves to Milosch as the champion of his people. At that crisis the old hero, Kara George, stepped forth from his exile with the design of breaking up the negotiation; but a few days later he was murdered in his bed. Peace was made with the Turks, and Milosch was recognized as head of his nation.

When Milosch, however, became a ruler, he ceased to be a hero. He grew insolent, stupid, and cruel. His rule became so oppressive that it effaced from the minds of his subjects the recollection of his services, and they drove him from their country. His son Michael succeeded him, but died soon after. His second son, Milan, came after Michael. He ruled so badly that his subjects drove him into exile in 1842. They then called Alexander Karageorgevitch, son of their first leader, to the throne. Him they exiled in 1858.

After this the Skouptchina, or National Assembly, recalled old Milosch Obrenovitch, who was living in Austria. He reigned for a year, and on dying was succeeded by his youngest son, named Michael, like the eldest. An English writer and journalist [1] who claims to have known Prince Michael well says of him: —

"A stancher, more straight-forward, and more single-minded man than Michael Obrenovitch III. I never knew, nor one whose decisions upon any issue submitted to his judgment were more uniformly dictated by a principle of rectitude. In any country he would have achieved distinction, so clear was his intellect and so indomitable his energy. For Servia, in which his lot was cast, he was a thousand times too honest, intelligent, and incorruptible. His virtues, in fact, were a standing reproach to his subjects by contrast with their vices, and the time came when, unable any longer to endure the rule of so virtuous and chivalrous a gentleman, they slaughtered him in cold blood."

[1] Monarchs I Have Met, by W. Beatty-Kingston.

Meantime, in 1862, a quarrel between some Turkish soldiers in the garrison at Belgrade and the Servian population of that city led to the bombardment of the town by the Turkish commander of the fortress, which Turkey had been permitted to retain as a concession to her dignity. After much diplomatic dispute Sultan Abdul Aziz resigned the stronghold, the most important military position on the Danube, into Prince Michael's hands.

The Turkish evacuation took place with great ceremony on April 12, 1867. Thereafter the prince bent all his energies to give to Servia a new and really independent life, and by his exertions she was placed in a better position than she had been since the fall of Stephen Dushan, five centuries before. Mr. Kingston says, however: "Prince Michael's throne was not lined with swan's-down. He had a great deal to put up with from his subjects, — as difficult to lead or drive as their own pigs." In a conversation with Mr. Kingston the prince said, not long before his death, —

"My father was a man of humble origin and but little instruction, but he was a genius, and performed what was little short of a miracle in raising the Servian nationality up out of the mire into which it had been trodden. I am no genius, but I was brought up abroad, under the influences of civilization, and I have worked very hard to profit by the advantages which Providence has bestowed on me. The sultan's generosity has made me a free prince of a free country. Never believe that I shall break my word to the sultan or fail to keep my faith to the Sublime Porte. But in many things my ministers and the leading men of the province are against me. As long as I believe myself to be right, I shall try to carry out my own convictions. God knows whether I shall succeed, for many of my own countrymen hate me, though I have never done any man a wrong willingly."

While Prince Michael was thus resolved to be true to his engagements to the sultan, Peter Karageorgevitch, the representative of Kara George's family, was in sympathy with Russia, and quietly conducted a conspiracy for a change of rulers and a change of policy.

"It was Prince Michael's custom to walk daily after his hours of work in the Park of Toptchidére, a lovely spot about three miles from Belgrade. Here he was wont to throw off all restraint, and accompanied by some of the ladies of his family, and perhaps an aide-de-camp, to spend an hour in the glades of the forest. In the afternoon of the 10th of June, 1868, the prince was thus engaged, when he met three individuals in European costume. As the park was open to any decent citizen this caused no surprise. They saluted his Highness and passed him. No sooner was his back turned than the crash of revolvers told of a tragedy. The prince fell, and the murderers rushed on him, stabbing and gashing the dying man with their knives. The two ladies, his relatives, were also attacked, one being desperately wounded, the other killed. Luckily the veteran minister Garashanin was within hearing, and when he had ascertained the cause of the pistol shots, he leaped upon a horse and galloped into Belgrade before the conspirators in that city were quite prepared. Having alarmed the authorities, got the troops under arms, and the police on the alert, the assassins and their accomplices were seized; and thus was a civil dynastic war averted, for it became evident that the movement was in favor of the deposed dynasty — the Karageorgevitch. A long trial of the conspirators ensued, and twenty suffered death for participation in the plot."[1]

Thus, mainly through the exertions of one man, the succession of young Milan, nephew and heir presumptive of Prince Michael, was secured; and Servia passed through the crisis without disorder or civil strife. A regency was appointed to guard the young prince and to govern the country during his four years' minority.

This lad, when ten years of age, had been sent to Paris for his education. He was placed at the Lycée of Louis le Grand, but he had also a private tutor. This personage was not deficient in learning, but he was very Bohemian in his tastes and associations. He frequented certain *cafés* in Paris, assembling-places of the class of men who subsequently became leaders of the Commune. There he would sit for hours talking politics and literature with Cluseret,

[1] British Quarterly Review.

KING MILAN OF SERVIA.

Courbet, Felix Pyat, Rochefort, and even Ferré and Raoul Rigault. The boy sat by his side, and listened while they talked. It was an unusual training for an heir-presumptive.

Prince Milan was fourteen when his uncle was assassinated. He grew up a handsome young man, rather too much addicted to the adornment of his person, but still princely and popular. When he came of age he indulged himself with a visit to Paris, where he found most of his old associates either shot or transported to New Caledonia. Marshal MacMahon, then President of France, gave him the Grand Cross of the Legion of Honor. He sowed a plentiful crop of wild oats during his travels, and has ever since been reaping them.

In 1875 he married Natalie de Keczko, daughter of a colonel in the Russian army. This lady soon became popular among the Servians. She was quick-witted and fascinating, and was devoted to her husband's interests, in spite of his notorious unfaithfulness and his habit of gambling.

During the last twenty years there have been two parties in Servia, — one aristocratic, or Austrian; the other, led by M. Ristics, radical or Russian. It was to this last that Prince Milan, on attaining his majority, seemed to incline. His early Parisian associations may have familiarized him with radicalism; the influence of his wife, and the persuasions of Russian agents, servants of the "mission," may have inclined him to Russia. Prince Michael said to Mr. Kingston : —

"It is constantly being impressed on me, and in a very urgent manner, as well by some of my most eminent countrymen as by Russian gentlemen who honor me with their visits, that Servia has to look to Russia for all manner of future benefits and aggrandizement, and that she is the only friend we have in Europe."

The revolt against the Turks in Bosnia and Herzegovina in 1875, which was at first rather a peasant rising against tax-gatherers than a rebellion, roused the Servians to fury.

"Hatred to the Turk," Prince Michael said, "is in their blood."

Austrian influence restrained the Servian government for a while from taking part in the quarrel; but Servia is only separated from Bosnia by the river Drina, and numbers of Servians passed over the frontier to fight the Turks, while pressure was brought upon the prince and his ministers to force them to reverse the policy of Prince Michael and take sides with the insurgents.

These councils, combined with popular enthusiasm, prevailed. War was declared with the Turks. Russian officers flocked into Servia to join the Servian army, and were much disappointed with all they found there. Then came the declaration of war between Russia and Turkey in the spring of 1877. Before that time, however, Servia, having been worsted in every encounter by Osman Pasha, had made peace, and took no part in the Russian War.

Servia was made a kingdom in 1882, chiefly through the influence of Austria, and after that the Western world seems to have lost all interest in her affairs for several years. She was supposed to be growing in order, peace, prosperity, and education. The only unsatisfactory rumors that reached the general public were reports of disagreements between Queen Natalie and her husband.

King Milan, after Austria had promoted his elevation, had changed his political views. He had become more aristocratic and more Austrian; less Russian and radical.

In 1886 Eastern Roumelia made a sudden revolution. She cast off the Christian governor assigned to her by the sultan, and implored Prince Alexander of Bulgaria to annex her to his dominions. This was no part of the policy of Russia. It seemed possible it would make Alexander of Bulgaria too powerful; and he was a prince loathed by the Russian emperor, as well as by the German chancellor. Neither was it the policy of Austria to increase the limits of Bulgaria, for the prosperity of that semi-Slavonic state might increase the restlessness of her own Slavonic population. She therefore encouraged King Milan to oppose the aggrandizement of Bulgaria, and (taking a leaf out of the rules and regulations of the Great Powers) to put forth a claim that if Bulgaria, by violating the Treaty of Berlin, acquired Eastern Roumelia, Servia should be compensated by acquiring two districts belonging to Bulgaria.

King Milan took the diplomatists of Europe by surprise when he declared war against Bulgaria. Two States recently emancipated from Turkey seizing each other by the throat, was a spectacle that disappointed philanthropists and disconcerted politicians.

Hostilities were very brief. Almost before the Western world had heard of the declaration of war, Prince Alexander with sixteen thousand men had defeated a much larger force of Servians at Slivnitza, a place nearly in the heart of Bulgaria. He had pursued them as they made a rapid retreat into Servia, and was going on to follow up his victory, when he was forced to make peace by Austria, who threatened to join the Serbs if he advanced into their country. "I cannot fight the whole world," he said, throwing open the palms of his hands in a deprecating manner.

The Servians were so disgusted with the war, and with the way their king had conducted it, that but for the popularity of Queen Natalie they would have dethroned him.

Instead of being grateful to his queen for her influence in his behalf, King Milan became jealous of her popularity, — not jealous in the French meaning of the word, for Queen Natalie's faithfulness as a wife had not been called in question, — but jealous of her political influence, which, now that he was in alliance with Austria, it displeased him should be exerted in favor of the czar.

Prompted by this jealousy he resolved on a divorce, but as this could not be procured by ecclesiastical means, he took King Henry VIII. for his example, and applied to a body of lawyers to grant him a release from the obligations of his marriage.

By this means he obtained a sham divorce, and exiled

Queen Natalie from Servia. She was followed to a German watering-place by agents of her husband, who forcibly abducted her son, Prince Alexander, then a boy ten years old, and carried him back to Servia, in violation of the rights of the State in which they found him.

King Milan, as an offset to his unpopularity caused by his domestic conduct, next endeavored to regain favor with the radical, or Russian party, led by M. Ristics; but his efforts to do this having failed, he took the world by surprise by his sudden abdication.

His son Alexander was proclaimed king, and a regency was appointed. The lad was forbidden to hold intercourse with his father or his mother. It is said he was deprived of playfellows, and confined strictly to the society of the regents who governed in his stead. Queen Natalie betook herself to St. Petersburg. King Milan went to Monte Carlo, where he soon lost at the gaming tables the large sum of money given him by the Servians to facilitate his abdication.

The regents were perplexed by constant intrigues; now they feared that in some way the mother's influence would be brought to bear upon her boy; now it was the father who was supposed to be conspiring for his own restoration. But on April 13, 1893, the toils, cares, responsibilities, and anxieties of these gentlemen came to an end. The young King Alexander, born Aug. 14, 1876, lacked four months of his legal majority. In view of his approaching manhood the restrictions imposed on him had been relaxed, and he was residing in the Royal Palace of Belgrade with considerable personal liberty.

Besides the continual uneasiness caused by the rival intrigues of the royal parents, public affairs in Servia had gone badly during the regency.

"For some months it had been a question whether under existing circumstances Servia would not relapse into anarchy, and the Obrenovitch dynasty give place to the Karageorgevitch, whose representative was supposed to be devoted to the interests of Russia. The aristocratic or Austrian party, whose

QUEEN NATHALIE.

followers had named themselves Liberals, was the party in power. The feuds between the Liberals and the Radicals were irreconcilable. The regents recently, to secure a triumph in the Skouptchina, had had recourse to force and fraud. The result of disregard of law in the highest quarters was general disorder and prostration of business. Society needed a savior, and a plan was formed by the young king which worked with all the precision of Louis Napoleon's famous *coup d'État*, save only that it was accomplished without bloodshed, and with as little violence as possible to personal liberty.

"King Alexander invited all the regents and all their ministers to a State banquet at the palace, on the evening of Thursday, April 13, to celebrate his having creditably passed the regular examination prescribed for Servian students. All came, and the banquet proceeded, Alexander occupying the place of toast-master at the head of the table. Meantime, police and soldiers occupied the houses of his distinguished guests and all the public buildings. A sufficient force was at the same time gathered about the palace in which the banqueters were making merry. After the third course, when the champagne had circulated freely, an aide-de-camp whispered to the king that all was ready. Thereupon Alexander, with great self-possession, rose and said: 'Gentlemen, for four years you have administered in my name the kingly power. I thank you heartily for the trouble you have taken. Now, however, I feel able to administer the kingly power myself, and I will exercise it from this moment. I beg you therefore at once to hand me your resignations in writing.' Needless to say the regents and the ministers were taken by surprise. They refused to comply with the young king's demand. He said nothing, but left the room. Presently the aide-de-camp returned, and called upon the regents thrice in the king's name to resign. Upon their refusing they were conveyed away under guard to another palace to spend the night. M. Dokitch was appointed Premier, a new cabinet of Radicals was organized, and writs were issued for a new election."[1]

The spirited action of the young king made him popular both with the army and the people. The new prime minister gave solemn assurance that neither Russia nor Austria,

---

[1] Baltimore Sun, April 28, 1893.

King Milan nor Queen Natalie, had inspired the movement; only the king and himself, he affirmed, were in the secret.

Another surprise followed this event. King Milan and Queen Natalie were reconciled, and are living, to all appearance happily, in a castle in their son's dominions; although the sham divorce occasions legal embarrassment, it being difficult to undo what it appears had never been done. King Milan asserts that he has never ceased to be in love with his wife. Queen Natalie professes herself willing to believe him. There are people who have hinted that King Milan, having squandered his resources at Monte Carlo, has found it prudent to be received back into his wife's favor, and to share her fortune.

The Kingdom of Roumania, once the Turkish provinces of Moldavia and Wallachia, is peopled by the descendants of Roman military colonists and of the ancient Dacians. Its religion is that of the Greek Church; its language is a corrupt Latin. To the north it borders upon Austrian Poland; on the east it is separated by the River Pruth from Bessarabia (a province given to it after the Crimean War, but restored to Russia by the Berlin Congress); on the west it borders on the Slavonic dependencies of the kingdom of Hungary; while the Danube is its southern boundary, and divides it from Bulgaria.

Under the earlier Mohammedan sultans its Christian inhabitants were granted the free exercise of their faith, and the appointment of their own prince or hospodar; but after Moldavia had been surrendered to Austria, and reconquered by the Turks in 1737, the Porte deprived its inhabitants of the privilege of appointing their own sovereign, and every seven years sold the dignity of *waiwode* (as the ruler was then styled) to the highest bidder among the Greek residents of Constantinople. The rule of these Fanariots, as they were called, from the Fanar, the Greek aristocratic quarter in Constantinople, was utterly distasteful to their subjects, and in 1821 the Turkish government tried appointing *boyards*, or native noblemen, with no better success. " Hospodar " was the title of these rulers in Moldavia, while " caimacan " (meaning " deputy of the grand vizier ") was the name of the governor of Wallachia, the sister State.

In 1828, after the Treaty of Unkiar Skelessi, Russia assumed a protectorate over Moldavia and Wallachia; but though one of the Russian governors displayed both energy and integrity, the rule of the Porte was preferred by the people to that of St. Petersburg.

The aversion of the Roumans, as the Moldo-Wallachians call themselves, to the Russians is two-fold. The Roumans are not Slavs, but consider themselves Romans; and the proudest of their ancestors in the palmiest days of the Roman Empire could not have been more disdainful of the barbarians of Scythia. They are of the Greek Church, it is true, but of the Greek Church of Byzantine origin; not that offshoot of it which, under the headship of the czar, is the religion of Russia.

There is in Paris, in the Rue Neuve de Berry, a beautiful little Russian church, erected shortly before the revolution of 1848. " What ! " cries a Moldo-Wallachian preacher, " Roumans to frequent a Russian place of worship? Is it then forgotten that they can never enter its walls? — that Wallachians who die in Paris declare that the presence of a Russian priest would be an insult at their tomb? . . . Our hatred is perpetuated by the difference of language. The Russian tongue is Slavonic; ours is Latin."

A Moldavian writer says: "There is less sympathy between the Rouman and the Slav than between the Rouman and the Ottoman. Any attempt to assimilate the Roumans, the Turks, the Slavonians, and the Greeks would be fruitless."[1]

Here, then, we are met full face with one of the difficulties of the Eastern Question.

[1] Blackwood's Magazine, 1858; Williamson's Wallachia and Moldavia.

From 1721 to 1828, a little more than a century, Wallachia passed through the hands of no less than forty governors. It was occupied by the Russians from 1770 to 1774, by Austria from 1789 to 1792, and again by the Russians from 1806 to 1812. The evils naturally arising from such a state of things weighed so heavily on the Moldo-Wallachians that they implored the court of Russia in 1792 to interfere in their behalf. This led to the Russian protectorate and the rule of the boyards.

We are in the habit of associating the word "boyard" with aristocratic ancestry and large landed estates. This, as concerned the Roumanian boyards, is entirely a mistake. Boyards in Moldo-Wallachia were made for life. They were of two classes, the great and the little boyards. The privileges of boyards were immense. They paid no taxes, were under no obligation to perform military service, and no punishment could be inflicted on them that was degrading. In 1858 there were in Wallachia three thousand boyards; in Moldavia six thousand. Not more than three hundred of these were of ancient families; the rest had been promoted from the middle class. Indeed, men of ancient lineage who respected their traditions declined to share a rank to which the reigning ruler of Moldavia had in that year (1858) promoted all his footmen.

For twenty years — that is, from 1834 to 1854 — both Wallachia and Moldavia were engaged in perpetual disputes with their rulers. Alternately they appealed to the czar or to the sultan. Sometimes they rose and drove their princes into exile. Among the worst of their governors was Michael Stourza of Moldavia, and Prince Stirbey of Wallachia. The latter was still reigning when the Crimean War broke out, and Austria sent into the principalities an army of occupation. She had declined to take any active part in the great war; but agreed to keep Moldavia and Wallachia from giving assistance to either side. Prince Stirbey, who up to that time had been almost a Russian vassal, attached himself at once to Austria, as the power in the ascendant in the principalities.

All accounts speak indignantly of the cruelties, the insolence, and the misdoings of the Austrian soldiers. They succeeded in rousing in the provinces bitter hatred to their country, — a hatred greater than the popular hatred to Russia, far greater than the animosity ever manifested by the Wallachians to the Turks, in spite of the misdoings of Turkish officials.

When the Crimean War ended, the Moldo-Wallachians had hopes that the Paris Conference would afford them some relief, and began to talk of union under a foreign prince as their only hope of order, independence, and prosperity. But the diplomatists at Paris did not seem inclined to consult their wishes. In Wallachia Alexander Ghica was restored to a throne he had forfeited by misgovernment; and in Moldavia two hospodars succeeded his brother, Gregory Ghica; until, in 1858, John Alexander Couza was called to the hospodarial throne. His father had been a wealthy Moldavian, who sent his son to Paris, where his irregularities of conduct were so outrageous that he was ordered home, and put into the Moldavian militia, where he again got into trouble for every kind of misconduct. He next went into politics, and took part in an abortive Moldavian revolution. For this he was arrested, and sent to Galatz to be delivered over to the Turkish authorities. He escaped, and was smuggled on board a grain vessel by the British consul. He came back not long after, when Gregory Ghica succeeded Michael Stourza. His private life, though disreputable in the extreme, did not prevent the Hospodar Vogorides, his boon companion, from appointing him to a judgeship, and making him his aide-de-camp. But Couza, who had resolved to bid for popularity, turned against his patron, and commenced a new public career as a disinterested patriot, — above all, the friend of the peasantry. In 1858 the liberal leaders at Jassy (the Moldavian capital), being at a loss for a candidate to propose for hospodar, were coerced into selecting Couza. When apprised that their choice had fallen upon him, he was playing billiards in a *café*.

"On learning what had come to pass he laughed aloud, observing: 'Very well. I accept. Perhaps after all I may make as good a prince as any of you.' Next day he was elected hospodar of Moldavia by a large parliamentary majority; and three weeks later the Wallachian chamber selected him to the like office in Bucharest, thus seizing the opportunity of securing the long yearned-for blessing of the union of the principalities."[1]

Prince Couza reigned eight years. He carried out his liberal intentions toward the peasanty, — gave them complete emancipation from serfdom, security in their landed possessions, and universal suffrage.

"The actualities of Couza's reign," says Mr. Kingston, "were, after all, of the highest importance to his native country. . . . The opportunity was presented to this dissolute but astute Moldavian of amalgamating the two provinces, already one in speech, religion, customs, and history; and he fulfilled this part of his self-assigned mission admirably, achieving a veritable triumph of diplomacy in inducing the Porte to confirm his nomination as hospodar of the united provinces. By this brilliant and unexpected feat he imparted the impulse to his country's destinies which carried Roumania irresistibly forward until she achieved absolute independence and the rank of a kingdom. His reforms, however, in favor of the peasantry roused against him the enmity of the wealthier classes, who felt that their only chance of establishing a stable government was to place their country under the sovereignty of a foreign prince, if one could be found suited to the position."

On the night of Feb. 13, 1866, Prince Couza was roused from his sleep by officers of the army, who laid an act of abdication before him, and ordered him to sign it. After some resistance he did so, and was forthwith transported to the frontier. He left twelve ducats in bullion in the treasury; the troops were unpaid, although taxes had been collected for that especial purpose; and the very horses of the cavalry were so starved for want of fodder that two regiments, personally attached to him, were unable to pursue the party who were carrying him over the frontier into Hungary.

[1] Monarchs I Have Met, W. Beatty-Kingston.

KING CHARLES OF ROUMANIA.

A provisional government was at once appointed, consisting of three of the principal conspirators. It was quietly accepted by all parties; and agents were despatched to the different courts of Europe to pick out a future sovereign. The leading men in Roumania had pledged themselves in writing to choose no Roumanian by birth, well knowing that none of their fellow-countrymen would be acceptable alike to Russia, Austria, and Turkey, and dreading local influence and local jealousies.

Prince Jerome Napoleon offered himself; but the Czar Alexander would not consent to his selection. Then the Count of Flanders, brother and heir presumptive of the king of the Belgians, declined the proposed honor.

"One day, during an audience granted by Napoleon III. to José Bratiano, the emperor, after passing in review the names of various august personages, eligible from the Roumanian point of view, and raising insuperable objections to each, observed: 'There is young Prince Charles of Hohenzollern, by the way, — why do you not try for him? I have heard him very well spoken of; besides, as you may know, he is a sort of connection of mine. If you should choose him, your choice would be agreeable to me!' On leaving the Tuileries after further conversation on the subject, Bratiano communicated the imperial hint to the triumvirate at Bucharest, by whom he was promptly empowered to open negotiations with Anthony of Hohenzollern, — the young prince's father, — and with the court of Prussia."[1]

Prince Charles was a second son, his elder brother being that Prince Leopold, whose selection for the vacant throne of Spain brought on the Franco-Prussian War. The tie of relationship alluded to by the Emperor Napoleon was the marriage of a Prince of Hohenzollern-Sigmaringen with one of the nieces of the Empress Josephine.

Prince Charles, at the time when the princedom of Roumania was offered him, was a captain of dragoons in the Prussian army, " highly esteemed in his regiment as an officer of conspicuous merit, devoted to duty, and a shin-

[1] Mr. Kingston.

ing example of good conduct in professional and private life alike. Roumania's good luck was decidedly in the ascendant when such a prince consented to take charge of her affairs. To him she owes the regeneration of her manhood and the amelioration of her morals, her national independence, the increase of her material prosperity, and the establishment, on a solid basis of victory, of her military reputation. When he took her in hand, she was, as a State, of 'no account' in the great European problems awaiting solution. Her army was worthless; her civil and judicial administration were rotten; bribery and corruption were rampant in every department of the State's service. A more hospitable, generous, and kindly people than the Roumanians could not have been found within the length and breadth of Europe, nor one less industrious, thrifty, truth-loving, and trustworthy."[1]

Shortly before the Seven Weeks' War broke out between Prussia and Austria, Prince Charles set out in disguise for his new dominions. At the frontier he was met by M. Bratiano, the leader of the liberal party, who has ever since been his prime minister. He made his public entrance into Bucharest May 10, 1866; and since then few monarchs have accomplished more for their people, or enjoyed a larger measure of well-merited confidence and popularity. The only distrust of him that has been ever manifested was in 1870, when the sympathies of Roumania were all for France in the Franco-Prussian war, and it was feared he might wish to take some part in it, being a Hohenzollern.

Prince Charles had been hospodar of Roumania three years and a half, when he sought and obtained the hand of one of the most highly gifted and accomplished ladies in Europe, whose virtues and talents have lent lustre to his throne. She was one of three daughters of Prince Herman of Wied, a tiny mediatized principality on the edge of the Black Forest. Prince Herman had written a book on metaphysics, and spent his time chiefly at the German

[1] Mr. Kingston.

QUEEN ELIZABETH OF ROUMANIA.

universities. His oldest son was with his regiment at Berlin, and his wife (a princess of Nassau) and his three daughters lived in the ancestral castle. Elizabeth, the eldest, devoted herself to study; reading poetry and philosophy, and rambling about the forest attended by two immense St. Bernard dogs. She grew greatly interested in folk-lore and in the habits of the peasantry. When she was eighteen her mother sent her to Berlin to spend a winter with good Queen Augusta. There she first met Prince Charles of Hohenzollern. When she was twenty-one she passed a year in Russia, but the climate did not suit her delicate health, and her chief pleasure was in a friendship she formed with Clara Schumann, sister of the composer.

She went afterward to Italy, and on her way paid a brief visit to a cousin, where she met Count von Moltke, who said in her presence of Prince Charles of Hohenzollern, "He is a young man who will take his place in life and be much spoken of."

Princess Elizabeth had made up her mind never to marry, but to devote her life to literature and philanthropy, when Prince Charles of Roumania again appeared, believing that in the young girl who had from the first attracted him, he should find a true helpmate in his difficult position.

The courtship was brief, but it was a very happy one. When her friends congratulated her on ascending a throne she said, "No throne would have suited me but that of Roumania, because in Roumania there will be plenty to do."

She was married November 18, 1869, and ten days later she and her husband reached Bucharest, their capital. A traveller before that day spoke of Bucharest as "a rural city, belted with pleasant meadows, and nestling in a network of vines and gardens." With every demonstration of delight its motley population of Roumans, foreigners, Gypsies, and Jews, received their young prince and his bride. Elizabeth was lost in delight over the beautiful scene.

At once she set herself to fulfil her duties, learning to take pleasure even in ceremonial. She encouraged education in every way, taking an especial interest in school-books and children's books, of which, up to her time there were none in the Roumanian language. She collected young Roumanian girls, daughters of noblemen, around her, and the first thing she taught them was *industry*. She and they wore always the Roumanian costume, and while she set them their tasks of needle-work, like a chatelaine of old, she read aloud to them and tried to inspire them with a taste for poetry, music, and general literature.

In those early happy days of her married life little Marie, her only child, was born. But little Marie died of diphtheria when she was four years old. "Only in work, in the great abundance of work, lies consolation," the sorrowing mother said in her affliction.

In 1876 the struggle between Russia and Turkey began by the occupation of Roumania by a Russian army. In 1877 Prince Charles was fighting as the ally of Russia. If occasionally Roumanians had been found who thought that their prince retained rather too much of the steady-going painstaking Prussian officer, they now learned how much those qualities contributed to their national importance. When they called him from his military service in Germany the Roumanian army was a mob of undisciplined men. In the war of 1877 the Roumanians proved themselves the best contingent in the Russian army. It was to the forty-six thousand men of the Roumanian reinforcement that the Russians owed their ability to retreat in good order after their first repulse at Plevna. Skobeleff complained, as we have seen, of their plundering propensities, but they fought admirably and appear to have been well officered.

Meantime in Bucharest the Princess Elizabeth came to be called by Russian and Roumanian soldiers "the mother of the wounded." "Wearing the simple garb of the Red Cross sisterhood she was to be found early and late in the hospitals. Whenever," says Mr. Kingston, "in my

PRINCE FERDINAND OF ROUMANIA.

flying visits to Bucharest I found time to look up some friend or acquaintance lying fever-stricken or wounded in the ward of a hospital I was sure to encounter by some poor fellow's bedside the merciful princess."

When the war was over Roumania was declared wholly independent of Turkey; and on October 28, 1878, the prince and his victorious army marched in triumph into Bucharest, received with showers of flowers, and singing a Battle Hymn composed for the occasion by Princess Elizabeth.

But a great disappointment was in store for the nation and its sovereign. Their reward for all that they had done and suffered was that the Berlin Conference took from them Bessarabia, giving them instead the swampy and malarious Dobrudscha. "Bessarabia had given to Roumanians the command of the mouths of the Danube; by losing it they impaired their chance for becoming a strong and prosperous nation."

Most writers of the period bitterly comment on the ingratitude and bad faith of the Emperor Alexander II., in consenting thus to despoil his own ally, but do not remember (perhaps did not understand) how terribly his own prestige was impaired among his people by the proceedings of the Congress, so that he dared not refuse any additions to Russian territory that the Powers were willing to offer him. Nor was he at Berlin during the Congress, being detained by the illness of the empress at Gatschina.

The international position of Roumania was confirmed and secured to her, and it was intimated to Prince Charles that Europe would gladly see him made a king.

He was elected to that dignity by a unanimous vote in both chambers March 26, 1881, and crowned king of the kingdom of Roumania May 22 of the same year. "The coronation day," says Mr. Kingston, "brought him a splendid reward for his long and steadfast devotion to the best interests of his adopted country."

The crown was made from the steel of a Turkish gun, taken by the Roumanian troops when they wrested a seemingly impregnable redoubt from the veterans of Osman Pasha.

Not long since a great sorrow fell once more on Queen Elizabeth, better known to many of us perhaps as Carmen Sylva; and her health, long impaired by excitement and overwork, seems now hopelessly shattered.

Among the young girls who sat at her feet and listened to her voice, and loved her as their inspiration and their guide, was a certain Princess Vacaresco. As the royal pair of Roumania have had no children since their little daughter died, King Charles selected as his heir presumptive a son of his brother, Prince Ferdinand of Hohenzollern. The young man resided at the Roumanian court that he might become well acquainted with the manners, the customs, and the language of his future people. At this court and in the society of its queen he met the Princess Vacaresco. They became deeply attached to each other. The queen favored their love and endeavored to promote their marriage. But the constitution of the kingdom of Roumania was against the lovers' hopes and wishes.

Not only had it been stipulated that no Roumanian should be considered an eligible ruler, but so great was the popular dread of awakening the jealousies of rival houses that a stipulation was added that no prince could bear rule in Roumania who married a Roumanian.

The throne had not been established long enough for an heir presumptive to disregard this provision. The lovers parted. The Princess Vacaresco withdrew to Paris, and after a period of sincere grieving for her loss Prince Ferdinand asked the hand of Princess Marie of England, granddaughter of Queen Victoria, daughter of H. R. H. Prince Alfred, Duke of Edinburgh, and niece to the present emperor of Russia. His suit was accepted, and the marriage took place January 10, 1893, at his father's family castle in Hohenzollern-Sigmaringen on the Danube. King Charles was present, but Queen Elizabeth was too ill to attend.

PRINCESS MARIE.

CHAPTER XVI.

THE BALKAN PRINCIPALITIES AND PROVINCES.

WE will end these sketches of Russia and Turkey and the kingdoms and the States now lying between them, — lands fought over and ravaged, outraged, contended for and still in dispute, — with some account of the obscure Turkish provinces placed by the Congress of Berlin under the protection of Austria, and of two principalities, one of which still acknowledges the quasi-suzerainty of the sultan, while the other, proud of having never been subdued, is entirely enfranchised.

This tiny principality is Montenegro, a land which Mr. Gladstone says " might have risen to world-wide and immortal fame had there been a Scott to learn and tell the marvels of its history, or a Byron to spend and be spent on its behalf." [1]

When at the close of the fifteenth century the Turks overran the ruins of Stephen Dushan's Servian Empire, the Montenegrin ruler, Ivan Tchernoievitch (ever since in his own land a popular hero) sought help from the Venetians. It was denied him, and with all his people he retired to the rocks and precipices of the Black Mountains, forsaking for the cause of faith and freedom the fertile plains that had been populated by their race for seven hundred years.

Prince Ivan built a monastery at Cettinjé, round which subsequently grew up the capital of Montenegro; "and,"

---

[1] Montenegro; a sketch by W. E. Gladstone. Nineteenth Century.

says Mr. Gladstone, "what is most of all remarkable in the whole transaction, he carried with him to the hills a printing-press twenty-eight years after the appearance of the first printed book in Germany."

George, the son of Ivan, had married a Venetian wife, and was persuaded by her to go back among her people; but finding soon after that his countrymen were in danger, owing to the unworthy conduct of his brother Stephen, who had become a renegade, he returned to his mountains, restored peace, and in 1516 retired finally to Venice, transferring his authority to the metropolitan bishop.

After this for three hundred and thirty-six years the government of Montenegro was carried on "by a long series of about twenty prelate princes, who taught in the sanctuary, presided over the council, or fought in the front of battle. There were among them those who were admirable statesmen. These were especially of the Nicgush family, which came in 1687 to the permanent possession of power, — a power so little begirt with the conveniences of life, and so weighted with responsibility and care, that it was never coveted, and seems never to have been abused."

After the accession of Prince Danilo, the first of the Nicgush bishop-princes, incessant wars were carried on between the Turks and Montenegrins for more than a hundred and fifty years; in other words, almost to the present day. The Montenegrins were alternately aggressors and self-defenders. Their raids on Turkey very much resembled those of the Highland caterans upon the Lowlands, — "raids," says Mr. Gladstone, "that we have learned to judge so leniently."

Whenever Austria or Russia went to war with Turkey the Montenegrins took that opportunity to attack the Turks, but they rarely reaped any reward from the Christian Powers for their assistance. The Russian government of late years, however, has paid a small subsidy to the prince of Montenegro.

By the Congress of Vienna the only seaport possessed by

the Montenegrins (that of Cattaro) was made over to the Austrians. Until recently the principality was no larger than one of the smallest dukedoms of Germany, but the Congress of Berlin added to its territory, and gave it in addition to Cattaro two seaports, Antivari and Dulcigno. It now contains seventeen hundred and ten square miles of territory, and has a population of about a quarter of a million,—one-fifth as much, let us say, as the city of Chicago. The surface of the country is a series of elevated ridges rising here and there into high mountains covered with forests. The population is entirely agricultural, and every man when he engages in field labor adheres to ancient custom and keeps his weapons by his side. The population was increased in 1865 and in 1875 by Christians flying from Turkish oppression in Bosnia and Herzegovina; but when peace was restored by the Berlin Congress these immigrants, for the most part, returned to their own fertile plains.

In 1782 Peter the Saint was prince or vladika of Montenegro. General Marmont (Duc de Raguse) offered him great inducements to join the French and Turks against the Austrians, but Peter firmly refused to place his people on the side of their hereditary enemy. Marmont, notwithstanding his disappointment, wrote thus: "This vladika is a splendid man, now about fifty, of remarkable intelligence and great dignity of manner. His legal authority over his countrymen may not be great, but his influence is unbounded."

"Down to, and perhaps after the time of this prince," says Mr. Gladstone, "the government of Montenegro was carried on like government in Greece in the Homeric age. The sovereign was priest, judge, and general, and was likewise the head of the General Assembly of the people, in which were taken the decisions which were to bind the nation as laws."

Prince Peter died in 1830 and was succeeded by his nephew Peter, surnamed the Poet, who was seventeen when called to the throne, and who three years later received at St. Petersburg episcopal consecration. He was nearly six feet eight inches in height and finely proportioned.

He proved himself a successful warrior and a somewhat stern legislator, being resolved, like James I. of Scotland, to put down among his subjects both brigandage and the vendetta.

Hero, statesman, and poet, he died in 1851. His recognized heir was his nephew Danilo. The reason Montenegrin princes were succeeded, not by sons, but by nephews, was that their sacerdotal character enjoined celibacy. In the orthodox Greek Church, priests *must* marry; bishops may not. Prince Danilo had become greatly attached to a lady in Trieste, and thence arose a difficulty. Either he must renounce his love, or break with the traditions of his race and refuse to be a bishop. The Council of his people whom he consulted advised him to marry, and to become, not their bishop, but their hospodar. With their consent he transferred his allegiance (what little of it was left) from Turkey to Russia, and sought investiture in his new dignity from the Emperor Nicholas.

He lived a happy married life for nine years, but in 1860 he was shot by an assassin, from some motive of private revenge, while standing on the quay at Cattaro. During the Crimean War he had declined to take any part in the struggle, much to the indignation of his subjects, who wished to help the Russians; but in 1858, after the war ended, Mirko his brother attacked the Turks and gained a signal victory. This fight was in consequence of an attempt of the Congress of Paris to force Montenegro (in return for the restitution of Cattaro) to acknowledge the suzerainty of the sultan. Prince Danilo refused. Prince Mirko gained his victory, and chiefly by the good offices of the Emperor Napoleon III. the Powers acknowledged the complete independence of the gallant little principality.

Prince Danilo left no sons. His widow and his daughter retired to Venice, a city which to Montenegrins of position has for generations been a gate leading from their mountain stronghold into civilized life. There the princess died not long since, much embarrassed by debt. Her habits were lavish and her resources very small. Indeed she could receive little aid from Montenegro. The whole revenue of the principality amounts only to two hundred and fifty thousand dollars.

Her husband was succeeded by his nephew, Prince Nikita, or Nicholas, son of Prince Mirko. According to a Montenegrin writer, Prince Nikita entered on his reign with two fixed ideas of duty: he resolved to carry on the work of civilization, and to assist in the liberation of other Slavonic peoples.

It would be of little interest to relate the varying fortunes of the guerilla warfare carried on with the Turks from July to October, 1876, when the Bosnians, Herzegovinians and Servians made peace, but their allies the Montenegrins refused to do so till they could treat as victors with the national enemy.

Prince Nikita is now (in 1893) fifty-two years old. He received his education in Paris, at the Lycée Louis le Grand, some years before King Milan of Servia was sent to the same institution.

"Napoleon III. took a great interest in him, invited him often to Compiègne, gave him pocket-money and presents, and on his coming to the throne gratified him with fifty thousand dollars."[1]

In his youth this prince was strikingly handsome; and he remains so still, although he has grown gray and portly. He is a poet as well as a soldier, and has composed some ballads which are popular wherever the language in which they are written is spoken. He is himself an accomplished linguist, speaking French, Italian, Russian, and Turkish with perfect fluency, and German fairly well. He is regarded by European diplomacy as the firm ally, almost the vassal of the emperor of Russia, and between them is

[1] Temple Bar.

the bond dearest to the heart of the Czar Alexander, — the prince and people of Montenegro are of the orthodox Greek Church, the branch that is the State Church of Holy Russia.

Prince Nikita married when seventeen the beautiful and gracious Milena, daughter of a Slavonian nobleman, by whom he has a large family. One of his daughters, the Princess Zorka (or Aurora) has been married to Peter Karageorgevitch, the pretender of the dynasty of Kara George to the Servian throne. This prince, who is a spendthrift and a vulgarian, lives at Cettinjé, and from time to time gives his father-in-law considerable trouble.

The Montenegrins all wear their national costume; all have the air of soldiers. Their dress is Oriental, — a sky-blue jacket, a scarlet sash, and spurred boots. Their prince throws over this a white mantle or furred caftan; and thus attired, with a jewelled sword at his side, he gives audience, sitting under a tree (like Saint Louis under the oak at Vincennes), two or three times a week to all who have anything to ask of him; and he administers justice off-hand.

Cettinjé is a town of about two thousand inhabitants. It is built aloft on a high mountain, the path up which from the seacoast is so steep that every article of furniture brought from abroad must be carried up on the backs of men or women.

The palace is like a mediæval castle. In it, besides the prince, his family and household, a hundred men of his body-guard are lodged. There is a large hotel, where members of the diplomatic corps reside together, or at least dine together and spend their evenings.

Prince Nikita is still constantly engaged in cultivating his subjects; but one idea of our *fin du siècle* has made no entrance as yet into Montenegro, — its martial men still look upon women as the Indian brave looks upon the squaw. The women accept the "dynastic tyranny of larger bones and stronger sinews" without a murmur.

An adventure in Montenegro told by Laurence Oliphant

seems to make the primitive simplicity that reigned there twenty years since so plain to me that I venture here to repeat it, especially as I think Mr. Oliphant's book, "Scenes from a Life of Adventure, or Moss from a Rolling Stone," is far less known than it deserves to be.

Mr. Oliphant had arrived in Montenegro in 1860, immediately after the marriage of Prince Nikita. He had passed through Hungary and crossed the Danube at Belgrade, "reaching it," he says, "on the day before Prince Milosch's death, and witnessing the very singular funeral of that remarkably able and very wicked old man."

"Thence I rolled on through Bosnia and Herzegovina, wilder and more turbulent in those days than they are now, abounding in brigand bands, enchanting scenery, and fleas, and in a chronic state of guerilla warfare with the Turks, which invested travelling through that country with the pleasing charm of perpetual risk to life and limb."

By way of Cattaro he reached Cettinjé.

"This little town did not in 1860 contain any hotel, properly so-called. The rare stranger who visited it was accommodated in a sort of lodging-house, in which there were one or two spare bedrooms; or if they were not actually spare their occupants turned out, I suppose for a consideration, on the arrival of a guest. The chamber assigned to me had apparently been thus vacated. Its former occupant had evidently been a man of modest requirements, for the whole furniture consisted of a bed, a huge chest, and a chair. I much wondered at the absence of a table, and at the presence of the chest; but the latter was better than nothing, and when a boiled chicken was brought to me as my evening repast, I spread one of my own towels upon it, in the absence of a table-cloth, and squatting uncomfortably upon the solitary chair proceeded to make the best of existing conditions. I was in the act of dissecting an extremely tough wing, when the door suddenly opened, and a stalwart Montenegrin, magnificent in his national costume, walked in. He addressed me with great politeness in his native tongue,—at least I gathered from his manner that he was polite, for I could not understand a word of what he said. As he was evidently a man of some position, — in other words, as he seemed to be a gentleman of Montenegro, — I rose, and bowed with much ceremony, addressing him fluently in the English language; upon which he drew an immense key from his pocket and pointed to the lock of the chest, thus giving me to understand that he wished to open it. In order for him to accomplish this, it was necessary for me to remove my dinner, an operation which was speedily performed. As he seemed a frank and engaging sort of person, without any secrets, and as I was possessed with some natural curiosity, I looked over him as he opened the chest, to see what was in it. To my astonishment it was full to the brim with bags of money. Not only this, but my strange visitor opened one of them and poured out a handful of gold. They were evidently all full of gold. When he had counted out what he wanted (apparently it was over one hundred pounds) he tied up the bag again, replaced it, locked up the chest, helped me, with many Slavonic expressions which I have no doubt were apologies, to lay my cloth again and spread my banquet, and with a final polite salutation vanished, leaving me alone, and in perfect confidence, with the untold treasure he had thus revealed to me. There was something almost uncanny in dining and sleeping alone with so much money. At night the chest seemed to assume gigantic proportions, and I felt as if I had been put into a haunted room. The absolute confidence placed in me, an entire stranger, — for I had not been in the place two hours and had not yet presented my letter of introduction to the prince, — appalled me, and I went to sleep vainly trying to unravel a mystery so very unlike any I had expected to find in the barren wilds of Montenegro. It was not solved until next day, when, dining with the prince, I met my visitor of the previous evening. I then acquired the information, through a Russian gentleman who spoke French, that the chest upon which I had dined contained the entire finances of the principality, and that the Montenegrin who had unlocked it, and had vacated his chamber on my behalf, was the chancellor of the exchequer!"

Herzegovina and Bosnia are countries that the ordinarily well-educated man or woman thinks it no shame to know nothing about. Up to the regulation of east European affairs by the Congress of Berlin in 1878, these provinces of Turkey were the western frontier of Mohammedan dominion, dividing it from the borders of so-called Christian civilization; but they were at the same time the most backward of all the provinces of the Porte in enlightenment. They lay west and southwest of Servia, interposing a savage population between the strip of Dalmatian territory that skirts the Adriatic, and the comparatively more civilized communities that dwell along the Danube. The land is rich in minerals of every kind. The soil of Bosnia is said to cover enormous coal-fields. The scenery is beautiful, game is abundant, and the valleys are fertile; but great darkness for centuries settled down upon their people, and in darkness no man is disposed to be active either in body or thought. Up to 1875 there were no roads throughout the country, except fragments of those highways made by the Romans when the country formed part of the province of Mœsia, and lay within easy distance of Byzantium, an imperial city.

When conquered by the Turks in 1485, most of the nobles of Bosnia preserved and indeed increased their hereditary privileges by turning Moslems; but the rural population, especially in Herzegovina, remained true to their Christian creed; while national feeling was kept up by the village system, common to all people of Slavonic race.

In Bosnia the renegade nobility became the oppressors of their people, but Herzegovina retained for a long while some of its popular rights. But in 1850 the Begs of Bosnia (the renegade nobles) became so insubordinate that the sultan sent Omar Pasha with an army into their land to put an end to their government.

In 1858 the celebrated Hatt-i-Humayoun, extorted from the sultan by the Powers after the Crimean War, raised the hopes of Christians throughout the Turkish Empire. It guaranteed them civil rights and religious freedom; but, as we know already, Turkish statesmen may put forth promises to "Christian dogs and unbelievers" upon paper, only to find that pashas and good Mussulmans are unwilling to perform them.

In Herzegovina, in 1875, Christians largely outnumbered the Mohammedans; in Bosnia they were in a proportion of two to one. Both provinces contained many Roman Catholics, whose sympathies were Austrian, but the majority of the Christians were what some call Pravo-Slavs,— that is, Christians of the Russian Greek Church; and one of their most bitter complaints against the Turkish government was that it set over them Greek bishops from Constantinople, who paid for their appointments.

In Herzegovina the harvest of 1874 was a bad one, and the peasantry foresaw a hard winter before them. Abdul Aziz was eager for an increase of revenue. To defray the expenses of his European tour, and his extravagant building projects, he had raised a foreign loan. His treasury was empty, and he could not escape the obligation to pay dividends to the foreign bondholders. The farmers of the taxes were pressed by the government to raise more money. In their turn they pressed hard upon the tax-gatherers, who pressed more heavily than ever on the unfortunate people.

The tax-collectors had always required the agriculturists to keep their crops standing until it suited their convenience to come and levy the tithe due to the sultan; and they invariably estimated the crop, however damaged, to be worth the highest market prices in Constantinople. But in one district the tax-gatherer did not make his appearance until January, 1875, by which time hunger had compelled the peasants to sell or to eat some part of their crops. The tax-gatherer estimated the tax at an enormous sum; the people resisted his demands; they were robbed, beaten and imprisoned, and their head men were threatened with arrest if they complained. Some fled to the mountains of Montenegro, sure of finding shelter among people of the same faith and the same race. The insurrection spread to other portions of the province. About the same time the emperor of Austria, on whom Roman Catholic Christians, when oppressed by the Porte, looked as their protector, chanced to visit his province of Dalmatia. The

Herzegovina peasantry at once began to hope that he had come to aid them. Soon every part of Herzegovina was aflame with insurrection.[1]

The governor of Bosnia went over into Herzegovina, and made some attempts to settle the dispute by pacific intervention; but in vain. The insurrection spread into his pashalik. Thousands of unhappy fugitives crossed into Austrian territory. Six thousand were sheltered in Ragusa, and the resources of that little Dalmatian city were strained to the utmost to provide for them. Their cry of distress reached western Europe, and in England and elsewhere societies were formed to send them clothes and money. Meantime both Servians and Montenegrins came to their aid, and Bulgaria showed symptoms of insurrection, which were repressed by massacre. But the Turkish armies had good leaders and trained soldiers; the insurgents seem to have had no leaders, and were without arms or military discipline. Their allies, the Servians, made peace with the Turks in 1876. Herzegovina and Bosnia lay at the mercy of the sultan. But at that moment the attention of the authorities at Constantinople was distracted by a change in the order of succession, and an impending war with Russia, besides plans and counter-plans for administrative reform. The war of 1877 took place, and when the Congress of Berlin took on itself the settlement of eastern Europe, Bosnia and Herzegovina were placed under the administration of the emperor of Austria, though they still, nominally, form part of the sultan's dominions. Austria has placed over them a military governor, and has garrisoned the country with fifteen thousand men.

So few travellers are attracted to these provinces, notwithstanding their abundant game and easy access, that very little is known about their present condition. It is, however, reported that the peasantry are very unwilling to submit to military conscription. Under the Turks no Christian could be a soldier. A tax was laid upon all male

[1] Cf. London Quarterly Review.

Christians, even an infant in arms, as a substitute for military service.

The chief town of Bosnia is Serajevo (in Turkish, Bosna-Serai). The chief towns in Herzegovina are Mostar and Trebinje. The population of the two provinces is about one and a half million, of whom less than one third are Mohammedans who appear to submit quietly to Austrian rule. They have, however, forfeited their privileges as the dominant race.

The Bulgarians naturally sympathized with their fellow Christians in 1875 and 1876, and we know already how the hearts of all men and women in western Europe and America were stirred by accounts of the atrocities committed by Turkish irregular troops and by Circassian settlers in Southern Bulgaria. The war of 1877 was to the Russians a Holy War, undertaken on behalf of their fellow-Christians.

When peace was signed, by the Treaty of San Stefano, Bulgaria believed herself to have gained her freedom. But she was disappointed. The Congress of Berlin divided her into two portions. That south of the Balkans, now called Eastern Roumelia, remained Turkish, having, however, a Christian governor. That north of the Balkans was formed into a principality.

The Bulgars are said to have been a Tartar tribe who settled in the southern part of Russia in the fourth century. Subsequently they moved southward to the shores of the Danube, which they crossed into the present Bulgaria, where they planted themselves afresh for the third time. They subdued the Slavonic races who at that time inhabited the region, and became a powerful people, waging cruel wars with the Greek emperors, one of whom after a victory is said to have put out the eyes of fifteen thousand Bulgarian prisoners in one day. The Emperor Basil drove the Bulgars out of Macedonia and Epirus, and forced them back to their own dominions between the Danube and the Balkans; and when the Turks poured over the lands that acknowledged the Greek emperor, they conquered the Bulgarians, who, though Christians, were of a kindred race.

That brilliant writer and army correspondent, Mr. Archibald Forbes, draws by no means a distressing picture of Bulgarians under Turkish rule, up to the time when the massacres of 1876 made them visible as an oppressed race to the eyes of the western world:—

"Taxed they were," he says, "no doubt heavily and arbitrarily, but they prospered. Annoyed, too, they must frequently have been by some Turkish *zaptieh* (or policeman) and the Circassian settlements were from the first a heavy grievance to an industrious population. The country, under Turkish rule, could hardly be said to be governed. As long as things went on quietly, the dominion of the dominant race acknowledged, and taxes quietly paid, the Bulgarians were not much molested by the Ottomans. They had plenty of churches, they were allowed to ring their bells. Their greatest grievance was that their bishops were despatched to them from Constantinople, and were not in accord with their flocks, even in creed, for the Bulgarians inclined to Pravo-Slavism. I do not mean to say that all was smooth and pleasant for the Bulgarians, or indeed for any of the Christian races of which the population of Turkey in Europe is made up; but their lot, from all that I have been able to learn, was tolerable enough. I think a Devonshire laborer, with his nine shillings a week and a few mugs of cider, would cheerfully have put up with the *zaptieh*, exclusion from the management of public affairs, and even with debarment from military service, for the sake of the rich acres of pasture and barley land, the cattle, and broad acres of the rural Bulgarian."

But there is no doubt that when Servia was at war with Turkey, and Bosnia and Herzegovina were in revolt, the Bulgarians were stimulated to plot against their Turkish masters. Then came the massacres in Southern Bulgaria, the intervention of Russia, and the war.

At the Congress of Berlin the Powers agreed on Prince Alexander of Battenberg as Prince of Bulgaria, and the sultan gave his assent. It was also agreed that no interference with the affairs of Turkey or of the Danubian States should be permitted to one Power, unless the others sanctioned what was done, or co-operated in it.

Alexander of Battenberg was one of four brothers, the others being Prince Henry, Prince Louis, and Prince Francis Joseph. Their father was a prince of Hesse, uncle to the present Prince Louis of Hesse-Darmstadt. He made a morganatic marriage with the daughter of a *waiwode*, or nobleman in Austrian Poland. The lady was made princess of Battenberg, and her sons, by courtesy, had the title of prince. The emperor of Germany and his great chancellor were much opposed to the pretensions of this left-handed branch of the House of Hesse. Not so Queen Victoria; and the empress of Russia, who had been born a princess of Hesse-Darmstadt, was disposed to favor her young connection, Prince Alexander, and in her will left him a considerable sum.

The choice of the Congress was not, however, agreeable to the Emperor Alexander II., though he acquiesced in it; but Russia thought it hard that, after all the blood and treasure she had expended for Bulgaria, her candidate for the honor of ruling it — Prince Dondoukoff-Koursakoff — was not even considered. However, this prince, who was then provisional governor of Bulgaria, said openly that, if he was not chosen to govern the country, he was going to make the Bulgarians adopt a constitution under which nobody else could. Accordingly he drew up for them the scheme of an ultra-democratic constitutional government, which to a people who did not know how to use political privileges, was very embarrassing. It is said, however, that the Bulgarians and their ruler got over the difficulty by paying the constitution as little attention as possible.

It is believed that Prince Alexander, whose appointment was, as it were, forced upon Russia, displeased the Emperor Alexander and his people from the first, by showing too little gratitude for what Russia had done for Bulgarians, and by discountenancing the expression of such gratitude on the part of his subjects. Others say that as long as Alexander II. lived, Alexander of Bulgaria was on good terms with the court of Russia (indeed he was one of the imperial dinner party at St. Petersburg on the day of the explosion at the Winter Palace); but undoubtedly when Alexander III. came to the throne a positive personal animosity soon showed itself on his part to his morganatic cousin.

Prince Alexander was a handsome man, of powerful but not ungraceful build; his bearing was military, and his features finely chiselled. His manners, also, were courteous and polite. The Bulgarians, by way of showing appreciation of their first independent ruler, erected for him in the late Turkish Quarter of Sofia, his capital, a palace of a somewhat novel kind. It is a rudely constructed, one-storied building, "differing little from other houses in Sofia, save in respect to superior cleanliness." The furniture was simple and tasteful, though not princely. The house contained three sitting-rooms, a reception-room, a study, and the prince's bedroom. At the back of the courtyard were two servants' rooms, an apartment for the Secretary of State, and the stables. There were four servants, all of them males and Germans, whom the prince had brought with him from his own country. There was, besides, the hall-porter, and a Montenegrin attendant, — a martial figure with a fiercely curled moustache. The prince's aides-de-camp were his old comrades, and a friend of his boyhood was his private secretary.

I have dwelt upon these details because they have some bearing on the subsequent history of Prince Alexander.

Sofia is the capital of Bulgaria; Philippopolis that of Eastern Roumelia. By the Treaty of San Stefano these two parts of Bulgaria had been united into one autonomous State. When this arrangement was set at naught by the Berlin Congress all the Bulgarians had been bitterly disappointed, and on September 18, 1885, a quiet revolution was effected at Philippopolis, by which the inhabitants of Eastern Roumelia threw off the Turkish administration and put themselves under the prince of Bulgaria.

Prince Alexander had not intrigued for this result; indeed it embarrassed him, and complicated an already difficult situation. He received the news when on his model farm near Varna, and at once set out in a light open carriage to see things at Philippopolis for himself. By travelling night and day he reached that place in forty-eight hours, having made, over rough roads, five hundred miles. He took the helm of government at once, and before night great satisfaction reigned in the capital of his new dominions. But the emperor of Russia was indignant. He was willing to protect and patronize the Bulgarians and Roumelians, but not their prince. It was not his wish to see a strong State, whose public feeling was opposed to Russian interests, built up between the Danube and Constantinople. Moreover, when the other Powers held him strictly to the observance of the provisions of the Berlin Treaty, it was exasperating to see those provisions, in six years, set at naught by so puny a power as Bulgaria.

Abdul Hamid, influenced by England, and by his own strong desire for peace (so necessary, as he conceived it, to foster his plans of reform), acquiesced in the new disposition of Eastern Roumelia; but the moment the news reached Servia, King Milan laid claim to two districts in Bulgaria, which he said were peopled by Slavs, and ought, if Bulgaria enlarged her borders, to be annexed to his dominions. At once he declared war on Bulgaria. The campaign lasted about a week, and was conducted with great ability by Prince Alexander. The Servians were defeated at the battle of Slivnitza, and pursued into their own territory. Then Germany, Austria, Russia, and Turkey intervened and forced an armistice, Austria threatening to take part in the war if the Bulgarians advanced into Servia, and Russia to invade Bulgaria.

Prince Alexander could not do otherwise than bow to the

will of the superior Powers; but his own people, proud of the success of their little army, saw in their prince a military hero, while the Servians resented the conduct of their king. Prince Alexander returned to his capitals, Sofia and Philippopolis, outwardly a triumphant conqueror, but inwardly perplexed and discouraged.

We have seen how according to the "will" of Peter the Great it was recommended that Russia should keep political missionaries in foreign capitals, and among Slav populations, to create Russian feeling, and promote Russian plans. Such an agent was M. Zankoff. His mission in Bulgaria was to do all in his power to make the task of government so difficult that the reign of Prince Alexander might end in confusion and abdication. With Zankoff was associated a General Kaulbars.

Prince Alexander had been faithful to Russian interests at the beginning of his reign, but when he had to choose between being a mere vassal of Russia or incurring her enmity he took the side of his people. The prince was aware of the intrigues carried on against him in his capital, but declined to take any extreme measures against the Russian conspirators, saying that there must be an opposition in every country, and that it was better to let the very small sore remain open than by severity to drive the canker inwards.

To appreciate the situation we must remember that the Bulgarians have been for centuries a nation of slaves. They are a people, thrifty, industrious, cheerful, and well capable of taking care of their own material interests, but so jealous of any dictation from foreigners, or interference with their affairs, that to this day they will not suffer any one but a Bulgarian to make their railroads or even to invest in them.

They had been provided by Prince Dondoukoff-Koursakoff with a complicated and unworkable constitution, and they and their prince were left to struggle with it as best they might. For eight years the government went on in a sort of happy-go-lucky fashion, which would have been entirely satisfactory to all parties had the Bulgarians been let alone. But Russian agents were at work and had command of Russian money. These missionaries are in no way accredited agents of their government. If they succeed they will have served their country; if they fail they will be discredited and disavowed.

The *rôle* that these agents took up in Bulgaria was one of advanced liberalism. Already in Servia the radicals had been the Russian party. M. Zankoff represented to all discontented spirits that Prince Alexander and his government were continually violating the constitution; but so great was the prince's popularity after his victories over the Servians that it was a common joke in Sofia that the Russian party consisted of M. Zankoff, General Kaulbars, and eight others. A conspiracy, however, against Prince Alexander was secretly matured, and this Russian nucleus was augmented by officers disappointed of promotion, and some who had personal grievances. Others were members of the Russian consulate, and the chief bishop. In the end the number of the conspirators amounted to fifty. When all was ready the minister of war, who was one of those concerned in the plot, sent the prince's body-guard to a distance and substituted a regiment whose officers had been gained over.

On the night appointed, August 2, 1886, the palace and the houses of Alexander's chief friends were surrounded. No officer slept in the palace, which was guarded by a few sentries and occupied only by the prince, his brother, and their servants. Resistance seeming useless, the prince surrendered when he found revolvers pointed at his head. Some of the officers who threatened his life had dined at his table the evening before. He was taken to the office of the war minister, who was in the plot, was there treated with indignity, and forced to sign his abdication. Subsequently this paper, having been found on the person of one of the conspirators, was restored to him.

Before daylight Prince Alexander was sent under escort

to a port on the Black Sea, put on board a yacht and taken to Reni in Russia. During his journey he was treated like a criminal, and when he reached Russian soil his treatment is said to have been still worse.

Having thus kidnapped the prince, the Russian party in Sofia seems hardly to have known what to do next. They probably waited for instructions from St. Petersburg. A telegram arrived assuring them that the czar took Bulgaria under his protection, would secure immediately its reunion with Eastern Roumelia, and that a representative of the Russian government should be sent to Sofia at once. But while the conspirators waited for the arrival of this personage the Bulgarians had time to recover from their astonishment. The prince's own body-guard, which had been sent to Slivnitza, marched back to Sofia, and recovered the capital without firing a shot. The army and the people declared everywhere for Prince Alexander. There was wild confusion throughout Bulgaria and Roumelia, but everywhere popular feeling was with the prince. A regency was appointed, and what might happen next was anxiously waited for.

Meantime Prince Alexander had been liberated and sent over the Russian frontier into Austrian Poland. At Lemberg the Austrian officials received him with due honor, and there he learned that he was still prince of Bulgaria, his subjects having appointed a regency to await his return.

Though physically exhausted by all he had gone through, he set out the next day for Bulgaria, and on his arrival in that country such a popular reception was given him, as probably never was accorded to a prince before. His people flocked as one man to bid him welcome. Never was enthusiasm more general or joy more sincere. Yet on his arrival at Sofia he made known his purpose of renewing his abdication. Perhaps he was hampered by some promise made during his captivity. He took such measures as he could to harmonize the different parties and to secure peace and order in the country, and then he departed amid such scenes of sorrow among the people and the army, "as" says an eye-witness, "can never be forgotten."

But Prince Alexander seems to have been thoroughly disheartened and discouraged. He knew that Russia, incensed against him before, would be more his enemy than ever; Turkey under temporary Russian influence seemed to have changed her policy; his people, loyal as they were to him, were apprehensive of the end, and party spirit raged more fiercely than before his abdication. The Russian party was now bold and noisy, denouncing the prince, and predicting his speedy overthrow. Alexander himself was in doubt whom he could trust in the army, and among those about him.

Some Shakespeare commentators have characterized Romeo as the man who was always unlucky. Luck went against him at every opportunity. Prince Alexander is the Romeo of contemporary history. Before he left Lemberg he had addressed a submissive telegram to his Russian cousin, intimating that he would thenceforward promote Russian interests if let alone. This telegram had no results except to injure his position.

He abdicated, believing that Bulgaria must succumb to Russia; but she did not succumb. She sent him a deputation, after he had reached his home in Darmstadt, imploring him to reconsider his resolution and return. When he gave an emphatic refusal to this request, she elected Prince Ferdinand of Coburg, grandson of Louis Philippe, as his successor.

Prince Ferdinand's father was a German prince and an Austrian officer; his mother was the wealthy and admirable Princess Clementine.

No choice probably could have been less agreeable to the czar, who wanted the Bulgarians to choose Prince Nikita of Mingrelia, a Caucasian principality. The dislike of the Russian court to King Louis Philippe and his family is well known. The revolution of 1830 destroyed the hopes and plans of the Emperor Nicholas for the attainment of Con-

PRINCE FERDINAND OF BULGARIA.

stantinople. Besides this, Prince Ferdinand, being an Austrian officer and accustomed to hold personal relations with the Austrian court, might naturally be expected to favor Austrian interests when they should come into collision with those of Russia.

It was in September, 1887, that Prince Ferdinand arrived in Sofia to assume his new position. Few people expected that he would be suffered to hold it long. If Prince Alexander, tried, and beloved, a brilliant general, a man of mature age, and of seven years' experience in the affairs of Bulgaria, had abdicated in utter discouragement, how could it be expected that Prince Ferdinand, who so far as the world knew, had shown no marked ability, should succeed, when his very election was a menace to Russia?

"I do not envy the man who may be called to fill the place of Prince Alexander," wrote an old resident of Constantinople when the choice of a new prince was yet unmade. "If he attempts to rule in the interests of Bulgaria he will be subjected to every insult, and thwarted at every step. If he is simply a Russian satrap he will be hated by his people."

Nevertheless Prince Ferdinand has held on his way without any more violent catastrophes than a new conspiracy which ended in the execution of a Russian agent, and the assassination of his finance minister. He has been prince of Bulgaria nearly as long as Prince Alexander, and feels himself sufficiently secure to have lately taken to wife Princess Maria Louisa of Parma. She is a descendant of the elder branch of his mother's family, — her grandmother having been the Princess Louise, sister of the Comte de Chambord.

Prince Ferdinand has been fortunate in his prime minister, M. Stambouloff, who was president of the provisional government during the change of princes. His fortunes are bound up with those of Prince Ferdinand, for whose acceptance of the Bulgarian throne he is mainly responsible. He is extremely popular in the country. That Russia is bitterly opposed both to him and his prince is probably an additional reason why they are beloved by the Bulgarians. Nevertheless the bullet that killed the unfortunate minister of finance had been aimed at M. Stambouloff; happily for Bulgaria it killed a man less important to the country.

Bulgaria has now her railroads, and, in the language of our time and country, "seems to be forging ahead." What may be in store for her no man can know.

Prince Ferdinand is a man of excellent education, far superior to that inadequate training which he said himself is considered sufficient for the scions of royal houses.

Alexander of Battenberg went back to Hesse where he bought himself a handsome country-seat, and the next thing the world heard of him was in connection with the sorrowful scenes that took place round the death-bed of the Emperor Frederic.

The Battenbergs are exceptionally fine young men, — men of a pattern it is hard to find as husbands for Protestant princesses. Queen Victoria, who likes match-making, has married two of them to her descendants, one to her daughter Princess Beatrice, another to her granddaughter the child of Princess Alice of Hesse-Darmstadt, and it had been arranged that Prince Alexander should marry Princess Victoria, the second daughter of the Emperor Frederic. They had been engaged some time and it was supposed that they were much attached to each other. The old Emperor William and his chancellor Prince Bismarck, exceedingly disapproved the match, and the marriage was postponed until the parents of the princess should have full authority. It was understood that if the dying Emperor Frederic lived till June, the young people, in spite of Prince Bismarck, should be married by his death-bed. But the Emperor Frederic died before June came, and Alexander's unlucky star prevented his marriage. It is said that it was not so much the czar's political objection to Prince Alexander that frustrated the match as the extreme personal dislike felt for him by the young Emperor William.

However that may be, while the luckless Alexander was still looked upon by the public as a fascinating and accomplished prince, robbed of his principality by the animosity of one emperor, and of his bride by the unreasonable prejudices of another, one fine morning he destroyed with his own hand his *prestige* as a lover. Again he descended from his pedestal and disappointed his admirers by marrying at the Prefecture of Mentone, a German prima donna, Madame Loisinger, daughter of a game-keeper in the service of the emperor of Austria.

It was subsequently reported that French law refused to admit the validity of the marriage, as the prince had represented himself under a false name to the prefect of Mentone. It has also been reported that, the marriage not having proved satisfactory, the prince has separated from his wife and entered the Austrian service as an officer of cavalry.

"*Chassez croissez,*" said De Morny when news was brought him that Cavaignac, late dictator of France, was occuping the rooms assigned the Prince-President Louis Napoleon when prisoner at Ham. And a similar change of places seems to have taken place in the lives of Prince Ferdinand and Prince Alexander. The ex-Austrian officer now occupies the throne of the prince; the ex-prince wears the helmet of the Austrian officer. Doubtless it sits more easily on the head of Alexander than on that of Ferdinand does the princely crown.

NOTE TO CHAPTER XIV.

RECENT accounts of the persecutions of American missionaries in Armenia, in accordance with a policy that apparently had its beginning in 1884, seem hard to reconcile with the character of Sultan Abdul Hamid, as he is described by all who have been brought into personal contact with him in Constantinople. Whether these persecutions have been inspired by the Russian government, which, in 1891, instructed its consuls in Asiatic Turkey to place obstacles in the way of missionary educational enterprises, or arise from the sultan's wish to keep the improved education he designs for his subjects in his own hands; whether it be the result of representations made to the Sublime Porte by unfriendly pashas; or, lastly, whether it has anything to do with a personal peculiarity of the sultan himself, — who can say? The personal peculiarity that I allude to is a disposition somewhat akin to the cryptographic mania which disturbed the world of letters in the case of Shakespeare. The sultan finds offence where it is quite impossible offence could have been intended, and an idea of the kind once having been entertained can never be removed from his mind. A clever Turkish writer, having translated the "Avare" of Molière, gave great offence by bestowing on Harpagon the popular name in Turkey for a miser. This name, it seems, had sometimes been bestowed in sport on Abdul Hamid by his brothers. Nothing could convince him that it was not intended as an insult; and on his accession it led at once to the disgrace and banishment of the unfortunate translator. I have said already that the expression "servant of his people" ("servant" being in Turkish synonymous with "slave") poisoned the mind of the sultan against followers of the policy of Midhat Pasha; and in the missionary schools of Armenia text-books on chemistry were suppressed because the symbol H_2O (denoting water) was supposed to indicate that Hamid II. was a cipher.

E. W. L.

INDEX.

INDEX.

A.

Aali Pasha, vizier, 201, 202, 208, 336.
Abdurahman, ameer of Afghanistan, 316, 317, 318.
Abdul Aziz, sultan, 199-206, 208, 210, 215-222, 230, 337-341, 363.
Abdul Hamid I., sultan, 68.
Abdul Hamid II., sultan, 205, 208, 228, 229, 230, 341-356, 396. His family, 353.
Abdul Medjid, sultan, 104, 197, 198, 199, 205.
Adrianople, 82, 257, 258; Treaty of, 82, 92, 215.
Afghanistan, 313, 316.
Akh Pasha (General Skobeleff), 247, 258.
Aksakoff, Ivan, 284, 296.
Alexander I., emperor, 16, 17, 18, 20-25, 27, 31, 70, 71, 83, 91, 92, 106.
Alexander II., emperor-liberator, 86, 153, 154, 167-171, 180-183, 193-196, 237, 251, 253, 254, 265-268. 279, 326; attempts on the life of, 184, 185, 186, 268, 269, 270.
Alexander III., emperor, 182, 183, 279-287, 289, 290, 291, 292, 300, 321, 322, 325, 328, 329, 334, 357, 379, 400; family of, 301, 302.
Alexander of Battenberg, prince of Bulgaria, 270, 366, 393-400, 402, 403.
Alexander, king of Servia, 368, 369.
Alexis, son of Peter the Great, 12.
Ali, pasha of Jannina, 70.
Alikhanoff, 318, 319.
Allied Armies at Gallipoli, 120, 121; at Varna, 122-127; reach the Crimea, 127-130; on the flank march, 130; before Sebastopol, 130-159.
Alma, battle of, 130, 134.
Alp Arslan, 44, 45.
Amurath I., sultan, 46, 51.
Amurath II., sultan, 55, 56, 57.
Anna Ivanovna, empress, 13.
Armenia, 354; missionaries in, 404.

B.

Bajazet I., sultan 51-54.
Bajazet II., sultan, 65.
Baker Pasha (Col. Valentine), 319.
Baku, oil-wells at, 319.
Balaclava, 137, 138, 139; battle of, 140-144.
Balance of power, 114, 232, 233.
Balkans, 233, 255.
Baltic Provinces, (Livland or Livonia, Courland, Esthland or Esthonia), 323-328.
Bashi-Bazouks, 237, 253, 335.
Batoum, 320.
Beckwith, Colonel, 131, 132.
Belgrade, 52, 57, 233, 363.
Beloochistan, 317.
Berlin, Congress of, 233, 258, 259, 260, 357, 379, 381, 392, 393, 395.
Bessarabia, 379.
Biat, 215.
Black Sea, 128.
Bokhara, 315.

408 INDEX.

Boski, railroad accident in Southern Russia at, 321, 322.
Bosquet, General, 145, 156.
Bosnia, 211, 233-236; history of, 365, 388-392.
Boucicault, Sieur de, 52, 53.
Boyard, 372.
Bozzaris, Marco, 76, 83.
Brailow, siege of, 80.
Brandes, George, *quoted*, 284.
Broniec, Marshal, 28.
Bucharest, 246, 377; Treaty of, 69, 80.
Bulgaria, 228, 233, 234, 236, 237, 392-403.
Bulgars, 392.
Burial certificate, 235.
Burnaby, Capt., his ride to Khiva, 313, 314.
Butler, Capt., 122.
Byron, George, Lord, 76, 77.

C.

Caimacan, 371.
Catherine I., empress, 12, 13.
Catherine II., empress, 13, 14.
Canning, George, 77.
Canning, Sir Stratford (Lord Stratford de Redclyffe), 109, 110.
Canrobert, 145, 155, 156, 157.
Capoleone, Doctor, 208, 217, 228, 230, 231.
Carmen Sylva, see Elizabeth, queen of Roumania.
Cattaro, 383, 385.
Caucasus, 94.
Cattinje, 381, 385.
Chancelor, Sir Richard, 10.
Charles of Hohenzollern, king of Roumania, 375, 376, 379, 403.
Charge of the Heavy Brigade, 141, 143.
Charge of the Light Brigade, 140-143.
Charlotte of Prussia, wife of Emperor Nicholas, 85, 86, 100, 101.
Chlapowski, general and dictator, 29, 36, 37, 39.
Cholera, 37, 125, 126, 127, 129, 131.
Circassia, 94.

Circassians, 236, 237, 335.
Cochrane, Capt. Lord (Earl of Dundonald), 76.
Codrington, Admiral Sir Edward, 79, 80.
Constantine, Grand Duke, 14, 18, 26-37, 86.
Constantine Palæologos, emperor, 58-62.
Constantinople, 52, 54, 58-62, 82, 111, 260; why coveted by Russia, 105, 106.
Coronation of Nicholas I., 33, 34; of Alexander II., 183, 184; of Alexander III., 284-290.
Cox, Hon. S. S., ambassador, *quoted*, 347-353, 356.
Couza, John Alexander, hospodar of Wallachia and Moldavia, 372, 373, 374.
Cracow, 97, 101.
Crimea, 24.
Crimean War, begun, 110-114, 116; rendezvous at Gallipoli, 120-121; armies sail for Varna, 122; sail for Crimea, 127, 128, 129; landing and flank march, 129, 130; hardships, 137-140, 146, 147, 148, 159; close of, 164; results of, 165, 166; generals in, 155, 156, 157; Russia after the, 165, 166.
Crusades, 103.
Cyprus, 260.
Czartoriski, Prince Adam, 27, 39.

D.

Daghestan, 94.
Dagmar, Marie, princess of Denmark, wife of Alexander III., 182, 301.
Danilo, prince of Montenegro, 380.
Danube, 238; passage of, 245.
Denmark, queen of, 297.
Dickson, Doctor, 221, 339.
Diebitsch, Marshal, 37, 80, 81, 82.
Dolgorouka, Princess, 183, 200, 267, 272.
Dolma-Baghtché Palace, 203, 206, 209, 215, 350.
Dondoukoff-Koursakoff, Prince, 259, 394, 397.

INDEX. 409

Dorothea, princess of Montbelliard, wife of Paul I., 14, 26.
Ducas, *quoted*, 61, 62.
Dushan, Stephen, 359.

E.

Edhem Pasha, 204.
Elizabeth Petrovna, empress, 13.
Elizabeth, queen of England, 10, 11.
Elizabeth, princess of Wied, queen of Roumania (Carmen Sylva), 376-380.
Elliot, Sir Henry, ambassador, 206, *quoted*, 337-341.
Emancipation of Russian serfs, 171, 172, 176, 177; compared with negro, 175, 176; of serfs in Esthonia, 326.
Eugene, Prince, 67.

F.

Ferdinand of Hohenzollern, crown prince of Roumania, 380.
Ferdinand of Saxe-Coburg, prince of Bulgaria, 400, 401, 402.
Finland, 17, 200, 201, 202, 205, 208, 326.
Forbes, Archibald, *quoted*, 251, 252, 253, 393.
Frederick II., emperor, 86, 402.
France, 40, 41, 69, 91, 92.
Fuad Pasha, vizier, 201, 202, 208, 336.

G.

Galitzin, Princess and Prince Dimitri, 24.
Gallipoli, 120, 121.
Geok Tepi, 261, 318.
George, king of Greece, 83.
George, Grand Duke, 289.
Georgia, 94.
Gladstone, Mr , *quoted*, 266, 381, 382, 383.
Goldenberg, assassin, 268.
Görgey, General, 102.

Gortaloff, Major, 244, 245, 246.
Gortschakoff, Prince, 133, 315, 316.
Gourko, General, 250.
Greece, 23, 70, 82, 83; revolution in 70-76, 80, 82, 83.
Greek and Latin churches; attempt to unite them, 55, 56.
Gregorius, Patriarch, murdered, 72.
Grudzinski, Count, 28.
Grudzinska, Janetta, princess of Lowicz, wife of Grand Duke Constantine, 28, 29, 30, 33-38.
Gustavus Adolphus, king of Sweden, 325.
Gustiniani, Gian, 59, 61.
Gwilt, Colonel, 158.

H.

Hairullah Effendi, sheik-ul-Islam, 211, 213, 217, 218, 228, 229.
Harold Hardrada, 9.
Hartman, 269, 270, 274.
Hassan Bey, 223-228.
Hastings, Captain Frank, 76.
Helfman, Hesse, 277, 278, 280.
Henry IV., Shakespeare's, 55.
Herat, 313, 316-319.
Herzegovina, 211, 228, 233, 234; history of, 388-392.
Hetairists, 22, 23, 70, 71.
Holy Alliance, 18, 23, 70, 71.
Holy places, 104, 105, 109.
Hospodar, 371.
Howe, Dr. S. G., 77.
Hungary, 101, 102.
Hunniades, 56.
Hussein Avni, 211-214, 216, 217, 221, 222, 223, 225, 226, 227.

I.

Ibrahim Pasha, 79, 93.
Ignatieff, General, 209, 280, 282, 300, 331, 335.
India, 43, 44, 315, 316
Inkerman, first battle of, 144; second battle of, 144.
Ivan the Terrible, 10, 11, 324, 325.

INDEX.

J.

Janissaries, 46–49, 58, 69, 77, 78.
Jassy, 70, 373.
Jews, persecuted, 291, 323, 328–334.
Juliana, princess of Saxe-Coburg, wife of Grand Duke Constantine, 26, 27.

K.

Kaiserli, 213, 217, 225, 226.
Kanaris, 76, 83.
Kashgar, 315.
Kara, George, 359–362.
Karageorgevitch family, 362, 363, 364, 386.
Kars, first siege of, 164; second siege of, 271.
Katkoff, journalist, 280, 282.
Kaulbars, 397.
Kennan, Mr., 303, 304; *quoted*, 306, 307.
Kératry, Count E. de, 197, 356.
Khanates, 314.
Khiva, 314, 315.
Kinglake, Mr., *quoted*, 106, 112, 113, 128, 130, 131, 134.
Kingston, Mr. W. Beatty, *quoted*, 362, 363, 374, 375, 376, 378, 379.
Krapòtkin, Prince, 268.
Kremlin, 284, 287.
Krüdener, Madame de, Barbara Julie von Wielinghoff, 18–24.

L.

Ladislas, king of Hungary and Poland, 56, 57, 58.
Lanin, Mr. E. B., *quoted*, 297, 298, 299, 328.
La Valette, Marquis de, 104, 105.
Leopold, king of the Belgians, Queen Victoria's letters to, 98, 99, 100, 113, 114.
Liprandi, General, 140.
Lowicz, Princess, see Grudzinska.

M.

Mahmoud II., sultan, 68, 69, 70, 72, 77–80, 93, 197, 199.
Malakoff and Redan attacked June 18, 1855, 158; evacuated, Sept. 5, 160–164.
Mamelon, 157.
Marie, princess of Darmstadt, wife of Alexander II., 169, 183, 269, 272.
Maritza, story of, 75, 76.
Mavroyéni, Doctor, 208, 351.
Mehemet Ali, khedive, 69, 70, 78.
Mehemet Reschid Effendi, 353.
Melikoff, Loris, 271, 272, 273, 280, 281.
Mentzikoff, Prince, 108, 109, 130, 131, 133, 139, 140, 154.
Merv, 318, 319.
Metternich, Prince, 108.
Michael Obrenovitch, prince of Servia, 362, 363, 364, 365.
Midhat Pasha, 211, 212, 213, 217, 224, 225, 226, 336, 337, 338, 343.
Milan, king of Servia, 364–370.
Millingen, Doctor, 339.
Milosch, Obrenovitch, prince of Servia, 361, 362–367.
Mingrelia, 94.
Mir, 172, 173, 174, 178, 179, 180, 304, 305, 307, 308.
Mohammed II., 58, 59, 60–65.
Mohammed, Nedim Pasha, 208, 211, 212, 335.
Moldavia, 32, 65, 71, 92, 93, 233.
Montenegro, history of, 381–385; adventure in, 386, 387, 388.
Morny, Duc de, 183, 184, 403.
Murad V., ex-sultan, 201, 203–209 212–218, 222, 223, 228–231, 350.

N.

Napier, Admiral Sir Charles, 112, 114, 115.
Napoleon I., 15, 16, 17, 18, 39, 83, 260.
Napoleon III., 105, 109, 112, 159, 167, 168, 185, 186, 375, 385.
Nasmyth, Captain, 122.

Natalie de Keczko, wife of King Milan of Servia, 365–368, 370.
Navarino, battle of, 79, 80.
Nesselrode, Count, 110.
Nicholas I., emperor, 32, 33; 85–89, 91, 92, 93; 96–100, 106, 107, 122, 123, 151, 152, 153, 167–169, 187; children of, 101.
Nicholas, czarevitch, son of Alexander II., 169, 182, 185.
Nicholas, czarevitch, son of Alexander III., 301, 322.
Nightingale, Miss Florence, and hospitals, 148, 149, 158, 159.
Nihilism, 155, 267–281, 290, 251, 294, 310, 311; Nihilists, 26, 155, 186–190, 290, 291; quotations from Nihilist writings, 187, 188, 109.
Nikita, prince of Mingrelia, 400.
Nikita, prince of Montenegro, 385, 386; his wife and children, 386.
Nisi Novgorod, 9, 20.
Nizam, 79, 81.
Norsemen, 9.

O.

Obrenovitch, Milosch, and his family, 361, 362–367.
Oliphant, Laurence, 134; *quoted*, 123, 124, 181, 386, 387, 388.
Omar Pasha, 116, 121; visit of the generals to, 123, 124.
Orkhan, 45, 46, 50, 51.
Osman Pasha, 243, 248, 250, 366.
Otho, king of Greece, 82.
Othman, 45; sword of, 216, 342.
Ottoman Empire, 45, 46, 54, 68, 83, 84.
Oxus, 313, 314.

P.

Padishah, 348.
Palæologos, John, 50, 51; John II., 55, 58; Manuel, 55, 56; Constantine, 58–62; the renegade, 64.
Pamirs, 322, 323.
Pan-Slavism, 259, 261, 295, 296, 357, 358.

Paropamisus range, 316, 319.
Paskievitch, Marshal, 29, 40, 80, 93, 95, 121, 122.
Paul I., emperor, 13, 14, 15, 16.
Pélissier, General, Duke of Malakoff, 118, 119, 157.
Perovskya, Sophia, 269, 276, 278–280.
Persia, Russia's war with, 93.
Pestel, 89.
Peter the Great, 9, 11, 12, 325, 326; will of, 89, 90, 91.
Peter II. and Peter III., 13.
Peter the Poet, prince of Montenegro, 383, 384.
Peter the Saint, prince of Montenegro, 363.
Philippopolis, 396.
Plevna, 243, 244, 247, 248.
Poland, 17, 18, 27, 326; revolution in 1831, 34–41, 101; rising of 1863, 181.
Pomacks, 335.
Pozzo di Borgo, 91, 92.
Probédonostzeff, minister, 298, 334.

Q.

Quetta, 317.
Queen Victoria, visit of Emperor Nicholas, 97–100; sees the Guards start for the Crimea, 113; reviews the Fleet, rejoices over the victory of the Alma, 133; sees General Canrobert in Paris, 157; distributes Crimean medals, 165.

R.

Radetsky, General, 250, 256.
Raglan, Lord (Lord Fitzroy Somerset), 112, 117, 119–124, 128, 132, 137, 151, 157, 158, 159.
Randolph, Sir Thomas, ambassador, 11.
Razumoffsky, Alexis, 13.
Rhodes, siege of, 64; second siege, 65, 66.
Romanoffs, 11, 85, 87.
Rose, Mr. W. Kinnaird, *quoted*, 240, 242, 243, 256.

Roumania, 370-381; religion in, 371, 372.
Roumanians in the War of 1877, 378.
Roumelia, 233, 366, 395, 396.
Ruchdi Pasha, minister for foreign affairs, 211, 212, 217, 225, 228.
Russia, 9, 85, 174, 175, 180; prophecies concerning, 43, 63, 103, 108, 251, 237; policy of, 107, 108; present plan of government in, 291-294.
Russian hatred to Turks, 168; invasions of Turkey, 80, 81, 111, 238; landed proprietor, a, 193-196; liberalism, 398; names, 238; officers and soldiers, 251, 252, 321; population, 294; public opinion, 294, 295, 296; railroads, 193, 306, 307, 313, 314, 320, 321; rural government of, 178, 179, 180; sects in, 191, 192.
Russia after the Crimean War, 165, 166, 167.
Russia after the Turkish War, 266, 267.

S.

Saint-Arnaud, Marshal Achille de (Jacques Leroy), 117, 118, 119, 121, 123, 124, 127, 128, 129, 140, 145, 146.
Salonika, 72, 237.
San Stefano, Treaty of, 258, 260, 395.
Samarcand, 313, 319.
Sardinians, 156, 159, 165.
Scanderbeg (Alexander Castriot), 58.
Schamyl, 95-97.
Scio, 73, 74, 75, 204.
Sebastopol, 25, 125, 126; attempt to give plan of, 135, 136; fleet destroyed, 136, 137; life in, during the siege, 154; scene during brief truce, 157, 158; evacuation of, 162, 163, 164.
Sedgwick, Miss Catherine, *quoted*, 73-75.
Selamick, 216.
Seljouk Turks, 44.
Senova, battle of, 255, 256.
Sergius, Grand Duke, 291, 301.
Servia, 67, 228, 233, 237, 238; its history, 359-370.

Severnaya, 162, 163.
Seymour, Sir Hamilton, 106, 107.
Shipka Pass, 255, 256.
Shumla, 80; visit of generals to, 123, 124.
Siberia, 306, 307, 308.
Siberian exiles, 192, 193, 267, 304-312.
Silistria, 121, 122.
Simpson, General James, 159.
Sinope, 111, 112.
Skobeleff, General Mikhail Dimitrivitch, 238-250, 253-264, 315, 316, 318.
Skobeleff, General Dimitri Nicolaivitch, 238, 239, 254, 261.
Slavs, 358, 359, 371, 372.
Slavophils, 295, 327.
Slivnitza, 396.
Sofia, 395.
Softas, 211, 216.
Solyman the Magnificent, sultan, 65, 66.
Stambouloff, M., prime minister in Bulgaria, 401.
Stratford de Redclyffe, Lord, see Canning.
Suwarroff, Marshal, 15, 26.

T.

Taganrog, 25.
Tcheragan, Palace, 218, 350.
Tchernaya, 139, 159.
Tekké (Turcomans), 261, 315, 320.
Tennyson, 143.
Timour, 52, 53, 54.
Todleben, General, 140, 160, 246, 250,
Tolstoi, Count Dimitri, minister, 273, 304.
Tolstoi, Count Lyof, 155; *quoted*, 157, 158, 160-164, 218.
Top Kapou Palace, 217, 222, 350.
Treaty of Bucharest, 69, 80; of Adrianople, 82, 92; of Unkiar-Skelessi, 93; of Paris, 178; of San Stefano, 258; of Berlin, 259, 260.
Trench, Mrs., from "Monthly Packet," *quoted*, 285, 286-289.

INDEX.

Trochu, General Jules, 128.
Troubetskoi, Prince, 87, 88.
Turcomans, see Tekké.
Turkish Empire, 42, 66, 67 ; race, 42, 43, 44, 45, 233, 234, 235 ; fleets destroyed, 79, 80, 111, 112; parliament, 343; population, 84; soldiers, 67, 116, 117, 354, 355; sultans, 49, 65, 66, 67, 69; viziers, 48; when Crimean War began, 166.
Turkestan, 260, 313, 320.
Turks, 42–45, 103.

U.

Unkiar-Skelessi, Treaty of, 93, 111.
Ural mountains, 306 ; railroad over, 306, 307.

V.

Valette, Marquis de La, 105.
Vambéry, Arminius, 320, 344, 345 ; *quoted*, 320, 345, 346, 347.
Varescovo, Princess Hélène, 380.
Varna, 80, 81, 122, 125, 127, 133.
Verestchagen, Alexander, 239; *quoted*, 239, 240, 241, 243, 255.
Verona, Congress of, 23.
Vicars, Capt. Hedley, 147.
Victoria, see Queen Victoria.
Victoria, Princess of Prussia, 403.
Vienna, 66; Congress of, 17, 230, 231, 380, 383.
Villagos, 102.
Vladimir, Grand Duke, 182, 302.
Vladivostok, 307.

W.

Wallace, Mr. Mackenzie, 175 ; *quoted*, 176–179, 193–196.
Wallachia, 22, 71, 92, 93, 233, 372; see also Roumania.
Waterloo, 22.
War, Russia with Napoleon I., 15 ; with Persia, 93; with Poland, 36 ; Crimean, 111–166; in the Caucasus, 95–97 ; with Turkey, 238–259.
Warsaw, 36, 38, 39, 40, 333.
Wœstyne, Ivan de, *quoted*, 263, 264.
William I., William II., emperors, 86, 201.
Witte, 300.
Woronzoff, Prince, 96, 97.

X.

Xenia, Grand Duchess, 286, 289, 301, 321.

Y.

Yarkand, 315.
Yildiz, 351.
Ypsilanti, Alexander, 22, 23, 70, 71.
Yusef-Izzeddin, 201, 210, 351.

Z.

Zankoff, 397.
Zaptieh, story of a, 235.
Zelony Gory, 247.
Zemstvo, 178, 273, 282, 291.
Zizim, Prince, 65.
Zouboff brothers, 16.

www.ingramcontent.com/pod-product-compliance
Lightning Source LLC
Chambersburg PA
CBHW031959300426
44117CB00008B/822